THE REV. J. W. LOGUEN,
AS A SLAVE AND AS A FREEMAN

THE REV. J. W. LOGUEN, AS A SLAVE AND AS A FREEMAN

A NARRATIVE OF REAL LIFE

INCLUDING PREVIOUSLY UNCOLLECTED LETTERS

J. W. LOGUEN

EDITED AND WITH A CRITICAL INTRODUCTION BY

JENNIFER A. WILLIAMSON

SYRACUSE UNIVERSITY PRESS

Syracuse University Press
Syracuse, New York 13244-5290

First Edition 2016

16 17 18 19 20 21   6 5 4 3 2 1

∞ The paper used in this publication meets the minimum requirements of the American National Standard for Information Sciences—Permanence of Paper for Printed Library Materials, ANSI Z39.48-1992.

For a listing of books published and distributed by Syracuse University Press, visit www.SyracuseUniversityPress.syr.edu.

ISBN: 978-0-8156-3446-1 (cloth)
978-0-8156-1068-7 (paperback)
978-0-8156-5369-1 (e-book)

Library of Congress Cataloging-in-Publication Data

Names: Loguen, Jermain Wesley, author. | Williamson, Jennifer A., 1978-editor.
Title: The Rev. J. W. Loguen, as a slave and as a freeman : a narrative of real life, including previously uncollected letters / J.W. Loguen ; edited and with a critical introduction by Jennifer A. Williamson.
Other titles: Reverend J. W. Loguen, as a slave and as a freeman
Description: First edition. | Syracuse : Syracuse University Press, 2016. | Includes index.
Identifiers: LCCN 2015045141 (print) | LCCN 2016003289 (ebook) | ISBN 9780815634461 (cloth : alk. paper) | ISBN 9780815610687 (pbk.) | ISBN 9780815653691 (e-book)
Subjects: LCSH: Loguen, Jermain Wesley. | African American abolitionists—United States—Biography | Fugitive slaves—United States—Biography | Antislavery movements—United States. | Underground railroad.
Classification: LCC E444 .L83 2016 (print) | LCC E444 (ebook) | DDC 326/.8092—dc23
LC record available at http://lccn.loc.gov/2015045141

Manufactured in the United States of America

CONTENTS

PREFACE

This edition includes a testimony by E. P. Rogers appended to the second edition of *The Rev. J. W. Loguen* as well as a poem by E. P. Rogers—African American poet and minister Elymas Payson Rogers, who also wrote a poem for the 1854 Jerry Rescue Celebration—and two letters appended to the third edition of the narrative, all of which were published sometime after 1859. The first letter was written by Mrs. Sarah Logue, David Logue's sister-in-law, in which she admonishes Loguen for running away, chastises him for financial hardships caused by this loss, and criticizes him as unfit for ministry. In response, Loguen blasts Mrs. Logue's appeals and refutes her moral points in a powerful indictment of her role as a slave owner.

It should be noted that the original title page remained unchanged in the two subsequent printings, so the second and third edition publication dates—during which the testimony, poem, and letters were appended—are unclear. Publication dates for the second and third editions are still listed as 1859, and Valerie Sallis, of the Syracuse Library Special Collections Research Center, theorizes that because printers J. G. K. Truair & Co. specialized in stereotyping, they may have chosen to reprint the book with additional materials without changing the title plate to save cost and labor or out of confusion over the legal requirements of the copyright statement.

Readers may find a clarification of Loguen's name helpful. As later discussed in the introduction, Loguen was originally named Jarm Logue. He later added the *n* to his last name to differentiate himself from his slave master father, David Logue, and adopted the middle name Wesley to reflect his Wesleyan Methodist sympathies. Loguen spells his first name both "Jermain" and "Jarmain." Because he signed letters and public documents with the initials "J. W.," it is difficult to determine his preference. Although references to Loguen in the newspaper also usually referred to him by his initials, on the rare occasion his first name was used, it appeared as both "Jermain" and "Jarmain." Unless included in a direct quotation, any mention of his first name will use the spelling "Jermain," which is the spelling in the preface and is utilized more frequently than the alternative spellings.

The text of *The Rev. J. W. Loguen* reproduced here is of the original stereotype edition printed in 1859. I have attempted to reproduce this volume faithfully, and I have preserved certain spelling eccentricities when they do not interfere with comprehension. Nevertheless, some minor corrections were deemed necessary for punctuation, consistency, and typesetting.

Loguen's explanatory footnotes have been supplemented by additional editor's footnotes for certain names and historical or literary references in the original text and appended letters. A comprehensive annotated version is not the goal of this edition; familiarity with or the ability to identify major abolitionist figures is assumed, and Loguen explains his connection to many individuals in his work. Where references are more obscure or difficult to access for the modern-day reader, additional information has been provided.

ACKNOWLEDGMENTS

This edition of *The Rev. J. W. Loguen* would not have been possible without the steadfast support and mentorship of an incredible group of scholars.

I am, first and foremost, grateful to Natasha Smith and Mike Millner at Documenting the American South (DocSouth), a digital publishing initiative sponsored by the University Library at the University of North Carolina at Chapel Hill. My personal discovery of Jermain W. Loguen began during my work with them as research assistant and editor for the North American Slave Narratives collection. They enthusiastically supported me, expanding what began as an essay for the DocSouth collection into a critical edition of the original work.

I would like to express sincere thanks to William La Moy, curator of rare books and printed materials at Syracuse University Library, who assisted me in translating the difficult handwriting of nineteenth-century letters. Visits to this archive were supported by summer fellowships from the Northeast Modern Language Association and the Graduate School of the University of North Carolina at Chapel Hill.

I am deeply grateful to Philip F. Gura, who encouraged this project from its inception and who reviewed—in the form of a seminar paper for his course on pre-1860 American literature—an early draft of what would eventually become the introduction to *The Rev. J. W. Loguen.*

I am forever indebted to William L. Andrews, who is an incredible mentor and has taught me so much about literary historical scholarship. Bill was exceedingly generous with his time as well as willing to share a wealth of knowledge and advice on the process of researching the rich history of slave narratives. Bill was an incredible sounding board and editor, and his encouragement to take this research project beyond the classroom and library to publication made the whole venture possible.

Heartfelt thanks go to the following colleagues, for the advice and encouragement they have offered along the way: Linda Wagner-Martin, Wahneema Lubiano, Rebecka Rutledge Fisher, Fred Hobson, Harry Thomas, Angie

Calcaterra, Meredith Malburne-Wade, Ashley Reed, Kelly Bezio, and Ben Bolling.

My thanks and appreciation also go to my family and friends, who cheer me on and are always ready to join me on the next literal or literary adventure. Special thanks go to my father, who instilled in me the belief that I can do anything; I'm grateful for the ways he makes it possible. To my aunt Martha, who cheers me at every step and constantly inspires me to broaden my thinking. To my late mother, who is always with me.

THE REV. J. W. LOGUEN,
AS A SLAVE AND AS A FREEMAN

CRITICAL INTRODUCTION

Jennifer A. Williamson

The Rev. J. W. Loguen, as a Slave and as a Freeman: A Narrative of Real Life was first published in 1859 in Syracuse, New York. Ostensibly the biography of a controversial and charismatic African American speaker, writer, and minister-activist, the narrative recounts Loguen's early life in slavery, his escape to the North, and his career as a minister and abolitionist in New York and Canada. Emerging evidence suggests, however, that this remarkable narrative is, in fact, Loguen's autobiography, the product of his own initiative and recollection, and thus a notable contribution to the fugitive slave-narrative tradition in the United States. *The Rev. J. W. Loguen, as a Slave and as a Freeman* represents an intriguing literary hybrid, an experiment in voice and style that enlarges our understanding of the slave narrative and the work of this African American leader in the antislavery movement.

Dubbed the "Underground Railroad King" in 1860 by the *Weekly Anglo-African* newspaper for his extraordinary efforts on behalf of fugitive slaves, Loguen made his home on East Genesee Street in Syracuse the central "depot" of the Underground Railroad in that upstate New York city. Loguen's uniquely defiant way of advertising his Underground Railroad efforts marked him as a lion among fugitive slaves and antislavery activists. He was eventually credited with helping more than fifteen hundred slaves escape to freedom. Loguen counted among his close friends and colleagues a virtual "who's who" of American reformers of the mid-nineteenth century: Frederick Douglass, Gerrit Smith, Samuel Ringgold Ward, James McCune Smith, Samuel Joseph May, and Beriah Green. Loguen also worked with other well-known abolitionists such as William Lloyd Garrison, William Wells Brown, Harriet Tubman, Henry Bibb, William Still, Charles Augustus Wheaton, Henry Highland Garnet, J. R. Johnson, Lucretia Mott, and Lucy Stone. Frederick Douglass praised his "esteemed friend" as a valuable and effective anti-slavery activist, the "imbodyment [*sic*] of manly energy, a kind-hearted, gentle, good man, naturally a lamb yet evidently capable of playing the part of a lion."[1]

Jermain Wesley Loguen was born around 1814 in Davidson County, Tennessee, to an enslaved mother named Jane, who was kidnapped from the free state of Ohio and renamed Cherry by her new owners. Loguen's father was his own master, David Logue, who had taken Cherry for a mistress. Originally named Jarm Logue, he later added the *n* to his last name to differentiate himself from his slave-master father and adopted the middle name Wesley to reflect his Wesleyan Methodist sympathies. Loguen was acknowledged as the son of David Logue during his childhood; he, his mother, and his siblings enjoyed a favored status until David Logue took a white mistress. Cherry had three children with David Logue, and after the dissolution of their connection, she was allowed to marry an enslaved man named Henry from a neighboring plantation, with whom she had another child. Cherry, Loguen, and the children were separated from Henry, however, when they were eventually sold to Manasseth Logue—David's brother and Loguen's uncle—to pay David's growing debts. They worked in the fields and distillery, suffering extreme physical abuse, particularly during Manasseth Logue's drunken rages. Loguen also witnessed two events that deeply affected him and recurred frequently in his abolitionist lectures to illustrate the horrors of slavery: he was present when slave traders came to take his brother and sister away and saw, firsthand, his mother's extreme grief over losing her children; he also witnessed the distress and anguish of his older sister, Maria, when she herself was sold away and forced to leave her own children behind.

In his early twenties, Loguen escaped from slavery and traveled through Kentucky, southern Indiana, and New England, before reaching Canada in approximately 1835. He eventually settled in upstate New York and enrolled in the abolitionist Oneida Institute in 1839. He began a lifelong commitment to education in the African American community, and he later established a school in Utica, New York, for African American children. He moved to Syracuse in 1841, founded another school, and married Caroline Storum, with whom he had eight children. Loguen was ordained by the African Methodist Episcopal (AME) Zion Church in 1842 and became increasingly involved with the abolitionist movement, transitioning from local ministry to working

1. Frederick Douglass, letter from the editor, *Frederick Douglass' Paper*, July 30, 1852, African American Newspapers (database).

with Frederick Douglass and Samuel J. May on the New England and Canadian lecture circuits. Loguen quickly developed a reputation as a powerful speaker and was in great demand. Newspaper reports of his lectures praised his "sparkling wit," eloquence, and emotional force.[2] His African American antislavery colleague Samuel Ringgold Ward recounted a lecture in which Loguen "thrilled the meeting with the most fervid outpouring of living eloquence I ever heard." Another leading African American abolitionist, William C. Nell, wrote in an open letter to William Lloyd Garrison that hearing Loguen speak was "a treat which will long [be] remembered." A journalist for the *Auburn (NY) Advocate* described Loguen as speaking "with an energy and pathos rarely surpassed."[3] Douglass, who frequently traveled with Loguen and co-lectured with him, so admired Loguen's abilities that he devoted an editorial in the *North Star* to one of Loguen's lectures:

> Brother Loguen and I addressed the meeting at much length. . . . The speech of my co-worker was on this occasion full of genuine pathos, moral force, and manly indignation. Slavery never looked more foul, cold blooded and fiendish, than while Loguen portrayed the sale and carrying away of his sister's children—a scene witnessed by himself, and had left in him an ineffaceable impression. His manly form shook, and his voice choked for utterance as he recalled and strove to bring before his hearers the thrilling scene. There were many tears and heart throbbings occasioned on his narration, showing that all feeling had not fled from Anti-Slavery meetings.[4]

Loguen tirelessly promoted the assistance of fugitive slaves, both as manager for the Fugitive Aid Society and as a "conductor" of the Underground Railroad in Syracuse. For Loguen, it was not enough to merely offer aid to fugitives—he built additional rooms on his house and supplied his basement with bunk beds to shelter fugitives. Publicizing these efforts to garner support led Loguen to public disagreements with Frederick Douglass and other more

2. "State Convention," *Impartial Citizen*, July 11, 1849, Black Abolitionist Papers, 1830–1865 (database).

3. Samuel Ringgold Ward, letter to the editor, *Impartial Citizen*, Nov. 2, 1850, Black Abolitionist Papers, 1830–1865; William C. Nell, letter to the editor, *Impartial Citizen*, Dec. 10, 1852, Black Abolitionist Papers, 1830–1865; "Rev. J. W. Loguen," *Frederick Douglass' Paper*, Jan. 28, 1853, African American Newspapers.

4. Letter from the editor, *Frederick Douglass' Paper*, June 23, 1854, African American Newspapers.

cautious activists, who urged the need for secrecy regarding Underground Railroad activities. Loguen boldly identified himself on his business cards and letters as an "Underground Railroad Agent," advertised his home address in newspapers as a refuge for fugitive slaves, distributed notices of fugitives received at his house, and published reports of funds donated to and used on behalf of the efforts of the Underground Railroad for public inspection.

Frequently, notices appeared in such newspapers as *Frederick Douglass' Paper*, *Douglass' Monthly*, the *Syracuse Daily Standard*, the *Syracuse Daily Journal*, and the *National Era*, informing the public as to the number of fugitives Loguen aided:

> keeper of the Underground Railroad Depot in the city, Rev. Mr. Loguen, is now busily engaged in providing places for the company of eight fugitives that arrived here on Friday night. He is determined to do his utmost for all who choose to seek his assistance under like circumstances.[5]

> Rev. J. W. LOGUEN was providing for a couple of noble fellows who fled from Baltimore. . . . So many passed through this city this week. The stream is constant. The number touching and receiving aid from Syracuse since January have been about one hundred and forty. The fields and kitchens of the south will suffer for hands. The agent of the road, Mr. LOGUEN has his hands full of this business. Hurrah for democracy![6]

> During the last three weeks, twenty-four of the children of Slavery have been cared for by the superintendent of the underground railroad at Syracuse, J. W. Loguen, and sent on their way rejoicing. One man sent his wife ahead in a box, which came straight through, was opened by Mr. L., and the wife found safe and sound.[7]

Loguen's audacity—especially given his own fugitive status—was unprecedented. He taunted Southern slaveholders in newspapers: "I would like to say to the Slaveholders and all others, just here, that the Underground Railroad was never doing a better business than at present. We have had as many as

5. "The U.G.R.R. Syracuse Station," *Frederick Douglass' Paper*, Aug. 3, 1855, African American Newspapers.

6. "Fugitives from Service," *Frederick Douglass' Paper*, Oct. 12, 1855, African American Newspapers.

7. "During the Last Three Weeks," *National Era*, July 23, 1857, African American Newspapers.

sixteen passengers in one week in this city. I speak officially, as the agent and keeper of an Underground Railroad Depot. Let them come; we have some true hearts ready to receive them, and God will raise up more."[8]

Loguen also offered public thanks to his contributors and supporters because he was able to provide such assistance only through donations of money, food, and clothing, given by various aid societies and private citizens: "In behalf of the many Fugitive Slaves who have passed through our city to [Canada] . . . I wish to return thanks to the friends therein, from whom 'they have received substantial aid and comfort.' They escaped from the land of mangled bodies and bleeding hearts, and found many among you to relieve their wants and strengthen their hearts."[9]

After lecturing in Canada, Loguen provided follow-up reports on fugitives who had successfully reached the British-controlled country in the North through the assistance of the Underground Railroad, describing meetings with former fugitives in his reports: "I saw many fugitive's [*sic*] whom [the Vigilance Committee] had personaly [*sic*] aided during their passage on the Underground Railroad. They were, with scarcely an individual exception, doing well and sent many heartfelt thanks to their good friends in Syracuse, whose kindness they can never forget."[10]

When the Fugitive Slave Act passed in 1850, Loguen not only denounced the law, as did many abolitionists, but also swore to defy it. "I don't respect this law," he says in *The Rev. J. W. Loguen*. "I don't fear it—I won't obey it! It outlaws me, and I outlaw it, and the men who attempt to enforce it on me." Loguen's militant antislavery activism spurred his leadership in the widely reported effort to rescue William "Jerry" McHenry in October 1851, a fugitive slave who was to be tried and returned to slavery in the South. Loguen was later indicted for his participation in the successful "Jerry Rescue" and forced to flee to Canada temporarily to avoid arrest and prosecution, which would put him in jeopardy for being returned to slavery in the South. He returned to Syracuse in late 1852 to resume his work on the Underground Railroad and on behalf of fugitive slaves, while also continuing his antislavery lectures throughout the Northeast. He had always been a champion of active

8. Jermain W. Loguen, letter to the editor, *Frederick Douglass' Paper*, Apr. 6, 1855, Black Abolitionist Newspapers, 1830–1865.

9. Jermain W. Loguen, letter to the editor, *Frederick Douglass' Paper*, June 8, 1855, Black Abolitionist Newspapers, 1830–1865.

10. Jermain W. Loguen, "Refugees in Canada," *Anti-Slavery Bugle*, Jan. 14, 1854, Black Abolitionist Papers, 1830–1865.

resistance, but with the passage of the Fugitive Slave Act, Loguen's views supporting war to achieve the abolition of slavery became more pronounced.

In the early 1860s, Loguen was appointed to serve as pastor to AME Zion churches in Binghamton, New York, and Montrose, Pennsylvania. The Binghamton church was a struggling congregation with little wealth, and Loguen helped raise funds for a new church building to be constructed in 1864 that would accommodate two hundred people. In addition to raising church funds, Loguen also helped recruit solders throughout central New York, and a black military company formed in Binghamton that was known as "Loguen's Guards" in response to state refusal to allow African Americans to serve. As the ongoing Civil War created more pressure on the federal government to accept African American soldiers, these recruits were ready to join the fight. After the Civil War, Loguen became active in establishing AME Zion congregations in Kentucky and Tennessee for Southern freedmen. Logan Temple, one of the churches he started in Knoxville, Tennessee, is named for him. His theological stance that Christianity and slaveholding were opposed informed much of his ministry and his writing. Loguen was named a bishop in the AME Zion Church in 1868. He supported the work of the Freedmen's Bureau as well as the American Missionary Association in the South. He died in Saratoga Springs, New York, in 1872.

At the time of the book's publication in 1859, *The Rev. J. W. Loguen* was greeted with enthusiasm. It was hailed as a narrative following the tradition of Douglass's *My Bondage and My Freedom* (1855) and a work solidifying the reputation Loguen had built through his antislavery lectures and activism. Syracuse's *Central City Daily Courier* advertised *The Rev. J. W. Loguen* enthusiastically:

> There are few men whose history is so marked with stirring incidents, instructive lessons, and encouraging examples, as Mr. Loguen's. It contains the peculiarities of Mr Loguen's childhood, his daring escape from bondage, the perils and hardships he endured in his passage to freedom, and the acts of subsequent manhood, which have honorably connected his name with the moral and political causes of the last twenty years, which, to a large extent, have made the subject of African Freedom the living topic of private and public circles, of the press, the pulpit, and the State and National Legislatures.[11]

11. "The Life of Jermain W. Loguen," *Central City Daily Courier* (Syracuse, NY), Mar. 29, 1859, Newspaper Archive (database).

The *Syracuse Daily Journal* called *The Rev. J. W. Loguen* "in all respects well executed" and predicted that "the sale of the book will doubtless be large and rapid," printing excerpts from the narrative to encourage the public's interest in purchasing copies. In 1860 "M.," a contributor to the *Weekly Anglo-African*, wrote a letter to the editor in which he glowingly described a lecture Loguen had conducted in Albany, New York: "He pictured most beautifully and truthfully the 'irrepressible conflict,' and how it strove even in the bondsman's heart. Oh! that every one would but read his life, furnished as it is in a handsomely bound book of four hundred and fifty pages, for only one dollar, and thus aid in carrying on this 'irrepressible conflict.'"[12]

Loguen's narrative remained in the public eye for some time; five years later, the *Christian Recorder*, an African American abolitionist newspaper, praised *The Rev. J. W. Loguen*, noting that the paper did "not claim to be the first to call attention to it through public print" and calling it "a wonderful book." The *Christian Recorder* recommended *The Rev. J. W. Loguen* because "this book narrates the life of Bro. Loguen as a slave with startling power. . . . [W]e have read enough to convince us that the history it gives to the public is a most striking and truthful one." Loguen's life story remained of interest to the public beyond the end of the Civil War and Emancipation. In 1872 the *Christian Recorder* advertised William Still's newly published *The Underground Railroad* by comparing it favorably to *My Bondage and My Freedom* and *The Rev. J. W. Loguen, as a Slave and as a Freeman*.[13] That the most prominent African American newspaper of the Reconstruction era paired Loguen's narrative with Douglass's autobiography as major touchstones of African American autobiography testifies to the honored place Loguen and his narrative held in the eyes of black America well after the slavery era.

Twentieth-century literary scholars have debated the import of *The Rev. J. W. Loguen* as to literary quality and authenticity. Whereas one critic extolled the narrative as "by far the greatest [slave biography] from a literary point of view," others dismissed it as an "obviously false account."[14] Much of the divided opinion on *The Rev. J. W. Loguen* can be attributed, however, to the different

12. "New Book," *Syracuse Daily Journal*, Sept. 28, 1859, Black Abolitionist Papers, 1830–1865; M., "Our Albany Letter," *Weekly Anglo-African*, Jan. 28, 1860, Black Abolitionist Papers, 1830–1865.

13. "Book Notices," *Christian Recorder*, July 9, 1864, African American Newspapers; "The Underground Railroad," *Christian Recorder*, Apr. 27, 1872, African American Newspapers.

14. Margaret Young Jackson, "An Investigation of Biographies and Autobiographies of American Slaves Published between 1840 and 1860," 3; Gilbert Osofsky, *Puttin' on Ole Massa*, 13.

perspectives from which it has been evaluated—as literary or historical artifact—and to its complicated position within the slave-narrative tradition.

As a literary tradition, slave narratives date back to the early eighteenth century, almost to the beginning of western European slavery itself. Forms and styles have varied over the centuries, but common themes and rhetorical similarities connect them. Although most slave narratives exist in the form of autobiographies, stories about the lives of slaves can be found in many formats, such as books, pamphlets, crime confessions, interviews, newspaper reports, meeting minutes, and court transcripts. At the most basic level, most slave narratives tell the life story of an individual who was born in Africa or was of African descent, endured the abuses of enslavement, resisted and escaped to freedom, and eventually publicized his or her experiences. Furthermore, slave narratives also employ several common rhetorical strategies and philosophical themes that developed throughout the late eighteenth and nineteenth centuries. It is a genre that is, according to William L. Andrews in *To Tell a Free Story: The First Century of Afro-American Autobiography, 1760–1865* (1986), "chiefly distinguished by its rhetorical aims."[15] Stylistic similarities within this tradition stem from a convergence of aesthetic, social, and political goals. Shared themes include the definition and redefinition of African Americans as fully human instead of chattel, the trauma of familial separation, temperance and the social evils of alcohol, representations of manhood and manliness, the use of journey or quest motifs to symbolize spiritual evolution, and interpretations of "true Christianity" as inherently opposed to slavery. *The Rev. J. W. Loguen* exemplifies all of these key slave-narrative themes through Loguen's personal experiences graphically and forcefully rendered. Loguen's narrative displays its originality in its focus on the author's ideas about African American manhood and manliness, the African American family and the effect of slavery on it, and Christian theology as a liberating gospel for oppressed African Americans.

As political and social circumstances changed, rhetorical styles in slave narratives responded. The earliest slave-narrative autobiographies strongly emphasized spiritual conversion, arguing for the humanity of the enslaved through their access to Christian salvation. Later narratives assumed access to Christian salvation and focused on reinterpreting Christian theology to show incompatibility with proslavery views or highlight the hypocrisy of slaveholders who claimed Christian beliefs. Whereas earlier slave-narrative authors

15. William L. Andrews, *To Tell a Free Story: The First Century of Afro-American Autobiography, 1760–1865*, 1.

argued for the humanity of the slave, such authors after the mid-nineteenth century focused instead on selfhood and individuality represented in words and deeds increasingly resistant to slavery. Although most early slave narratives were published on behalf of slaves who had been denied access to education and therefore needed white editors and amanuenses to transcribe their stories, African Americans like Douglass, Wells Brown, and Loguen mobilized their literacy so as to write and publish their own life stories. Formerly enslaved authors often included "Written by Himself" or "Written by Herself" in the titles of their narratives to emphasize their literary independence and political self-determination as free men and women determined to tell their stories honestly and freely.

When *The Rev. J. W. Loguen, as a Slave and as a Freeman: A Narrative of Real Life* was first published, it bore neither the name of its author on its title page nor an explicit indication in its title that it was, in fact, an autobiography. The narrative did present to its reader, however, a facsimile of Loguen's portrait with Loguen's signature underneath, facing the title page, which indicated Loguen's close association with and approval of the work. Because the narrative was written in the third person, with occasional editorial interruptions and direct quotations from Loguen, it appeared to be a biography. Yet no author or editor of the biography was named, and no one later claimed the honor. Therefore, although some newspaper advertisements called *The Rev. J. W. Loguen* a biography, because of Loguen's close association with the book the narrative was generally understood to be an autobiography. Questions about authorship lingered because of the lack of evidence conclusively providing who the narrative's author was. Slave-narrative scholars John W. Blassingame and Philip Foner classified Loguen's narrative as genuine autobiography, while critics Margaret Jackson and Milton Sernett proposed an anonymous author, although Sernett credited Loguen with close involvement in the composition process.[16] In a genre where authenticity was paramount because the story was judged both on its style of telling and on the truth of its facts, this uncertainty has created problems for scholars and readers who are uncertain about how to understand this narrative—whether the facts contained in the narrative could be verified, the degree to which the "voice" of the text was Loguen's, and

16. John W. Blassingame, *Slave Testimony: Two Centuries of Letters, Speeches, Interviews, and Autobiographies*, xxxxviii; Philip S. Foner, *History of Black Americans*, 2:279; Jackson, "Investigation of Biographies and Autobiographies," 3; Milton C. Sernett, "A Citizen of 'No Mean City': Jermain W. Loguen and the Antislavery Reputation of Syracuse."

the degree to which Loguen's story had been altered or mediated by another author or editor. These questions about who actually authored *The Rev. J. W. Loguen* became particularly important as twentieth- and twenty-first-century scholars began to analyze the ways in which African American voices in slave narratives had been mediated, edited, or altered by the—at times well-intentioned—efforts of white editors and amanuenses as well as the ways African Americans asserted their own voices within such texts.

The question of "voice" and authorship in slave narratives has been essential to the genre throughout its development. From their inception, the authenticity of slave narrative texts was of constant concern because skeptical reviewers were quick to point out what they termed were exaggerations or lies in order to undermine abolitionist arguments and support counternarratives that presented slavery as a benign institution. The question of authorship and authenticity was a paradoxical problem, particularly in the first half century of slave-narrative publication, because enslaved individuals were generally denied the opportunity to learn how to read and write—to publicize their stories required a mediator. Slave narratives were often published with the help of an amanuensis—who was usually white—to whom the individual dictated his or her story for transcription.

Despite the emphasis on authenticity as essential to a slave narrative's antislavery argument, the mediating process often meant that the voice of the original storyteller was moderated or altogether altered based on the perceptions or intention of his or her white editor. As John Blassingame points out, the perspective and voice of the editor affected the presentation of the narrative: "On occasion a narrative contained so many of the editor's views that there was little room, for the testimony of the fugitive. Sometimes the accounts were so romantic and focused so heavily on the flight from bondage that they were more akin to Indian-escape literature than slave autobiographies. . . . There can be little doubt that the abolitionists interjected some of their own ideas into the narratives."[17]

Over time, an increasing number of slave narratives were self-authored because of expanded educational opportunities in the North as well as the symbolic significance expressed in being able to tell one's "own story." Andrews points out that Douglass's *Narrative of the Life of Frederick Douglass, an American Slave* (1845) and subsequent autobiographies were "textual declarations

17. John W. Blassingame, "Using the Testimony of Ex-Slaves: Approaches and Problems," 83.

of independence" that "implied that the writing of autobiography was itself understood to be an act of self-liberation. . . . Instead of existing as the theme of the text, that which the slave narrative is *about*, freedom becomes the crucial property and quality *of* a text—not just *what* it refers to, but *how* it signifies."[18]

In a 1989 article that was expanded into a chapter in her 1993 book about Loguen's life, historian Carol M. Hunter claimed that the narrative's actual author was John Thomas, a white abolitionist whom Loguen met in 1844 while fund-raising in Cortland, New York. By the time *The Rev. J. W. Loguen* appeared, the two men had known each other for at least fifteen years. Thomas, a lawyer and an editor of the *Liberty Party Paper*, was, like Loguen, a recipient of funds from antislavery philanthropist Gerrit Smith. Although Hunter concedes that "no one doubts that Loguen was literate and capable of writing an autobiography," she cites references from the narrative to a third-person author that refers to Loguen in the third person, which in her view suggests that the book was likely compiled through a series of interviews with Loguen. Hunter also points to correspondence that "indicates that [Loguen] did not like to write," because in numerous letters—to Frederick Douglass he claimed that "writing is not my forte"—Loguen begged leave for the poor quality of his writing. However, by mistaking modesty for lack of ability, Hunter fails to account for both Loguen's wealth of experience as an antislavery lecturer as well as the sheer volume of writing Loguen produced and published. As Andrews points out in *To Tell a Free Story*, by the 1840s many slave narratives were being authored by preachers and antislavery speakers who had become popular on the abolitionist lecture circuit: "In their roles as preachers from the antislavery pulpit, slave narrators gained valuable training for their literary careers." Furthermore, Loguen willingly and regularly agreed to publish reports of his lecture tours and open letters about his views on abolition in *Frederick Douglass' Paper*. He also frequently sought to have his letters and notices—absent of any self-deprecations—reprinted in "all papers friendly to colored men."[19] Loguen's letters, particularly the ones that treat a political or theological dispute with a critic, were eloquent, passionate, and sophisticated.

18. Andrews, *To Tell a Free Story*, 103–4.

19. Carol M. Hunter, "The Rev. Jermain Loguen: A Narrative of Real Life" and *To Set the Captives Free: Reverend Jermain Wesley Loguen and the Struggle for Freedom in Central New York, 1835–1872*, 20 (quote); Jermain W. Loguen, letter to the editor, *Frederick Douglass' Paper*, Apr. 4, 1854, Black Abolitionist Papers, 1830–1865; Andrews, *To Tell a Free Story*, 100; Jermain W. Loguen, "Gerrit Smith's Land," *North Star*, Mar. 24, 1848, Black Abolitionist Papers, 1830–1865.

Many of his letters evinced poetic descriptive powers, particularly when he discussed escaping to freedom and the torment of leaving his family behind. Other letters developed thoughtful arguments for African American education and vocation as key aspects for racial uplift, anticipating the late-nineteenth-century views of Booker T. Washington. Loguen also published letters in which he engaged in meticulous theological debates, such as his public feud with Rev. H. Mattison in 1856. Loguen not only showed the reasoning of an educated, intellectually engaged minister who explored the finer points of biblical interpretation, but also meticulously fleshed out his argument that Christianity was antislavery and rhetorically defended himself against a proslavery minister who had openly insulted him.

A letter from John Thomas to Gerrit Smith dated August 24, 1859, indicates that Thomas was certainly involved in the narrative's publication. But in this letter Thomas acknowledges having received a three-hundred-page manuscript from Loguen, which it was Thomas's job to edit. From Thomas's account, it is clear that Loguen created the original manuscript of his autobiography and then turned it over to his white associate to shape into publishable form. Thomas makes no secret of his motive and role as Loguen's hired editor: "When Loguen, finally, offered me $300 for the manuscript, I grabbed at it, because I was poor & wanted money to live on. I instantly set to work & cut it down, & that is what I am doing to it now, besides hurrying the printers that I may get it off my hands."[20] Thomas's contribution to Loguen's narrative, therefore, appears to be the kind of editing that Lydia Maria Child provided to Harriet Jacobs as *Incidents in the Life of a Slave Girl* evolved into Jacobs's 1861 autobiography. In both cases, the white editors worked with a preexisting manuscript authored by a fugitive slave, which each editor helped to shape and revise in ways typical of the prepublication editorial process then and now.

On March 23, 1859, five months before Thomas's letter to Smith, Loguen sent Gerrit Smith a letter to inform him that "I am trying to get out a book. What think you of it. I hope you will feel friendly to the idea." Loguen's motivations for publishing his life story were to raise money on behalf of fugitive slaves and to help sustain his family while he dedicated his efforts full-time to that work. He depended primarily on donors to provide for the needs of the hundreds of fugitives whom he aided through the Fugitive Aid Society and

20. William La Moy, curator of rare books and printed materials at Syracuse University Archives, assisted me in translating the difficult handwriting of the letter.

the Underground Railroad. Because he was employed full-time ministering, lecturing, and conducting charity work, he needed help to meet the needs of his large family as well. Whereas abolitionists promoted the publication of slave narratives in order to publicize the atrocities of slavery, many slave-narrative authors also declared proceeds would go toward their particular charity works—some dedicated profits to building African American schools or churches as well as fugitive aid societies—toward purchasing freedom for themselves (or family members), or toward making up for financial hardships incurred by their fugitive status. Loguen's letter to Smith signaled a hope for the philanthropist's financial support of the project. Newspaper circulars providing advance notice of the book reiterated Loguen's precarious financial position, stating that *The Rev. J. W. Loguen* was about to be released "but for the pecuniary responsibilities incident to its publication. . . . When $1,000 is thus subscribed, the Book will be immediately published and subscribers will receive the amount of their subscriptions in Books, if they wish. All over that sum Mr. Loguen will himself assume." Loguen had taken full financial responsibility for the publication of *The Rev. J. W. Loguen*, and a way to relieve such a heavy burden was to advertise for subscribers to help offset the costs. In November 1859 an advertisement appeared for *The Rev. J. W. Loguen*, instructing readers to order copies directly from Loguen or L. J. Ormsbee, "wholesale dealer in stationery, watches, and fancy goods."[21]

One of the clearest insights into Loguen's choice to publish *The Rev. J. W. Loguen* comes from a correspondent to the *Weekly Anglo-African*. As mentioned above, "M." wrote a letter to editor Thomas Hamilton, reporting on a visit Loguen made to Albany, New York, in January 1860. In his letter M. not only enthused about Loguen's lectures, during which "never was so thrilling and heart-rending a scene brought directly home to the heart of slavery as it is, as one depicted by him. . . . Scarcely a dry eye could be seen among the females, and even many were unable to repress their sobs," but also encouraged all readers of the *Weekly Anglo-African* to purchase a copy of *The Rev. J. W. Loguen*. While Loguen's life story was powerful in revealing the horrors of slavery, M. also pointed out that Loguen had taken a stand by personally financing the publication of his narrative:

21. Gerrit Smith Papers, Box 25, Special Collections Research Center, Syracuse Univ. Libraries; "Life of Rev. Jermain W. Loguen," *Central City Daily Courier* (Syracuse, NY), Mar. 23, 1859, Newspaper Archives; "A New and Interesting Book," *Syracuse Daily Journal*, Nov. 5, 1859, Black Abolitionist Papers, 1830–1865.

> There is one important fact connected with this book that every one ought to know. . . . Mr. Loguen has refused most tempting offers on every hand from enterprising publishers, who, desirous themselves to reap the profit, have sought to blow the wind and publish the work and make it go off with a rush. In the face of this, that his own brethren might be joined with him in reaping the profit, if any, he has refused to appoint any but colored agents, himself having everything in his own hands, publishing, &c., although attended, of course, with vast expense. But the grand object is by this achieved, that by thus doing he himself reaps the benefit—not some great publisher—and divides it by per centage among his own people as his agents.[22]

It is unlikely that such a busy man would keep "everything in his own hands" and exert so much effort to publish and distribute a ghostwritten story, particularly a story ghostwritten by a white man, even one who shared his abolitionist cause. It seems clear that Loguen was determined to make the publication of his life story a publicly identified black enterprise, right down to returning profits from the sale of his book to the African American community. Loguen was willing to hire a white editor to assist him, but the evidence surrounding the genesis, publication, promotion, and sale of *The Rev. J. W. Loguen* indicates that Loguen provided the initiative, the original manuscript, the direction, and the marketing plan for his narrative.

Loguen's motivations in lecturing, writing, and publishing were all an integral part of his antislavery and pro–African American community efforts. He was involved with the production of the narrative from its creation to its publication and distribution, and he maintained total financial responsibility for the work, listing his name as the official copyright register to Congress in the text's imprint. Having been engaged as an agent to sell Frederick Douglass's autobiography *My Bondage and My Freedom*, Loguen knew the power of written personal testimony. He not only exercised control over the publication his own work, but also deployed his narrative with a deliberate political purpose. As M.'s letter indicates, Loguen shared this intention publicly, connecting the oft-repeated content of his abolitionist lectures with the life story told in the autobiography. Although John Thomas helped Loguen shape *The Rev. J. W. Loguen* into its final form, Thomas indicated in his own letter that he received a manuscript from Loguen, and no other individual was as

22. M., "Our Albany Letter," *Weekly Anglo-African*, Jan. 28, 1860, Black Abolitionist Papers, 1830–1865.

closely connected to the narrative, from beginning to end, all of which supports Loguen as primary author.

Published in 1859, *The Rev. J. W. Loguen* appeared at a critical moment in abolitionist and slave-narrative history. The passage of the 1850 Fugitive Slave Act had immeasurably heightened tensions among pro- and antislavery forces in both free and slave states, and it was followed by years of public debate, high-profile fugitive trials, rebellions, and sentimental publications leading up to the Civil War. Loguen, along with a large group of antislavery activists, participated in the notorious "Jerry Rescue" in 1851 to demonstrate defiance of the law and stir up feelings of resistance in Syracuse. Harriet Beecher Stowe's sentimental novel *Uncle Tom's Cabin* was published in 1852, achieving runaway success as a work of fiction and striking a blow for abolitionist ideals. Antislavery activists were acutely aware of the persuasive power of Stowe's novel, welcoming this text into the growing canon of abolitionist literature:

> Our thanks and our gratitude are due to Mrs. Stowe, for the great and good work, while the most commanding intellects of the age are merely exerting their [talent] to amuse the people; her's [*sic*] have been exerted to instruct them in the path of duty—to enlighten their moral reception—and to excite their sympathies in favor of a helpless and oppressive people. Uncle Tom has paid a visit to almost every family in the country; and his earnest and tearful appeal to all of the best, and purest, and noblest feelings of human nature will never be forgotten by those who have given him a candid hearing. This leaven is silently, but surely working its way to the hearts of the great mass of the American people.[23]

As she acknowledged in her *Key to Uncle Tom's Cabin* (1853), Stowe's novel not only was inspired by the real-life stories of slavery found in slave narratives, but also reflected the nineteenth-century emphasis on fiction that contained Christian, morally instructive, sentimental elements that inspire sympathy and feeling in the reader in order to bring him or her into a correct understanding. Abolitionists called this process "moral suasion" and had attempted to turn the public against slavery through such means for many

23. James L. Taylor, letter to the editor, *Frederick Douglass' Paper*, Sept. 30, 1853, African American Newspapers.

years, arguing for moral suasion over the use of violence. *Uncle Tom's Cabin* became their most effective tool in this fight. As a result, numerous antislavery sentimental novels followed in the style of *Uncle Tom's Cabin*.

Not all abolitionists, however, were content to rely on moral suasion, and fractures had appeared among abolitionist groups as early as the 1830s over the effectiveness of moral suasion versus direct action. On October 16, 1859, John Brown led a small group of volunteers on a raid against an arsenal in Harpers Ferry, Virginia, in an attempt to incite an insurrection and destroy the institution of slavery. Brown dismissed the pacifist views of William Lloyd Garrison, advocating violent action to achieve the end of slavery. By the 1840s Loguen had also broken with the Garrisonian doctrine of nonresistance, and by 1854 he had joined the Radical Abolition Society. In 1858 he joined Brown on the first part of his journey from New York into Canada on his way to Chatham, where Brown held a convention to set up a provisional constitution prior to the raid at Harpers Ferry. A letter Loguen wrote to Brown after the trip indicates he knew of—and supported—Brown's plans:

> My dear Friend and Brother:
> I was glad to learn that you and your brave men had got on to Chatham. I have seen our man Gray and find it as I feared—that he was not ready yet. I do not think he will go to War, soon. Others that would go have not the money to get there with and I have concluded to let them rest for the present.
>
> Have you got Isaac Williams with you? Have you got Harriet Tubman? Let me hear from you soon. As I cannot get to Chatham, I should like much to see you and your men before you go to the mountains.
>
> My wife and all unite in wishing you great success in your glorious undertaking. May the Lord be with you is our prayer.[24]

In 1860, after Harpers Ferry and Brown's subsequent execution, Loguen wrote to Frederick Douglass, celebrating Brown's "noble sacrifice" and exclaiming: "The 2d day of December, 1859, will hereafter be looked upon as a sacred day to the holy cause of human freedom. . . . We thank God that ever such a man as John Brown lived. And though Virginia may think she has put him to

24. J. W. Loguen to John Brown, May 6, 1858, in *Speak Out in Thunder Tones: Letters and Other Writings by Black Northerners*, edited by Dorothy Sterling, 274–75.

death, yet he lives—lives in the hearts of every liberty loving individual in our country. Yes, in the hearts of the poor, crushed, bleeding slave, for whom he sacrificed life. . . . And he himself said 'he could not better serve the cause he so much loved than to die for it.'" Despite the general fear of slave insurrection that Harpers Ferry struck in the white population, in the same letter Loguen describes approval of the event among his antislavery acquaintances, showing increasing support for active resistance:

> In all my travels among our people, I find but one feeling in reference to this matter, namely: a universal endorsement of John Brown's operations at Harper's Ferry, to the fullest extent. This, to my mind, is encouragement. . . . [T]he blow struck for liberty at Harper's Ferry is bringing the genuine lovers of impartial freedom to the surface. . . . I hope, dear friends, that we as an outraged people, may use this well begun work, so as to achieve the glorious designs proposed by it, namely: the liberation of the slave, and his religious elevation in the scale of being.

Loguen also enclosed a brief letter he had received from John Brown, written on May 17, 1859, in order to show that "Brown's religion did not commence after he was taken at Harper's Ferry; and that long before that event occurred, other measures, looking to the moral and religious elevation of our downtrodden people, were in contemplation by the good man." In his letter to Loguen, Brown likens their efforts to a ministry: "I have no doubt you will soon have a call from God to minister at a different location. I trust you will obey that call."[25]

The Rev. J. W. Loguen, appearing at the height of pro- and antislavery agitation leading up to the Civil War, reflects a convergence of two opposing branches of abolitionist propaganda in its hybrid literary form. It resonates with Loguen's fiercely held doctrine of active resistance while also attempting to capture the sentimental appeal and rhetorical style he had found so effective in his antislavery lectures. Although based on Loguen's life and centered on factual biographical details, *The Rev. J. W. Loguen* employs storytelling methods of nineteenth-century American sentimental fiction, revealing a desire to access the social and political power that was available through that kind of narrative. Through the novelized style, Loguen was able to introduce readers to more than just his individual suffering; he was able to reveal the hearts and

25. Jermain W. Loguen, letter to the editor, *Syracuse Daily Journal*, Feb. 18, 1860, Syracuse Univ. Archives.

minds of participants at every level of the system of slavery, underscoring the humanity and suffering of slaves, revealing the complexity of relationships between Southern slaves and whites, and promoting abolitionist philosophies that echo throughout the text from the mouths of a variety of characters.

Loguen's style allowed him to address the theme of manliness and manhood in a way that differed from previous straightforwardly autobiographical slave narratives. Slave narratives written by men often conflated the acquisition of literacy with freedom and manhood. Although earlier slave narratives written by men depicted scenes that emphasized family or community connection, they often strongly represented the male author as an independent, self-made man in order to counter feminized associations with family, community, and victimhood. Frederick Douglass, an exemplar of this style of masculinity, included a scene in his *Narrative of the Life of Frederick Douglass, an American Slave* and *My Bondage and My Freedom* in which he wins a violent confrontation with overseer Covey, after which he declares, "I was a changed being after that fight. I was *nothing* before; *I was a man now*." However, while Loguen emphasized the formation of manhood throughout his text, he defined it differently. Rather than developing a self-made, independent manhood, Loguen associated manhood with reason and intellectual awakening inspired by community connection. His physical pivotal confrontation with his master resulted not in Loguen realizing his own manhood but instead in forcing Manasseth Loguen's recognition of it. Loguen had previously understood his own manhood through reason and community connection and then, because to be abused as less than a man became insupportable, asserted himself through action—the fight "opened [Manasseth's] eyes to the positive, manly, and uncompromising character of his slave."

Loguen also showed a correlation between manhood and womanhood in his portrayal of his family relationships. By emphasizing close familial relationships and dramatizing the highly sentimental, wrenching pain of separation—and maintaining its recurrence as a theme in his abolitionist work—Loguen's narrative challenges cultural beliefs and standard critical interpretations that have tended to view feeling as a feminized quality. Loguen embraced feeling as an integral part of his identity and a significant motivation for his desire to escape, become educated, and fight slavery. Loguen connected literacy, freedom, and manhood with feeling, community, *and* action, utilizing the sentimental genre to create more complex gender presentations and disrupt the established male-female slave binary. Similarly, as Loguen defined his masculinity as an identity that requires both feeling and action, Loguen's narrative revised concepts of African American womanhood in his presentation of the ways such women meet sentimental ideals while also being systematically prevented from enacting them. In this way, his text anticipates the complex presentations of African American womanhood explored in such later works as Harriet Jacobs's *Incidents in the Life of a Slave Girl.* Cherry is idealized as a loving mother desperate to protect her children but who is left vulnerable to the sexual and physical abuses of slavery. Loguen portrayed her as both a sentimental ideal—the loving mother—and a woman of Amazonian physical strength who taught him the (masculinized) value of resistance, but who was nevertheless ultimately powerless to prevent or escape the abuses of slavery.

The style of *The Rev. J. W. Loguen* also allowed Loguen to expand on antislavery theological themes in a way that made them more comprehensible to the average reader. Conversations between characters provide opportunities for readers to follow the logic behind abolitionist Christian arguments. Conversations between David Logue and his neighbor Joseph, during which Loguen himself is not present, allow readers to overhear both sides of a theological debate—between a proslavery advocate who wishes to continue his practices and an antislavery Christian who kindly points out the errors and fallacies in David's beliefs. Similarly, when Loguen is temporarily hired out to the Preston family, he recounts their conversations around the dinner table, when the young Loguen heard the Preston children ask their father about his theological views. Thus, not only does Loguen reveal how his own Christian beliefs were shaped in a time of youthful ignorance, but the conversations gently instruct readers in the foundational views of this form of Christianity.

Many passages of *The Rev. J. W. Loguen* are devoted to conversations between individuals who sift through fine points of abolitionist theology. By incorporating a range of characters—from conflicted slaveholders and curious children to ardent pro- and antislavery advocates—Loguen is able to address multiple viewpoints. Rather than position Loguen as the authoritative narrator who articulates lengthy sermon-like explanations of abolitionist philosophy, the text places those philosophies in the mouths of characters who interact with other less supportive or informed characters and engage them in debate. This process breaks down the complex ideologies into more comprehensible statements for a reader, while modeling ways in which these ideas might be challenged or supported, strengthening their potential impact.

Though *The Rev. J. W. Loguen* appropriates the power of sentiment for several good reasons, the text demands not only fellow feeling with the slave but also direct and forceful action. Even as it builds audience sympathy for the oppressed in bondage, Loguen's text prepares readers for an eventual call to arms by incorporating the theme of resistance in key sentimental moments, beginning with Loguen's mother, who first teaches her son the Jeffersonian-adapted motto that would become Loguen's mantra, "Resistance to tyrants is obedience to God." Accordingly, readers are prepared for later outbursts of Loguen's frustration at the lack of progress in freeing African Americans from slavery. Loguen repeatedly connects the themes of familial separation and legally sanctioned abuse to his emotional outbreaks, elaborating upon them in order to galvanize his audience from emotional identification to support for real-world action:

> What other motive can God employ to stir me to mortal resistance, beside those that are burning my heart and seething my brain this moment? My wife and children trembling for their outraged husband and father, surrounded by trembling white men almost as timid as they—my mother, brothers and sisters, and kindred and race embruted—the very color God gave us made a mark of dishonor by the tyrant whose blood my revolver thirsts for! The tide of progress rising, too, and breaking its waves at Syracuse and elsewhere, and bellowing above the storm, "NOW OR NEVER!" Come bloody battle, I say—I care not how bloody, if these outrages continue!

Such calls for "bloody battle" could have, no doubt, offended and distanced a contemporary audience who loved to cry over the death of Little Eva and the goodness of Uncle Tom. But Loguen sensed that a heightened emotional identification with the outraged manhood and violated families of African American slaves was the spark needed to ignite a crusading moral fervor among whites. The autobiography demands a move beyond sympathetically shared suffering. In the spirit of John Brown's call to arms, *The Rev. J. W. Loguen* builds upon the feelings of its audience and asks readers to recognize the limits of sympathy by transforming those feelings into a real-life battle against slavery, either through legal means or through actual war: "I tell you the evil is past endurance—the Justice of God cannot endure it. . . . Heaven's gathering vengeance waits your decision to-day—my poor oppressed countrymen are charged with it to the brim. . . . If our rights are withheld any longer, then come war—let blood flow without measure—until our rights are acknowledged or we perished from the earth."

The Rev. J. W. Loguen uses moral, religious, and emotional themes of sentimental fiction to justify its call to arms, altering traditional slave-narrative patterns to become a hybrid of the biography, autobiography, slave narrative, and sentimental novel that seeks to intensify reader identification with its antislavery directive. *The Rev. J. W. Loguen* builds upon the tradition of the slave narrative and appeals to sympathy for the abused slave and fugitive while also acknowledging the futility of sympathy without action. The literary and historical silences surrounding this work may be a result of its lack of conformity to genre classifications or its passionate endorsement of "resistance to tyrants." Examining this narrative, however, raises important questions about the relationship between the forms, aesthetics, and political functions of sentimental fiction and autobiographical slave narratives. *The Rev. J. W. Loguen* should encourage us to further consider the interrelationships among traditions of white abolitionist writing, women's writing, and African American writing as well as fiction and nonfiction that occurred in the nineteenth century.

Bibliography

Andrews, William L. *To Tell a Free Story: The First Century of Afro-American Autobiography, 1760–1865*. Urbana: Univ. of Illinois Press, 1986.

Blassingame, John W. *Slave Testimony: Two Centuries of Letters, Speeches, Interviews, and Autobiographies*. Baton Rouge: Louisiana State Univ. Press, 1977.

———. "Using the Testimony of Ex-Slaves: Approaches and Problems." In *The Slave's Narrative*, edited by Charles T. Davis and Henry Louis Gates. Oxford: Oxford Univ. Press, 1991.

Foner, Philip S. *History of Black Americans*. 3 vols. Westport, CT: Glenwood Press, 1983.

Hunter, Carol M. "The Rev. Jermain Loguen: A Narrative of Real Life." *Afro-Americans in New York Life and History* 13 (July 1989): 33–46.

———. *To Set the Captives Free: Reverend Jermain Wesley Loguen and the Struggle for Freedom in Central New York, 1835–1872*. New York: Garland, 1993.

Jackson, Margaret Young. "An Investigation of Biographies and Autobiographies of American Slaves Published between 1840 and 1860." PhD diss., Cornell Univ., 1954.

Osofsky, Gilbert. *Puttin' on Ole Massa*. New York: Harper and Row, 1969.

Sernett, Milton C. "A Citizen of 'No Mean City': Jermain W. Loguen and the Antislavery Reputation of Syracuse." *Syracuse University Library Associates Courier* 22 (Fall 1987): 33–55.

Sterling, Dorothy, ed. *Speak Out in Thunder Tones: Letters and Other Writings by Black Northerners*. New York: Da Capo Press, 1998.

1. Unknown artist, pen-and-ink portrait of J. W. Loguen, published in *The Rev. J. W. Loguen*. Courtesy of the Gerrit Smith Papers, Special Collections Research Center, Syracuse University Libraries.

THE

REV. J. W. LOGUEN,

AS

A SLAVE

AND AS

A FREEMAN.

A NARRATIVE OF REAL LIFE.

SYRACUSE, N. Y.:
J. G. K. TRUAIR & CO., STEREOTYPERS AND PRINTERS,
OFFICE OF THE DAILY JOURNAL.
......
1859.

2. Title page to *The Rev. J. W. Loguen*. Courtesy of the Gerrit Smith Papers, Special Collections Research Center, Syracuse University Libraries.

TO THE FRIENDS
OF THE
UNDER GROUND RAIL ROAD
IN
AMERICA AND EUROPE

The subject of this book has had the charge of the Under Ground Rail Road at Syracuse for many years—therefore we dedicate it to the friends of that Road on both sides of the water, hoping they will be charitable to its blemishes and defects, and countenance its circulation to the extent of its merits.

THE EDITOR.

PREFACE

Every book has its preface. A book without a preface, would be like a city without a directory, or an animal with part only of the organs necessary to its existence.

We have proposed to write the Biography of Rev. JERMAIN WESLEY LOGUEN, and we have given its features in the following pages accurately. We took the features from him and filled up the picture. We began with his parents, infancy, childhood, and traced him from the Southern prison through the wilderness, and Canada, and back to the United States again, to fight the enemy all through the anti-slavery war to the end of the Jerry Rescue—giving the particulars of that Rescue, with the names of persons engaged in it, on one side and on the other.

The latter half of the life of Mr. Loguen stands out before the world. The other half is buried in the cimmerian night of slavery. Defective as is our taste and ability in giving the former, it will be allowed that we have been true to it, because the world has seen it. It is that portion in the folds of slavery only that may be questioned and criticised. It will be more likely to be questioned, because some few facts, circumstances, and discourse, not connected with Mr. LOGUEN'S experience with slavery, have been supplied to connect the real facts of his life, and furnish variety for the reader. Whoever reads such portion, or any portion of this book will remember, that not a fact relating to his, or his mother's, or brother's, or sister's experience with slavery, is stated, that is not, literally or substantially, true. Those facts were history before they were written; and they were written because they were history.

We have adopted the popular form or style in our narrative, in respect to popular taste; and, as aforesaid, occasionally supplied vacancies in his southern life from our own fancy; but in every case that we have done so, the picture is outside Mr. LOGUEN'S experience with slavery—and the picture, be it fact, opinion, or argument, may be adopted, and all we have given as his slave life will remain true. The reader, therefore, will test every such case by the question—"Does it involve Mr. LOGUEN'S experience of slavery, or that of his mother, or family, or any one else?" If it does involve one or the other of them, it is substantially, if not literally, true, as related.

Again. For obvious reasons, we have not always used real names when writing of real persons; for we would not involve living friends, or their families, for their good deeds. We refer now to Mr. LOGUEN'S life in Tennessee, not to his life in New York, or Canada. In Tennessee, slavery rules the tongue, the press, and the pen. In New York and Canada, these are given to free judgment and discretion. At the north, men are answerable for such judgment and discretion to the law only. At the south, they are amenable to an overgrown monster that devours alike law and humanity. At the south, we give Mr. LOGUEN'S connection with slavery, and therefore conceal names. At the north, we give his connection with liberty, and therefore give names of friends and enemies alike.

Because the circuit of Mr. LOGUEN'S activities has been large, we have necessarily followed him all around the course; and have been obliged briefly to note the growth of public opinion in favor of freedom, until freedom snapped her cords in Syracuse, and in the country around Syracuse, and in other places. In doing so, we have given particulars, and used the names of friends and foes with absolute truthfulness.

Though we have spoken freely, we doubt not there were other persons, equally, if not more deserving of honorable notice, than some we have named. Modest and retiring men are often most effective when bravery and strength are needed, but, nevertheless, they blush at a record of their own qualities. They vote, or strike, and retire out of sight. When justice opens a picture gallery to display the faces of those who have done much for African freedom, we shall see many noble faces in it, which are now obscure, in our villages and towns. If an artist would pass through those villages and towns, and engrave those faces in a book over a sketch of their deeds and lives, he would have a book posterity would love to look at. It would be a book of great thoughts, great hearts, and great men—men who were the receptacles in the body politic, to receive the inflowing life of Heaven, and diffuse it over the system, and bring it to life again—the real Saviours of the country.

We have put into the mouths of some of the characters, religious counsels, ideas, opinions, and sentiments, which may not, and of course cannot, coincide with the divided and distracted theories of the age. All we ask of the reader in regard to these, is, that he will be as charitable to them, as they are to him. Those counsels, ideas, opinions, and sentiments, are responsible only to truth, and conscience, and reason; and we kindly ask the reader to submit them to those heavenly vicegerents, and not charge them as a sin upon the Editor, or anybody else.

But the enquiry may be made—"What is the call for such a book; are we to have a book for every man or woman who is good and useful among their fellows?" Our answer is, it would be well if we had. This is not only a reading age, but it is a new age, and it is well to occupy our youth with its philosophy and facts. Men do not think, or labor, or travel, or live, as they did fifty years ago; and still the change is onward. For a long time invisible mental powers have been turning society on its hinges to let in a new dispensation of learning, religion, and life. There is a spring in all departments of humanity for a "long pull, a strong pull, and a pull all together," to move mankind on to a higher and a better level; and our young readers should know that colored men furnish a quota of the mental and physical muscle that produces the motion. Society is in process of incubation, and we should know whence is the heat and substance that embody and cherish the embryo. We should keep an eye on the formative elements, to see what portion is subsiding and dying, and what portion is combining to form the substance and life of the coming age. The African element contributes largely to the causes that agitate mankind, and must have its place in the product. The vital powers are attracted to it by force of the charities that make them vital, and are amalgamating with that element to form a new basis for society—a basis on which it will stand in the order of heaven, humanity, and religion—when men may look at it, and not start back affrighted.

We have come, therefore, to consider and honor a new element in the social state, and for that reason a man like Mr. LOGUEN becomes a subject of speculative and philosophical enquiry. At such a time, colored men are divine instrumentalities for Divine ends. Hence, so many of them have dodged their masters and their chains,—broken through the clouds, and become conspicuous in the intellectual and moral firmament.

In a mere preface, it becomes us not to anticipate history; but in answer to the question, "Why should the history of LOGUEN be written?" we may say, that though God has distinguished other colored men, by genius, learning, eloquence, and high deserts, he has distinguished LOGUEN more than all others with that noble and enlightened courage, which, at the earliest moment, turned upon the tyrant and defied his power. Instantly upon the fugitive slave enactment, and before that even, he proclaimed, with a voice that was heard throughout slavedom—"I am a fugitive slave from Tennessee. My master is Manasseth Logue—the letter of the law gives him a title to my person—and let him come and take it. I'll not run, nor will I give him a penny for my freedom." He was an example of courage to white and black men alike, to set slave laws at defiance, and trample them under his feet,—at a time, too, when such an example was needed, to mesmerise the drowsy spirits of both classes, and move them to break the crust which pro-slavery usages formed over them, and let the waters of life flow freely.

It needs little observation to see that the tide of affairs has reached the point, when men of power are needed, with moral courage to face the false and selfish, and in regard to slavery, the devilish policy and usages of the world, and avow in a manner to arrest the attention and legislation thereof, that "Human Rights" are the limits of Divine, and, of course, of all human law,—and that all enactments beyond those limits are void. Precisely at this point in the order of Providence, the men, the God-appointed men to do so, appear. We need not name them. Some of them are among the dead, many of them are among the living. They are the lights of the age, and saviors of the country—the monarchs of progress, in politics, in morals, and religion. By these, politics, and morals, and religion, are being regenerated, and society is evidently in prosperous effort to attain its natural and heavenly basis.

But if men are selected and gifted to impress the law of freedom, it is needful also that somebody be gifted with the sublime qualities, that shall lead him in defiance of penalties, to tread upon the enactments and constitutions that transgress such law. Pity, amazing pity, there are so few among white men gifted and commissioned to do so. As if to vindicate the deserts and dignity of all races, God has taken from the ranks of the severest bondage, JERMAIN W. LOGUEN, representing equally the blood of the slave-holder and the blood of the slave, the extremes of inverted humanity, and qualified and commissioned him, and made him alone conspicuous among black men, and most conspicuous among all men, practically and personally, to nullify all slave laws, and boldly to defy the enemies of human rights to enforce them.

Therefore, his name is entitled to a place upon the record.

CHAPTER I

We must devote a brief chapter to the parents of Mr. Loguen.

The genealogy of an American Slave may be traced with certainty to the mother, rarely to the father, never beyond them on the male line. It is the condition of the mother *de facto* that makes the slave. She is mother *de lege* only to the intent that her offspring may be an outlaw. As to the progenitor on the male side, he is rarely known as the father in fact, never in law. The slave has no father. Slave legislation has no use of a paternal line, and refuses to acknowledge one. It acknowledges a mother; not in respect to any natural relation, but for accommodation, as the medium of titles, not of affections and obligations. Legally speaking, the slave has neither father or mother.

Slavery, of course, has no records of conjugal relations. Should the clairvoyant translate and publish the secrets of its history, the domestic relations of the South would be broken up, and society sink in the abyss of vulgar passions. It owes its existence to the fact that its sexual history is faintly shadowed in the varied colors of the abused race.

It is hardly proper to pass by those familiar truths, while placing upon the record the life and character of Jermain W. Loguen. It is to be presumed that his physical, intellectual and moral qualities, partake of the character of his ancestors, and that they were modified by the influences that surrounded his childhood.

The mother of Mr. Loguen is a pure African. Her skin is jet black, and her hair short and curled to the head. She is now, if living, near as can be determined, about seventy years of age. In her youth and maturity her face was fair, and her features marked and regular—her bodily proportions large, symmetrical, round, and muscular—presenting a model of health and strength, and a specimen of the best of her race.

Of her parents and kindred of any kind, she is perfectly ignorant. The extent of her recollection is, that she was free in her infancy, in the guardianship of a man in Ohio, by the name of McCoy, with whom she lived until about seven years of age. She remembers that she was out of sight and hearing of Mr. McCoy's house, alone, when she was such little girl, and that a bad man got out of a covered wagon and took her into it with one hand about her body and the other upon her mouth to prevent her screams—that when she got into the wagon, he held her in his lap, and told the teamster to drive on—that there were several other little colored children in the wagon with her—and that they were taken over the river together in a boat; probably into Kentucky.

This story she often repeated to her son, and kindled in his boyhood the intensest indignation against the institution which so outraged the mother he loved. All other memories were drowned in the sorrows and terrors, which at that time overwhelmed her spirit, and the brutal associations and treatment she received afterwards.

Thus all recollection of parents, kindred and friends of every kind, were merged in the clouds which the kidnappers drew about her; and she has not heard the name of any one of them pronounced from that day to this. She is as if she never had any parents, or kindred, or, as if they were all buried and forgotten. That she was once free, she has the most distinct remembrance, and a flickering recollection of happy days in early childhood, still faintly illumines the dark horizon of her memory.

She does not remember the precise number of wretched little children, boys and girls, who were in the wagon with her, but thinks they were about her age, and all involved in the intensest grief. She remembers that their cries and sobs, like her own, were silenced by the terrors of the lawless villains who had them in charge.

We may be allowed to remark that these colored orphans illustrate the helplessness of the whole colored race, in a country where slavery is guarded as lawful and sacred. In proportion as slavery has the protection of law, do the persons of all colored men, women and children, lose the protection of law. As the condition of the former is hopeful and secure, is the latter desperate and exposed to outrage. Not only does the colored man suffer from the contempt and insolence of the favored class, but his or her person is outlawed to the limited and unlimited abuses of the conscienceless men who make them their prey. Developments of such enormities, incidentally and occasionally appear, as specks of light through "the blanket of the dark" upon the black volume which is out of sight.

These unhappy little ones were at the age, when childhood carols its joys with the birds, and bounds like lambs in the pastures at the touch of angels. For long and weary days and nights, not a motion or sound of delight, not a joyous look or laugh varied their depression and wretchedness. The oblivion of sleep was the only solace of the little sufferers; and even this was often tortured by the pressure of misery, and the silence of night broken by their sighs and sobs. Whether, like the mother of Mr. Loguen, they were stolen from their parents, or purchased from those who should have protected them, is unknown. Their story is untold or it is forgotten, and their history is a secret only to him who gathered little children in his arms to represent the kingdom of God.

After they passed the river, the kidnappers sold them, one after another, as they could light of purchasers on the road. The mother of Mr. Loguen was left or sold to three brothers, David, Carnes, and Manasseth Logue, who lived in a small log house on Manscoe's Creek, (so called) in Davidson county, about sixteen miles from Nashville, Tennessee. They were large, rough, and demi-civilized young men, the unmarried owners of a miserably cultivated plantation, and (what was at that time in that part of the country of better repute than a school or meeting house,) a whiskey distillery.

Whether these brothers were a link of a chain of kidnappers, extending through a part or the whole of the free and slave states, and claimed the poor girl as a Pirate's portion; or whether they purchased her for money or other thing, she does not know. Of one thing she is certain, so soon as the ruffians left her, she had an interview with her purchasers which made a lasting impression upon her person and memory.

There was nothing in the aspect or conduct of the Logues that showed aught but sympathy for her manifest wretchedness. Such was the tenderness and concern with which, at first, they seemed to be touched, and the obvious natural humanity which in their countenances, concealed and gilded the quiet ferocity of their natures, that she ventured to tell them how she was stolen, in the hope that they would return her back to her friends in Ohio. She had but begun the story when every expression of sympathy vanished, and their faces were covered with frowns. Their kind words changed into threats and curses. Nor was this all, or the worst. One of them took a slave whip that hung on the wall of the cabin and whipped her. Of course she could but beg and suffer, and at the conclusion promise she would never again repeat the offensive fact of her freedom.

Thus was this innocent child, according to the customary mode in such cases, metamorphosed from a human being into a chattel. To cover the transaction and make the change more complete, the name by which she had always been called, "Jane," was taken from her, and that of "Cherry," the name by which she has ever since been called and known, was given her.

Of course it is not the intent to give more of the history of this woman than shall serve to illustrate the maternal influences which nourished the spirit of her son. Though the enchanter's wand touched and changed her into a slave *de facto*, the terrible lesson did but adjust her habits to a prudential exterior. While it checked the growth of the sympathies and virtues of artless childhood, it awakened and strengthened animal energies, which under better influences had ever slept. The Logues intended her for a useful slave. The whipping and threats and extorted promise were designed for that end—and whether they were aware she had been stolen or not, her treatment would have been the same. They had no unkindness farther than they intended that neither her tongue or name should lead to evidence, by accident or intent, by which they might be deprived of their property; all memory of which they hoped would be overgrown by the habits of servile life.

Free colored persons have no right or privilege beyond a permitted residence in slave states, and such residence gives them nothing that deserves the name of protection from the wrongs of white men. The kidnapping and enslaving this little girl therefore, could not be looked upon as very bad, by men like the Logues, and the body of slaveholders, whose morals and humanity are so inverted, as to suppose, that by making her a slave, they raised her from the lowest to a higher condition, and furnished her with protection and privileges not to be enjoyed in a state of freedom. This fact will be illustrated in the course of our history, and we have mentioned it, incidentally, to relieve the Logues from the inference that their principles and habits were barbarous beyond public sentiment and the laws of the land.

Not slaveholders only, but slaves in the slave breeding States, as a general truth, regard theirs as a favored position, compared with the condition of free colored men and women at the South. Mr. Loguen, whose biography we write, is not the only one who says from experience, "If I must live in a slave State, let me be a slave."

Thus was Jane, who we shall hereafter call "Cherry," at the age of seven, robbed of all her rights, even of a knowledge or the names of her parents, and every one of her kindred, and placed under the tutelage of the rude habits and passions, and unscrupulous avarice of David, Carnes, and Manasseth Logue. These three brothers, lived with their widowed mother in a small log house, and Cherry was put in a pretty cabin, with other slaves, a little distance from them.

As her physical strength developed, she became their main dependence, in the house, the distillery, and in the field. Without losing her feminine proportions, she grew to a masculine hardihood. Among her other accomplishments, she became expert in the art of manufacturing whiskey, and was often employed day and night with other slaves in the distillery. On the plantation there was no hard service, whether it was driving the oxen, loading, lifting, plowing, hoeing or any other thing, to which she did not do a man's days' work. There was no man on the plantation, upon whom her masters more depended in all the departments of labor, and at all times, and in all weathers.

Cherry had now arrived at the condition her masters desired her to occupy. She was a faithful, skilful and able slave. She however felt the condition as a necessity, and submitted to it with the same contentment that the young Leopard feels under the restraints that cages and tames him. Her natural disposition was gentle, affectionate, kind, and confiding; but these qualities reposed upon a spirit, which, when roused and chafed, was as resolute and indomitable as the tigress in the jungles. She knew no fear, and submitted only to passion, interest, and necessity. Nothing but the lamb-like sympathies she always manifested under decent treatment, and her inestimable personal services, saved her from the legal and usual consequences of desperate resistance to those who would outrage her person.

It is believed that ten thousand slaves have been whipped to death, shot, or otherwise murdered, for transgressions not half so offensive as hers. But ignorant and brutal as were her masters, they respected alike the natural loveliness of her affections, and her indomitable impulses under wrongs, which no chastisement could subdue. But what most contributed to her safety, was the fact, that she was a first class laborer and slave breeder, and finally the mistress of David Logue, the youngest of the three.

This spirit of resistance, caused her many and some bloody battles and scourgings—the marks of which she will carry on her person while she lives. She would never allow a woman or any number of women to whip her. Nor could she be subdued by any ordinary man. When women sometimes inconsiderately engaged with her, they were obliged to call in a posse of stout men to bind her.

Jermain W. Loguen, whose heart even now, is as tender as a child to the touch of pity, when a little boy, and afterwards, has seen her knocked down with clubs, stripped and bound, and flogged with sticks, ox whips and rawhide, until the blood streamed down the gashes upon her body. When released from the place of torture, she never retired with a subdued spirit, but passed from a scourging to her labors like a sullen tigress. Her habits and character in this regard will be more unfolded in connection with the life of her son.

Compelled, as she was, to endure violence from her masters, and comparatively cautious in resisting them, she never endured it from others. White or black, male or female, if they attempted liberties with her person, against her consent, she not only resisted, but fought with a spirit and force proportioned to her own estimate of her rights and wrongs.

In describing the person of Cherry in the ripeness of robust youthful development, it may be inferred she was not destitute of attractions for the casual lust of the vulgar slaveholders who lived along the banks of Manscoe's Creek. The black distillery was the common resort of that class of lawless men. David, Manasseth, and Carnes Logue, her masters, were of the same class. They were all hard drinkers, and the distillery was a convenient place for coarse enjoyment and low carousals.

Though Cherry made the fire-water, she never drank it. Her nights and days were often spent at work in the distillery, and of course she was in the sight and hearing of these vulgar men, and often the subject of their brutal remarks. But outside the family of Logues, woe to the hand laid upon her person with lascivious intent. The body of a female Slave is outlawed of course to the white man. All the law she has is her own arm, and how Cherry appreciated that law may be illustrated by the following incident.

When she was about the age of twenty-four or five, a neighboring planter finding her alone at the distillery, and presuming upon the privileges of his position, made insulting advances, which she promptly repelled.

He pursued her with gentle force, and was still repelled. He then resorted to a slaveholder's violence and threats. These stirred all the tigers blood in her veins. She broke from his embrace, and stood before him in bold defiance.

He attempted again to lay hold of her—and careless of caste and slave laws, she grasped the heavy stick used to stir the malt, and dealt him a blow which made him reel and retire. But he retired only to recover and return with the fatal knife, and threats of vengeance and death. Again, she aimed the club with unmeasured force at him, and hit the hand which held the weapon, and dashed it to a distance from him. Again he rushed upon her with the fury of a madman, and she then plied a blow upon his temple, which laid him, as was supposed, dead at her feet.

This incident, though no portion of the biography of her son, is introduced to show the qualities of the woman who bore him, and which those acquainted with him will infer she imparted to him. This, and like scenes, formed the cradle in which the infant spirit of Jermain W. Loguen was rocked.

Cherry, unterrified by the deed we have related, did not flee to escape the application of the severe laws she had violated by striking a white man. She left the now passionless and apparently lifeless villain, bleeding not only from the wound inflicted, but from his nose and ears also, to inform her masters of the encounter, and meet the consequences. She told them she had killed the wretch, and the whole family of Logues hastened to the distillery to look, as they supposed, upon the face of their dead neighbor. They found him laying in his gore. But upon raising him and washing his wounds, he showed signs of life, though it seemed likely he would die.

To curtail a story which may seem an interpolation, after the most unremitting care and skilful attention of the best surgeons and physicians they could procure—and after the lapse of many weeks, during which time he was stretched on a sick bed, and racked by pains and fevers—after drinking to the dregs as severe a cup as ever touched a slaveholder's lips, he recovered.

In the meantime Cherry was shielded from harm, partly by the shame of her violator—partly by her masters' sense of justice—more because they had a beastly affection for her as a family chattel—more still because they prized her as property—but most of all because she was the admitted mistress of David Logue, the father of Jermain, then about six years of age.

He (Jermain) well remembers the case and the excitement produced by it in the family and neighborhood. His memory was refreshed with the rehearsal of it for years by the family and the negroes.

When Cherry arrived at about the age of twenty-eight, she was the mother of three children. To this period, she had never passed through the ceremonial sham of a negro marriage, but for years, as stated above, had been the admitted mistress of David Logue, the father of her children.

Here we may be permitted to record a fact well known at the south, and allowed by most white men, and by all slaves, to wit: that a young negress is often her master's mistress, until childbearing and years render it tasteful or convenient to sell the offspring from his sight, and exchange her for another victim. Such was the relation Cherry sustained to David Logue, and such too her fate.

At this point we drop the mother to consider briefly the character of the father.

It is rarely possible for a slave to identify his father with so much certainty as in this case. In a society where promiscuous intercourse is allowable, as at Manscoe's Creek, the chastity of white men of course does not transcend the chastity of black women; and the conspicuity of virtue, is apparent, only, in the fidelity of the slave girl to her condition of mistress. On this point the conduct of Cherry was a bright example and her fidelity to that relation was confessed and allowed, not by the parties only, but by the family and neighborhood.

Jarm, as Mr. Loguen was called when a slave, remembers when a very little child he was the pet of Dave, as his father was also nicknamed, that he slept in his bed sometimes, and was caressed by him—he also received from him many little favors and kindnesses which won his young heart. As his body and features grew to fixedness and maturity, all who knew them both, instantly recognized a personal, and even a spiritual resemblance.

On his recent visit to the fugitive slaves in Canada, Mr. Loguen met a fugitive from the neighborhood of his old master in Tennessee. She informed him that she was struck with his resemblance to his father—that his size and form—his walk and motions, every thing but his hair and complexion, was a striking expression of him—that from his walk, alone, she should take him for the same man at a distance, if his face was concealed.

Thus was Mr. Loguen taught by his mother, by the treatment of his infancy, by the admitted fact in the family and neighborhood, by family resemblance, not of person only, but as we shall see by the impulses of his spirit, that David Logue was his veritable father.

With his other brothers, David lived at the paternal mansion of their widowed mother, when Cherry came into their possession. They were all three, young men. David, the youngest, probably not over eighteen years of age. Jermain never saw or heard of a schoolhouse or school, or meeting house, at Manscoe's Creek, nor does he believe there were either. Many of the planters were ignorant of letters. Their Sundays were spent in sport and dissipation. Their agriculture resembled the Indian culture on the Onondaga Reservation in the State of New York. Mr. Loguen never passes through that Reservation in the Summer, without being sensibly reminded of the scenes of his childhood. The houses were all log houses, and the people even more destitute than the Indians of the means of intellectual, moral, and religious culture.

Nevertheless, the father of Mr. Loguen was not devoid of noble and generous impulses. He was full six feet high, sprightly in the use of abundant muscle; an impulsive, drinking, and chivalrous rowdy—unscrupulous in his pleasures—but ever ready to help a friend or smite a foe. Had he been cast amid the privileges of northern culture, instead of the creature of passion and indulgence that he was, his excellent physical and intellectual qualities might have blossomed into the highest use—the public might have honored him as a benefactor, and Jermain loved and revered him as a father. Even now, bowed down, as it is said he is, by poverty and dissipation, it would be a real pleasure to Mr. Loguen to contribute to his father's necessities—and help the infirmities of his sin smitten and rapidly declining age.

We need not dwell longer upon the father and mother of Mr. Loguen. We have given enough for the purposes of our story, and their character and condition, will, of course, be further illustrated by facts to appear in the history.

CHAPTER II

In the ordinary and acknowledged relations of life, the mere naked facts attending the infancy of any man or woman, are the farthest removed from romance or interest. They must be the result of an individual or social departure from the order of nature, to claim a slight attention. Nevertheless, we must devote a little, attention to the infancy of Loguen.

The fact that shocks us in the infancy of a southern slave, is, that its story cannot be told. No facilities are provided to mark its steps or preserve its memories. A slave baby is the offspring of brute passion and the subject of brute neglect and suffering. It claims no greater sympathy and care than any other animal of the sty or the field. The angels, who delight to touch the delicate fibres of the brain, and communicate the joys of heaven, and paint them on an infant's face, are driven away by oppression, that the most perfect medium of Gods converse and conjunction, with man may be tortured and distorted by devils. Black and damning will be the record of the crimes and cruelties by which thousands of these little innocents are let into heaven.

The above remarks are made, not because they apply to the infancy of Mr. Loguen, for they do not—but because they do apply, as a general truth, to the great body of children who are born as Mr. Loguen was. We should do injustice to history, did we present his infancy or childhood other than as an exception to the general rule. He has every reason to believe that his infancy was cared for by the strongest maternal affection consistent with his mother's servitude, guarded as he believes it was by the instincts of a lawless, but naturally susceptible father. Multitudes of kindnesses, partialities, and unquestionable loves, are indelibly written upon his memory, which he thinks contributed to the formation of his character. They are lessons which even now temper and molify his passions, as he sees them through the sorrows and trials and outrages and storms that are piled upon his pathway.

"Jump on my back, Jarm," half whispered Dave, as, rifle in hand, he stepped lightly down the bank of the creek where little Jarm was playing with the pebbles, suiting his bulky frame to the body of a child three or four years old.

Well did the child understand the accustomed ceremony, and he clasped his little arms upon his father's shoulders.

"Be still now—say not a word and you shall see me shoot a deer."

"Where is a deer?" said the child, while Dave neared a bunch of bushes, and pointed to an animal the former took for a pet calf which had grown up under his eye, and for which he cherished a child's regard.

"Don't say a word now—you will scare the deer away if you do," repeated Dave.

Jarm was obedient, while Dave with his load, which was scarce more than a fly on a giant's shoulder, crept slyly into the jungle, and crouching by a log, rested his rifle on it, and drove a bullet through the body of the beautiful animal. The deer with dying energy, leaped and poured his mortal bleat upon the air, then staggered and fell.

Poor little Jarm was in an exstacy of grief, and made the plantation echo with his screams, and brought the whole swarm of whites and blacks to his relief. His cry was "He has killed the calf," "he has killed the calf." Even old "Granny," as Jarm called the mother of the Logues, hearing the screams, came to see what mattered the little favorite chattel.

Ere they assembled, Dave had the game, bleeding from the deep gash his knife had made in the throat, at the feet of the child, and was soothing him with the tenderness of a father's love.

The boy soon saw his mistake, and was laughed and petted into a tremulous composure; but the shock of seeming cruelty made an indelible impression on his spirit and memory. To others, it was an amusing and vanishing incident—to Jarm, it was a lesson of life.

Life, truly and philosophically speaking, is the form and embodiment of thoughts and affections. In its uninterrupted current from the uncreated fountain, it creates and vivifies material receptacles in the form of angels, and also of all that is healthful, beautiful, lovely, innocent and correspondent of heaven, in animal and vegetable nature. But when that current is intercepted, and passes through the medium of infernal loves, it creates and vivifies other receptacles of monstrous forms. Hence all the noxious plants, and loathsome insects, and poisonous reptiles, and ferocious animals, and hateful men, correspondent, all, to the varied passions of Hell. Hence the slaveholder and the slave.

The life of little Jarm blossomed in the shape of an angel, but receptive of the disordered affections and monster passions around him. The problem must be solved, whether he should resist those surrounding affections and passions, and preserve his virgin life, or be deformed into a monster. The incident just related was the first shock upon his spirit which he remembers. It is introduced to show the condition of his childhood, but may be noted as the commencement of incidents which were to form his manhood. The forms of feeling and consequent combinations of thought, which are the life of a child, manufacture the spiritual cable which holds him amidst the storms and tempests of the world, or leaves him a wreck upon its waves. To change the figure, they are the causes which ultimate the hero, the despot and the slave.

The first ten years of Jarm's life was to him a period of much freedom. He was as well fed and housed as any other little savage. A single loose, coarse cotton garment covered his burly body, and he was left in summer to hunt mice and chipmunks, catch little fishes, or play with the ducks and geese in the creek, and tumble down and sleep in the sun or shade if he was weary; and in the winter, covered only by the same garment, to sit in the corner and parch corn, scatter it among the fowls and pigs, (his peers in the sphere of plantation rights) and occasionally ride on Dave's back or trot by his side, to the great house, (about the size of a moderate log cabin on the Onondaga Reserve) and have a frolic with him and "Granny," and perhaps stay over night.

It was the only schooling he ever enjoyed—for he was left to his own thoughts and invisible instructors. And though doubtless he came to as valuable intellectual results as any boy, it must be confessed the school was better adapted to physical than mental development. His tender muscles swelled and hardened with the severity of his voluntary exercise, and no boy on the plantation or in the neighborhood, black or white, could measure strength with him. Personally, he suffered no treatment from his masters which hinted to him that he was a slave.

But he was at school, and was not to eat and drink, and sleep and grow only—but to think also. The story of the deer was the first item in life's reality, gently pictured on the Canvas, which, ere long, was to be covered with black, ugly, and unendurable forms. As the days and months increased, the items multiplied. He saw little boys and girls brutally handled for deeds, and even no deeds, which he knew would not attract censure had he been the subject. In his day dreams, it puzzled him to know why he was secure and petted, while they were insecure and abused.

Forbearance and forgiveness, or any of the virtues of charity, find little root in the soil of slavery; but passion, revenge and violence come up as in a hot bed, and are familiar to every eye. The oft repeated sights, instead of darkening, sharpened the eye of Jarm, and stimulated his enquiry. They made him think the more. When, as near as he can guess, he arrived at the age of seven or eight years, loitering on the bank of the creek at the close of a summer's day, he saw his mother coming with unusual steps. It was obvious to Jarm that she was in distress, for her head, usually erect, was downcast, and her sighs and sobs were borne almost noiselessly on the light wind to the heart of her son.

"What is the matter?" with animated voice exclaimed Jarm.

The poor woman, absorbed by grief, had not noticed her darling; and was even thinking not to shock his young heart by appearing before him, until the depression which bent her down, and the crimson signals upon her person, had disappeared in the waters of Manscoe's Creek. The idea came too late. All trembling with indignant sorrow, surprise and love, at the sight of her boy, she rushed towards him, raised him from the ground, and pressing him to her bosom exclaimed in a voice of hysteric earnestness:

"Oh my poor boy, what will become of you?"

Jarm felt there was sadness and significance in her emphasis, altogether unusual, which, with the tremulous pressure of her embrace communicated a nervous sympathy to his heart, and was already changing his spirit by the influx of a new idea.

"What is the matter, mother, and what makes you bloody?" instantly asked the little boy.

"You will understand such things too soon. Don't ask me about it," replied the mother, as she sat him on his feet again, and let fall a drop of blood from her brow on the face of the child.

He wiped the stain away on his coarse shirt, and plied the enquiry with a concern which could not be resisted.

Fearing he would pursue the subject at the house, with the slaves, with Dave, and even with Carnes, and thereby involve himself and perhaps forfeit his future security by an alarming independence which was increasing with his years, and which was less likely to be indulged as her attractions and intimacy with Dave were failing, she determined to improve the occasion for his benefit. She trembled lest his unrestrained spirit should be an inconvenience to her oppressors, and that Dave would consent to the breaking it, by the same brutal treatment that other little colored children of the plantation suffered—or what was worse, that they would sell him at a distance to rid themselves of an annoyance—therefore she determined to satisfy his enquiries, and if possible, determine him to a prudent silence.

"Where is Jane?" a little girl two years younger than Jarm.

"I have just sent her to the house with the babe," replied Jarm—"but what is the matter, mother? do tell me."

"Well, I will tell you" said she, "and I tell you that you may not speak of it to anybody, and especially that you do not let Manasseth, Carnes, or even Dave, know that you know it. If you should speak to them about it, they will not treat you so well as they have done; and I fear they may whip you as they whip me; and what is very dreadful, I fear they will sell you to the slave drivers and I shall never see you again."

Cherry had not yet known the deep grief of parting with any of her children, and the fear of that heart-rending experience often tortured her spirit. She knew there was no dependence upon Manasseth and Carnes, and that her peril increased with the increasing dissipation and consequent embarrassment of all the white Logues.

Jarm had never seen his mother stricken, and his blood boiled when she gave the cause of her wounds and misery, and he asked fiercely "who whipped you?"

Cherry had effectually roused the indignation of her boy, and saw before her precisely the presence she feared he would one day exhibit to her masters, in view of the outrages inflicted on her or on himself. A change of relations which was being more apparent every day, made it not unlikely he would manifest the same spirit to them, and bring on himself one of those awful flagellations employed to crush the budding manhood of a slave. No premonition warns the undisciplined wretch of his fate. A display of just feeling and manly spirit, precisely what Cherry now saw in the swelling muscles of her son, was sufficient to subject him to cruel torture. To be a slave, he must cease to feel that he is a man.

The evidence of deep feeling which her words and appearance produced in the child, induced her to make him acquainted with his true condition, so far as he could comprehend it, and if possible set him on guard against invisible dangers.

In answer to his enquiry, "who whipped you?" she said Carnes struck her on the head, and made the wound from which the blood dropped. She said that Manasseth and Carnes often whipped her, and even Dave had lately treated her roughly. She explained to him, his and her helpless condition—how she was stolen when a little child like himself, and left with "Granny," and the white Logues—how she was cruelly whipped for innocently stating her case to excite their justice and pity—and again charged him, with great earnestness, not to let it be known at the house that she had told him this, or that he knew anything about it—assuring him, that if the white Logues knew she had told him these things, they would whip him also, and may be sell him to the slave drivers, as they did little "Charley and Fanny," a few weeks previous. She told him that though Dave and old Granny now loved him, they would certainly hate him, if he pestered them with complaints regarding her wrongs—and that his doing so would bring upon her greater wrongs, and in the end upon himself the most terrible chastisement, and perhaps they would sell him away from her forever.

Jarm was now fully possessed of one other shocking idea, which though it determined his prudence as it excited his pity and fear, did not repress the swelling and burning current in his veins, which swept before it every lamb-like feeling. The case of the deer, shocked his pity deeply, but did not forbid utterance—but now, at the sight of his mother brutally mutilated, suffering, and bleeding, he was taught to stifle his sympathies and passions, clamoring, swelling, and almost bursting his heart for utterance. The incident was burned into his memory by the fire it kindled, and the incident and the fire will remain there forever.

Cherry went with him to the creek and washed the stains away as well as she could, then assuming an erect and cheerful position as possible, took her course, towards the cabin, requesting him to wait a while, and then follow on. Her interview with Jarm was a relief to her sad heart—she partook of her coarse meal, hugged her babe to her breast, and then care-worn and weary, cast herself on her bed of straw, and lapsed into oblivious and healing sleep.

Not so Jarm. This second chapter in the slave's life, weighed upon his spirits and disturbed him. He was not old enough to comprehend its full import, but his understanding was sufficiently mature to receive and plant it deep in his memory, and shape his manners to its terrible demands. It had full possession of him, and it was sometime ere sleep closed his memory, and laid the surges of sorrow and anger that swelled within him.

The morning found Cherry composed, and Jarm too was soothed and refreshed by [un]disturbed slumber. She went to her usual labors in the field, and he, after a breakfast of corn bread and bacon, sauntered away alone, to reconsider the lesson which was taught him, and study its philosophy and bearings. His daydreams and buoyancy were laid aside, and that day was spent in studying the alarming reality which stared him in the face.

Thus early was he forced to revolve matters of grave importance. His treatment by the white Logues was most difficult to reconcile with the perils which his mother thought was present with him. To his inexperience, the enigma was inscrutable—but the conclusion was irresistible, that he and his mother were linked to a common destiny, and he felt his heart grappled to hers with a force greatly increased by sympathy for her sorrows, and a strong conviction of common dangers. The causes which attached him to her, weakened his attachment to her oppressors, which no evidence of kindness or affection on their part could prevent.

From this time forward, though left to dispose of his time and body as he willed, the clouds increased and thickened around him. Dave's favors and caresses were less frequent as the months and years came on, and in perfect recklessness of his presence, the most shocking and brutal outrages were inflicted on his mother. His masters were late at their carousals, and became more and more embruited as their affairs became embarrassed.

It was about this time that the family and neighborhood were agitated by Cherry's brave resistance and almost death of the licentious villain at the distillery, which were circumstantially related in the last chapter. This also served to confirm the story of his unhappy mother regarding the condition and danger of both, in the mind of her precocious and considerate child. The conversation among the slaves as well as among the whites, assured him, that not only his mother, but himself also, was at the mercy of every white man, and in case he or she resisted them, be their intents never so murderous, the whole power of Tennessee was pledged to their destruction. It was much talked of and well understood at Manscoe's Creek, that poor Cherry, had forfeited her life to the law, and that she held it at the mercy of the ignorant, and passionate, and unscrupulous people about her.

The distance between Jarm and Dave widened as the intimacy between Cherry and Dave ceased. He soon brought to his home a white woman, who resided with him as a wife or a mistress, and by whom he afterwards had children. Nor did Jarm regret the separation from his mother. The events of every day convinced him that their intimacy and connection was forced and unnatural. His boyhood was social and buoyant, but it revolted from family relations which seemed pregnant with evil, and obviously destitute of mutual trust, affection and support. The current of causes was forcing the affections of the mother and son to a common center, and fusing them into one. He felt that she and their little ones were all the world to him.

He sympathised deeply with those who were in like condition with himself, but to his mother, brother and sisters he was attached by ties which none can appreciate, but those, who, in like condition, have felt them.

The spiritual changes which were now gradually forming the great gulph between him and the white Logues, allowed him more leisure for thought and physical development. His time was nearly all his own; and with maturer judgment, and greater strength, he pursued his game on the land and in the water. The harmony of woods and fields, of birds and flowers and bounding animals, gave birth to ideas that chimed with the angelic counsels of his mother but which, in the family of his oppressors were never felt or imagined.

CHAPTER III

Marriage (or what is called marriage) between slaves, is sometimes accommodated to the affections of the parties—always to the interest of the slaveholder. As its end or intent is his interest, the feelings of the parties are indulged or compelled as the interest varies. Legally, and strictly, there is no such relation as husband and wife among slaves, because the law adjudges them to be things, and not men and women. They are chattels in law, and their sexual relations in contemplation of law are the same as any other animals. The whole affair is in the hand of the master as a means of the increase and improvement of stock. Other important motives sometimes blend with it and subject it to ulterior views. But the end or purpose is the same. The slave being "property to all intents," is subject, of course to the laws relating to "things," not to "persons."

The strongest affections grow up between male and female slaves, for they are men and women, the law to the contrary notwithstanding. Masters too become tenderly attached to their female chattels, and have children by them without once thinking they are guilty of the crime against nature. That they are not thus guilty follows from the fact, that nature acknowledges the connection and the offspring as her own, which she ever refuses to do when the parties are not adapted to the highest human uses.

Cherry was already the mother of three children by David Logue. They were eminently perfect in their physical proportions, a case quite in point, (if one is needed) to show the parties eminently human. Besides, Dave pledged a slaveholder's word to Cherry that Jarm should not be a slave, but that he should be set free. So "Granny," as Jarm always called the mother of the Logues, often told him he was not to be slave, like other colored children, but was to be free—thus showing that the Logues also considered that the law, not Dave and Cherry, was the criminal against nature.

Since Dave took to his home the white woman, his intercourse with Cherry ceased, while she was yet in the vigor of young womanhood. In respect to her profitableness as property therefore, as well as a protection against disturbing domestic influences, it was thought best she would have a man, who, in the eye of his white family, would represent a husband and father.

Where, among a large portion of any community, children are propagated as other animals, without the acknowledgment of marriage relations, or the care of law, it follows of course, that the moral feelings and prevailing habits of the law-makers are on a level with the indulgence which their laws and habits protect and sanction. And as the laws which sanction slavery are made by white men alone, it follows that the chastity of a majority of the slave legislators does not rise above the level of the chastity of black women, who they purposely expose to their polutions. Hence, the secrets which the former labor to keep from their wives and daughters, canker their morals in other respects, and are a ceaseless source of jealousy and discontent.

Dave had now successively purchased the interests of Manasseth and Carnes in the paternal estate, including the slaves, and became the sole owner thereof. Manasseth had moved to the southern part of the State, and Carnes had gone, it is not known where. Dave and his white family and mother occupied the paternal mansion alone, and the delicacy of his condition as father of the colored Logues forced on him an external regard to proprieties.

In the neighborhood of Dave's plantation lived a planter of unusually high character among colored people, and among all people, by the name of Barry. He was unusually humane and indulgent to his slaves, and they were strongly attached to him by reason of such indulgence. As a consequence, his slaves were more industrious, thriving and happy, and the plantation better improved and was more productive than any other in that region. The peace, industry, and thrift of this family were the subject of general remark among all classes of people.

This Barry owned a man by the name of Henry. He was a stout, well-built fellow, about thirty years of age, perfectly sound, having never experienced a day of sickness to his remembrance. Barry, of course, valued him highly as a most faithful servant and an honest man.

Henry was a kind, warm-hearted fellow, but he had seen such sights of misery in the disruption of families, the separating sometimes husbands from wives, and sometimes parents from children, that he had resolved never to expose himself to such misery, by becoming a husband or father. To be free of those endearing relations is the only freedom a male slave can enjoy. In his person, the apostle's rule is inverted, he had better not marry, and very many considerate ones so determine, and abide by the determination. Had Jermain W. Loguen remained a slave, he was sworn never to be a husband or a father. To a sensitive and reflecting spirit, the greatest curse of slavery is, that it is doubled, and more than doubled, with every domestic relation. Alone, the slave suffers personal wrongs only; but as a husband and father, his heart strings are exposed to, and his imagination tortured by suffering which can never be described.

But the laws of nature are not easily controled or evaded. Henry's coarse and untutored nature was pervaded by powerful susceptibilities, and ere he was aware of it, his spirit adhered to its conjugal counterpart in the spirit of Cherry. The spiritual relation was formed before Henry's prudence was sufficiently on guard to forbid the banns.

This attachment between Henry and Cherry so favored the purposes of Dave, that he approached Mr. Barry on the subject, and asked his consent that Henry and Cherry be acknowledged as man and wife. Mr. Barry consented to the proposal, on condition that Henry should be consulted and his wishes pursued.

Henry accordingly was sent for. When the subject was broached to him, as if awakened by an important crisis, his prudence was aroused. He confessed his willingness that Cherry should be his wife, only on condition that neither he or his wife, or any children they might have, should ever be separated by Dave or Barry at a distance of more than ten miles from each other.

Both Dave and Mr. Barry readily pledged themselves to the condition, and Cherry was sent for and presented to Henry, and he joyfully embraced her as his wife.

Mr. Barry was perfectly trustworthy as to his engagement, nor was Dave less so if he continued solvent, for he never intended to part with Cherry or her children. He was by nature and habit a kind and generous hearted man, and such was his relation to Cherry and the children, that he would not think of separating from them after he had provided against suspicions which disturbed his domestic peace.

This event was to Cherry like a morning sun after a dreary night. A genial atmosphere warmed and healed her bruised heart. It was the gentle breath of spring melting icy fetters to admit the influences of heaven upon her soul. Her daily labors, she was habited to as a portion of her life. She felt them not as a burden, now she enjoyed her hours of refreshment and repose with Henry. The attachment and joy were mutual, and for two happy years Cherry was scarce disturbed by one of those jars, which before, and often, left indelible marks upon her person. They lived in the aura of their own affections, without a single care beyond the faithful execution of their tasks, and inventions within their means for each others happiness.

At the end of the year their union was blessed with a darling boy. The rustic bosom of the innocent and noble natured Henry swelled with the heavenly influx of parental love. The very condition of slavery seemed to defend them against the invasion of every evil, and in an exstacy of delight they were prepared to adopt the delirious dream of the sailor boy—"O God, thou hast blest me. I ask for no more!"

Another year rolled away and left them in the same blessedness—another month and a startling light disturbed their dreams—another, and "the gay frost work of bliss" was gone forever.

CHAPTER IV

All unseen by Cherry and her little ones, affairs at Manscoe's Creek were now verging to a crisis. The most important and stirring events in a slave's life were pressing to the surface. For a long time there had been quiet at home and in the field. Jarm had digested the lessons which had been taught him, and the balsam of peace was healing the wounds upon his spirit. But could he have looked behind material to spiritual causes, he would have seen it was the quiet that preceded the storm—the repose that enveloped the lightning and the thunder, which were to break upon the heads of his oppressors, demolish the circle of his loves, and drift him to a distant part of Tennessee.

As a prelude to a disaster, the community on Manscoe's Creek was shaken by one of those astounding acts of barbarism which occurs in no country but where chattel slavery exists, and which is there only occasionally permitted to demonstrate the inherent atrocity of the slave system.

At a small distance from the Logues, on the opposite side of the Creek, lived a savage man by the name of Betts. He was the proprietor of a large plantation and a number of slaves. He was also an habitual drunkard, and proverbial for his passion and malice and cruelty; and for such excesses, was despised, even by the slaveholders of the neighborhood.

On a beautiful spring's morning, (and none more beautiful ever infolded the rays of divine goodness, than those which pour their blessings upon the monster growths of nature and man in the valley of Manscoe's Creek)—Jarm, having neared the age of ten years, was leisurely sauntering amid the green grass and blossoming fields, and regaling his senses with the music of birds and insects, and the outspreading beauties and harmonies of nature, which ever enter a receptive spirit, and with "a still small voice," announce the presence of an unseen God—then, when all was quiet within, and all beauty and bliss and harmony without, there arose from the opposite bank a howl of agony which thrilled his soul, and forced him, as it were, from heaven to earth again. Screeches, and screams, and cries for compassion, followed the sounds of the unfeeling instrument as it fell from the hand of the murderer Betts, upon his unhappy slave. The charms of nature in a moment vanished, and the voice of God was drowned by the cries of misery.

Jarm's compassionate soul comprehended the thing at once, and instead of fleeing with terror, as small boys of that age would, covered by the brush which formed a deep fringe on the bank of the Creek, he sped swift and noiselessly as possible, and sheltered by the outer verge of it, had a clear view of the infernal act on the opposite bank, which so rudely and suddenly changed a celestial picture into an image of hell.

Nothing could excuse the detail of a scene like this, which disgusts and crucifies good taste, and all refined and humane feeling, but the necessity of descending to the depths of this terrible system, to display its frequent and horrible monstrosities. It is to be borne in mind, that such scenes formed the life of Jarm in his boyhood, ere he was thrown into the crushing jaws of slavery.

The distance from bank to bank across the river at this place was about four rods. The sky was unusually clear, and Jarm had a distinct view of the whole transaction after he arrived. The sufferer was a young man about twenty years of age, by the name of "Sam"—a good-feeling, kind-hearted fellow, who Jarm well knew, and who, a few weeks before, saved him (Jarm) from drowning in the creek when it was swelled by the rain.

This poor fellow was stripped quite naked, hooped, and lashed by cords to a barrel on the steep bank of the stream. His head almost, if not quite, touched the ground on one side, and his feet on the other—the fleshy part of his body being exposed above, covered with gore, while the blood dropped upon the barrel or ran down his back and legs to the ground.

Whether the barrel was filled in whole or in part with liquor, Jarm of course could not know. The flesh of the poor wretch was quivering in the sun, and painting its pure rays red, while Sam was moaning and pleading for pity with a depth of feeling which would move any heart.

Beside the barrel stood a man without a heart—a stout, square-built, burly, bushy-headed fellow, of about forty years of age, whose face resembled an intoxicated fury. He had on neither hat, coat, or vest, and his shirt, open at the collar, fallen loosely away, showed a broad, sun and whiskey-burnt chest, which seemed a fortress of strength. His sleeves were rolled up like a butcher, and his right hand clenched an instrument of torture, known nowhere under the sun but in the slave States, called a *paddle*, which he fiercely flourished over the heads and faces of some half dozen negroes who stood trembling by.

Such is a poor description of the murderer Betts, and the wretched objects around him, when Jarm took his position in the bushes. The villain, as he brandished the bloody paddle, filled the air with his curses, and threatened the slaves with the same and even a worse vengeance than he was inflicting on the fainting Sam.

The instrument called "a paddle," was the only article of southern manufacture that Jarm knew of—and its existence might have remained a secret to the rest of the world, had not he, and others like him, escaped to declare and describe it. It is a firm board, shaped like a huge Yankee pudding stick filled with small auger holes, and of a heft to do the most execution upon the flesh it bruises. It is the most savage and bloodletting instrument employed to torture the slave. Every blow, the sharp wood on the circumference of the holes cuts into the flesh, and the pain and the blood follow, in proportion to the number of such holes and the force of the blows.

The monster having finished his speech to the negroes, turned to glut his vengeance on poor Sam, with a rage and energy that seemed provoked by his cries, and the sight of his own barbarity. As he grasped the paddle and swung it from his shoulder to increase the force of his blow, Sam begged with all the strength of nature. The slaves turned their faces to the ground or covered them with their hands—and Betts, with an oath, brought the weapon down with his might—blow after blow followed, and screams, and howls of agony, and cries for mercy, followed with them.

Jarm, overcome with the misery of his friend and the cruelty of his tormentor, hid his face on the ground and covered it with his hands, and refused to look upon the scene.

Betts continued the blows until he was weary, and then ceased them to repeat his threats and curses to the negroes.

Thus he alternated his violence upon the one, and threats and curses upon the other, until the voice of Sam growing hollow and faint, convinced the listener that nature was failing. The last sentence which he articulated was, "O Lord! O Lord!" and he continued to utter it until utterance failed, and no noise broke the stillness around but the sound of the infernal weapon upon the insentient and motionless body. When the monster saw Sam ceased to speak or move, he also ceased his blows.

At this time, when all was silent, Jarm raised his head from the ground and saw Betts place his foot against the bleeding body, and with a savage curse and malignant force, set the barrel and body rolling together down the steep bank into the river. As they reached the water, he (Betts) turned to the negroes and said, fiercely:

"There, you d—d dogs, go and bring him back again, and unbind him and let him go."

Quick as lightning the compassionate fellows sprang to the water, unbound him, and laid him on the bank—but it was too late. Life ceased to animate the poor man—his soul was set free, and his mutilated body, already wrapped in its bloody shroud, was prepared for its funeral.

The poor fellows looked meaningly at the brute Betts as he stood at the Creek washing the sweat from his brow and arms, and then, with sad countenances stood motionless around the corpse.

"What are you doing there, you d—d villains," said Betts.

"Sam be dead, massa," said one of the circle.

"I'll bring him to life," said Betts, and coming rapidly up the bank, gave him a brutal kick upon his ribs. Not a muscle stirred—sensation was gone forever—his last breath was spent with his last prayer, and the life and the prayer together were already infolded in the infinite heart, to which, in the last extremity, the wronged and outraged never plead for protection and repose in vain.

"Take the d—d dog and bury him," were the last words that Betts muttered, as he turned and walked heavily away.

Thus closed the last scene of the tragedy, and Jarm, faint with contending emotions, bent his way homewards. Any more teachings on the subject of the slave's helplessness, and hard fate, were now superfluous. Boy as he was, he comprehended all from Alpha to Omega. Any other lessons, he saw could only vary the manifestations of the diabolical principle, which nulified every right, and exposed the slave to every outrage. His first lesson was the dying deer—the last, the dying slave. He shuddered to think that by a change of masters he might be murdered as Sam was. His heart was tortured with the intensest hatred of slavery, and concern for himself, mother, brother and sisters.

Now, for the first time, he revolved the possibility of escape, and if an opportunity occurred, determined to improve it at any hazard.

On his return, his soul was locked up to its own perceptions. He saw only the world within him and had no eyes or ears for the world without. The flowers flung their fragrances on the breeze as before—the birds sung as sweet—all nature was redolent with divine goodness when he returned, as when he went out; but he heeded them not. This scene, connected with corresponding reminiscences, filled him with new and harrowing thoughts and passions, which were regenerating him. Young as he was, it needed but that to stir a new life in him. From that moment he felt a flame enkindled which made him a new creature—a flame which all the demon fires of slavery could not countervail—a flame which, at the expiration of another ten years, forced him from his mother and kindred, bravely, to stand at the mouth of the infernal crater and throw his shackles in it.

Of course, Jarm's verdict in the premises was qualified by what should be the conduct of white men in the case. He knew the Logue family well enough to know that they would revolt at this deed of nameless and murderous atrocity. He thought all white men must feel as he did, and it remained to know that they would act also as he would act in the case.

Jarm instantly informed Cherry of what he saw. Smitten with terror by the story, and by the danger to which she feared he would be exposed if he breathed it aloud, she hushed him to a whisper. She assured him the deed would be known through Bett's slaves, and charged him to say nothing about it lest he be involved as a spy. She said the absence of Sam in the neighborhood and on the plantation would confirm the report, and there would be abundant opportunity to know the effect of the murder upon the white people. In thus charging him, she was prompted more by an over anxiety for the safety of her boy, than by any real danger which she saw could result from his making the story public.

This tremulous caution, which was so common on her part, had a nervous effect upon Jarm. While it determined him to secrecy, it increased his sense of insecurity, and deepned his hatred of the web in which he felt himself involved. Cherry, however, informed him he might set his mind at rest at once as to the effect of the disclosure. It would create a tempest of passion soon to pass away, and the slaves would remain unprotected and Sam unavenged.

As foretold by Cherry, so it came to pass. Before the sun went down of the same day, the murder and all its particulars were known to every slave and every white person on the plantation.

The secret was first communicated by one of Bett's men, to a slave girl belonging to the Logues, who was much attached to Sam, and who expected to be his wife. She declared it aloud, and sobbed in all the demonstration of grief.

The family of Logues were stirred to madness by the hellish deed, and swore Betts should be lynched and driven from the neighborhood. They communicated the facts to the white people about, and a flame blazed forth which threatened for a time to wipe the murderer from the earth. They did not expect, nor did they wish, the judicial tribunals to furnish a precident of punishment for the murder of a slave, which was impossible (by the express terms of the law,) if the murder occurred "by moderate chastisement"—nor could it be proved by colored witnesses. They preferred rather that he should be a victim to the lawless vengeance which their chivalric notions allowed to trample on the laws of the land.

As Cherry predicted, the tempest of passion perished in its own effervescence, and in a little period Betts was as safe, and the negroes as unsafe, as ever.

CHAPTER V

The appearance of Dave since his connection with the white woman and purchase of the paternal estate, was a great improvement upon his previous life. He was a drinker, to be sure, but more regular in his hours—more sober in his demeanor—more attentive to business than before.

To the poor slave who is blind to everything not on the surface of affairs, the inference was quite natural that he was growing in the right direction. He had carried on the estate some three or four years, alone, with an attention to its interests which showed his mind active above the level of his past life. The labors of the plantation were conducted with more order, peace, and profit. The Logues always denounced the economy of pinching the stomachs of the laborers, and sufficiently provided them with coarse food and clothing. In fact, the slave began to value his breath—the only property he could enjoy—more than he had done.

Strangers, too, some of them evidently of the better class, began to call on him, sometimes to leave papers, sometimes to chat on politics and business, and taste his hospitality; while Jarm, then in his eleventh year, tended their horses with grass and grain.

As these calls increased, Jarm thought he perceived they were not always agreeable to his master. He wore a frown sometimes when he saw them coming, and there was an evident dash of servility in his face and manners after they arrived. His demeanor seemed sometimes strained and unnatural in their presence.

On one occasion he was closeted a long time with one of these gentlemen, who, though a stranger to Jarm, seemed to be an acquaintance of Dave's. When their interview was concluded, they approached Jarm in company as he was holding the horse. The faces of both wore a jocular expression, which seemed to indicate anything but ill-will. But Jarm was somewhat expert at reading countenances. Face expressions were the only letters he had ever set to learn. He was quite sure their careless pleasantry was a cover to other and graver feelings.

"This fellow will answer—I guess, I will take him," said the man, as he came up to Jarm and put his hand on his head.

The joke did not drive the smile from Dave's face, but it changed the color of it, and he quickly replied:

"This is a bad business, anyhow, Joseph. I trust you will consult my convenience. It will be an extreme case that separates me and that fellow."

The Sheriff—for such was Joseph—raising a searching eye from Jarm to Dave, broke into a laugh, and said:

"A dash of the Logues—don't deny it, now. Ah, you have been a sad boy, Dave!"

Dave was in no condition to relish a joke in that direction—his voice and expression sank together, and adroitly as possible he changed the subject.

There are no such highways in that neighborhood as are used in the north. The path through the plantation was mainly used by travellers on horseback, and occasionally an ox cart picked its way along. Dave and his friend walked on foot, conversing as they went along—while Jarm led the horse a few paces behind them.

"I tell you what, Joseph, I don't know but I made a blunder when I bought this property; we were reckless boys, and I don't know but I was most reckless of the three; we suffered the estate to be embarrassed. I have a strong veneration for it—in it are the bones of my father—my old mother has lived on it from the day she married him—all the negroes were derived from him, except the mother of the boy behind us and her children. I bought it in to save it, and I mean to save it. I have been very attentive to business for some time—the plantation has never yielded half so much as it does now, nor looked as well. I have given up every luxury except an occasional glass with a friend—by heaven I won't give up that. I have done well for the last three years—the negroes have done well—their hearts are grown to the soil and to each other—we are a happy family without these accursed debts, which are killing me. If my creditors will indulge me another crop, I can twist out of this infernal case. It will be mighty hard for me to give up any of these boys—it will break their hearts, I know, and will almost break mine—but some of them must go. Humanity to the rest demands it—'the greatest good to the greatest number,' you know, is our democratic doctrine."

"If it was expedient that one man should die to save a nation, I suppose you think it is expedient that some of your slaves be sold to save the rest—that is your argument, is it not?"

"Exactly."

"All fudge!"

"No fudge about it. How am I to get along if I don't part with some of my slaves?"

"And if you could get along by doing so, it does not follow it would be right. Nor does it follow if you sell some of them that you will thereby save the rest—or that you or they will be the better off. That was the argument of Caiphas, a Jewish old fogy and incorrigible hypocrite. The Jews adopted his counsel and killed Jesus in obedience to your infernal doctrine, 'the greatest good to the greatest number.' But did they thereby secure good in his sense of the words? No. I tell you good can only come from doing good—and we can never receive good unless we do right. Come, I am going to preach. No good can come from wrong. Good to one is good to all—and evil to one is evil to all. Caiphas lied when he said that. He was blind to everything but—self. He gave up his church and country to be murdered when he gave up Jesus to be murdered. It needed just that to seal their doom. Jerusalem, which symbolizes the Church—and the Temple, which symbolizes the Lord himself, fell by that sin from among them. The foundations of the former were plowed up, and not one stone, that is, not one truth, remained upon another, after they had crucified Jesus. Falsehood was ultimated and triumphed in the decapitation of the Lord of the Church."

"Always a preaching—but how do you make out that the Jewish Church fell with the Jewish State? There is scarce a large city in the world without one or more synagogues in it—you are out there."

"No church can survive its Lord—its form may remain, as the Christian church does now, like the broken shell when the chick has flown. When it excommunicated the Lord, its life went with him, of course. The old church committed suicide to let in a new one. Fi! Dave—don't believe these preaching, praying, and chanting assembles in synagogues and meeting houses, are, of course, genuine churches. They may be forms without life—mere husks and shells—mere human organizations, made by men for men—not by God for God. There is but one church and that is 'the Lamb's wife'—in other words, the Lord's wife—the Lord has not got two wives. He maintains no Harem. He acknowledges no Presbyterian wife, nor Methodist wife, nor Baptist wife, nor the thousand and one things that claim him as husband. They who live to do good to others, be they Christian or heathen, 'lean on his bosom' and are his wife, and 'he is their Lord.'"

"Do you mean to say that the Church instituted by the Lord Jesus Christ can lose its life, and be as a husk or shell, as the Jewish Church is?"

"Indeed I do. When it becomes as the Jewish Church was, its fate must be the same, by the laws of order. The Apostolic Church was no more the

Lord's Church, than was the Adamic, Noatic, and Israelitish churches, before them—and they successively performed their uses and perished. When a church ceases to honor its Lord by a life devoted to his uses—when it is a covering for selfish and worldly aims, it has like the Jewish Church excommunicated its Lord—it has conspired with Judas and sold him—it has, in other words, lost its life. It may preserve truths—but they will be without good—they will be truths in petrified forms after life is gone—their light will be the light of winter shimmering in the face of death. Of what use is light without heat—truth without good—or what is the same Faith without Charity?"

"Now, Joseph; I am no Christian, and know little of Divinity—but you surprise me—do you mean to say that Christianity is a failure, and that the Lord has no Church in the world?"

"No, no. No church ever was a failure. All were adapted to the age they were instituted. They performed their uses and perished—they are the ages or dispensations that have come and gone."

"I am not satisfied—I want one reason why I am to believe that the first Christian Church, as you call it, has perished?"

"Well—I will try to give one. Christ founded his Church on Peter, on a Rock, on Truth—in other words, on Faith. After Christ arose from the grave, he had a talk with Peter—the Rock, the Truth—Faith—for in the language of the ancients the former words mean Faith. In that talk he described the doom of his Church in the following striking prophesy: 'When thou wast young thou girdest thyself and walkest whither thou wouldst—but when thou shalt be old, thou shalt stretch forth thy hands and another shall gird thee and carry thee whither thou wouldst not—'"

"But that was said to and of Peter."

"Don't interrupt me—have I not just said, that in the correspondential language of our Lord, *Peter* means *Faith*? It's literal, is *Rock* or *Stone*, and in such language, they both mean *Truth* or *Faith*. Christ did not establish his Church on Peter as a man. He was a very unreliable man. In ancient times things had their names from their qualities—Rocks and Stones represented Truths—and Peter is another name for Rock or Stone, the Divine meaning of which is Truth or Faith—and the Bible is to be read in its Divine or spiritual meaning. The things of nature represent God's thoughts, and were clearly seen and read by unfallen men. And because Peter or Stone is a Divine representation of Truth or Faith, therefore it is said to be the head of the corner. Christ used the word in the Divine sense, as it was used before letters were made."

"When he spoke of Peter then, he spoke of a New Church he come to establish—was that it?"

"Yes. It was a prophecy. 'When thou wast young,' means when the church is young—'thou girdest thyself,' means, it thought for itself or had a mind of its own—'walking whither thou wouldst,' means that such church was free to obey God according to its own mind and will—'when thou shalt be old,' means when the church is decaying—'thou shalt stretch forth thy hands and another shall gird thee,' means that in its decline it will give its power and honor to another (for hands mean power)—to the Pope, to the Bishop, the Presbyter, the Council, the Synod, &c.—that these shall dictate its doctrines and creeds—'lead thee whither thou wouldst not,' means that the Church will become a servile, fashionable thing, without understanding or will of its own. Now, when Peter, or Truth, or Faith, has given its understanding and will to another—don't you see it can't obey the command 'follow thou me'—that faith is gone, and the church is defunct, when it follows another?"

"But Christ said that to signify what death Peter should die."

"So he did. But natural death is spoken of only because it corresponds to spiritual death, just as stones correspond to truth. The former is the external and natural, the other the internal and Divine sense."

"Is that the way you read the Bible? I have always understood the Bible as it reads, and have never read it much. Then you will have it, God did not mean that Adam should die on the day he eat the apple?"

"No—indeed,—he did eat the forbidden fruit, but did he die a natural death on the day he eat it? Not he. God set him to tilling the ground,—sufficient evidence *that*, to satisfy everybody that God intended a different sort of death. He lost the Divine life and image—that was death enough. Natural death is purely normal; our natural bodies are no part of us. The spiritual body is the man, and it takes on this body of flesh, and puts it off like a worn-out garment—and then lives on, and on, on forever in a higher sphere of existence. To suppose that God declared that Adam should die a natural death on the day he ate the fruit, is to suppose, not that the serpent or devil, but that God was the liar. Not so. God was true. Adam lived naturally, but not spiritually."

"Do you suppose mother Eve was seduced by a serpent?"

"There it is again. If we take the natural sense of the letter to be the Divine meaning, our God will be little better than the gods of the heathen. Adam and Eve, the man and the woman, represent the bride and the bridegroom, the lamb and the lamb's wife—the church, in the Divine sense. The serpent is a hieroglyph, representing the sensual principle in man ruling his affections—as woman does the Church itself under the dominion of the higher principles of his nature. So the serpent was understood by the ancients, and so figured on the pyramids and rocks, the books of the ancients. The serpent crawls upon his belly, and cannot raise its head to see or assail the higher principles of man's nature. It aims only at the heel, the lowest natural principle—it can't reach higher. But, be it remembered, the sensual principle is a Divine element in God's nature as well as in man's, for man is an image of God—and being so, it is an essential element in man. In its place, under the dominion of the understanding and will, the higher principles of the human soul, it is absolutely necessary for human uses. Separate from those principles, it becomes an enemy, a serpent. It is beautifully represented by the rod of Moses. In its proper place, in his hands and power, it is a staff to help him in the Divine walk or life—but released from his control, it is a snake, whose bite is death, and that is what it means. The Woman, that is the men and women of the church called Adam, gave themselves to the dominion of the sensual principle, and of course separated from higher and Divine principles, and sought light and wisdom through the senses. They threw the rod of God upon the ground, and of course came under the dominion of the serpent or sensual principle, and perished."

"But how will this carry out? If Peter's name had such significance, what is the meaning of JOHN? His name, too, is used in this connection. Has that an internal meaning, too?"

"O yes—John, as represented by the ancients, means 'the Life of Charity,' or love true to its impulses, and never swerving from its duties. John never forsook the Lord of the Church, though Peter, and all the Apostles, who represent all the other qualities of the Lord and of the Church, forsook him. Charity is ever faithful, leaning on the Lord's breast. What a beautiful emblem of Charity that! John, or Love, followed the Lord into the High Priest's Palace, when every other disciple fled, and Peter, or Faith, stood at the door *without* and denied the Lord three times. John stood at the Cross and saw his Lord die, and received his last words, 'Woman, (or church) behold thy son'—then to John (or charity) he said, 'Son, behold thy mother.' Charity is born of the Church (or heaven) as its mother—and now mark 'from that hour that disciple (Charity) took her (the Church) to his own bosom and preserved her,' to use the Lord's expression, 'until I come,' that is until he came in the spirit to form a New Church. Christ came only to form a new church. If you want to find the church, look for John, not Peter."

"Well, you may be right in all this business, Joseph—but what do you mean by it? Do you mean I am not to sell some of these slaves to save me from bankruptcy?"

"I am not your judge, Dave. You will judge your own case, as I shall mine. That is the order of Heaven. But mind you, 'with what judgment ye judge, ye shall be judged.' If you seek the good of others, then ye will have good for the deed—but if ye seek your own good, disregarding the good of others, then will ye have evil. I shall take your receipt for this slave, but I will never sell him. I am sick of my office and shall resign it. I don't like it, any way. What I cannot do for myself, I will not do for the state."

They had now come in sight of the slaves at their work. Joseph endorsed one of them on his execution against Dave and took his receipt for his delivery at a future day, and they separated. The slaves were as ignorant of it, as if they had been hogs or horses.

CHAPTER VI

The course of events soon satisfied David Logue that he could not relieve his estate from the pressure of the claims upon it. His creditors had the fullest confidence in his industry, honor and intents, and would gladly indulge him a reasonable length, but some of them feared that others would press their claims for the sake of precedence. They could not trust each other. Suits were, therefore, commenced to obtain a priority of lien, and thereby all his creditors were about to be let upon him. He was likely to be ground to powder by the merciless principle that the law favors the vigilant and not the slothful creditor. His real estate was considerably encumbered, and such was the pressure of his creditors that he foresaw he must sell his slaves, as well as his plantation, to escape hopeless bankruptcy. He had intended to keep the mother of Jermain and her children, but now, he saw he could not. He had promised Cherry and Jarm that he would give Jarm his freedom—nor could he do this and be solvent.

It became now inconvenient to redeem his promises, and they were of no avail opposed to his convenience. Being chattels, Henry and Cherry and Jarm could not be parties to contracts. A deed of freedom supposes all the rights of the slave vested in the master, and he gives those rights as by a new creation.

When Dave saw the storm gathering, and clothing the thunderbolt over the heads of his slaves in its black folds, he was deeply grieved; but not so much grieved that he was willing to adopt the only expedient that would avert it. His interest overbalanced his sympathies and good intents. He dreaded hopeless bankruptcy more than that thunderbolt and the unutterable woes its fall would produce. It would be unjust to say his feelings were not pained by a struggle between pride and poverty. They were deeply pained; but such was the force of pride and perversity of education, that they overcame his justice and instincts, and compelled a determination to convert his slaves, and even his own flesh and blood, into money to pay his debts.

All his plans and purposes and promises of good to Jarm and his deeply-wronged mother, were nullified by the selfishness that nourished his chivalry.

He might have taken them out of this dark land into a free State and given them freedom—or have put all his slaves in charge of the British King in Canada, and plead the claims of justice and humanity against his creditors in justification of the act; but in such case he would also be obliged to take up his abode at the north, as he supposed, in naked poverty.

In such circumstances, Dave determined to sell all his slaves the first opportunity, and to the best advantage.

In the meantime, the poor negroes were cheerful at their labors, not dreaming of an event that was soon to separate them forever, and scatter them through the southern country. The terrible secret was carefully kept in the bosom of their master. He was cautious that not even a suspicion of their fate should be awakened until he had sold them, and they were fairly in the power of their purchasers.

But, notwithstanding this determination, he mediated the possibility of so providing for Cherry and her children, that their fate should be as endurable as possible and never relinquished the hope, that, by some means, at some time, he could secure the freedom of Jarm. He had already accepted a proposition for the sale of his plantation, on condition he did not refuse it in a limited time, which refusal depended upon his disposal of his slaves to his liking in that time. Slave traders often drove through his plantation, but it required time to find a purchaser for so large a stock.

It was in the fall months, after the crops were harvested, and the slaves were looking forward to the leisure and pleasure of the holidays, and a comparatively easy winter life, that such an opportunity occurred.

Quite late in the season, his affairs called him to Nashville, where he found a trader willing to return and spend a day with him on the plantation, and make him an offer for all his slaves. He was to be at Dave's in the character of a visitor and acquaintance, and inform himself of the quality of the chattels without creating a suspicion of his intent.

On the evening of the same day, Dave and his visitor concluded their contract for the sale of the entire stock of slaves, not excepting Jarm. He learned that the purchaser, on his way to Alabama, would pass the residence of Manasseth Logue, in the southern portion of Tennessee; and it was a condition of the bargain that he should sell the Logue family to Manasseth, in case he, Manasseth, would pay the sum at which they were valued in the Bill of Sale.

At the time the contract was closed, Henry had just arrived, as usual, to indulge a few moments of comfort with Cherry and her boy, and the whole circle of slaves were seated around their cabins, in the same social and happy contentment they enjoyed since Dave was the separate owner of the estate;

little suspecting this was the last time they would be thus assembled, and that the shades of the evening were shutting from their eyes the scene of their comforts and labors forever. To them, a slave trader was an object of supreme dread; and the caravans of misery which such traders drove by their poor homes, were the most shocking of all scenes. Their course was always towards the deadly sugar and cotton fields. The sad and moaning coffles stirred the depths of their souls and discovered the last soundings of human misery. With the planters interest as well as sympathy usually combined to keep families together; but the poor negroes knew, as well as others, that these trading vagabonds were ruled by interest only; and that they separated families with as little feeling as professional cattle traders separate other animals. By a sale to these soulless men, they knew they were literally thrown into the jaws of avarice.

In the dead of night, when they were locked in sleep, the negro quarters were surrounded by stout men, armed with revolvers and shackles. The strongest and bravest of the negroes were manacled in their slumbers—and because of the prospect of frantic agony, and desperate bravery, and strength of Cherry, they put the irons on her also, as the best means of managing her. The other women and children were easily secured.

The victims, taken unawares, were in the power of their captors. Cherry waked from her slumbers, her infant sleeping at her side. Her imprisoned limbs revealed her helplessness, and a consciousness of the cause sent a chilling horror through every avenue of feeling. Her first utterance was a shriek, responsive of the deep agony of her soul. For a moment, her spirit was swathed with black despair, and then she raved with the fury of an imprisoned tigress. She called for *Dave* and she called for *Henry*, and no voice responded to her call but the voices of savage wretches who stood over her and the rest, armed with whips and pistols.

She was told that Dave had, that night, started on a journey—that she no longer belonged to him—that she was the property of the ferocious-looking man who stood in the centre of this group of sorrow, clenching a whip in one hand and a pistol in the other—that Henry would meet her on the road—that she must "shut up at once, and take her babe and come along"—that she would meet Dave at Manasseth Logue's, in southern Tennessee, where he resided. The speaker said Manasseth would take her and the children off their hands.

This was quite possible, for he (Dave) had already started on his journey to see Manasseth, to prepare him to redeem this wretched family, who were mostly his own flesh and blood, in pursuance of the arrangement with the purchaser. The fact, like the lie in regard to Henry, was repeated to the miserable woman only to pacify her. The cowskin had failed to answer the purpose. Her body, insensible to assaults, was already seamed with bloody stripes, and the lie and the truth, so far as there was truth, was adopted in lieu of the lash for the sake of convenience, not compassion.

It is left to the imagination of the reader to finish this night scene, and fill up the picture of horrors which drew their dense folds, blacker than the night, about the minds of these miserable chattels. They were about twelve in number; and suffice it to say, that ere the signs of morning light appeared, the coffle, consisting of the men and women who it was thought best to secure, with the exception of Cherry, were chained together and to the wagon, as usual in such cases, and ready to start on their dreary journey. Cherry was fettered with irons which were fastened with a lock, and placed, with the children, in a covered wagon, which occupied the van of the procession.

About the time the sun began to change the color of the eastern horizon, the procession started. The purchaser and his adjutants, having refreshed with bacon and whiskey, and distributed coarse eatables to the captives, armed with whips and pistols, mounted, one of them the wagon which was drawn by four horses, and the others, each a horse, in front and flank and rear of the prisoners, and started on. The crack of the driver's whip over the backs of the horses gave the first notice, and a like crack over the heads of the slaves, gave an irregular start to the dark and wretched coffle in the rear.

It seemed as if some of them were fainting with sorrow, and scarce able to march in order. But the noise of the terrible lash awakened their activities, and brought them into an even step with the dragoons by their side. The thought that they were leaving the spot, which, in spite of its sorrows and trials, was dear to them, without being able to see it—and that they were parting forever from acquaintances and relations in the neighborhood, under circumstances the most awful to their conceptions—for a country and condition which they knew not of, and to be scattered they knew not where, among cruel strangers who had even less sympathy for the slave than the man who sold them, threw them into paroxysms of grief. Many of them mourned aloud, and their sighs and sobs, mingling with infant's screams, the crack of whips, and the curses of the drivers, made as discordant and infernal sounds as ever shocked the ear of night.

The sky just began to grow gray when the procession started. The wagon was closely covered with canvas, which shut out every appearance of light, and the blackness within was made more gloomy and sad by the scraping and rustling of the brush against the sides of the wagon, as it picked its way along the narrow path in the forest. Every spot was familiar to Cherry for miles around, and these sounds of familiar and stationary objects in contact with her rolling prison, seemed like the voices of the spirits of Manscoe's Creek speaking an everlasting *farewell.* The bottom of the wagon was covered with clean straw, just harvested and threshed by the hands of the prisoners, and she could have been comfortable, if it was possible for her body to rest when the miseries of hell were let loose upon her soul. She knew these slave dealers were the most truthless men, and placed no confidence in them. She never expected to see Henry or Dave again in the world. All thought was drowned in a phrenzy of despair. Agony had taken full possession of her spirit, and she groaned aloud. On the very brink of sanity she was startled by a gentle whisper in her ear, which, as by enchantment, laid the surges of her soul.

"Where is Ohio, mother?"

Jarm, not comprehending the circumstances of his condition as did Cherry, but yet sufficiently comprehending it to know it was insufferably bad, felt most keenly her sorrows—he had quieted the babe to sleep in his arms, and laid it with the other children who were asleep by his side. Thus relieved of his charge, and full of a sense of his incomprehensible dangers, he revolved the possibility of escape from them. He called to mind the fact, often told him by his mother, that, when a little child, younger than himself, she was taken by force from a free land called Ohio, and left in slavery with the white Logues. Intensely moved by her present sufferings, he impulsively breathed in her ear the above startling question. The flood immediately passed off from her spirit and she was herself again. She paused a breath or two and asked—

"Is it you, Jarm?"

"Yes, mother."

"Did you ask mc where is Ohio?"

"You told me you were free in Ohio, and that you were stolen from there when a little girl and made a slave. I want to know where Ohio is."

"Why do you want to know where Ohio is?"

"Because, I hoped we were moving that way—and may be we can get away from these wicked people and go to Ohio and be free."

"Hush!" said Cherry, "we can never get away from these people. Besides, I don't know which is the way to Ohio. I am very sure we are not going that way. The slave traders always drive their coffles toward the land of slaves, never to the land of freemen. These bad men intend to sell us at the far south, and I fear they will sell you from me. They will sell us all apart, so that we shall never see each other again, if they can make more money by our separation."

The conversation continued for some time in this manner, Jarm suggesting the possibility of escape, and his mother resisting it, until sleep overcame the boy and laid him beside the little ones, and Cherry was left to her chains and reflections.

When Jarm awoke, the golden light of an autumn sun poured through the mouth and crevices of his prison, and showed him a scene that moved him to tears. His mother, in her fetters, was feeding his little half brother, the son of Henry, from her bosom, and the other women and children were either crying or deeply sad; but his mother, the saddest of them all, resembled the image of disappointment and misery. At such a sight, Jarm could not resist the sympathy which burst the fountain within him, and vented itself in sobs and tears. It was broad day, and the sound of merry voices in the streets, and of birds in the trees, speaking the mercy and goodness of God to all outside the hell in which he was caged, communicated to his inmost soul the certainty that Nature, and the God of Nature, were outraged in the persons of the prisoners.

It was now the turn of the mother to comfort her son, and pacify her little ones. The sweet office of affection relieved her own suffering spirit. Jarm's fountain of tears was soon closed, and he and his mother lapsed into a state of rational sadness, which seemed to say, "We will make the best of it."

The captain of this band of robbers took his coffle to a sort of slave pen or tavern, near Nashville, where he refreshed his company and fed his victims; and thence made his way again over the wretched roads and through the uncultivated scenery, which is the everlasting inheritance of the land of slaves. Days and nights the caravan pursued its monotonous course until it reached the borders of Alabama. It would be useless to detail the incidents of the road, nothing having occurred to vary the usual character of the journey. The older slaves were habituated to their imprisonment and severe exercise under the lash of the driver, and had looked their wrongs and prospects so long in the face, that they were drilled into a state of sad contentment; whilst the younger ones, let loose to play among the beasts which held their fathers and their mothers, ignorant of their doom, were pleased with the journey.

Jarm, now grown to a stout boy, was the pet of savage men; and, though he never forgot his wrongs, he put on a cheerful face, and was rewarded by favors and privileges beyond his companions. He had just begun to learn to ride and manage a horse, and was clothed only with a single coarse shirt. To relieve and please him, they occasionally put him astride the leader, where, whip in hand, his bushy head exposed to the sun, and his fat legs and unshod feet clinging to the horse's ribs, he whistled his time away. Sometimes, to give him company and contentment, and to gratify Cherry, they placed behind him his brother, a chubby little fellow, who kept his place only by clasping his tender arms as firmly as he could to Jarm's back.

These human cattle drivers, as well as other cattle drivers, understand full well that it is better to amuse and coax and flatter their chattels, than cross their tempers and passions by unnecessary violence. Thus it is, that what seem to their victims as favors, are often means of economy and expedition, rather than a manifestation of humane feeling.

It should not be inferred, though, that mild expedients are the only ones adopted to hasten along these poor people. The driver's whip, followed by the groans of the sufferer, occasionally started the rabbit and the partridge from the brambles, and announced to the weary ones, that, whatever the inconvenience, their steps must respond to the will of their drivers. Expedients, which we need not name, were adopted to strengthen and cheer their languid spirits, in aid of their bodies. But now and then, one, less able or fortunate than the rest, from foot-soreness or weakness, sank beyond the power of the lash, and was taken into the wagon as the only means of getting him or her along.

It need not be stated that such a condition as this slave coffle, which has its likeness in all the roads of the south, dispenses, by necessity, with all the decencies and moralities which men and women, even in a state of savage freedom, instinctively preserve. The imagination, for decency's sake, must fill up the pitcher, if the true idea of the horrible exhibition is obtained. Suffice it to say, that in this way, this wretched coffle dragged its length along, until it arrived at the Little Tombigbee, on the northern borders of Alabama.

The slaves were encouraged to more than usual speed during the day on which they arrived at this place, for the reason, that they had been promised a respite of rest and refreshment at this spot. Cherry had been particularly told that there she would be met by her old master and her husband, and that she and all her children would be left with them. As we before said, her experience taught her that a negro trader's word, and more especially a negro trader's word to a slave, under the circumstances she and her children were placed, was worth nothing; nevertheless, she knew their pretence was possible, and the hope that it might be true, was some relief to her tortured spirit.

It was about an hour before sunset that the coffle arrived at the Little Tombigbee, and stretched its length under the shade upon its banks. The owner, some time before the arrival, had parted from it, and hurried his horse toward three log buildings, which nestled like Indian wigwams in a half cultivated forest, half a mile distant from the company. Cherry seated herself on the banks of the stream, with Henry's babe in her arms, her children by her side, and waited with keen anxiety the fulfillment of the promise the robbers so often made her, that she would there meet Henry and Dave, and that she and her children and Henry were to remain there together.

It was not long before she saw three men, in the direction of the three log houses, approaching on horseback, and behind them, a wagon, with two horses, driven by a colored man. The two former she recognized as the Captain of the band and Manasseth Logue. This was the first actual evidence that the affirmations of the barbarian might be true. She hugged her babe to her bosom with convulsive transport, thinking that, though Dave was not along, Henry was actually approaching with the wagon to take her and her children to their quarters. How sad was her disappointment, as the wagon neared her, to see that it was another man, and not Henry, that was driving the horses. Still she hoped. Manasseth and the captain rode near where Cherry sat with the children, and the latter, pointing to the dark circle, said, "There they are; Cherry, Jarm, and the others described in the Bill of Sale."

Cherry, slave fashion, dared not raise her head, but sat looking humbly, sadly, but hopefully, at her image in the water, and seeing only Henry in it, but had not courage to ask the question, the answer to which would relieve her aching heart, to wit, as to the whereabouts of her husband. This, she concluded, would be too great presumption, and might lead to bad results. She, therefore, said nothing, but hoped on.

"Why, how these children have grown," said Manasseth. "This boy," said he, pointing to Jarm, "will make a profitable servant, if he is not spoiled. Come, Cherry, get up into the wagon with the children, and Jack will show you to the quarters."

When the wagon had gone out of the hearing of the white men, she enquired of Jack for David Logue and Henry, explaining to him that the former was her old master, and that the latter was her husband.

Jack told her that David Logue had, that morning, started on his return journey to Manscoe's Creek, and that no such man as Henry was now, or ever was, on the estate to his knowledge.

It was now clear to Cherry, that that portion of the promise regarding Henry was made for the occasion; and she vented her disappointment in loud expressions of grief and indignation. Now she felt that the separation between Henry and her and their child was eternal—the last hope vanished, and she settled down in sullen despair.

Cherry and the little ones were soon deposited at the negro house, which was one of the three buildings spoken of. A few rods from it, in different directions, was a small smutty distillery, and the family mansion of her new master—all which, as has been said before, were log houses, and the only buildings in sight.

It was now dark, and Cherry, weary with grief, labor and disappointment, cast herself and babe on her bed of straw, and, notwithstanding the shock she received the evening previous, for the first time for many days had a night of repose. The healing angels closed her senses in absolute oblivion—"raised from her brain the rooted sorrow, and cleansed her bosom of the perilous stuff that weighs upon the heart." The history of her relations to Manscoe's Creek was all told, and she was now to enter upon a new chapter of life.

When she awoke in the morning, it was with a new spirit—bent, but not broken. The instructions and endurances of the past, strengthened and tempered it to meet the conflicts before her with greater skill, prudence and courage.

CHAPTER VII

It was said at the conclusion of the last chapter, that the sale and abandonment of the colored Logues by David Logue concluded an important epoch in their lives. The two families parted to encounter temptations and conflicts in different directions. But the temptations and conflicts of the colored Logues were an accumulation of wrongs, which did not break them down, but instructed and strengthened them rather, for others to come. Not so with poor Dave. He had unwittingly cast away the only anchor which, hitherto, kept his barque right side up amid life's waves. Had he not yielded his natural kindness of heart to false pride, and a perverted public opinion, instead of the victim of poverty and low indulgence which he afterwards became, he might have risen as his son J. W. Loguen rose, a conqueror on the waves of life, and defied its storms. The anxiety to save his slaves, especially Cherry and her children, had, for years, held him, in a measure, obedient to the duties of life. In separating from them, he cut with his own hand, the cable that preserved him, and without an anchor was driven by the winds, and shortly sank into the gulph he labored to avoid—and there remains, without the hope, and probably without the wish to escape.

The fate of this generous, chivalric, and noble natured man, the only saving clause in the history of the white Logues, has a counterpart in thousands who die to all good, like the mercies of heaven in the soil blighted with the crimes and cruelties of slavery.

Poor Dave had not willingly parted with Cherry and her children, and therefore the memory of the act remained to dog his footsteps, and torture his brain like "a rooted sorrow." Though he partnered with his brothers Carnes and Manasseth in the crime that kidnapped her when a little child, he remembered with keen remorse, that, with one exception, he was the father of the hale and lovely children by her side, and that he was in fact responsible for the wrongs and miseries each and all of them had suffered hitherto, as well as those they might thereafter suffer. The excepted link in this circle of wronged ones was the child of Henry. His memory, too, which would awaken delight in an angel, had clinging to it a barbed curse. The cherub face and innocent smiles of the boy, often crept into David's mind's eye in connection with the compact he made with Henry at his nuptials, as if they were the living seal of his perjury and dishonor.

As before said, after his bargain for the sale of his slaves was perfected, David left Manscoe's Creek for Southern Tennessee. He started in haste, and in the night, that his eyes might not witness the misery he had produced, and hastened to Manasseth to arrange with him a plan for the redemption of Cherry and her children. Manasseth and his wife had become brutes, and like other brutes, their minds and hearts were unadapted to the mercies and business of life. David Logue knew full well that, without the aid of his genius and industry, his kind intents to prevent Cherry and her children being driven to Alabama, could not be executed. And not until the morning of their arrival at the Tombigbee had the plan been completed. To avoid again the sight of Cherry, Jarm, and the rest, on their arrival, and to hasten to the relief of his affairs at home, which actually and strongly demanded his instant attention, he started without delay to Manscoe's Creek.

He started on horse back of course, the only mode of travelling in those days. Except in the immediate neighborhood of Columbia and Nashville, his journey was through a new country, and such a thing as a pleasure carriage or wagon had never been seen there. His way, mainly, was through gigantic forests—occasionally broken by fields of girdled trees, and sometimes by lots partially cleared of large timber, where the sparse settlers, with their negroes, had begun to grow corn and tobacco.

Like the early settlers of N. York and Ohio, the early settlers of Tennessee did not, as a general thing, clear off the heavy timber and fence their lots before they commenced cropping. More like the aborigines, the negroes girdled the large trees, and cleared off the underbrush, leaving the large trees to die, and then planted their seed. The trees thus girdled were left to rot in their natural position, until blown down by the winds, and then they were not cut by the axe, but burned into sections convenient for logging, and consumed.[1] If the wind was high, the negroes were careful of falling trees and limbs, which occasionally prostrated the corn or other crops. It was a rare

1. [Loguen's note:] The first settlers of Western New York had a similar practice. After falling the large trees of hard wood, they not unfrequently chopped a place in their trunks and made a fire there, on the top of which they placed another hard stick called a "nigger," which they occasionally stirred to increase ignition—and in that manner they made the fire work for them, and burnt the trees in pieces, while they used their axes on other trees.

thing that those southern pioneers attempted the labor of clearing the fields entirely, as is customary with the pioneers of the north. In the neighborhood of such fields might be seen two or three log cabins, which served for the dwelling of the whites and blacks, and shelter for horses and cattle.

It may be safely conceived that Tennesseean agriculture made a haggard aspect on the face of noble nature. The people were mostly emigrants from Virginia and North Carolina, and had none of the habits of industry, which at the North harden and embolden the farmer, whilst they perfect his skill to change the forests into pleasant fields and cheerful residences, for the use and comfort of men.

It was a chilly morning when Dave sallied out on his homeward journey. The tops of the large trees were already shorn of their leafy honors, and numerous squirrels sported on their branches and trunks near the cornfields, and served for a time to divert him. The external pressure which for years held his mind and body in painful durance, was broken by the denouement of this last enterprise, and left him to his contemplations. The event which he most dreaded, and which he in vain supposed "was done, when it was done," to wit, the deliverance from his slaves, and their value deposited at Nashville, was accomplished—and he rode into the forest thinking he was alone with nature.

The traveller in Tennessee at that day, and particularly at that season of the year, was rarely disturbed by other travellers. He jogged on his way with all the expedition consistent with the ability of his horse—but not alone did he travel. Always moved by external and sensuous things, he had never looked into himself, or dreamed that his mind was an interior world, peopled with angels and devils from whom he derived every thought and desire, and that the mutable things of the outer world were but the incrustation of the substantial and indestructible things within it. He did not dream that "the kingdom of God was (really) within him," and that that kingdom was a heaven or a hell in proportion as his affections were like or unlike the angels who love or hate him. He never dreamed that every struggle of temptation, every sensation of conscience, was the touch of the Almighty's finger from God's throne within him, indicating every tendency of a departure from the law and order of that kingdom. He supposed he would be alone in those wild woods and unfrequented paths—that his mind and body, relieved of care and labor, would be refreshed by the pure air of the mountains and vales through which his journey lay. His philosophy never taught him that the solitude of nature was the aura of the spiritual world, in which good angels from within talk with bad men without, and mirror before them their crimes and deeds until prevailing goodness wins them to repentance, or prevailing evils harden their consciences to the touch of infinite mercy. He little thought he should meet Cherry and her babes in the wilderness, pointing to their wrongs and sorrows, from the day she was kidnapped, and pleading for his justice and mercy, and compelling him to a decision which would save or damn his soul. He did not know that the throne of eternal judgment was within him—and that, under God, he was to pass upon his own bad deeds the sentence which would consign him to the infernal fires which engendered them—or that other sentence which would change those fires into a love which was life eternal.

But so it was. The change of scenery diverted him until the novelty ceased, and his mind was wrapped in the inspiration of the wilderness. A feeling altogether new came over him. He seemed in the vestibule of another world, and in the midst of those with whom his life had been connected. He was let into himself, to see his own spirit daguerreotyped in his life. His slaves were impersonated in their wrongs, and for miles and hours, he was tortured with the ghosts of memory. The evils which were past, plead for rescue from evils to come. Most clearly of all, did Cherry and her babes rise before him and appeal to his charities. It was in vain he attempted to avoid them. Like the ghost of Banquo, they would not down at his bidding. The various ways in which he could save them from coming calamities were opened to his consciousness. He might declare their freedom, for she was really free, and the condition of the children followed her condition by pro-slavery law—he might return her to her friends in Ohio—he might flee with her and hers to Canada on the north, or to the Mexican settlements on the south—he might concoct a plan with Manasseth for their deliverance, which would avoid the claims of his creditors. Every consideration of mercy and justice and compassion, was pressed upon him, until the light which presented them was gradually intercepted by the veil of selfhood, and they disappeared like dissolving views, and the things of sense and nature reappeared, and he was back to the outward world, whose deepning shadows covered the light within, and he was spiritually blind—externally all was light and beautiful—internally, all was night. It was a fatal triumph. Overcome by pride, sensuality and ambition, he turned his back again upon the immutable truths which would certainly save him, be the peril ever so great, and embraced the mutable things of sense and nature, which would certainly sink him, against any amount of human foresight.

As he approached Nashville, the country was more cultivated, and travellers more frequent. He was in the full enjoyment of fancied freedom. He felt relieved of a double bondage—the claims of his creditors upon his property, and the claims of his slaves upon his humanity. He fancied he saw the end of all his embarrassments, and his light spirit was busy building castles in the air.

The Genii which released him from spiritual visions, surrounded him with other "pictures which fancy touched bright." Spellbound in delicious dreams of the future, he was suddenly startled by a voice behind him—

"Well, Dave, I have found you at last."

"Good!" said Dave. "You, Joseph, are the man I wanted to see. I am prepared for you. The money is in the hands of my banker, at Nashville, for the payment of those infernal executions, and I am anxious to cancel them and have them off my mind."

"All right. But you look better—more cheerful than you have done. What turn of fortune, pray, has wrought the improvement on your spirit?"

"Why, sir, I have been horribly under the load. To be burdened with debts and pursued by creditors as I have been, is, enough to make any man solemn; and the way and only way I had to discharge them, was calculated to intensify that solemnity to torturing and unbearable pain. Thank God it is all over now. I have sold my slaves, and they are out of my sight and out of my heart. The burden is all gone, and I can pay my debts, and have a balance to begin anew, I hope. I am in a new world, Joseph. The Lord is on my side, I believe. The sun, and the world it encompasses and vivifies, are as bright to my eyes as to yours, now. Thank God I shall be free."

"Of course the Lord is on your side; but are you on his side?—that is the point."

"Why, that is what I mean."

"You are happy?"

"Yes."

"May you not learn that your happiness is a delusion."

"How can it be a delusion? I feel it—I know it,—there can be no mistake."

"Well, I want you to be happy. I want to be happy myself, and see others happy—but allow me to say to you, that the buoyancy that comes of relief from debt may be a wretched counterfeit, after all. I hope, sincerely, that your experience may not teach you that yours is spurious."

"This is a matter in which I, alone, am the witness, and can, of course, alone decide—and I will prove my happiness to you over the best bottle of wine in Nashville, after those executions are discharged."

"Ah! my dear fellow, I appreciate your generosity—but I fear you do not appreciate your own state."

"How is that?"

"You have forgotten what I told you when last we met. There are two kinds of happiness—the one comes of the love of self, and the other of the love of the neighbor. Both are real, but not genuine. There is a broad difference between them. One, in fact, is infernal—the other celestial. The source of your joy, and the assertion of yours, that *you* are the *only* witness in the premises, leads me to fear the quality of your delight."

"There you are—preaching again—but I love to hear you preach. You talk philosophy and good sense. I wish our clergy would preach as you do—go on—I want to hear you. And first of all, tell me what difference it makes, whether my happiness is my own only—the pleasure that comes from the love of self, or the love of others. If I am happy, I am happy—come the gratification whence it may. It belongs to me alone, not to another—it is in me and not in another, and another cannot speak of it, of course."

"Difference! It is the difference between Heaven and Hell! In one case you delight in the happiness of others, and are in Heaven—in the other, you delight in sensual and worldly things, for the sake of self, and are in Hell."

"Go on—do you propose to make out I am in Hell?"

"I don't propose anything about it. I was but contrasting my notions of happiness with yours. I spoke of Heaven and Hell incidentally. They are states in a man, not places *outside* of him. He, who, forgetting self, delights in good done to others, and lives in the happiness of his neighbors—who feels their happiness within him, not thinking of his own—whose joys are their joys, that man is in Heaven. Place him in any natural condition you will, and all the devils and flames of Hell cannot hurt him. On the other hand, he who seeks his own happiness, in himself, and for himself, forgetful of his neighbors, of necessity, hates all who conflict with himself—and though he may have moments of delirious delight, he is, in fact, in Hell—and cannot fail to come into conflict with others—and in the end, sink into the flames of his own passions and lusts."

"Joseph, you are a better philosopher than Divine. 'Charity begins at home,' is a truism as old as mankind. The charge of the apostle is founded on it—'if any provide not for his own, especially for his own house, he has denied the faith, and is worse than an infidel.'"

"There are those who are indeed worse than infidels—worse, because wilfully blind to truth. They are those who falsify the Word for the indulgence of self love—who provide 'for the flesh to fulfil the lusts thereof.' 'Provisions,' in the sense of the Scriptures, are *truths* and *goods*—the *treasures* of the mind, which is the *house*, the *Heaven*, the *home of God.* The children of such house, are the products of such truths, goods, and treasures, begot by use. 'Provisions,' in the sense of your interpretation, are *falses* and *evils* and their offspring, tenants of that *house* when self love has changed it into a Hell. Christ begins by driving those evil and false things out of his home, and fitting it for Heaven's uses.

You libel charity which 'seeketh not its own,' but begins in use to others, and ends in joys which result from such use. Those only who do good to others are man-like, Christ-like, God-like. The Lord never taught a doctrine at war with his own likeness."

"Go on—may be you will make me a convert. What sect do you belong to? I should like to know."

"I don't belong to any sect; my religious platform, which is 'charity,' can have no foundation in sect, and no abode but in 'truth.' Charity disarms sects, and merges them in a common brotherhood. Would to God you were converted to my opinions, and lived their, not my life—theory is one thing, and practice quite another thing—'life is everything.'"

"You are a singular man—you don't talk religion like other folks. What is religion?"

"Religion is Love to the neighbor manifested in the Life."

"If that is religion, there are a blessed few religious men and women in the world—you may bet your life of that."

"And for that very reason it is necessary to build a new ark, or new church, and gather into it, again, the beasts and birds and living things, representatives of affections, which have been seduced away. The old church has died out, and the Lord comes in the new, just as fast as he disappears in the old—just as fast as the world is willing to receive him. There is just as much religion in the world now, as there is love to the neighbor, and no more. Religion is Life—it is love to others, in action, for their good. The Lord never left his church—he never left anybody. It is they who leave him. The story of his ascension and return in the clouds, is symbolic and prophetic language. It asserts apparent, not real truth, just as when it is said 'God is angry.' The Lord, of course, can never leave men, or be angry with them. Men leave him, though, and change his light into dark clouds, and his pure love into infernal hate. They make their own lives—and the clouds in which the Lord appears and disappears, are in the mental, not the material world."

"What do you mean by men making their own lives?"

"A man's life is his ruling love—it is himself. In general terms, life is love. What we love, we do. Take from you your love, and you cannot speak or think, or act—you are annihilated—your love is your life. If your ruling love leads you to mercy, justice and goodness, you are spiritually alive, and are in the way to regeneration and Heaven. On the contrary if your ruling love overrides your inclination to mercy, justice and goodness, you are spiritually dead, or dying, and on your way to Hell. That is to say—in each case you will be giving to your affection a state, or form, which will determine the character of your acts and desires, forever. Our love remains with us after death, and rules us forever. Heaven and Hell are states of the soul."

"Your divinity always captivates me, Joseph, but it thwarts my purposes and feelings cruelly. Nevertheless, I always feel in a good atmosphere in your company. Your philosophy is beautiful, but it begets a painful conflict within me, between duties and inclinations. When I leave you, I have no peace until I forget it all in my affairs."

"For God's sake, don't let that conflict cease, until your inclinations side with your duties. It is the process of regeneration. It is the spirit with you in the wilderness, as it was with Christ. He was a man, and his victory over his lusts which hungered for indulgence, made his humanity divine. Such a victory would make you an angel of Heaven—defeat, will sink you into a devil."

"Almost thou persuadest me to be a Christian. What if I was one?"

"If you be a Christian, it will be your joy that you are useful to others—your joy will be *in* the use. And again, mark me—whether you will or no, infinite wisdom will make you tributary to merciful ends. Uses on the earth, are the same as uses in the Heavens, to wit, doing good to others. The joys of Heaven and the joys of earth, are not in the states of the soul merely, but in the actual uses which the soul performs—it is the *use*, the happiness of others, which makes heavenly joy."

They had now arrived at Nashville, and the colloquy ended. The last remark of Dave was—

"How I regret that this conversation must end here. May we have another opportunity to continue it to the end of the chapter. There are various topics I want your advice upon, and I shall delight in an opportunity for that advice."

"I shall always be happy to talk with you; but if I have given any light to your mind, set it down to the Lord himself—it is his light, not mine. It is now twelve o'clock—meet me at my office at half-past two."

"Dine with me, Joseph."

"I can dine nowhere—I have 'uses' to perform, which I must attend to. Remember—just half-past two."

Joseph emphasized his declaration of 'uses' with a smile, indicating both playfulness and sincerity, and waving his hand, departed.

Dave had his heart full and running over. Whether intended to that end or not, the words of his friend fell like fire upon his conscience. He felt them to be true, and because they were true, they lay where they fell, and burned like hot iron. But he passed into a cold atmosphere. That fire soon ceased to burn—and another fire, congenial to his interior state, healed the wound it made. Though naturally impressible to the kindest sentiments, his life had been a succession of self gratifications, and whatever might have been his misgivings during the talk with Joseph, they soon vanished in the storm of passions which clamored for indulgence.

CHAPTER VIII

Jarm now felt, for the first time, what it was to be a slave. He was turned into the fields with the other hands, without experience, to do his part, according to his years. Unfortunately, his personal appearance and strength were beyond his years, and led his overseer to expect more of him than is usually exacted from boys of his age. By the instruction and assistance of Cherry, he was soon able to accomplish all that was required of him, and more, had there been motive to prompt him to do more.

Manasseth Logue purchased a plantation on the Tombigbee, where he lived after he sold out to his brother David, as stated in the previous chapters. Beside his plantation employments, he kept at his old trade of manufacturing whiskey. Had he been a manufacturer and vender only, it had been better for his character, habits, property and family. But unhappily, he and his wife were large consumers also, and sank together into intemperance. Their original virtues, if they had any, were lost, and they were very drunken, passionate, brutal and cruel. As a consequence, their habitation, and the habitations of their slaves, were neglected, filthy and uncomfortable. They had several sons and daughters, most of them older than Jarm—all idle, ignorant, unlettered, and gross in their manners and habits, following fast in the steps of their miserable parents. Those parents belonged to that unfortunate class of drunkards, whom liquor makes mad—and when in it, as a general thing, fight each other, abuse their slaves, and every body else who come in their way. Jarm has frequently seen them fly at each other with great fury,—chase each other with stones, clubs, tongs, or whatever other thing was handy—and rave, and curse, and threaten, like mad ones.

When such scenes occurred—and, alas! they were too frequent—the slaves were particularly careful to be out of sight—or if in sight, so to demean themselves as not to attract the attention of the furies. If, by any unlucky act or word, in such cases, the wrath of their master or mistress was attracted to the slaves, it was as steel attracts lightning, and the innocent victims were beaten, without sense, reason, or limits. Thus they were often maimed and bruised shockingly, and sometimes left almost dead. The poor negroes never knew when they were safe in the presence of Manasseth and his wife, when they were in such condition. And they never were safe, except at those rare times when their tormentors were not in liquor. And when their master and mistress were without liquor, their minds and bodies were so shattered by the frequent and severe tests to which they had been subjected, that they were nervous, irritable, and easily excited to deeds of excessive violence.

About the second spring after Jarm was consigned to these barbarians, an event occurred illustrative of his condition, and of the safety of all the human chattels in their possession. He was at work in the cornfield with other hands, Cherry not being among them. Manasseth was present, and in a condition to terrify them all.

The article used as a hoe by a Tennesseean planter could hardly be acknowledged as a hoe by a northern farmer. It was a thick, heavy, pyramidal piece of flatted iron, with a large eye on the top for a clumsey handle.

All were excited to the utmost carefulness, not to attract the attention of this terrible man, and very attentive at their work to avoid him.

Unluckily for Jarm, as he raised it to strike, his hoe handle became loose, and the hoe fell to the ground. This was enough to stir the devil in this wicked man; he raised a stone and hurled it at the head of the boy, charging him with culpable negligence in his tools, in terms too vulgar to repeat. Jarm dodged the missile, and crazy with excitement, raised the hoe and put the handle in it. His master ordered him to go into the yard, near by, and wedge the handle on, and at the risk of his life, never to expose his carelessness in that way again.

Already had Jarm partaken largely of the alarm which made all around him tremble with fear. He obeyed the command promptly and returned to his work. He spared little time for the purpose, well knowing if he did not return quick, the tiger would be after him. In his haste and fright, he thought to fasten the handle sufficiently for the time his master was by, and to finish it when he had gone. The wedge he drove into the handle stuck out of the end of it an inch or two, and he went to work with his hoe in that shape.

The instrument answered the purpose for a short time, when, most unluckily, he struck the wedge against something, and knocked it out, and off went the hoe again. Alas! poor Jarm!

The last unlucky event threw the intoxicated beast into a phrenzy of passion. Blazing with alcohol and Hell within, he picked up the long wedge, and swore the boy should swallow it. As if to compel him to do so, he ordered Jarm to open his mouth. Jarm instinctively demurred to the absurd proposition, but Manasseth was inflexible. So soon as Jarm hesitated, his enemy struck him a blow on the side of the head, with his fist, which brought him to the ground.

The brute, with increased passion, leaped on him, and held him down—and in that condition charged the boy to open his mouth, on peril of his life—at the same time pressing the wood against his lips and teeth. Jarm, fearing he would break in all his teeth, opened his jaws, and the wretch immediately crowded the wedge in until it reached the roof of his mouth, before he could stop it with his teeth. He began to pound it in with his heavy fist. Not withstanding Jarm held on with his teeth, the wedge driven into the roof of his mouth, and mangled it frightfully. The blood flowed down his throat, and profusely from his mouth.

So soon as Jarm found his teeth were likely all to be broken, and that there was no hope of sympathy from the intoxicated wretch, he obeyed the instincts of nature, and by a sudden and powerful effort, he seized the wedge and the hand that held it, and turning his head at the same time, delivered his mouth from the instrument, and turned it towards the ground—resolved, if he was to be murdered, he not be murdered in that way. The heartless man then commenced punching the boy with the sharp end of the wedge, on his head and mouth, making bloody gashes—Jarm dodging, as well as be could, to avoid the blows.

This cruel transaction, from the time of the first attack to the close, lasted some minutes—when, tired with the effort, Manasseth rose from the body of the boy, and ordered him to get up and learn how to wedge a hoe.

Jarm was weak and bruised, and his lips and mouth shockingly mangled and covered with gore. With some difficulty he rose to his feet, wiped the sweat and blood from his face and lips, spit the blood from his mouth, and returned to the yard, to fasten the handle to his hoe again. At the same time, his master, with dreadful oaths and curses, muttered against his hands, and Jarm in particular, turned his face to the distillery, and soon disappeared—to the great relief and joy of Jarm and all the other hands present.

This experience was valuable to Jarm, for it revealed to him his positions and relations to slavery, which he ever afterwards remembered with perfect distinctness. He was now about fourteen years of age, of excellent strength and health, and saw there was no other way for him, but to bear his trials with all possible discretion—and if an opportunity occurred to escape, to embrace it at whatever peril—but if doomed to remain a slave, to die struggling with his tyrant, when driven to the last extremity. To this resolution he was always obedient—ever mindful of the occasion that induced him to make it.

For many days it was with difficulty that Jarm swallowed his food or performed his tasks. Without the sympathy and assistance of his mother, and the hands, with whom he was a favorite, he would probably have failed in his labors. With their assistance, he was restored to ability and soundness, and had full opportunity to digest the terrible instruction this transaction furnished.

Cherry, fortunately, was absent when this outrage was committed. The slaves who were present, would have interfered to prevent the cruelty, had they not supposed their interference would expose themselves to greater evils than might be inflicted on Jarm, without the hope of lessening his wrongs. But, had Cherry been there, nothing would have restrained her uncalculating and indomitable courage from pitching into the fight. Jarm esteemed it fortunate that his mother was absent.

Such was the state of things in this unhappy family for a year after the above outrage, when they were awakened, at dead of night, by a glaring light which filled every cabin, and made their dark rooms brighter than day. They all sprang in terror from their miserable beds, and saw the old distillery buried under a pyramid of fire, which spread a sheet of light in every direction over the country around. The first moment of alarm having passed, they saw the flames had progressed to a complete victory over the establishment. The negroes were delighted, first at the beauty and sublimity of the scene, but more from the hope, that, as the cause of their daily peril, terror and suffering came from that distillery, its destruction would be to them the beginning of better times.

Nor were they mistaken. Manasseth, and his wife and children, walked around this blazing hell, and witnessed with horror the bursting barrels spurting their burning contents, which flowed in flaming rivulets around the base of the pyramid. To them, it was a shocking sight. At first, they could not look upon the ruin of so much of the "dear creature" without sympathy for their aching apetites and failing revenues. With all their sottishness and negligence, they never lost sight of their property—and though they did not, and with their habits could not, accumulate property, they did not sink their avarice in a thirst for liquor. They "held their own" in that respect, while they were fast giving their souls and bodies to the evil one. Having surveyed the sad spectacle for some time, the following colloquy ensued:—

"All gone to the devil!" said Manasseth.

"Good riddance!" said the old woman.

"A thousand dollars in a single night," he replied.

"Good riddance, I say," responded the old she bloat, as the pale light of the fire reflected from her blood-swollen cheeks.

"What do you mean by that?"

"I mean we are better without than with the infernal thing. It has made brutes of you and me, and has been fast making brutes of our children. I am heartily glad to see this fire."

"But I tell you here is a great loss of property."

"The loss is gain, I tell you. Had it been burned as soon as built, and remained burned, we should be better off as to property this moment, besides being decent and respectable people. We should not then be the miserable creatures we now are. I am glad to see it burn."

"Why, do you mean that you will live without whiskey?"

"I shall try it—you may bet your life of that. I had rather die for the want of it, than be burned up by the accursed stuff soul and body together. I rejoice that there is no other place where it can be had for many miles around."

"But the property—were it not for the value of the property, I could rejoice with you—for I allow it has been a curse to us almost as great as absolute poverty."

"Infinitely greater, Manasseth. How much happier would we be in absolute poverty, with sound minds and bodies, and peaceful affections, than in the Hell where we have been burning for years—and dragging our children there, too. Like the Rich Man, I have been in agony for a drop of water to cool my tongue for years, and now feel it drop upon my soul from the light of this fire. We have property enough left—let us employ the brains we have left, to turn it to better uses, for our own good and the good of our children."

"It is the first sensible proposal you have made in eight years. And now, how do you suppose the distillery took fire?"

"Can you doubt about it? Of course those spoiled boys yonder did it. They won't tell us—but the truth is, they were late here last night, and no doubt they left fire so carelessly that it fired the building. We are ruining our children, Manasseth, and the Lord has burned the building to wake you and me to business of saving them—which can only be done by leaving this hateful thing in its ashes, and living like sober people. I am glad it is burned, I say, and I pray Heaven it may stay burned."

"Then you have sworn, in earnest, to have nothing more to do with liquor?"

"I have so sworn."

"D—n the stuff—I'll join you," said he.

"Boys, give three cheers for the old distillery!"

This took the negroes by surprise; but they joined the white Logues, and sent up a 'Hurrah' which filled the country around with a jubilant demonstration. This was the first time for years, that the presence of their master and mistress was tolerable to the slaves—but now their presence was not tolerable only, but joyous. They joined in the loud *hurrah* with eminent gusto, for it honored a compact, which, fulfilled, would deliver them from the greatest terror of their lives.

It was the whiskey from that distillery that made beasts of their master and mistress. Left to their own natures, which were not lovely, they were endurable—because the slaves knew how to find them, and could act intelligibly. Subject as they had been to fits of intoxication, which occurred almost, if not quite every day—sometimes one drunk, and then the other; and sometimes, and often, both drunk together, and always under the influence of liquor, the negroes never knew when they were safe—and they never were safe in the presence of their master and mistress—and often suffered the most terrible injustice and cruelty. The slave must fit himself to the will of his master. This he can never do if his master is a drunkard—and if he is an ugly drunkard, as were both of these, then is the poor slave literally delivered over to be tormented by devils.

This chapter might be lengthened to any extent, with details of cruelties and outrages inflicted by Manasseth and his wife during their intoxication. But they are too atrocious and disgusting to be recorded. The above outrage on Jarm must suffice as a specimen—but by no means the worst specimen of their numerous and shocking barbarities.

The reader may easily infer that the slaves were happy to witness this compact of their tormentors, and will not wonder that *their* voices, louder than the rest, rolled upon the clouds, and reverberated from the hills and woods.

Thus, this event, which the slaves supposed would drive their master and mistress to madness, to be vented, as usual, on them, put the latter in possession of their reason, and the former in comparative safety.

Slaveholders are in their own place, and of course creatures of sense. From necessity, they are licentious and intemperate, or are in kindred evils. Their sensuous spirits look downwards to the earth, where they hold their human chattels only as instruments of their pleasures, and never upwards to the heavens. Did they turn their affections upwards, they would bear their slaves aloft with them, into the region of religion and liberty. Instead of holding them for selfish ends, their slaves would be only instruments of higher use to them. "A servant is the Lord's freeman," and the Lord's injunction is, "neither be ye called master, for one is your master," and "whosoever would be chief among you shall be your servant." Slavery is a state, corresponding to the inner man. It is the inner man in ultimates. Lust and cruelty and murder are as incident to it, as heat is to fire, or as love is to life. In other words, it is the exterior and natural form of internal love which makes the master a spiritual bond slave to the greatest tyranny in the universe. As slavery is the inverted order of humanity, so is a slaveholder an inverted man—the opposites, each, of God and Heaven.

CHAPTER IX

Not long after the events related in the last chapter, a circumstance of great importance occurred, which favored the agreement Manasseth and his wife made in their own strength.

Notwithstanding the injustice and wrong which all her life long had been inflicted on Cherry, and though outside of Henry and her children she had always been surrounded by examples of fraud and sin, in trying forms, still she preserved an internal consciousness of right, and was ever receptive of religious impressions. Doubtless those outrages and examples, taught her there was no power on earth upon which she could rely for support and happiness, and led her to look above the earth for repose and comfort.

The Methodists largely prevailed in this portion of Tennessee; and in the neighborhood of Manasseth's plantation was a notable camp ground for their great gatherings. At those annual gatherings, the inhabitants of the surrounding country assembled in great numbers, in their best costumes. As a general thing, the slaves also were there, as servants of their masters and mistresses, or to enjoy a holiday of personal relaxation and pleasure, or to sell the fruits some of them were allowed to raise on their little patches of ground. The free blacks and poor whites were there also, with meats, fruits, and liquors of various kinds, to sell to the white aristocrats, who, from pride, or fashion, or religion, were attracted to the place. The camp was the universal resort of lovers and rowdies, politicians and pleasure seekers of every kind, as well as religionists, who gathered about the preachers, or promenaded in the woods, or refreshed at the booths, where the poor whites and blacks exposed their provisions for sale.

For years the old distillery monopolized the entire wholesale liquor trade on those occasions. The poor people aforesaid purchased it of Manasseth at a whole-sale price, and retailed it at a large profit, to the world's people and christians who attended the meetings.

These circumstances regarding the camp meetings are related as preliminary and explanatory of the events which follow. Cherry invariably attended the meetings, when the claims of her master and mistress did not require her stay at home. Not long after the events in the last chapter, a religious awakening occurred in the camp, which spread at a great distance over the country. Cherry was one of the first to feel and acknowledge the divine presence. In the agony of her convictions, she fell upon the earth, and begged forgiveness at the throne of mercy, in tones of impassioned earnestness. Her master and mistress, touched by the sight of their poor slave in such a condition, left their place among the whites, and stood near her, to hear her words and watch the result.

It is proper here to remark, that, though religion in a slave is always a marketable quality, and therefore their masters are always desirous their slaves be converts, for the supposed increased value which religion gives them; still, we would not convict Cherry's master or mistress, on this occasion, of a motive so unworthy. Nevertheless, it is not unlikely, if they had searched their bosoms closely, they might have found at least a dormant motive of that sort, because it is inseperable from the condition of master and slave.

Manasseth and his wife stood behind the praying slave, and received every word from her lips. She first plead for herself—and then, as if caught by a new inspiration which left self out of sight, she besought the divine spirit to fill every soul of the great assembly. Warmed by the increasing fervor of her devotion, and forgetting every presence but her Lord, she descended to particulars, and prayed for her children and husband, and for divine assistance that they and she might act with a becoming and christian spirit in their trying circumstances—and finally, as if moved by the soul of charity, she embraced her cruel master and mistress, and bore them to the throne of pardon and grace, and continued her prayer for them, until the influx of divine love was so thrilling and potent, that nature yielded to the spirit, and she fell amongst the throng that crowded about her, in a speechless delirium of spiritual scenes and joys. To adopt the style of this class of christians, Cherry became converted, and had "the power." Though covering many subjects, her prayer, on this occasion, was not long, but direct and earnest, in the simple but touching words of an unlettered slave.

The angel of mercy which had smitten Cherry down, like a mighty contagion, marched through the crowd, numbering as his victims, blacks and whites together in his course. For days and nights, the groans of sinners mingled with the songs of converts and the shouts of saints. The great assembly swelled hourly by the attraction the awakening produced, and the whole country around was convulsed by the divine spirit. In the progress of events, the hard and stubborn heart of Manasseth, first touched by the prayer of Cherry, relaxed in the fervor of the excitement, and melted into penitence, and *his* harsh voice also mingled in the cry, "What shall I do to be saved?" His wife, also, was soon flooded with convictions of her awful sinfulness, and the husband and wife trembled and groaned together, in view of the eternal and awful Hell the preachers hung out before them. Long continued habits of intemperance, but just abandoned, left their nerves in a state eminently susceptible of the impressions which the skilfully selected words of the preachers employed to play upon them. So soon as their minds received the fearful picture of their depravity, and the startling horrors of the damned which awaited them in their then condition, a flood of emotions bore them into the vortex of the mighty maelstrom, in which they sank to come up saints.

We are as much in the dark as to the number of converts on this occasion, as we are to the evidence of their after lives of the reality and genuineness of their conversions. Nominally, they were blacks and whites—slaves and slaveholders—rich and poor, of both sexes, and in great numbers. Had they all been truly christian converts, the valley of the Tombigbee, by the power of God displayed in the camp, would have been changed into a picture of almost universal regeneration, and presented no faint image, of Heaven. But alas for repentance without a change of life, and for conversions which leave the converts where they were.

That some of the converts, with the help of The Lord, commenced a life of combat with inherited and welcomed evils, there is little doubt. That such was the case with Cherry was never doubted by those who knew her. Nor could it be denied that the lives of others were essentially modified and improved by impressions received at those meetings. Such, obviously, was the case with Manasseth Logue and his wife. If the impressions they received did not serve to clench the nail upon the compact they shortly before made at the burning distillery, it did effectually bend the nail in the right direction. But, alas, as a general truth, in a few weeks after the noise of the multitude, and the eloquence of the preachers died on the ears of the people, there remained on their memories and on the morals of society, no greater effect than was produced by a bygone thunder storm.

In stating such conclusions, it is not to be understood that the number of religious professors was not greatly increased, and that there were not many praying men and women where there were none before. Multitudes, of all colors and sexes, made open profession of religion, and engaged in public and private worship. Among those, and in the same church, were Cherry and her owners, who were baptized together in the name of the Father, the Son, and the Holy Ghost.

From that time forward, so long as Jarm remained in Tennessee, Manasseth daily assembled his family and slaves in the evening for Scripture reading and prayers, and himself and wife and Cherry were in good standing in the

Methodist Church. With what propriety he was classed with Christians, the reader will judge from what follows.

Such changes had been produced in the industrial and pecuniary affairs of Manasseth, by the loss of the distillery, that he hired out, or mortgaged, a few of his slaves to a neighboring planter, as a matter of personal economy, or as the means of raising money. Among the slaves thus leased or mortgaged, were Jarm and his mother. This occurred in the spring after her conversion. The precise length of the term of the lease, or the condition of the mortgage, Jarm does not remember. At any rate, it was determined, so far as they were concerned, in a short time, and they were returned to their master.

This temporary change in the condition of Cherry and Jarm is worth noticing only for an incident which occurred therein.

It was early in the spring when they were transferred to Mr. ——. As regards severity of labor, a hired or mortgaged slave, in possession of the mortgagee, is always in the worst condition. The interest of his owner of course regards his health and strength as of the greatest pecuniary importance, but if he is held by a mortgagee or lessee, the interest changes from the person of the slave to the amount of labor to be obtained from him. This Mr. ——, therefore, through his overseer, sought from Cherry and Jarm the greatest amount of labor he could consistently realize from them. Whether so directed by the proprietor, or not, it was obvious to Cherry that such was the aim of the overseer, and she bore with as much patience as she could the increased hardships upon herself and son.

Some two months after they had been in the employ of Mr. ——, Jarm was doing a man's days work, with all the hands, hoeing corn. The overseer stood a reaching distance behind the drove of weary laborers (it being the latter part of the day) with his heavy long lashed slave-whip in his hand. Fancying that Jarm was slighting his work, and while he (Jarm) was altogether unawares, the overseer brought the lash down upon his almost naked body, with a—"Look out, there! you black rascal! Do your work better, or I'll take your hide off! Take that!—and that!—and that!"—raising his arm to repeat the blow. Cherry rushed between the overseer and the boy, hoe in hand, and told the overseer he should not whip Jarm, for that he was not to blame.

This but increased the rage of the mad coward, and he again brought down the lash with increased force, which Jarm easily dodged; and then, changed ends with the instrument, to inflict a blow on Cherry with its leaded butt. She raised her hoe and made toward him. Knowing her amazonian strength, and cowering before the resolution which was manifest on her features, the craven rascal turned and run.

By this time the indignant spirit of Cherry was at its height, and she ran after him, and put forth all the speed she could to overtake him. For a time it was doubtful which was getting ahead, but at the moment he was passing out of the field, Cherry, because she supposed she could not overtake him, or because she was weary of the chase, threw her hoe at him, exclaiming—

"I'll learn you to strike a boy of mine, when he is not to blame, and is doing the best he can!—do it again at the peril of your life!"

Should the reader infer ought against the Christian character of Cherry from this act, they should remember that her religion was not of the passive sort, and as yet had not taught her to discredit the first doctrine she found among the instincts of her nature, to wit, "*resistance to tyrants is obedience to God.*"[1] Of course she belonged not to the non-resistant school.

It would be natural to suspect, that, according to the usages and laws of slavery, Cherry now would be the subject of some terrible chastisement. Had not Manasseth interfered, and had she remained at Mr. ——'s she probably would have been. As before said, it was the latter part of the day when the above transaction took place, and the overseer did not that day again return to the field. On that very evening Cherry and Jarm were returned to their old master, Manasseth Logue.

About three days after their return, an event occurred too terrible to record. Indeed, it was so shocking in its details and in its results—so internally and spiritually diabolical, that the material world has no symbols, or letters, or figures, to give but a faint idea of it. The skill of the painter, poet and historian is displayed in portraying the features of the soul to outward nature. After all, their best efforts are poor sketches of internal realities. The symbols which nature and language present to the mind through the natural sense, are but correspondences of thoughts and affections, which are rarely seen by the spiritual senses until the mortal coil is put off. The simple facts in the case are all that will be given. They are, perhaps, as gentle a picture of Manasseth Logue's christianity in particular, and of southern christianity in general, as we can give, or as genuine charity will be willing to look at.

1. [Editor's note:] "Rebellion to tyrants is obedience to God" was Thomas Jefferson's personal motto; he proposed it for the coat of arms for the state of Virginia, and it was written on his seal. Saul Padover, in his biography *Jefferson* (New York: Harcourt, Brace, 1942), indicates that Jefferson was inspired to adopt this motto after hearing Patrick Henry's "If this be treason" speech, while other scholars have attributed Ben Franklin as the original source. On February 24, 1823, Jefferson wrote Edward Everett that he believed that the maxim originated with one of the regicides of Charles I of Great Britain.

It will be remembered that Manasseth Logue, his wife and Cherry had been baptized at the same time, into the same Church, and on the Sunday previous to the case to be related, had partaken of the holy sacrament together; both being in good and regular standing in the Church. The family and slaves, after supper, assembled, as usual, at the family altar and listened to a chapter from the Bible, read by Manasseth—and then Cherry, with her little children by her side, fell on her knees with him and his wife, and joined in prayer to the Father of Mercies, for his pardon and blessings on their souls, and a copious influx of that love which binds together the Church on earth, and the Church in Heaven.

The next morning, Manasseth sent the adult negroes (including Cherry) into the fields at their labors, detaining all the children at the house. The arrangement, though unusual, was made in such a manner as to excite no surprise. Nor could they have supposed, that in his change of character and relations, his heart was susceptible of the diabolical intents he must have cherished over night, and felt in midst of his impious devotions.

Some hours after the mothers had gone into the fields, and while the children were sporting in the yards about the premises, two or three men on horseback rode up, and at the request of Manasseth dismounted and came into the door-yard. The occurrence was rare, and the appearance of the strangers so marked, that they attracted the notice of the children who left their sports and stood at a respectful distance to eye them.

After a short conversation with the strangers, during which time the eyes of Manasseth and his companions were turned toward the children, he called all of them into the yard, and commanded the oldest of them, in a stern voice, to stand perfectly still, and say not one word unless spoken to, while the strangers examined them. In giving this injunction, Jarm noticed the eye of the master particularly bent on himself, who was one of the oldest and stoutest of the boys. After this order to the children, he then told the men to examine the children and take their choice.

The elder children instantly knew the men were negro traders, and the horrors of the scene at Manscoe's Creek flashed upon the memory of Jarm. Now it was apparent that some of them were to be sold to these traders, and that their mothers had been sent out of sight and hearing in the fields, to avoid the scene the separation would produce if they were present.

The rude men immediately began to examine the bodies and limbs of the children—who had been taught by their mothers that the touch of such men was more dreadful than the touch of wild beasts. They soon selected Jarm's brother and second sister—the former about thirteen, and the latter about eight years of age. They were beautiful and lovely children, and unspeakably dear to Jarm. They had been the objects of his affectionate care during infancy, and were his companions during childhood. He had taught them to walk and sing and play; and the happiness of his life had been cherished by their attention and caresses. He had never been separated from them, and their society seemed inseparable from his existence. The sister not daring to move, on hearing the fatal decision, turned one imploring look at Jarm, and then broke into tears and sobbed aloud. They were immediately brought together, and the wrist of the right arm of one fastened to the wrist of the left hand of the other with a strong cord.

So soon as the ruffian put his hand on the little girl to bind her, no longer able to repress her terror and anguish, she shrieked at the top of her voice. The voice of the terrified girl sank into the souls of all the children present—and they rushed through the enclosures, screaming with fright; and in spite of the commands of Manasseth, fled into the fields and woods in the direction of their mothers, and the valley echoed with their cries. Jarm, only, remained with his poor brother and sister, as if he had been rivetted to the spot by speechless sorrow and dispair.

The mothers heard the wail of their children, and came running through the fields to know the cause and relieve them. Learning, by the way, that the slave drivers were at the house binding the children, and as they approached, seeing, at a distance, a long coffle of little children (to which Jarm's brother and sister were to be attached) marching towards the house, they broke into howls and screams and groans, which filled the air.

"We'll have a fine time of it, now!" said Manasseth.

"I thought you was going to put those black b——s out of sight and hearing."

"I thought I had done it."

"They always make such a muss, when we take their children, that it is often quite an inconvenience. Never take the calf in sight of the cow."

"You will find this the worst case you ever had, I fear. That she devil ahead, there, is the mother of these children. She is an amazon in strength—knows no fear—loves her children to madness, and will fight like a tigress, if she takes a notion, come life or come death; but she is of great value as a worker, and is a breeder No. 1. And mind you, I don't mean to have her disabled or killed—I can't afford to lose her."

"A few cracks of the whip, and it will be over. There are seventy-three children in that drove, picked from about twenty-five families. We had three or four scenes, but in most cases dealt with the children only, and got along easy. These two (pointing to Cherry's children) make our complement, and we can afford to have a frolic with the black devils—though I had rather avoid the trouble. It is incident to the trade—let it come."

"You will have a nice one now—that drove of children and these crazy ones, with Cherry at their head, meeting here, will make a hell not easily managed—and here they are upon us!"

Manasseth had just completed the delivery of the children, with the bill of sale, to the trader, who had mounted his horse and held the rope fastened to their hands, as Cherry bounded into the yard, and throwing her arms about the children, in a plaintive but firm voice, said—

"They shan't take you away!"

This new scene opened the wounds in the memories of the little sufferers all along the coffle, and their sobs, chiming with the groans and sighs of the surrounding negroes and children, and the moans of the agonizing mother, and the harsh voices of the traders, made a concert which, in connection with the parties, presented an exhibition not to be described.

"Let go of those children!" said Manasseth, "they belong to that man."

"They shan't go away from me!—they are my children!" said Cherry again, in the same sad voice.

"Get away, you black b——h!" said the trader, seizing her by the hair, and attempting to pull her away, and dragging the children along with her.

"They shall not be taken away from me!"

"You will have to use force," said Manasseth.

The trader then raised his terrible lash, and repeated the command—"Let go, or I will cut you in two." The command and the motion had no other effect on the frenzied mother, than to make her repeat the same sad words—

"They shan't be taken away."

The trader then let fall the heavy lash upon the naked shoulders of the unhappy Cherry. The blow produced a gash from which the blood flowed freely. But so fused were the mind and love of Cherry with the minds and love of her terrified children, that they were as one spirit which felt only the danger of separation. Her senses were all absorbed by the danger of the crisis and the greatness of the outrage, and the lash was no more felt than if it had fallen upon a corpse. Blow after blow followed, but not a motion of the muscles—not the least appearance of pain was produced, or the least relaxation of her hands—linked, as they were, like iron upon the backs of her children. The single garment which she wore was saturated with blood, which flowed down her limbs upon the ground. Still she stood there, holding her children in her strong arms, and leaning her head upon their heads, repeating the same soothing, moaning words—

"They shan't take you away."

Finding the whip made no impression upon the woman, the ruffian fell into a rage, and was about to give her a dreadful blow upon the head with the loaded butt of his whip, when Manasseth, fearing that his most valuable chattel would be disabled, and perhaps destroyed, interposed, and told the trader he would separate them without disabling her.

He then commanded two of his stoutest men, who stood at a distance, to come forward and release the children from their mother. The blacks came forward, but hesitated to obey the cruel command. He charged them to obey, at the peril of their lives. Forced by a fear of consequences, they set about the work, and failing to succeed without mechanical aid, they pryed her arms apart, and released her children. Finding herself separate from her children, she fell into a frenzy of grief and passion. Charged by their master to hold her, with great effort they succeeded to do it—while the hardened trader led the screaming children to the coffle, and fastened their bound wrists to the large rope that ran through it. Then, after the coffle had started, because she took advantage of the carelessness of the keepers—or because they were willing she should again embrace her children—she broke from them, and, ere she could be retaken, flew to the coffle and locked her children in her arms again—repeating the same moaning words—

"They shan't take you away from me!"

Again were they pryed apart as before, and the caravan of children, fastened in front to a large wagon, were dragged along in one direction into the darkness of the evening which was coming fast on, while Cherry was dragged by main force in another direction. The former were soon lost to the sight of the frantic mother forever.

That she might not follow her children, Cherry was now taken into the room which was used for weaving coarse cloth for the negroes, and fastened securely to the loom, where she remained, raving and moaning, until morning.

This scene, which is now as vivid as life in the memory of J. W. Loguen—whose words are as truthful as any man's living—was witnessed by him, without the possibility of remedy. Upon being asked what were his feelings on the occasion, he said to the writer—"So overpowering was my sense of the wrong and cruelty of the transaction, and so desperate my helplessness, that I was dead to all consequences. I was willing to be sold away, or die upon the spot." It is not difficult to see that such must have been his state.

It is philosophically true, that a man's love is his life. If it were possible for the slaveholder to destroy all the objects of the slave's love, he would have no will or motive of thought or action. He would be naturally and spiritually dead—and when this poor boy saw the objects of his affection tortured and crucified, he was necessarily driven to the verge of vitality. Motive, the wick from which life's flame derives its oil, was perishing. But because the slave is a spiritual as well as a natural being, the extinction of his natural or external motives, often flings him a stupor which is akin to death, or into a desperation which prompts him to terminate his natural existence, that his mind and heart may have scope and indulgence in another world.

The reader will wish to hurry over the denouement of this horrible outrage. Cherry, stiffened by confinement, and covered with wounds and gore, was no more reconciled in the morning than in the evening. She refused all food and rest, and raved and mourned for her children. The reflection that the voices which so sweetly answered her call, were wailing in that dreadful coffle—or that their bodies might be bleeding from the lash which drew her blood—that she could not go to them, or they come to her, almost made her crazy, and overcome every other feeling, and deprived her of food and comfort, until exhausted nature sank under the load of oppression, and she fell into a brief oblivion of sleep; then awoke, burdened with sorrows, and tortured by pain and burning fever—which deprived her of strength, and laid her upon her hard couch for days. A kind-hearted old slave woman washed her wounds and nursed her, and by the soothing attentions of her oldest child, Maria, and the affectionate sympathy of Jarm—who occasionally saw her—she was restored to health, and sadly took her place among the hands in the field—to her, the only place of sympathy during the day.

This was the first time Cherry was compelled to part with any of her children. The terrible circumstances under which she was robbed of these, obviously affected her mental constitution—and she was occasionally melancholy, and always nervous and suspicious of danger. The separation, with its aggravations, made a perpetual wound upon her spirit, which time could not heal. Her heart clung to her remaining children with tremulous earnestness. Her daily labors were performed with usual strength—but without the self-possession and sense of security, which, even in servitude, extract from labor its evils, and impart to life its blessings.

CHAPTER X

We will not dwell upon the sad particulars of the life of Jarm during his stay in bondage. We sketch them as features of life in a slave land, which, becoming rapidly visible, are multiplying results beyond its limits. They present a rude picture of the school in which the multitudes who flee from it are trained, to invigorate the growing sympathies in their behalf, at the North and elsewhere. Fugitive slaves are now objects of general regard. The public eye is turned towards them, and public feeling extended to them as they pass through northern thoroughfares. Crippled as are their minds, and scarred as are their bodies by lashes and wounds, they present a sample of a strong and hardy and bold race—whose manly qualities the severest tyranny cannot subdue. It may be doubted whether, in like circumstances there is another people on the face of the earth who could preserve their nature less impaired or subdued than they.

It is this sort of hard discipline which accounts for all their offensive peculiarities, and forces upon our notice the grand specimens of mind and courage which occasionally flash from their more gifted ones amid the cultivations of northern freedom. Disgusting as is the story of their wrongs, they are a necessary and important part of history. They are generating a new element of life, which is rapidly infusing and regenerating the masses, and lifting them to a higher and holier sphere of thought and action.

Jarm was now approaching manhood, with a body sound, strong, and active, and a mind capable of appreciating treatment and calculating for the future. He had come to the age when the slave is subjected to the severest process of being subdued by hard service and cruel discipline. But he was one of the class which it was not easy to subdue. Given to the unrestricted dominion of a tyrant like Manasseth Logue, it is easily inferred that his case was a hard one. Passing a multitude of examples of such discipline we sketch one now, only to show the character of his condition, and open a view of its miseries, and leave the reader to imagine what the full picture must be. Though Jarm might not have been faultless on this occasion, the measure and quality of the discipline he received will show his early training, and shed light upon his encouragement to fidelity.

It was in the fall of the year when the process of fattening the hogs was given to his charge. The corn was scattered in the ear upon the ground, which at this season was damp—and the place where they were last fed was often made muddy by the nuzzling of the swine after the last kernel of the meal.

One rainy Sunday morning, Jarm proceeded to feed the hogs as usual; and judging that the place where they were last fed was as fit a place to feed them as any—or not caring whether it was or not—he poured down his corn upon that spot. The consequence was, it became dirty and muddy, and the animals fished for it under unfavorable circumstances. Manasseth, learning the fact, fell into a frenzy of passion. He seized the hominy pestle—a thick, solid, heavy wooden instrument, used to pound the corn in a mortar into hominy—and rushed upon Jarm. He did not strike him transversely with the instrument, which would be comparatively harmless, but bolted the end of it against his head and knocked him down. Jarm attempted to rise, but Manasseth bunted his head again with the pestle, and continued thus to bunt his head until he was helpless and insensible.

Before his senses left him, Jarm thought from the repetition and heft of the blows, that the wretch intended to murder him, and that he was in the act of dying when he became insensible to feeling.

Jarm awoke from death, as it were, and found himself, at evening, lying in the loom-room—his mother washing the blood from his head and face with cold water. The water restored his senses, but the pain in his head was so great, that he was nearly crazy, and he groaned sorrowfully.

"Hush!" whispered his mother; "don't groan!—your groans will make him mad, and he will come and kill you!"

The sound of his mother's voice fell upon his ear like a drop of comfort upon an awakened sorrow. His head was covered with wounds—the blood flowed from his ears, nose and mouth, and run upon his face and neck—but Cherry wiped it away and staunched it to the best of her ability. He could not repress his anguish—and his mother repeated most earnestly her prayer that he would not groan; for that his groans would certainly bring on him again his mad master, and she feared he would kill him.

"I'm almost dead now," said Jarm, "and I had rather die than suffer the pain I do!"

"For my sake—for the sake of your poor mother—don't make a noise—don't bring him on you again—he has been drinking, and he will certainly kill you."

Though Manasseth did not make whiskey now, and though he and his wife were under a solemn compact to let it alone, and though they were in good standing in the Church, they occasionally procured whiskey, and drank it and became partially intoxicated—but by no means as often and deeply so as before. But a small quantity of whiskey was needed to drive the malignant passions of Manasseth to the unfeeling excesses which he had just perpetrated upon the body of his slave. There was no place for compassion or reason in his head or heart on such occasions; and his unresisting and helpless bondsmen were exposed to his unbridled fury. Cherry was familiar with his symptoms, and by no means mistaken as to his present condition, or the effect of Jarm's groans upon his irascible nature. Therefore, she urged upon Jarm the utmost care not to disturb him by a groan—well knowing it would again irritate his hatred, and drive him to uncontrollable excesses.

For the sake of his mother, Jarm suppressed his groans, though they seemed the only relief to his almost intolerable pains.

After the evening had set in, Manasseth eat his supper and called his family and slaves around him for family worship. Manasseth and his wife had been absent all day at the Sabbath meeting. The sacred time spent in holy worship should have sufficed to cool his passions, and fitted him for the prayer he was about to make in the presence of his family and slaves.

It was dark and still as death in the room where Jarm lay—and Cherry, that her absence might not remind the tiger of her almost dying boy, retired to the praying circle. Of course it was compulsion, not choice, that led her there—and while Manasseth was reading his Bible lesson, her ear watched intently in the direction of Jarm, to catch the least sound that might proceed from him.

Some considerable time elapsed—the chapter was finished, and the heartless monster was paraded on his knees before his family and high Heaven in mockery of prayer, and Cherry fondly hoped Jarm would live out the desecrated moments without a moan, when she knew Manasseth would retire, and the horrid stillness be succeeded by the usual motion and noise—under cover of which she might protect her son from the dreaded passions of her master.

The room where Jarm lay was attached to the negro house, a little distance from the habitation of Manasseth. Cherry, desirous to imprison his aching breath, had prudently closed the door upon him, and would have closed the only aperture through which light and air entered his room, had she the means to do it.

Manasseth had but begun his form of prayer, amid the most perfect stillness—when Cherry fancied a sound floating on the brooding silence and indistinguishable therefrom, which awakened her auricular nerves to painful intenseness. Again, and again, and again, the sound came at intervals, with increasing distinctness, until it was certain it entered the ears of the praying man, and diverted his thoughts from God to the suffering boy in the negro house. His voice was choaked—and his words, at first indicating embarrassment from distracting objects and contending emotions, were finally silenced by the overpowering devil within him, and he cut short the impious formality with an abrupt "Amen."

Hate is love perverted; Hell, the love of angels inverted. In the act of opening his bosom to the influx of divine affections, Manasseth suffered the tempter to interpose between himself and his Maker, and set him on fire of Hell. He rose from his knees, bloated and burning with infernal fires. His anger against Jarm was swollen to a burning torrent, which rushed him in blind rage, through the darkness to the negro house, and bounding into the room where Jarm lay, he muttered—

"I'll make you grunt for something, you black devil!"

"Kill me, master, and put me out of pain!" groaned the boy, at the same time.

"That is what I intend to do," said his master, grinding his teeth with rage, as he kicked Jarm with all his force against his shoulders—and he continued to kick him, sometimes stamping his heel upon his head and breast—while Jarm, unable to evade the blows, only repeated his prayer, "Do kill me—do kill me!"—his voice growing fainter and fainter—when, suddenly, a flood of light filled the room, and the cry of "Fire! Fire!" from many voices without, alarmed him. He sprang to the door, leaving the motionless and voiceless Jarm in his gore—the sight of which, by the terrific glare, stamped its horror on his memory as the Hell fires that produced it sank back to their source, and another fire, equally intense broke out from the same source, to wit, the fire of mammon.[1] "Fire! fire! fire!" he cried, as he saw the blazing column above the top of his house, on the opposite side, spreading sparks and cinders on the dark clouds, and showering them upon every thing that was inflammable about.

Cherry, with a pail of water in her hand, stood most conspicuous, with two or three other negroes, a little distance from the fire, when her master came

1. [Editor's note:] *Mammon* is a word from the Aramaic language meaning "wealth" or "property." It is derived from the Christian Bible and most often personified as a deity. Matthew 6:24 states, "No one can serve two masters. He will either hate one and love the other, or be devoted to one and despise the other. You cannot serve God and mammon."

up. So soon as she saw him, she made one cry of "fire!" which arrested his notice, and brought him to her.

"It is too late," said Manasseth; "don't waste your water, but watch the sparks, and see the house and barn don't take fire. Every one of you be ready with water, and keep your eye on the corn and wheat. Take care of that cloth," pointing to a large quantity of coarse cloth, which Cherry had herself manufactured for the negroes' wear.

Cherry handed her pail of water to one of the standers by, and ran to the cloth and filled her arms with it, and took it into the cloth room. The greatest confusion now prevailed. The whole family, blacks and whites, were spread in different directions about the premises, watching the falling fire, and extinguishing it when it fell in places to do damage, guided by their own discretion.

Cherry's expedient worked to a charm. She was in agony for the life of her child. She knew that Manasseth, when he got up from his prayers, was an intoxicated madman, and that Jarm's life was no more safe than if a mad bear was springing upon him. Therefore, to divert his attention from Jarm, and to extinguish one passion by another, she set fire to a load of straw that lay on the opposite side of the house, to the intent, that, so soon as the storm which it would produce was up, she might hasten to Jarm and save his life.

When she had deposited the cloth, she did not leave the room—which was light as day—but hastening to her bruised and bleeding boy, who lay in his blood as still as a corpse. To her great joy, she found him yet alive, but in a state which greatly alarmed her. He could not speak, and was insensible to her attentions. Again she procured water and cleansed his wounds, and took him to his bunk. After some soothing attentions, his sensibility was partially restored, and fancying his cruel master still with him, he whispered—

"Kill me! kill me!"

"No, my son, you must not die—I am with you, and you shall not die," said Cherry.

The sweet sound of his mother's voice restored him, but so great was the pain in his head and body, that he was bereft of reason—and in spite of his mother's affectionate attentions, he raved like a madman.

"Kill me!—do kill me!" was his loud cry.

The attention of Manasseth was too much engrossed by the fire to think of Jarm, or hear his ravings, for a long time. It was late in the night before the fire was so far extinguished that it was safe to leave it. Manasseth and his wife, children and servants watched the decaying embers and sparks, which the wind occasionally blew about—while Cherry, unminded, watched her boy, and in vain strove to quiet him. At a late hour of the night, Manasseth, now perfectly rational, approached his wife and began to enquire into the cause of the fire.

"How do you suppose this fire came?" said Manasseth to his wife.

"It is the visitation of God."

"Could it be possible that any of the negroes intentionally set this load of straw on fire?"

"If so, they did it as ministers of God," said his wife. "God is angry with us both, for breaking our solemn compact to drink no more—and is especially angry at you, for getting drunk and beating Jarm as you did—and he would not hear you pray, and sent Jarm's groans to drive you from your knees, and sent the spark into this straw to divert you from a murder, which would have kindled a fire in your soul to burn forever!"

"I believe it," said the repenting wretch.

"Hark!—what sound is that?" said Manasseth.

Cherry was greatly terrified when she could not prevent Jarm's loud ravings, and hoped her master would be so occupied as not to hear him until his (Manasseth's) reason was fully restored—when she hoped his interest, if not his compassion, would be awakened for Jarm. Such was the state of things in the negro house, when the ravings of the boy reached the ears of his repenting master and mistress, as they stood by the fire and heard him cry, "Kill me!—do kill me!" &c.

"My God!" said Manasseth, "it is Jarm still crying 'Kill me.' He thinks I am with him yet—the boy is crazy—where is Cherry?"

"I don't know."

"I am bound she is with him. Go in a hurry," said Manasseth, "and see how the case stands; I can't go there. Take the remaining whiskey with you—it may be useful to heal the wounds it has made. I have almost killed him, I suppose. We cant afford to loose him—he is worth a good deal of money—go, quick! I will stay here and try to make peace with God—for I verily believe he is angry with me."

A complete change had come over Manasseth. He was in deep concern for Jarm—the horrible impression which the last sight of him made on his memory—the consciousness that he had been driven by intoxication to the verge of murder—that he had violated sacred pledges, and angered God by misusing the power which the law gave him over the person of his slave—in the light of the providence which spoke from the ashes around him, and howled in his ears from the negro house—produced an overpowering reaction, cast him into the profoundest penitence, and convulsed him with a tremor of excitement in the opposite direction. Most earnestly did the poor man beseech Heaven's mercy for himself, and help for Jarm. So great was his agony and concern, that he did not think of retiring to his bed, but waited for his wife's return, that he might learn how the case stood with Jarm.

After a time, Mrs. Logue returned to her husband, and informed him that the boy was dangerously bruised and wounded, and insane by internal and external pains—and that he must have a physician without delay, or they must lose him.

With all possible expedition, Manasseth sent for the doctor. In the mean time, Cherry and her mistress watched the patient, and bathed his wounds with whiskey, and tried in vain to soothe and quiet him.

The doctor found his patient in the condition before described, and immediately took from him a large quantity of blood, gave him a soothing opiate, which quieted him, and he fell into sleep. Cherry and her mistress watched by his side until morning.

We will here close the details of this chapter in the slave's life. It is needless to specify the trials and watches on the part of his attendants, and the bodily and mental sufferings Jarm endured during a protracted illness, before nature assumed her place and composed his frame to her undisturbed dominion. The moral effect of these transactions upon Manasseth and his wife was decisive—at least for a time. The following day was celebrated by a new covenant between themselves and their Maker, thus:—

"It is just a year," said Manasseth to his wife, "since the distillery was burned."

"Yes—and just a year next Wednesday," she replied, "since we made public profession, at the camp, that we were converted to Christ."

"In the first place, we vowed we would drink no more whiskey, and in the second that we would be true to the Lord, who had mercy on us."

"And most unmercifully have we broken both of those vows," said Mrs. Logue.

"We made the first vow over the ashes of the distillery, and the second at the camp," said Manasseth.

"And now," said his wife, "we must renew them over these ashes, and confirm them at the camp on Wednesday."

"Yes," said Manasseth, "and may the Lord have mercy on our souls."

"But the Lord will not have mercy on us if we don't have mercy on others."

"That is the very thing this terrible lesson has taught me," said Manasseth.

"What is mercy?"

"I should have thought that a very simple question, but for that blessed tract which Joseph sent us some time ago, which, in my folly, I laid on the shelf for a more convenient season. I took it down and read it this morning, and found in it the very thing I needed," said Manasseth,

"Does it tell what mercy is?"

"Yes—and I will read the definition given. It struck me with great force—and it seems as if I had proof of its truthfulness constantly in my inmost soul, since four o'clock this morning."

Manasseth took up the tract and read as follows:—

"Mercy is God in us—God is mercy itself, and love itself, and goodness itself, and they constitute his essence."

"But if God is mercy only, how can he be just?"

"The Book answers the question thus:—

"A poet hath said, 'A God all mercy is a God unjust.' The sentiment is neither poetry nor philosophy. Justice is an ingredient of mercy, and cannot exist without it. A merciful being cannot but be just. Mercy seeks the good of others with all the light it has. Infinite mercy, therefore, is infinite wisdom and infinite justice. By separating wisdom and justice, from goodness and mercy, the truthless poet adopted the absurdity of a cotemporary and degenerate theology, which dissects the indivisible God into three equal persons, and crucifies the good and merciful one to appease the anger of a just one. It was the infinite mercy that propagated himself on his own image and lived among men in the person of Jesus Christ, whose inmost was Jehovah or Father, and whose external derived from the mother, was the Son—who possessed all the infirmities and lusts of humanity without sin—because they were overcome by the Father and the God within, to whom the Son was conjoined when the conquest, called his glorification, was complete. Thus the child prayed to the father until he was merged in him and became one in spirit with him."

"But if God is only love and mercy and goodness, why are not all saved?—why is he angry with us when we do wrong?—why do you become drunk and cruel?—and why is Jarm beaten to a mummy, and left to groan in the negro house?"

"Here your question is answered again," said Manasseth, taking up the tract and reading—

"God is life itself. All men, animals and things derive their life by influx from him—the source from which all life proceeds every moment. Coming from him, it cannot be less pure than his own love, which is his life. It is the same yesterday, to-day, and forever. But man's freedom perverts it to selfish uses and he thereby becomes a beast, and gives himself to the control of angry, selfish, lustful and cruel passions. It is man, not God, who changes. The latter loves alike the evil and the good. His sun and rain are shed alike on all. Good men receive his love into unperverted wills, and are like him. Bad men receive it into perverted wills, and become satans and devils. Hence, it is obvious that God, being love itself, loves his enemies, and cannot hate them, or be angry with them—for his word teaches that anger resteth in the bosoms of fools. And he further teaches us to love our enemies; and he would not prescribe a rule for us to live by which he did not obey himself. Men are led by their ruling loves to Heaven and Hell. Hell is a condition of perverted love, and men progress into it, not because God puts them in it—but because they love its horrible evils, and choose to go into it in opposition to his love."

"O, how truly that pictures my case! I, not God, was angry. Yes, I was in Hell yesterday—and all these evils are the result. I bless God that I am a changed man, and that he has not changed—that he loved me when I was angry and murderous—and now I pledge myself never again to drink a drop of liquor, and to love and obey my Savior. Will you join in the pledge?"

His wife made the same pledge.

Poor creatures! They had not begun to comprehend the depths of their selfishness, much less to look it in the face and overcome it. Conscience, which is the touch of God's finger within, had called their attention to evils they had eyes to see—but could not alarm them by the sight of still greater evils to which they were blind. They had not begun to think that their slaves were equally entitled to life, liberty and happiness with themselves—and that by holding them in slavery, they cherished in their hearts the complex of all evils, which must break forth in varied forms of evil life, and torture them with infernal fire, which all the love, and wisdom, and power of God, without their repentance, could not quench.

CHAPTER XI

During the year succeeding the events of the last chapter, Manasseth and his wife were measurably true to their agreement to abstain from liquor. Their attention to the forms of religion were regular, their habits generally natural and stable, and life on the plantation was as endurable as its inverted order would allow. He was a hard man in his best states, but the slaves might now anticipate their treatment, and regulate their conduct by his usual and known temper and life. The curse of their condition was more than half relieved by being disburthened of uncertainties. Jarm was treated with special indulgence, and he grew to man's strength, and became his master's most trusty and reliable slave.

Alas for the frailty of humanity! As the year was drawing to a close, Manasseth and his wife occasionally yielded to the liquor demon, and they and their servants were in danger of sinking to their former state and habits. Those occasions were not frequent, however, and their dependents, most of the time, were in the hands of a surly, selfish man, instead of a drunken beast.

Cherry, nor Jarm, however, during this period, suffered special injustice from his harsh temper. Indeed, the outrage upon Jarm, detailed in the last chapter, wrought a change in his conduct towards him. He not only refrained from abusing him, but allowed him privileges and favors, as a sort of atonement for the murderous outrage. Now, for the first time, he had a hat and shoes, and a Sunday suit—which he was allowed to earn by extra labor and small trafficking on his own account. Verging on manhood, with a fine person and social temperament, he begun to feel the pride of youth, and indulge his social propensities with young companions, of both sexes, in the neighborhood.

Though depressed and degraded beyond measure, the social instincts of the slave cannot be subdued short of the destruction of his ability and usefulness. Therefore, opportunities of social enjoyment, under harsh restrictions, are allowed from necessity. Of course such enjoyments, though eminently social and affectional, are, as a general thing, merely animal. The slave's education is the remains of destorted nature left to sensual indulgence, and farthest removed from mental or moral culture. Slavery cannot extinguish the affectional qualities God implanted in the African's bosom—though it crushes his intellect and robs him of moral motive. In the circles of rustic gaiety, for a brief hour, the negro dismisses sorrow—and though he emulates the civilities of the whites, he has no motive to regulate the indulgence which nature prompts and tyranny solicits. It is rare that the male or female slave seeks a higher level of chastity and purity than their masters. But notwithstanding those virtues are sins in slave life, there are instances in which they are cherished in spite of education. In the slave's bosom, God's voice is not always so hushed, that its demands are disobeyed in respect to domestic relations. It is not possible, if it were profitable, for slavery to reduce the blacks to the level of the animal herds—and it is forced, therefore, by policy and economy, to obey the plan of Providence and sanction a distorted relation of husband and wife.

Jarm had now arrived at that period when the only personal freedom allowed a slave is to debase his spirit by demoralizing instincts. Bereft of all other gratifications, he would doubtless have plunged to the bottom of the abyss, but for causes to be developed. For the last eight years he had not listened to words of kindness, friendship or compassion from a white man or woman, and was forced to regard them as enemies. His hopes had been crushed in every direction. On the verge of manhood he stood on the brink of moral desolation. But an event occurred at this time, which set him right, and rescued him from danger.

The season of the year came around, again, when it was convenient for the slave owners to attend to religion. The fall fruits were harvested, and the immortal camp-ground was to swarm again with worshippers. It was fitted up with cabins great and small to receive them. Free negroes and poor whites, as well as slaves, had prepared their booths, and filled them with meats, and melons, and fruits, and liquors for the occasion. The poor whites and free blacks ever look forward to it as a market for the surplus products of the little patches of land which they hold by lease or in fee, that they may have means to keep their families through the winter. The slaves look to it as a market for the products of like patches, which some of them improve, by the will of their masters, to get them extra clothing and comforts.

Jarm was on his way to the camp, in his best attire. It was one of those beautiful autumnal mornings, in Tennessee, when the spiritual world reposes on the surface of external nature, and gives an etherial impression to each sound and scene—which surrounds the soul with a mysterious aura, and infils it with a tranquillness which forgets earth. He was alone, and precisely in that state when the mind turns from objects without to undying thoughts and things and forms which open upon the spiritual senses in the vast world within him, where the kingdom of God is.

Little did the poor slave think—little do the rich and wise and learned think—(pardon the digression)—that they live in two worlds—the external and the internal—the natural and the spiritual; and the only reason they do not recognize the latter as real and more substantial than the former, is, because they have fallen from the spiritual state in which God placed them, into a sensualism that acknowledges nothing real that does not respond to bodily senses. Little do they think that their spiritual senses sleep, to wake when they merge from their bodies among the ever living thoughts and objects and forms which they now regard as visionary things. Little do they think that the flowers and fields, animals, birds and insects, and all material things, are external forms of the thoughts and affections that devised and projected them—and that they will remain in the atmosphere of thought and affection, and their significance be studied as the word of God, and their qualities loathed or loved, as they correspond to things of Heaven or Hell after time and space are forgotten. All unknown to himself, Jarm was in that world where the despot's arm cannot reach, and where the free soul is left to its own undisputed wanderings.

He had scarce entered the border of the woods which encompass the camp ground, and was out of sight of the cleared land in the rear, when he heard happy voices and sounds of horses feet behind him. He inferred that a cheerful party was approaching, on their way to the great gathering. The voices harmonized with the silence of the forest and his own emotions.

He stopped a moment, to look and listen, and a lady on horse-back appeared at the bend of the path, a few rods behind him—while the voices of her companions indicated they were not far off. She was travelling on a slow gallop, evidently exhilarated by the exercise, and the soft breeze that swept the locks from her forehead and exposed a beautiful face. She was of the superior race, and of course out of the reach of Jarm's aspirations—nevertheless, he thought her the most beautiful person he had ever seen. To appearance, she was about eighteen years of age, of graceful and full proportions, and rode her horse—of which she had perfect control—like a queen.

Jarm stopped only long enough to daguerreotype the delightful vision upon his memory, and then passed along. In a moment she was by his side, and the slave boy with a more willing heart than ever before, raised his hat, slave fashion, to the charming apparition. She checked her horse into a walk, and in a sweet voice, which was evidently natural, compassionate and harmonious with every expression of her face, enquired:—

"Are you going to the camp meeting?"

"Yes, madam."

"How far is the ground from here?"

"About half a mile, madam."

"I will be there in four minutes," said the girl—and she applied the whip to her spirited horse.

At the second bound, the animal made an unusual effort to overleap a gulch in the path, and the girth of the saddle broke by the swell of his strong muscles. The girl felt the breach, and a terrible sense of danger drove the color from her cheeks. With a convulsive effort she pulled the reins upon the bounding animal, and checked him—but a motion transverse the centre of gravity slid his body from under her, and she fell, screaming with fright, into the arms of Jarm—who, quick as lightning, sprang for her security. Disburthened of his load, the horse passed on a few paces, and commenced browsing the bushes—while the fainting girl, unable to stand, clung convulsively to the bosom of her deliverer, and was borne to a small bank by the road side, whence issued a spring, whose waters, in crossing the path, occasioned the mishap.

With all delicacy Jarm laid his precious burden on the bank, and remembering, from his own experience, the beneficence of water in such cases, dipped his hand into the cold, pure element, and sprinkled it upon her face. The beautiful girl instantly recovered, and turned her large blue eyes upon him, with an expression of unmistakable thankfulness. By this time the other portion of the company came up, and the dilemma and the denouement were told them by the artless girl, emphasizing the part Jarm had taken in the transaction, as worthy of something more than thanks, which she expressed with evident sincerity and generous simplicity.

It was a company of two brothers and three sisters, some older and some younger than Jarm, but not far from his age—who were on their way to the meeting. After they were informed of the facts, they warmly seized Jarm's hands, ladies and gentlemen alike, and overwhelmed him with kind emotions, which were as visible as their lips and faces. Besides, they contributed from their limited purses two dollars in cash, which they said was a trifle far below his deserts—and begged him to take it, with the assurance that they would gladly give more, if they were prepared to do it.

Jarm was thoroughly confounded by the naturalness, frankness, familiarity, kindness and humanity of their uncorrupted and loving hearts. They treated him as if they had no suspicion of difference of caste and color, and made him feel that he was on the level of friendship and brotherhood with them. It was the first time in his life that he had seen the sun in that direction.

So unlike anything before seen was this company of brothers and sisters—so unadulterated were they by vulgar and corrupting habitudes and passions, that they seemed more like angels than like men and women. Poor and needy as he was, the money they offered him—which in his sight was a large sum—bore no comparison in value to the soul treasures they emptied from their overflowing bosoms into his. In spite of all efforts to suppress it, the fountain within him broke and dashed its waters on his eye-lids.

Jarm accepted the money, and the parties separated, with mutual and undying good will. But the moral of this transaction lives to-day in Jarm. The innocence, purity, sincerity, kindness, justice and charity so transparent in his new acquaintances, impregnated the germ of his being, and it budded and swelled upwards—and aided by events hereafter related, gradually uplifted the cold and massive rock which lay upon it, and rolled it away—and broke into the free air and sun light. His life and character are much indebted to this transaction and its sequents.

Jarm soon arrived at the exterior of the camp, among the rude saloons where refreshments are sold by poor whites and free blacks and privileged slaves, to the mixed multitude. He was in the midst of the crowd of eaters, drinkers, gamblers, prostitutes and of every class, who swarm around these places. The most rude and lawless of the male portion of this motley mass, are the scions of the large proprietors in the neighborhood, who are the oligarchs of these ecclesiastical purlieus. Next to them in influence and power are the petty slave merchants—backed, as they are, by their masters, whose interest is to make the slave feel that his condition is preferable to that of a free black or poor white man. The free blacks and poor whites are the lowest grade of society in a slave State—and if either has advantage over the other, it is so trifling, and the grade of both so contemptible, as to be unworthy of notice.

"Glad you have come, Jarm," said a stout, fat and sleek negro, who thrust his arm through the evergreen boughs that surrounded a space of a rod of land, enclosed on all sides but one, and plentifully stored with melons, whiskey, &c.

"What do you want of me?" said Jarm.

"I want to get rid of that black nigger there. His stores are larger and better than mine, and he takes all my custom."

"Well, how do you expect to get rid of him?"

"I am determined he shall be driven off."

"What have I got to do in the matter?"

"I mean to set the young Massas on him—and what I want you to do is, to speak to Massa James, and get him to put Massa Charles and others upon the black rascal, and break him up."

James was a rowdy sprig of Manasseth, and ripe for a scrape of that kind. But Jarm was not in a state to entertain such a subject. He immediately replied:—

"I shall do no such thing. That is Jacob, the free negro that occupies the little patch near Col. Pillow's plantation. I know him well—he is a clever fellow—and I shall lend my hand to no such thing."

"What business has the poor devil to come and pile up his melons by my side, as if he was somebody? Such poor scamps should keep a respectful distance, and not crowd among gentlemen—it is an insult, and he shall budge!"

"Isaac," said Jarm, firmly and sorrowfully, "I shall do nothing to disturb that poor man. He has spent the summer to gather those stores from his little patch of land, and depends on their sale to take his family through the winter. It will be very cruel to disturb him—you must not do it. You have nobody to provide for, and are better off than he is—why, then, disturb him? I want you should let him alone to sell his things."

"By Gippers!—I'll rout him," said Isaac. "Poor folks have no business here. There comes Massa James, Massa Charles, &c.—I'll set them on to him—they will want no better fun than to use up his pumpkins."

Massa James, Charles and two or three others now reeled into the enclosure. Isaac immediately entered into a low conversation with them, and Jarm saw they were already sufficiently liquored for a cruel frolic. Having finished their low talk, they poured each a glass of whiskey and drank it, and with flushed faces, started for the poor colored man's booth.

"He'll catch it," said Isaac, looking significantly at Jarm.

"It is mean," said Jarm, "and you ought to be ashamed to injure that poor man."

Slaveholders, especially those of this stamp and in this condition, are always mad when they have a mind to be. The rowdies bounded into the poor man's booth, seemingly in a rage, exclaiming:—

"What are you doing here, you d——d black rascal?"

"I'll learn you to be civil to gentlemen!" &c., &c.

In such like language each of the rowdies addressed the poor fellow, who was astonished by their fierceness—and in the humblest manner plead his innocence of any wrong or intention of wrong—and begged them to say what he had done to offend them or any one else. But such as they, when they propose to teach a free negro that he is beneath their slaves, don't wait to hear his supplications. One of them began to pommel him over the head and shoulders with a stick, and the others to kick and stamp upon his melons—the negro begging all the while—

"Pray, Massa—Pray Massa!"

In two minutes the poor fellow's fine melons, bottles and liquors were all destroyed, and his booth prostrated—and the gallant olligarchs turned away, saying:—

"Clear out, now, you black rascal—and don't be seen about here again!"

The poor fellow stood a moment, looking upon the ruin of his hopes and labors—with his eyes downcast, he seemed the picture of desolation. The large tears started into his eyes—and he turned and wiped them away, and retired. Jarm was deeply grieved at this injustice, and was about to proceed after the poor fellow and attempt to comfort him—when he felt a tap upon his shoulder. He turned, and saw his master at a cane's length from him, in the crowd.

"I want to see you," said Manasseth. "Follow me."

Jarm followed his master from the crowd, and then his master said to him:—

"I want you to return home immediately."

"Won't you let me stay here until evening, massa?" said Jarm, anxiously—greatly disappointed by such a command.

"Don't make any words—go directly home, I say. I shall be there in the evening, and tell you why. I can't talk about it now."

The villainy perpetrated upon Jacob, and Jarm's pity and resentment thereat, immediately sank in his disappointment—and he turned sadly in obedience to his master, and retraced his steps to the Tombigbee. He was grievously downcast. He had reckoned much upon seeing his new acquaintances at the camp, and could not relinquish the idea without regret—which was aggravated by the fear that this strange order of his master boded some new calamity.

CHAPTER XII

Jarm was in painful suspense until the intent of his master was explained—nor did the explanation set him at rest. There was nobody at home when he arrived there, to sympathise with him. Cherry, and all hands but his mistress and the children, were absent. On the way home, the burden on his mind annihilated space and time—but there was nothing to kill time after he got there, and the moments were wofully long. He could not relieve himself of the thought that something bad was to happen to him.

At last his master came, and Cherry also. Immediately his master told him to make ready to go the next morning to live with Mr. ——. (He shall be nameless now.) The order was given with the indifference that he would order him to feed the hogs.

"Am I sold to Mr. ——?" said Jarm.

"No—you will work for him until I call for you."

"Where does Mr. —— live?"

"About fifteen miles from here. Put on your best clothes, do up your duds, and come to me in the morning—and I will direct you on the road."

As a general truth, there is no confidence between master and slave in any matter relating to his sale. The slave knows, as well as the contractors, that they are controlled by money considerations, as certainly as if they were dealing in hogs or horses. If there are exceptions to the rule, Manasseth Logue was the last man to vary from his interest in the matter of selling, mortgaging or hiring a slave, and Jarm knew it. Hence, any assurance he might give in the case, could not quiet Jarm's anxiety, which was intense.

Bound to such a wretch, it might be supposed he would be willing to risk the consequence of an exchange of masters, upon the presumption that he would not fall into worse hands. But Jarm had no experience of other hands. He esteemed all slaveholders unjust and cruel, and did not suppose a white person could entertain a fellow feeling for a colored man, until he came upon his white friends in the last chapter—and those he considered exceptions among the entire race. Besides, he had always lived with his mother, brothers and sisters, and was bound to them by the strongest love. The African is the most affectional of all God's creatures, and the slave the most affectional of that affectional race—for the reason that the love of kindred is the only indulgence spared him—and that is spared only because slavery cannot take it away. It is a great annoyance. Manasseth's command to prepare to leave his mother, brothers, sisters and companions, and go he knew not where, touched Jarm where he was most sensitive—and he went aside and wept like a child; and his mother, brothers, sisters and companions came and wept with him. They feared a trick to get him away from them into a trap, where he might be seized and taken to the dreadful south, as his little brother and sister were. Such fear worries the slave all the while, but most intensely when anything unusual occurs, as in this case. He worries of it when awake, and dreams of it when asleep. It is the Hell that haunts and tortures and shapes his spirit into an embodied fear, that startles and trembles at every point.

Of course Jarm's case required little preparation. In the morning, after breakfast, he packed up his working clothes, and appeared before his master in his best suit, according to order, and said:

"I have come, massa."

"Take this pass and go to Mr. ——'s. He lives about fifteen miles from here."

He then gave him directions as to the road. It was the same road he travelled the day before, to the woods where the camp was, and there he was to cross the track of his kind young white friends. He had hoped, when he found the direction he was to go, that he might fall into their path, and perhaps see some of them on the way. But that was eclipsed by the order to cut their path at right angles. His master also told him to make enquiries of anybody he might meet after passing that road, and they would direct him.

"Go there directly—don't stop by the way—I shall hear from you to-morrow morning. Your new master will be looking for you, and if you are not there by two o'clock, he will be after you, and call you to strict account—and I shall, too."

"How long am I to live with Mr. ——?" said Jarm.

"I don't know—it is uncertain. I shall come after you one of these days."

These were designed for the last words of the hard hearted uncle to his sad and outraged nephew on this occasion. Jarm returned to the negro house, where were his mother, brothers, sisters and companions, prepared to take a final leave of him. With aching hearts they clung together and wept together, until their savage master broke in upon them with his slave whip, and laid it over their bodies indiscriminately—and drove Jarm into the road upon his journey.

Of course he left his friends with no good will to slavery. Could he have taken his kindred with him, he would gladly have gone anywhere out of the reach of all slave-holders. Every day of his life repeated the lesson of unbearable wrongs, and much as he loved his kindred and friends, he had long since resolved to leave them to the care of Providence if a chance of escape occurred. His eye was ever open in that direction—but all was dark around him now. Could he have seen the path to freedom though clouds and darkness covered it ever so densely, he was in a mood to rush into it. But he could see nothing. He knew the north star, and that freedom lay that way,—but there was no light on its path. All was black as night. He knew darkness was light to the human beasts that guarded the negro's path to freedom, and that he was as liable as other runaways he had seen to stumble upon them, and be brought back and tortured and sold to the cotton fields.

It was a heavy heart he took with him that morning—and all alone as he was, it drew around him dark shadows. But dark though it was without, the life of his childhood stirred in him, and like a morning star, inspired his sickly hopes. He could see nothing externally but the cold walls of his prison house. His case was sad indeed.

For three long hours he dragged his heavy chains. They had never felt so heavy as they did that morning. He came to the road where his young white friends turned into the woods the day before. It was ten miles from his starting point, and he was weary and thirsty and heart sick. The spring which revived the frightened girl was but a few rods off, and he went to it, drank of its cold, fresh water, and sat down for a moment's rest and reflection.

The place was identified with the persons, transactions and sentiments of the previous day. The natural scenery was beautiful—but it was dead, and cold, and unmeaning, and unnoticed, in the presence of the original scene, which opened to his mental eye in all its parts, significance and freshness. Jarm saw nothing but the interview of the day before, and that stirred the depths of his soul. For the moment he was entranced by it, and knew not that he was in the body or out of it. He stretched himself at full length on the green sward by the pure fountain, and the circumstantials of that interview passed before him. Plainly as before he heard again the same happy voices and sounds of horses' feet, and saw kind and joyous faces about him. But his natural senses soon felt the touch of material objects, and he awoke to see the same natural and material faces about him, radiant with kindness and delight upon finding him so unexpectedly.

Jarm immediately rose to his feet and took off his hat, as is the custom of slaves in the presence of white persons.

"Put on your hat, my friend—we will not allow you to take off your hat to us, unless we take our hats off to you."

Jarm bowed confused—but they insisted he should put on his hat, and he did.

"How happened it we did not see you at the camp?" said two or three voices at a time.

"I went to the camp, but my master immediately sent me home."

"Then you are a slave?" said the artless girl who met with the mishap.

"Yes, madam."

"How sorry I am for you—my father will never own a slave."

Jarm did not reply.

"You made no effort to find us at the camp, then?"

"I thought much of seeing you at the camp. It was my intent to make it my first business to find you—but so soon as I arrived I was ordered home."

"We were all anxious to find you—we looked everywhere through the grounds yesterday and to-day to find you—and as the meeting was to be dismissed at three o'clock to day, and we were obliged to return to help our father and mother, who left on important business yesterday morning before we arrived—we gave up all hope of seeing you, and are most happy now to find you here. But how came you here—and where are you going?"

"I am going to Mr. ——'s, about five miles from here, to work a time for him."

"What!" exclaimed all of them.

"Here is the pass my master gave me," said Jarm, putting it in the hand of one of the company. "He gave me this pass, and directed me to go to the house of Mr. ——, and work for him until he called for me—and as I did not know the way from this spot, he directed me to make inquiries of whosoever I should meet after I crossed this place, and they would direct me—and I shall be pleased if you will tell me the way."

They all exclaimed at a time, "Mr. —— is my father, and you are going to our house!—how happy we shall be!"

Jarm was confounded, and for a moment silent, then he inquired:—

"Have you any colored people at your plantation?"

"None," said one of the young men. "Our father and mother work themselves, and we work. With the help of the sons and occasional hired help, father does all the field work—and with the help of her daughters, our mother does all the house work. We have nobody to attend to but ourselves, and have plenty of time for study and amusement. We are very glad if you are to live with us. If you are as good as we believe you to be, we will share and share alike in our labors and pleasures. But how come it about?—let us hasten home and find out about it."

Jarm knew not what to say in such unusual circumstances. Nor did he say or do anything. He stood confounded, thrilled and mute. Overjoyed at the turn of things, he dared not give expression to his feelings. He yielded passively to the circumstances, and was translated as in a dream of delight to the plantation of Mr. Preston.

Hitherto we have left a blank for the name of the gentleman to whom Jarm was consigned. We have filled the blank with a fictitious name. The reason for so doing is, the persons are real persons, and the transactions to be related, however fabulous they may look to the reader, are true in substance and matter of fact.

For aught that is known, all the parties are now living. They were the kindest and best people Jarm ever found anywhere. The parents he loved as his parents—the brothers as his brothers—two of the sisters as his sisters, and the other he loved better than a sister. Public opinion at the North nor at the South would sanction the intimacy, familiarity and affection which grew up between Jarm and Alice, (the girl Jarm saved from falling,)—chaste and delicate and refined as an angel's love, and known and approved by her brothers and sisters though they were. It is because this record may be read by their friends and acquaintances—and we sincerely hope it may—that we withhold their real names—that their generous and noble natures may not suffer from the distorted public opinion of the country. Nor would these delicate secrets be spoken at all, but to illustrate the respect to color in a slave land—and for the still more important reason, that the intimacy, familiarity and affection that grew up between these young people, and especially between Jarm and the beautiful Alice, cultivated his self-respect—brought forth the manly qualities of his nature—overcame every tendency to gross indulgence—brought him into love with virtue, chastity, purity and religion—refined his manners—elevated his aspirations, and armed him for the unseen trials and conflicts that were before him.

We name these young persons John, Charles, Susan, Alice and Charlotte Preston. On their return, they took a path transverse the one which entered the forest, and thus undeceived Jarm as to the direction of their habitation.

"Here is a singular case," said Alice to her father on their arrival. "This stranger met me in the woods, and saved my neck from being broke—and you, without knowing the fact, immediately take him home to be one of the family."

"What!" said Mr. Preston.

Alice then related to her father and mother her peril in the forest, and the service rendered by Jarm on the occasion, together with the particulars that followed.

The affections of the father kindled at the recital—he embraced his daughter fondly, and stretched out his hand to Jarm.

"Welcome, my good fellow," said he. "I little thought I was providing for the deliverer of my child when I took a conditional assignment of you, yesterday, from your master."

Jarm bashfully and awkwardly yielded his hand to the warm and hearty grasp of his new master. He was quite unprepared for it, and knew not how to behave. The act was in tone with the treatment from the children—and though he shrank from the familiarity—its earnestness, sincerity and kindness thrilled through his nerves.

Each of the young persons now took part in the conversation in lively terms—giving some fact or feeling they wished to express—while Jarm stood a silent, confused, awkward and delighted listener.

Mr. Preston was a red haired gentleman, of middling stature, and about fifty years of age. His frame was strong and healthy, his forehead high, his complexion light, his eye mild, bright and searching, and his countenance marked with sincerity, kindness, mental activity and energy. His appearance and address convinced the stranger at once that he valued public opinion only in subordination to principle—and though his temperament was ardent and active, he was little influenced by the fashion of society around him.

Mrs. Preston, also, might be taken for about forty-five years of age, of dark-brown hair and face, of robust habit—gentle, affectionate and confiding, and evidently marked with the simplicity of a country which carefully avoided a mixture with the world.

These people made their own society, educated their own children, and did their own work. Their religion was as peculiar as other things about them. They were educated Methodists, and attended Methodist meetings—nevertheless, their opinions and lives were quite independent of sects and creeds. Their domestic and social habitudes, as well as their labors and aims, were evidently obedient to interior forces that the people around them knew nothing about, and cared not to know. The centre and circumference, and every part of their religious philosophy, was *use*,—use to others, and use to self for the benefit of others, was the beginning and end of their creed.

"God's kingdom," said Mr. Preston, "is a kingdom of uses, and is spiritual—that is, it is within us,—in the affections, the understanding, and the will. The human body, as a whole, corresponds with it as a whole—and the parts of the body to all the parts of that kingdom. Each part of the latter, like the parts of the body, works for every other part. The brain labors for the foot, and the foot for the brain—and each part for every other part, in perfect obedience to the law of heaven, 'Thou shalt love thy neighbor as thyself.' Every muscle and part of the body (which is an image of God's body,) is performing uses for its neighboring muscles and parts. And so every inhabitant of Heaven, which is but a muscle thereof, and every society of Heaven, which is but a combination of muscles thereof, work, not for themselves, but for every other person and society in conformity to the aforesaid law of charity. That law is the basis principle on which all nature and all Heaven reposes—the law of all laws—the soul of God's government of both Heaven and Hell. If you wound your flesh, God within, is in instant effort to heal the wound. If you wound your spiritual body by sin, he is in instant effort to accelerate repentance, or a return to the law of charity, which is its only cure. God is love, and he works by love in Hell as in Heaven. He loves his enemies, and it is this principle which makes enemies neighbors, and works for their good—that keeps in motion and life the material and spiritual universe."

Such a man, of course, yielded nothing to the claims of slavery, and only conformed to its externals, to such extent, as was consistent with his residence in a neighborhood of slave-holders. Of course there was no negro house on his plantation; but the family residence, though made of logs, seemed to Jarm a palace; for as yet he had seen only log houses. The number, convenience and neatness of the rooms and furniture, plain as they would appear to him now, surpassed his then conceptions of architectural excellence and provision for family comfort. It was surrounded with a green court yard, which was enclosed, and separated from a garden in the rear by a neat picket, and ornamented with flowers and choice shrubbery and fancy and fruit trees.

"All for use," said Mr. Preston. "I would have nothing in my house, or on the heritage my Heavenly Father gives me that is not useful. The useful only is beautiful. So it is in God's great home and domain, and our affections should copy their features and provisions in the little world we make for ourselves. What is useful represents charity to the neighbor, and is a correspondence of Heaven. What is not useful, represents self, and is a correspondence of Hell."

We are particular to give the character of this man, his family and possessions, because, among them Jarm's thoughts and affections first felt genial influences, and began to take on a new life.

As near as he can judge, there were about sixty acres of cleared land in Mr. Preston's farm, surrounded by an unbroken forest. How much of that forest belonged to it he knows not. In approaching the messuage for a quarter of a mile, it seemed to him that he was leaving cultivated fields in the rear, and going into the bowels of the wilderness. The sun was completely intercepted by the frost-bitten foliage which shed its cold shadow on his track. The farm was a sunny spot in the dark woods. It broke upon his view like the light of the morning, when one awakes from sleep. The contrast of light and shade was more than equalled by the contrast of the industrial picture before him with that he left behind. The fields were perfectly and neatly cleared and fenced—the pastures and meadows green and beautiful, and finely stocked—the orchards of apples and peaches, some of which still hung on the branches, were a treat to the eye as the fruit was to the taste. Nothing was neglected—everything cared for and truly spoke of use.

To his companions, these beautiful surroundings awoke the sensation of home scenes only—but they came upon Jarm's soul like a vision of paradise, and he could not help whispering to himself—"O that my mother, brothers and sisters might live here with me and these good people forever!"

CHAPTER XIII

Jarm's arrival at Mr. Preston's was beginning a new life to him. All the time he lived with Manasseth, he had been driven along from day to day by dread of physical suffering, and the hope of escape from it. His affections were not allowed a moment's repose. It was ever a fearful looking for of outrage of some kind, attended by an impracticable determination not to bear it. His highest aim was to dodge the lash of a tyrant—his daily prayer, that his mother, sisters and brothers might not be subjects of new wrongs. So habited was he to wrongs, that he met them without disappointment, and endured them without complaint. Steadily looking for an opportunity "to stake his life on any point to mend it or git rid on't"—without an effort on his part the scene was changed, and his affections found a home. Kind hearts and smiling faces greeted him in the morning, met him at noon, and blessed him at night.

"Your name is Jarm?" said Mr. Preston.

"Yes, master."

"You must not call me 'master'—call me Mr. Preston. Well, you have come to labor with me a spell—I don't know how long. If you do well, you will live as well as the rest of us. I hope and believe we shall like you. We shall have to show a deference to the habits of the country. I never owned slaves, though I occasionally hire them. You will have a table in the same room with us, where you will take your meals; but you must go to work and make your own house to live in. Your table will be as well provisioned as ours, and the goodness of your house will depend on your taste, skill and desire. Do you know how to make a log house?"

"Yes, master."

"You call me 'master,' again. I am no man's master—you forget. Well, you shall have a team and all necessary implements and help—but you will do the hewing, chopping and fitting, alone. Remember it is for yourself alone—and yet it will be well to make it sufficiently large for two or three others. While suiting present use, it is well to regard future convenience. You are used to team and tools, of course?"

"O yes, sir."

"Here is the place for your house, and yonder the oxen—you will find tools in the barn. Your first business is to build this house. Being at work for yourself, you will need no overseer—and now come to breakfast."

This conversation occurred on the morning after Jarm's arrival. The remark about his being his own overseer, was said with a significant smile, as Mr. Preston turned and walked to the house, and Jarm followed him.

Jarm found a small table set for himself, apart from the family table, in the same room. It was covered with linen white as snow, on which was a plate, knife and fork, coffee cup and saucer, milk and sugar.

"You will sit here," said Mrs. Preston, addressing Jarm with a pleasant smile, and placing her finger on the little table at the same time.

The family placed themselves around the large table, and Jarm sat down at the little one. They then bowed their heads while the father repeated a brief prayer, of which the Lord's prayer was much the largest part. When the prayer was concluded, the two oldest young ladies brought the bacon and potatoes and coffee to the table, and at the same time divided a portion to Jarm from the main dishes, and poured out his coffee.

There were no little ones in this family. All were old enough to take a part in its sociables. Indeed, their religion cultivated the social as the means of ultimating good affections. The shadows which popular religion too often shed on the innocent enjoyments which come up spontaneously in the path of life, were never seen by them. According to Mr. Preston, men build their own life, and he taught his children that the life they loved at death, they would always delight in. If it was bad, God would never interfere with it, only as he now does to prevent injury to others—that God's providence and government in the spiritual, were the same as in the natural world. "Men change their states," said he. "God and his laws never change, in this world, or in that."

Educated as Jarm was, his condition was very embarrassing. He had been taught, in the severest school, that he was a thing for others' uses, and that he must bend his head, body and mind in conformity to that idea, in the presence of a superior race—and that it was treason to aspire to the condition he was then in. Of course he never believed in anything of the sort, but he supposed white people did. Whether they did or did not, it was all the same—for they ever acted upon that absurdity, and he was compelled to shape his life to it. Therefore, he knew not how to act in this new condition. He would have been glad to slink away with his breakfast to a private place, that he might eat it out of sight of those kind people. Hungry as he was, he hardly knew how to eat in such circumstances.

"Take hold, my boy," said Mr. Preston. "You have a job that requires strength, and you will be good for little if you don't eat. A man's breakfast is a part of his day's work—and if he don't do that up well, he will be likely to come short in the other parts. Remember, you are at work for yourself to-day, and you had best make a good beginning."

Jarm received the words as a command, and commenced eating. The charm being broke, he lost his reserve in the conversation of the family, who he supposed were occupied with themselves alone, and he ate heartily. His inference was precisely what their kindness designed—but so soon as he had finished his coffee, Alice was by his side filling up another cup—a fact which showed that their seeming inattention was a benevolent regard to his embarrassment, and that he had been really kindly watched. Thus he found that instead of being a waiter upon the family, they were in fact waiting upon him. This inversion of the rule of his life did not please him—but there was no help for it for the present.

Mr. Preston was a plain man, and in common acceptation, uneducated. Yet a stranger hearing him converse, might esteem him learned, and on some abstruse subjects—and particularly the philosophy of religion—class him with the profound in wisdom and science. He had but few books, and they treated mainly of such matters, and he studied them attentively. They professed to explain the literature of the Bible and the philosophy of Christianity, as taught by a great master. They represented the Bible as a revelation of God's thoughts, affections and intents, in the creation, preservation and regeneration of mankind. Its literature, they claimed, was hieroglyphical, symbolic and correspondential, a mode of writing adopted by the Ancients when things were known and visible representations of thoughts and affections before letters were known or needed. Every tree and plant and flower—every mountain, hill and valley and wilderness—every stream, lake, sea and ocean—every animal, bird, fish and insect—every other thing, simple or complex in nature, was an expression of a divine idea, which was read and understood by the most ancient people—as they are now and ever will be by angels, who "see thoughts in the trees, sermons in stones, books in the running brooks, and God in everything."

"God's Bible," said Mr. Preston, "is in his own language, not in man's. It is composed of pictures of his ideas, translated from external nature. Its letter, thus translated, is of course human—and the secret of its meaning is not in the words, for they express men's thoughts and affections—but in the symbols, historicals and parables described, which are God's letters and words, and express his thoughts and affections."

Mr. Preston's books maintained that the Bible has an external and literal, and at the same time an internal and spiritual meaning—that the internal dwells in the external, as the soul in the body—that it is divine—that it is God. The Apostle had his eye on this fact when he said, "The letter killeth, but the spirit maketh alive." And again—the whole Biblical literature and philosophy is expressed by Paul in these words, "The invisible things of him, from the foundation of the world, are clearly seen—being understood by the things that are made." Not the letter, then, but "the things that are made," infold the spirit and intent and life of the word. The most ancient people were born into a knowledge of this science of things, called by them "the science of correspondence." As they became sensuous, or in other words, aspired to know good and evil through their senses, and to be governed by their own king, they invented and adopted their own literature and laws. That is, as they gradually fell from the state in which God placed them, they gradually lost that science. It lingered long in Assyria and Egypt, and finally disappeared, and was buried in scientific inventions adapted to a race whose spiritual senses were closed, and who received knowledge through their natural senses only—whose thoughts and aims were outward—who saw the exterior earth and heavens without a perception of the sublime thoughts and affections that gave birth to them, and to which they correspond as language does to thought—and which, with their inhabitants, are a complex embodiment of the divine mind. Mr. Preston's books professed to reveal this lost science, and open the way to the internal truth of the word—making the clouds, that cover it and refract its rays so that they fall in different angles on mental eyes, glow with glorious light—and bend and blend various opinions by the law of charity into the beautiful bow of Heaven. Indeed, the "bow in the cloud" is a hieroglyph expressing that idea.[1]

"Now, Children," said Mr. Preston, "You have told us some things about your meeting expedition, we should like to know if there is anything more you can give us."

"Beside the mishap," said one, "we had a beautiful time on the road—the birds sang, and we sung and laughed, and enjoyed ourselves—and converted the occasion and the rich sunlight to our uses. 'Everything for use,' you say."

1. [Loguen's note:] Varieties of opinions are features of Heaven, as variety of things in the outer world are features of nature. But since those opinions are grounded in charity there, they do not distort or divide, but vary its harmony "as the light varies colors in beautiful objects, and as a variety of jewels constitute the beauty of a kingly crown."

"Very well—it becomes us to harmonize with nature. The joy of the birds comes of the fact that they are in harmony with the laws of order. They are in their heaven, and may sing and be happy. True joy, in man or other creatures, is the fruit of harmony with the divine plans. When you are in unity with the divine heart, as the birds are, you will be as happy as you can be—because you will delight in divine uses."

"The little birds have nothing to do but sing and be happy," said Lottie, a bright girl of fourteen, and the youngest of the family. "Every thing is provided for their support and comfort, and they have the sweetest sun to play in."

"Those externals are essential to their comfort, and of course, to their joys—but do you suppose their joys are derived from those external things?"

"Certainly—their little bodies being well and needing nothing, how can they be other than happy?"

"Ah, my dear child, your conclusion is quite natural, and no doubt is approved of popular science and christianity—but I am satisfied it is a mistake. These external things which appear to make the birds happy, are only conditions for the reception of divine love—and it is the influx of divine love itself into those conditions, which makes them happy, and makes them play and sing in the trees and skies. Those conditions are dead things, and impart no feeling—it is the life within them that makes their joy—and inasmuch as that life inflows from God's life (which is love) every moment, when the conditions for its reception are perfect, therefore their happiness is perfect. It is divine love, or life, stirring in all their internal receptivities which creates their joys. It comes from internal perception and life, and cannot come of external matter, whatever its conditions. Don't you see it must be so?"

"I must admit that what you say is very natural," said Lottie; "but does the same rule apply to men?"

"Of course it does. God has but one law of life, and all life flows from him constantly."

"Then what is the difference between man and other animals?"

"The difference is precisely this—man is born with a faculty to know, and an inclination to love, but without either knowledge or love. Other animals are born into their particular love, (which is their life) and into all the knowledge necessary for the gratification, of that love—and of course cannot progress beyond such knowledge and love. The implantation of knowledge and love at birth sets boundaries to progression—but the implantation of faculties and inclinations only, sets no such boundaries—therefore, a man is capable of growing more and more perfect in science, intelligence, and wisdom forever:—that is, he is capable of growing more and more a man forever. But a beast must remain in the knowledge and love which nature prescribed for him. His intellect attains its perfection with his body. The spider makes his web—the bee her hive—the bird her nest—and the fox his hole, with as much science the first time they attempt it, as at the hundredth—while man begins in absolute ignorance, with only the faculty and inclination to learn, and therefore progresses through eternity."[2]

"There is another important difference, it seems to me," said Susan. "The bird and beast being limited to their particular knowledge and affection, which they possess in perfection, they of course have neither freedom or rationality—they are shut up, in their own state, and can by no possibility change it. Their particular love and knowledge are the internal condition of their lives. Not only can they not be happy, but they cannot live in any other. On the other hand, men are gifted with freedom and rationality—and make and change their spiritual states as they will. Therefore, the latter are responsible for their spiritual conditions, while the former are not."

"Well said, Susan," said the father. "I would have said the same as an inference from what I did say—but you have happily done it for me. I only add—men are responsible, not for life itself, which flows into them from God, but for the quality of their lives. Not so with other animals—they do not have ideas and think as do men. Their acts flow spontaneously from the influx of life or love from the spiritual world; that influx is called instinct. Their heads and brains, the habitations of life, are so formed that the spiritual influx is precisely adapted to the particular natural, sensual, and corporal love which belongs to each."

"I see where you are coming," said Lottie. "The birds and animals are vessels, or organs, shaped for the reception of the natural love or life peculiar to each—which flows into them from the spirit world. And man, also, is an organ or vessel to receive the influx of life—which he shapes as he likes. Is this influx

2. [Loguen's note:] The distinction between men and beasts is well described by Rev. E. D. Rendell, in a very learned "Treatise on Peculiarities of the Bible." He says:—"The faculties for knowing and loving God, and the consequent organization through which they act, are the peculiar inheritance of man. They belong to the discrete degree of life, with its interior forms, which is above the endowments of the beast. Hence, beasts perish while man lives. Beasts, indeed, have souls, because they have life—but they are not immortal, because they have not the spiritual organization by which to know God, or to love anything respecting him. They have no interior link, by which to connect, in spiritual union, the finite with the infinite. They therefore cease to live when their bodies die."

what is meant in the Bible, by God's breathing into man's nostrils 'the breath of life,' and 'he became a living soul?'"

"Certainly," said Mr. Preston. "In a normal and regenerate state, man is an image and likeness of God, and receives in finite proportions, all the qualities or attributes of his Heavenly Father. Unlike other animals, he has freedom, and therefore power to close up some of the avenues through which some of the qualities of the divine life enters his soul, and so becomes a devil or beast, as the Revelator calls him. He excludes a portion of the qualities essential to humanity, and becomes a personified self love, like an inferior animal, and lives only for its gratification. Such are the covetous—the licentious—the drunken, and all other profane persons."

"Men, then, form their own lives or loves," said Lottie, "but other animals have theirs given them."

"Yes—but I want you to understand that God's life or love is equally present with the evil and the good—the good receive him, and he enters and abides with them in his fullness—whereas, the wicked exclude him from a portion of their habitation, and become monsters, not men."

"My life, then, is not my own," said Lottie.

"By no means," said the father. "It seems so—but it is not so. Life or love is uncreated. The Lord only hath life in himself—he, therefore, only gives life. Hear what he said:—'As the Father hath life in himself, so hath he given to the Son to have life in himself.' Were your life your own, you would be independent of God, and could live without him—could you not?"

"Why, yes—but if life is uncreated, then all the life of the world flows into it from God—that is, if I understand you correctly, God's life or love flows into minerals, vegetables, animals, men and angels—all of which, in their external forms, are organs receptive of life from the spirit world. Indeed, the universe is a complex receptacle of divine love."

"Certainly,—you remember the Lord said—'I am the life,'—'he that followeth me shall have the light of life.' And how John said—'In him was life, and the life was the light of men.'"

"How is it that minerals have life? I thought stones, rocks and the like were merely dead matter."

"So the philosophers have taught; they find their premises in nature, and to them 'the things of the spirit' 'are foolishness.' They walk by sight, and not by faith—that is, by the senses, not by internal and rational principle. They recognize only the external forms and properties of stones, rocks, &c., which affect the senses. They have not attempted to find the invisible forces which hold them together. The stones and rocks and mountains are held together by God's laws, as truly as the universe. Those laws are spiritual and invisible, and have force from the divine presence and mind. Every particle of matter, therefore, is vital with the Omnipresent and Omnipotent life of Deity. In the antediluvian literature—which is the literature of the word—a stone stands for truth—a rock for the Lord himself—and a mountain, for the highest spiritual state. Hence, Christ is called 'the corner stone,' and the place where God dwells is uniformly called a mountain. The foundations of Heaven are living stones. Since you are so interested in this conversation, I would be glad to extend it. Indeed, I am as much interested as you are," said the father—"but our day's work is before us—our co-laborer, Jarm, has finished his meal, and we have finished ours. The food we have taken into our bodies and spirits, needs digestion, and the best help for digestion is work."

"There is one question I would like to ask," said Lottie.

"Put it, then—we must be brief."

"If all animals and birds correspond to affections of the mind, how are we to know what those affections are?"

"Your question has a large circumference. I will briefly say—before the fall, every thing in nature was seen to be the immediate outbirth of the divine mind, and to be 'very good,'—every mineral, vegetable, insect, fish, bird and beast was, and was seen to be, an expression, each, of a thought—one of God's thoughts, and of his love, too—for there is no thought without an indwelling affection. At that time, men had as free use of their spiritual faculties as of their natural faculties, and could see not only the external and material quality of things, but their internal and spiritual qualities. When they saw a flower, a tree, or an animal, they not only knew it was an expression of one of God's thoughts, but they knew what that thought was. They did not need letters and books then. They are induced by the fall. The earth and the heavens were radiant with truth. The light and charities of Heaven were seen in 'the things that are made,' and sparkled before their eyes like precious stones of the New Jerusalem."

"Is this what is meant by God's bringing all the cattle and fowls to Adam, and his naming them?"

"Precisely—to name a thing in antediluvian language, was to express its quality or essence. Names of men, or animals, or any other thing, corresponded to and expressed quality only, in the infancy of the world—and men saw the quality in the name as well as in the thing itself. The Bible is written in that language. Hence, Christians are said to be 'baptized into the *name* of the Father,' &c. Hence the expression—'A cup of cold water in the *name* of a Disciple'—'A prophet in the *name* of a Prophet'—'Justified in the *name* of Jesus'—'A name above every other *name*'—'Whose *names* are in the Book of Life'—'Keep through thine own *name*,' and a thousand like expressions. Hence, also, the different woods and precious metals in the ark, the tabernacle and temple—all expressive of spiritual and celestial goodness and truth, qualities of the Lord. Hence, too, the animals sacrificed by the Jewish code.[3] Those animals and things were not arbitrary names, as the Jews blindly supposed. They corresponded to the charities of Heaven. They had a special signification and relation to Human Regeneration. And now, child, ask no more questions. Let us suspend conversation until other duties are done in their order," said the father.

Jarm heard all this talk, but it was Greek to him. He had been bred in darkness, and his faculties were all undeveloped. This was his first day with his new master, and it seemed to him as if he had been taken away from devils and placed in Heaven. He had formed no higher conception of God and happy beings than this family. If their talk, which he had just heard, was beyond his ken, he could feel the aura of their pure and blessed spirits, and wished no higher enjoyment or better companions.

Never did mortal man go to a day's work with greater good will than Jarm did that morning. Mr. Preston went with him into the woods, and described the limits within which to fell his timber.

"I make no blows upon the forest," said he, "except where I intend to clear. To do so, would be to invite the birds and winds to sow wild grass and weeds in the openings, and expose the standing timber to the tempest—it is bad farming."

Jarm marked a few trees with his eye, and fell to chopping. Few men in Tennessee had a stronger arm than his, or could wield an axe with greater

3. [Loguen's note:] The clean animals and birds offered or sacrificed, represented pure and innocent affections. The ceremony of sacrificing them was a lesson in an ancient language, that we should hold the affections symbolized sacred, and live them, in our actions and lives. The Ancients knew well enough that God "desired mercy and not sacrifice; and the knowledge of God more than burnt offerings." (Hos. vi. 6. Math. ix 13. xii. 7.) But the Jews were so thoroughly sensuous that they lost all the significance and intent of the sacrifices, and thought God was pleased with the literal transaction only. And there are some Christians who have no higher opinion of those ancient ordinances than the Jews had, and really believe they are done away by the advent of Christ—and are of no use either in their letter or intent. Whereas, in truth, they are as binding now as they ever were. "Love God and thy neighbor, for that is the law and the prophets," is only a transcript or translation of those ancient enactments.

skill. Mr. Preston stayed with him to witness the beginning of his work, and then left him, with the charge to trim the tops of the trees and pile the brush.

He was not disposed to be long in getting the timber to the site of his habitation—for the treble reason that he wished to confirm the favorable opinion his new master had of his fidelity and ability, and to shorten the period of his separation from his co-laborers, for whom he cherished great respect and attachment—and for the further reason that he wished to come into the possession and enjoyment of a house he was to call his own, and use as his own. Of course, with his ability and means, the materials were on the spot without delay, and he was busy hewing and fitting them for building.

"Jarm, you don't do that work as well as you should do it," said Mr. Preston, as he was chipping and hewing the logs for his house.

"Why, sir?"

"Can't you finish it off nicer than that?"

"O yes—but this is nice enough for a poor slave."

"No, no, no,—you should do work for your own use as nice and well as if you were doing it for my use. Remember it as long as you live—be as particular to do your work nice for yourself, as for me, or any one else. Never slight anything. I say this for your life-long benefit. Will you remember it?"

"O yes, sir."

This was a memorable lesson to Jarm. It had a revolutionary effect on him. He had been bred to believe anything good enough for a black man—that his condition allowed nothing to taste or ambition, and very little to comfort—but here was a concession that the poor slave had the same claim to any and all these as his rich master. It was seed sown in his understanding, that set him to reasoning in a way that awakened and encouraged his self-respect, and made him begin to think not only, but to feel that he was a man. He thought of that remark all day—went to sleep with it in his mind—and there it still is, strong in its growth and rich in its fruits. It awakened a consciousness of his individuality. It was a concession to his manhood, and he felt more and more that he was a man as he dwelt on it.

It is scarcely necessary to say Jarm's work was no more slighted. The small house was soon finished, with a skill and neatness that surpassed his master's house. The growth of a young and unbroken spirit is rapid when the weight that crushed it is taken off. A few days, only, sufficed to give Jarm's body and mind a manly shape and bearing—and he entered his humble cabin with a keener exaltation and greater gratitude than a monarch feels when he takes possession of a new palace. Here his bed was placed, and other things for his comfort, as if he had been of the blood of the Prestons.

When he sat about the job, he wanted to complete it, that he might retreat to it from his friends and be at ease. But his nature was eminently susceptible and social, and ere he finished it, he was not only at home in this dear family, but his soul was knit to them all by reciprocal kind feelings and growing intimacy—and the thought of leaving the same roof over night, even, was unpleasant.

CHAPTER XIV

Though the Prestons had a qualified title to Jarm, and, in contemplation of slave law, he was a thing for their uses, nevertheless, he was indulged no less than the sons. Do unto others as you would have others do to you, was the rule of life to the parents and to the children. Under such influences, Jarm's spirit quickly developed into manhood. The sense of servitude and danger which bent his soul and body to degrading forms, passed away, and he stood erect in the manly proportions of his nature. On Sabbath and holydays, when young and old appeared in their best attire, he was dressed as well as the rest, and rode by their side to the meetings. The religion of the Preston's did not condemn the sects as wicked.

"It is not heresy, but an evil life that is condemned. A man may err in doctrine and live a life of charity—and he may know all truth and live an evil life. It is the life that determines his religious qualities and state. Worship is not attention to Sabbath and religious forms or ordinances—it is obedience of the commands—it is life."

Such were their views of the substance and forms of religion and religious worship. They attended religious assemblies, therefore, not in respect to creeds and sects, but in respect to the charity which is the soul of all religion.

It is said above, that Jarm rode with the Prestons to the meetings, but it was not every Sabbath that they all rode, or that they all attended meetings. Whether he rode or walked with them, though a slave in law, he became master of ceremonies in fact. He was particularly attentive to his personal appearance and address, and no body-servant handed a lady from his palm to the saddle with greater ease or grace. The slaveholders looked upon him as a liveried slave—the brothers embraced him as a boon companion, the sisters admired his personal appearance and kind attentions. Caste, and pride, and prejudice of color were given to the winds, in the house and in the field. Nor did they make any concessions to slavery in their intercourse and habits, except that Jarm eat and slept separate from the family. The Preston family and estate were a little commonwealth by themselves, which shed their influence upon society, but received nothing in return. No family in that region was more respected, few more wealthy, and none so distinguished for morals and happiness.

It was not strange, therefore, that Jarm was happy in his new condition. He was living, in the order of Providence, upon an oasis in the great Southern Desert. Alone, among white people, his color, instead of excluding sympathy, attracted it, and was a guarantee for the freedom of his faculties and rights. The children had even less regard than their parents for southern sentiment and society. The parents felt their pressure and influence; they did not. For the sake of safety, the former were compelled to respect their forms, while the latter, educated in the domestic circle, found nothing without that circle so genial to their young hearts, and therefore lived and loved it, thoughtless and fearless of the hostile elements that ruled and ruined society around them.

"You will go without your dinner to-day," said Susan playfully to Jarm, on a time when Mr. and Mrs. Preston were absent, "if you don't eat at our table."

"Yes," said Alice, "and supper too, and breakfast and dinner to-morrow."

"Why, you have not set my little table to-day. No matter, I will be a good boy, and wait upon you, and eat when you have done. It will be a pleasure to me."

"You shall do no such thing," said John; "come along and sit here and eat with us. We will adopt our own customs now father and mother have left us to our own responsibilities."

"I would do nothing to displease them."

"Neither would we," said one and all, "but acting on their principle in a thing like this, we should displease them, did we not live out our own sympathies, wishes, and convictions when left to ourselves."

"How is that?" said Jarm.

"Take a seat here and we will talk the matter over."

"I submit to authority of course," said Jarm as he smiled and took a seat between John and Charles at the table.

"We will have a fine time now the government is in our hands," said John.

"Of course we will," said Susan.

"And now let us eat, and talk, and each one free their own mind," said John, as he fell to carving the meat and handing it around.

"But don't we always free our minds?" said Lottie.

"Why yes; we are pretty free to speak and do what we think is about right; that is, we are."

"Who then is not free?"

"To be frank, with great respect to father, I think he lacks a little freedom."

"How is that?"

"I believe if he acted his opinions and wishes he would not have one table for us and another for Jarm."

"Why then does he do it?"

"It is in complaisance to the laws and customs which use and abuse colored people."

"Do you believe that father has any respect for those laws and customs, or the people who make them?" said Lottie, with some spirit.

"By no means; father believes the laws are wrong, and that the people are wrong, and because the people are wrong they make bad laws. So wrong are they, that they do not always regard law or right; as a matter of caution and prudence, therefore, he defers to the customs and prejudices of his bad neighbors, for the safety of his person and property, as well as other things."

"It is hardly just to say that father lacks freedom in the premises. I would rather say he acted from motives of wisdom and prudence."

"But is it wise and prudent to do anything that appears to countenance so bad a thing as slavery?"

"Father does no such thing, we all know. And here we see how unsafe it is to judge a man for a single act or omission, without a knowledge of all the motives that induced it. Our father makes no distinction between Jarm and us, except as our relations or merits vary; and hating slavery as he does, he gives him a table by himself as a seeming concession to the enemy, but as a means in fact of annoying and destroying the enemy."

"How so?"

"It is well known in the country around that father disapproves of slavery; but were he unnecessarily to war with it at points where it is most sensitive, he would gain nothing for freedom, but would lose all opportunity to befriend it; he would destroy the wheat with the tares. An enemy has done this thing, and God's plan is to let them grow together until the judgment; or, in other words, until the means of destruction are certain. That is the order of Providence; it is wise."

"What is wisdom?" said Lottie.

"It is the form of love; in other words, it is the form of which love is the substance."

"But is there no wisdom without love?"

"No, indeed."

"Why not? We have great and learned men, who supply the world with knowledge, and facilitate the business and comforts of life; are they not wise men?"

"If love to man prompts them to communicate the light they get, then are they wise; but if they employ genius to get wealth and fame, or for any other selfish end, then may they have wealth and fame, the thing sought—but the rewards of wisdom, however great the good that results to society, belong to another. They are due only to the influx of divine light which formed and conducted their powers, and of which they were all unconscious. The end of wisdom is good; it is but the external form of love, as truth is the form of goodness, and as faith is the form of charity."

"Knowledge then with charitable ends is wisdom, is it?"

"Certainly. A man may have all knowledge; if he has not charity he is only a tinkling cymbal. He is like light without heat; like the light of winter, which locks nature in ice and glistens on its cold tomb; like faith alone. But wisdom united with love, or faith united with charity, which is the same thing, are in the spiritual world what heat united to light is in the natural world; the heat diffuses a genial warmth through nature, the buds open, the earth teems with vegetables and insects, the birds and beasts marry and multiply and fill the air and fields with life and joy. Love, unregulated by wisdom, would consume mankind with its heat. So light, untempered by heat, would reduce the material universe to a vast ice-berg. They must be united, or the spiritual and natural world will perish."

"But if it is wise and proper for Jarm to eat at that little table, and we at this, when father and mother are here, how is it proper he should eat here, now they are gone? Mind, you, Jarm, I would consent to no other arrangement than this, but I want to understand this affair, that is all," said Lottie.

"All right," said Jarm. "I know you all mean to act properly, and as I am a learner, I am glad you put these questions, for I also want to hear the answer. You will remember that your family is the first school I have been in that had any real regard for me."

"I will answer the question," said John. "It may be as proper for Jarm to sit there now, as when father and mother are at home; but their absence is brief, and the government is in my hands, mainly, while they are gone, and I don't feel bound to violate my feelings or wishes, or yours, in this matter. There is an impropriety somewhere. Father is not responsible for my course. Nobody can make complaint, but the wronged one, and if Jarm's old master don't like it, let him help himself."

"You need not be scared, my good fellow," said Jarm, "If I see any body coming here, I shall certainly arise, and put myself in a position that will not subject my friends to harm."

"You might do so if you pleased, or sit if you pleased, it would please me that you should sit here with us, in such case—but if any such thing occurs, it must be after this, for I now declare this meeting adjourned to evening."

The above is a sample of the conversation of these young people the first time their parents left them alone at home. There was no guile in the young Prestons. They were intelligent and generous and brave. They had no secret in the premises, but duly informed their parents of everything important for them to know.

"Here is a good long winter evening, and how shall we improve it?" said John, after they arose from supper and gathered about the large fire.

The light of day had already disappeared and the candles were lighted. "Give me your pocket handkerchief," said Alice, addressing Jarm. The fair girl bound the handkerchief close about the eyes of its owner, so that she believed he could see nothing, and said:

"There; let us see how expert you are at *Blind Man's Buff*."

"And what am I to do, Alice?"

"You are to catch one of us and tell the name, and then the one caught will be blinded and yourself released; and now do your best."

Although Jarm was nearly domesticated with his young friends, he was not so perfectly so as to be free from embarrassment. Under any circumstances he could not address Alice but as a superior being. For so humble and degraded a thing as he, purposely to put his hand on her person, seemed to him like trespassing on an angel. Nor did he regard Susan or Charlotte with less veneration. Such a commission from the lips of Alice, the most beautiful of the three girls, confounded him. He stood awkwardly for a moment to gather courage, when Charley cried out:

"Stir about my good fellow! You must make an effort or never see the light."

Whether so intended or not, the suggestion had a talismanic effect; it fell upon his ear like the voice of prophecy; his condition as a slave came upon his nerves like a heavy hand upon a stringed instrument. Just at that moment he felt a soft hand upon his back which was instantly removed, and his ear followed a light step and girl's laugh into a corner of the room.

"By the heavens above me!" thought he, "these are delivering angels. Why should I fear?"

He immediately began to move about slowly in the direction of the sound. The bird had flown though and twittered in another place. He then began to feel about and acquaint himself with the room, and becoming used to it, he spread his hands and moved intelligently after his game, which was active and skillful, sometimes dodging under his arms and hardly escaping his touch, until finally practice made him expert, and he had them all fleeing before him, and then at his sudden diametrical move, the girls screamed, finding there was no escape, and Charlotte, and Alice, and Charles were enfolded in his strong embrace. Jarm could not mistake their persons, but as Lottie was the first named, it was voted that she should next be blinded.

The little party now became crazy with excitement, and Jarm, as if in a dream, forgot his condition and embarrassment in the general delight, which was as new to him as visions of a new world. The play was continued—until wearied with its monotony, they took another, and then another, and tried all the child's plays within their knowledge. The fact that Jarm was not of the family, and was a novice in such things, of amiable temperament, and fine appearance and address, though ignorant of letters and society, subjected him to many penalties, and made him the instrument of redeeming many pledges which were forfeited by the rules of these homely amusements.

At precisely ten o'clock, with one accord, the young Prestons dropped their plays, in obedience to the rule on such occasions, and after a brief relaxation and small talk, they all retired to their places of rest.

The experience of a few weeks, ending as the week just passed by Jarm at Mr. Preston's, was like a dream. The rays of the morning, after the scenes just described, had life in them, but it was new life. It entered his soul through those rays, as they softly crept into his eyes and produced sensations such as infants feel, when new light shines into them—with this difference, his mind was intoxicated and dizzied by the effulgence that sped him through the track of lost time towards a tangible, intelligent, and lofty manhood. He could reason, they could not.

Jarm did not as usual drop to sleep that night almost as soon as his head touched the pillow. The facts of the evening stirred in his memory like living things, and combined in his imagination in exciting forms. When morning came, it was difficult to say he had or had not slept; though dreamy and unreal as his state seemed, his energies swelled with delirious power, and he leapt from his bed at an early moment, to restore the order of his brain by actual contact with material things.

"How did you sleep last night?" said Alice, as they were approaching the breakfast table.

"It is difficult for me to say I slept at all."

"Why so?"

"I was playing Blind Man's Buff and other plays all night."

"Of course you were dreaming; did your dreams break your rest?"

"O, no. I could have rested in my dreams until now, if the light had not pried my eyes open."

"Persons as active and robust as you, are generally sound sleepers."

"I rarely know anything two minutes after my head touches my pillow."

"Now, Ally, let me ask you a question. What is the use of the frolic we had last night?" said John.

"You call it a frolic. Well, there is no virtue in terms. You may as well ask what use for children to play in the nursery; the lambs and calves and colts to play in the fields; the kittens to play in the barn; and the chickens in the yard. Our play last evening was obedience to the innocent instincts of nature; an external response to the influx of divine love into the soul; things to be varied or restrained only by sinful loves or harsh tyranny. There! are you answered?"

"How happened it, then, that it kept Jarm awake or plunged him into dreams? There is no use in dreams."

"No use in dreams! Brother, you forget yourself, are not yet quite waked up. Have not our father and mother taught us; do not those books on the shelf teach us; does not the Book of books teach us; and does not our own reason confirm the truth, that there is nothing in Heaven or Hell, nothing in the whole kingdom of God, be it good or bad, that does not perform uses; is it not the fundamental principle of the government of God? Dreams are useful, to prove that the spirit is a substantial, living and acting thing, that the flesh clothes."

"Is that all they prove?" said Lottie.

"No. Among other things, they demonstrate that it is the spirit and not the body that sees, and feels, and smells, and hears, and tastes, as well as thinks and reasons; and that the body, in itself, is as senseless as a corpse. It is the house the spirit makes to live in. If a man's spirit is all sensitiveness when the flesh that covers it is locked in sleep, so also is it when the flesh is locked in death. They are an argument that man never dies. They are daily witnesses of immortality; a constant declaration that the life of man is in the spirit only; that his flesh has no more life in it than the clod on which he treads."

"But if our play was useful and innocent, how happens it that it kept Jarm awake, against the demand of nature for sleep? You have not answered that question yet."

"It may be a necessary experience to teach him what you and I already know. Jarm himself, has told the story; his life explains it; life is not natural with him yet. But if Jarm was kept awake by a new aspect of life, did not you and I sleep the sounder? Did not we give our hearts to our heavenly father with a sweeter confidence for having yielded to his laws?"

"But I want to know, if it made Jarm wakeful to play as he did with boys and girls he never played with before, why did it not also make you wakeful to play with a boy you never played with before; if it made him dream, why did it not make you dream? Many a young lady has been made a dreamer by more trifling incidents than those within your knowledge last night."

"I see what you are at, brother. I appreciate your compliment; but I think it too comprehensive and significant to consist with delicacy for the feelings of others. I hesitate not to say, that, to us, our amusements last night were as truly the bread of life as this toast I am now eating."

"Pardon me, sister. You have gallantly triumphed over my thoughtless badinage. I acknowledge myself defeated and instructed. You are right, and have been all the way through; and since you have done so well, you must instruct to the end. You have now touched a most important point in science as well as theology—and for the sake of your naughty brother and our juniors here, I hope you will say 'What is the bread of life?'"

"It is Goodness. To eat it, is to incorporate it with the spirit or life. Hence, the Lord said, 'I am the bread of life.' 'He that eateth me even he shall live by me.' 'He that eateth my flesh and drinketh my blood dwelleth in me and I in him'—and except ye thus eat and drink 'ye have no life in you.' Flesh and blood correspond to truth and goodness, and those qualities constitute the Lord himself; they are the uncreated substance of God. To eat goodness and truth is to live them and make them ours. Goodness, which is the bread of life, belongs not to a man until he does it. Then he eats it. It forms his will, which is his life. It is incorporated with his spirit."

"But I don't understand," said Lottie, "how our amusements last evening were truth—the bread of life, and all that."

"Whatever is in divine order is good, and of course true. Our amusements last night were in divine order—that is, they were spiritually good—therefore they were true. If you would ascertain whether a thing be true or not, whether it be good—if it be good, it is true—if it is not good, it is false—for truth is but the form of goodness—that is the test. Our amusements were in harmony with every word that proceedeth from the mouth of God, and are therefore a portion of that word. 'The word was made flesh,' the nutriment of the natural man, that we might know there is spiritual substance, life, nutriment, in every word that comes from it."

"Do you mean that God's words are really to be eaten?"

"To be sure I do—not that they can be eaten as we eat flesh. The spirit is nourished by thoughts and affections—the will receives them and lives them out. God's words are truths embodying divine affections, which are the life of angels and good men—the flesh and blood of the scriptures."

"I never could see what nourishment there was in words."

"It is because you don't understand the spiritual body."

"Do make me understand it, then."

"Well, I'll try. If you had been wicked, and told your mother a fib, to keep the truth from her, do you not feel that your spirit would be faint and weak?—that you would be a very coward?—and that innocence and truth only could give you strength to appear before her?"

"Certainly."

"You must come to relish goodness and truth in such case, and receive them into your will, and act them, before you would feel a restoration of courage and strength—before you could present your face to your father on earth, or your Father in Heaven."

"I begin to take the idea. If I love goodness, my heart will take in the elements that compose it, and they will become a part of myself—my spirit will be formed of them, and I shall will and live them all the while. They will be my strength, my life—or, rather, the bread that sustains my life."

"That is it."

"Is that the meaning of the Lord's prayer—'Give us this day our daily bread?'"

"It is nothing else."

"Well, now I understand it—it is beautiful."

"The blessed feature of it is, that God is constantly giving us this bread, and we only eat it when we give it away."

"What?"

"The bread is God's—it comes down from Heaven. It is ours when we live it, do it. Faith without is dead, and charity seeks not its own. Hence the bread is never appropriated until we give it to the hungry."

"O yes, yes, yes! The more you eat of it—that is, the more you give to others—the more you have to give. Is that what is intended by 'the loaves and fishes,' and the 'seven baskets of fragments,' and the 'widow's handful of meal in a barrel,' and 'a little oil in a cruse?'"

"Of course it is."

"But were they not real miracles?"

"Very likely. As regards the truth taught by them, it matters not whether they were or not. They are hieroglyphs—pictures of ideas, or truth in allegory, in the ancient mode of teaching—before letters were used. The greatest miracle is, that the words have an external and internal meaning—and the entire word being so written, makes it an entire miracle."

"Are miracles good for nothing?"

"They compel natural belief, but not rational and spiritual belief, or faith. They cannot be forced. The Jews were so natural and sensual, that they would have profaned the word had it been given them in their own language. Therefore, Christ spoke to them only in parables—the literature of the Ancients, or truth in correspondences—to the intent that the record might be preserved by the few to whom it was 'given to know the mysteries of the kingdom of Heaven,' and to them he explained the parables as they could bear them."

"How do we know that the divine ideas of the Bible are expressed in the pictorial language of the most ancient people?"

"Christ says so, in effect—'I will open my mouth in parables—I will utter things that have been *kept secret from the foundation of the world*.' These are the mysteries that were buried in the fall. Besides, the lost science of correspondence has been found, and modern scholars have corroborated it by the hieroglyphic literature of Egypt and mystic images of Nineveh—a science which exhumes the temples of ancient learning, and deciphers the symbols by which the truths of Heaven were known before the fall.[1] This discovery, shows the Bible to be written according to this lost science, and can be truly understood only in its light—a light which melts the sects into one by the heat of charity, and forms the letter of the word which divides men's minds, into a harmonious and heavenly philosophy."

"According to this, every person must feed from the dish, and eat the same morsel—and each one's appetite increase in proportion to the food he appropriates."

"Certainly—that is the law of charity. The spirit grows in strength and capacity in proportion to the good it imparts. It is that which makes the angels so strong that 'one can chase a thousand (wicked ones) and two put ten thousand to flight.' Spiritual food and natural food differ as spirit and matter; the former is affectional, and of course occupies no space or time; the latter

1. [Editor's note:] Nineveh was a great city in the Assyrian Empire. In the Bible, it is first referred to in Genesis 10:11: "Ashur left that land, and built Nineveh." It is also mentioned in the book of Kings, the book of Chronicles, and the book of Jonah.

is natural, and subject to the laws of matter. The former is substantial and imperishable—the latter material, unsubstantial, without life or motion. But we must defer the conversation for the present."

These young persons now departed to their daily duties—nor did any of them need an overseer, to compel them to perform them.

CHAPTER XV

In Mr. Preston's neighborhood lived a planter by the name of Wilks. He was wealthy, and owned many slaves. He was proverbial for his humanity—particularly for his humanity to colored people. He was thus humane from religious principle, and was as tenacious of the external letter of the Bible as Mr. Preston was of the internal spirit of it. According to Mr. Wilks' notion, the spirit of the word actually lay in the letter. So scrupulous and conscientious was he in this regard, that he maintained the duty of Christians to wash each other's feet, as Christ washed his disciples' feet, related in the 13th Chap. of John. He was a man of eminent sincerity, and by the attractions of his wealth and singular religious persuasions, he drew around him a short lived Christian sect. He built a small chapel for public worship on his own estate, and placed in it a large basin; and every month took his family, slaves and all, there, and they washed each other's feet in the water in the basin for that purpose—literally following the example of his Lord.

In this ceremony of feet baptism, there was no distinction of master and slave. The ablution was mutually performed with equal respect to all conditions, colors, ages and sexes. The master washed his slave's feet, and the slave washed his master's feet—and altogether, they obtained in the neighborhood the sectarian title of 'The feet-washing Baptists.'

When it was reported that a slave was about to be separated from his kindred, by a sale at a distance, it was quite common for this good Mr. Wilks to purchase him (or her) and bring him into this church.

But this church was not composed of Mr. Wilk's family alone. It embraced the whites and blacks all around, bond and free, who were permitted and willing to come into it. It would have covered the whole black population, but for the slave-holders. They despised a sect which condescended to forms so humbling, and which was a manifest reproach upon their lives. The principle obviously demanded a common brotherhood which they could not allow between themselves and the negroes. For such reason, this feet-washing sect was unpopular with slave-holders, and for the further reason that slavery in this church was nominal only—and it was generally understood and believed, that Mr. Wilk's will emancipated his slaves—a sectarian feature eminently odious to the slave owners.

Not many months after Jarm's arrival at Mr. Preston's, Mr. Wilks died, and his church, with its charities, died with him.

On opening his will, in lieu of giving freedom to his christian brothers and sisters, a provision was found in it, ordering that his slaves be sold by families, and not singly, if sold at all. The disappointment of the negroes in not being set free, was pacified by the consideration that they were not to be separated from family connections—the prospect of which fills them with more terror and distress than all the calamities incident to slavery. Death to them is not so terrible. If they become fugitives, they hope to hear from their kindred, and even to see them again—but if they are sold away, hope is extinguished in absolute despair.

In process of time, the Executors of the Wilk's estate advertised its personal property, cattle, horses, hogs, slaves, &c., for public sale. As his personal property—particularly his property in slaves—was known to be large, multitudes from far and near attended on the day of sale. Jarm was there with Mr. Preston, assisting the Executors to collect the dead articles at the auction block. There, too, were the notable slave dealers of Tennessee and Alabama. They had a seat by themselves, and were indifferent to everything until the negroes were brought to the stand.

Among those dealers, Jarm saw the identical fellow who brought him from Manscoe's Creek. His gray hair, and other marks of age did not conceal the antitype prefigured on Jarm's memory. There, too, he saw that other wretch, more hateful still, who purchased and tore from his bleeding mother his little brother and sister.

The poor negroes were chatty and cheerful while the auction was going on—not doubting that they would be sold in families when their turn came. What, then, was their horror and agony, when they found the direction of the will utterly disregarded, and themselves forced on to the block and sold singly. Such shrieks and misery were never before heard, of children, and even babes, torn from their mothers—husbands and wives, parents and children, separated forever!

Col. Wilks, the acting Executor, venerated his father; but he regarded the direction in the will as advisory only, and there was no legal power to enforce it. He was a man of susceptibility and sympathy and predominant love of money. He retired a little from the scene of sorrow, that his eyes might not see it, as the Ostrich hides his head to get away from danger. Thus was this little church of feet-washing Christians broken up and scattered to the winds.

There was one of this ill-fated number who made his mark on this occasion, and deserves a place in history. His name was Jerry. He was about thirty years of age, over six feet high, of the most critical beauty of proportions, quick of motion, of iron muscle and gigantic strength. Shakespeare would say he had the eye of Mars, the front of Jove, and the arm of Hercules. He was a husband and father, but his wife was free, and of course his children, also. Put upon the block, Jerry saw he was about to be struck off to an Alabama trader. He told the trader, in a solemn manner, not to buy him, for that he would never leave his wife and children, and be taken to Alabama.

The trader made no account of Jerry's warnings, and bid him off for the sum of $1250, and handed one of his bullies a set of irons to put on him. Cases of this sort are often met by the bullies and disposed of in short order—for the reason that the slave has too much prudence, or too little pluck, forcibly to assert his manhood.

The bully paid no attention to the threats of the insulted negro, and proceeded at once towards him to iron him. So soon as the bully came within the reach of Jerry's arm, he fell from his fist to the ground, and lay as lifeless and senseless as if he had been kicked under the ear by the hoof of a racer. To all appearance he had fought his last battle, and was taken up for dead. His defiant conqueror now braved a host of enemies, led by his new master, who rushed on him with bludgeons.

Bravely and powerfully did the lion-hearted black man carry the war into the dense ranks of his opposers. At Jarm's stand point, he was seen over their heads, his eye flashing fire, and his strong arm mowing them down and piling them in heaps about him, doing his best to sell his life dear; and, if possible, from their broken bones and bruised bodies, force upon them the lesson, 'He that taketh the sword shall perish by the sword.' But, alas, the heavy blows he received from all quarters were too much for him. Covered with gore, he was about to fall under a dozen heavy and probably fatal clubs, when Col. Wilks, who was also a strong and brave man, learning the condition of his heroic slave, rushed among the assailants, with streaming eyes, exclaiming:—

"Hold up!—for God's sake, hold up!"

"What do you mean, Col. Wilks?" cried a dozen voices.

"I want to compromise this matter, and save this man—there is no use in killing him."

"He has done his best to kill us, and has nearly killed many of us."

"There is nobody killed yet, and the poor fellow now can do no harm," said Col. Wilks, pointing to Jerry, who was bending under his wounds against a post for support, while the blood dropped down his limbs. "Let me see you a moment," he added, turning towards the trader who purchased Jerry.

Col. Wilks was a man of influence, and greatly respected. With one consent the battle ceased, while the trader and the Colonel held a conference apart from the crowd. The conference was soon closed, and they returned and took a position beside the bleeding man, where the trader proclaimed that the affair was amicably adjusted—that he had sold Jerry to Col. Wilks for $1350, and hoped that all parties would be satisfied with the arrangement.

Upon this announcement, a murmur of applause went through the crowd, and though there was no demonstration, it was evident the tables were turned, and that the bearing and bravery of this noble slave had told largely on the sympathies of the multitude.

It was gratifying to Jarm to see respect and homage, so bravely earned, instinctively bestowed upon a fellow slave by white people. It was a lesson to his pride, and helped to nourish in him the already growing American sentiment, 'Resistance to tyrants is obedience to God.'

Poor Jerry, bleeding and wounded as he was, came off victor in the battle. Every gash upon his body, and every drop of blood therefrom, testified to his manliness, and furnished aliment to the ceaseless terror of slave insurrections. Jarm, therefore, felt the victory was partly his own, and almost envied poor Jerry when he saw Col. Wilks supporting him to the little cove in the brook, where the foot-washing slaves performed ablution preparatory to the sacred washing in the temple. There the good Colonel, with his face literally bathed in tears, washed Jerry's wounds until the cove blushed all over with his blood. "When the slave is brave," thought Jarm, "his liberty is secure."

After Col. Wilks had cleansed the poor fellow, he led him to his own house, provided for him nurses and comforts, until his wounds were healed, and then placed him upon an estate—telling him that so soon as he should return $1350, his cost price, he should be free.

"A shocking day this has been on the Wilks estate," said Mr. Preston, while at supper with his family that evening.

"Why so?" inquired Mrs. Preston.

"Don't you believe," said he, "that all the slaves on that estate are sold in different directions, without regard to families?—the children one way and the parents another; and the brothers and sisters another—perfectly regardless of the mind of the testator? And such a scene of distress I never saw before, and never intend to see again."

Here Mr. Preston commenced and detailed all the particulars of the day to his deeply sympathizing family. When he came to the case of Jerry, whose wrongs and manliness he described minutely, particularly emphasizing his noble daring, Susan broke in upon him with the exclamation:—

"Poor, brave fellow!"

"How cruel and wicked to treat people so!" said one and all.

"Ah!" said Mr. Preston, "neighbor Wilks made a bad mistake."

"Why so?"

"At one time he really did intend to emancipate his slaves; and at last, perhaps innocently, because ignorantly, he changed his intent into a plan to keep them together in families, as being the only practical blessing; and now, every good he designed is lost, and their condition is dreadful. His duty was to emancipate his slaves himself. He had no right to intrust their freedom to any being under heaven. God made it a sacred trust to him, and he was bound to execute it—he had no power to transfer it. This blunder has cast a burden upon his spirit which will be difficult to bear."

"Do you believe the spirits of departed men know what is going on in this world?—think you old Mr. Wilks saw the shocking things you saw at his old homestead?"

"To be sure I do. That is the world of causes—this of effects. Angels or good men rejoice when men repent, and do what they can to make them repent. Of course they know what is going on. Devils or bad men in the spirit world feel and work the other way. Don't you remember that the angel, John was about to worship, said to him, 'I am thy fellow servant and of thy brethren?' &c. Good men in the other world are companions and co-laborers with good men in this world—and so with bad men. We are unconscious of it as a general thing, because we are gross and sensuous, and have sunk our spiritual in our natural senses—which is the fall. Now, men look outward through natural organs only, and see exterior and natural objects alone, and have no faculty to perceive the principles which constitute the interior life and essence of those objects. They hardly know that they are spiritual beings—but death will open their eyes, and show them where they are, and who are their companions, co-laborers and servants."

"Did a bad spirit, or devil, as such are called, put it into the head of old Mr. Wilks to change his intention to free his slaves, or did he do it of his own accord?"

"Most undoubtedly it was the work of a bad spirit."

"How, then, is it the work of Mr. Wilks?"

"It is not his work, nor is he responsible for it, unless his love or life harmonized with the love or life of the devil who suggested it. Death separates a man from his sins of ignorance. If his spirit does not approve them, the impassable gulf lies between him and such sins. Sin adheres to those only who love it—it has no hold of those who hate it, though they have been misled to commit it."

"Why, then, should it be difficult for Mr. Wilks to bear it? If he is a good man, will not a consciousness that he is good make him happy—though he be a guiltless instrument of mischief?"

"My words deserve qualification. I said Mr. Wilks had burdened his spirit—the burden may be a blessed one, after all. It is not difficult to see that the greatest joy of the righteous consists in nullifying evils they have done, and in bringing good out of them, from a spiritual and heavenly stand point. The happiness of Mr. Wilks does not result from his own conscious innocence of intent, but from the good he does for the injured. But mind you—the Goodness is God's goodness, not his. It is uncreated, eternal, and flows into men as they are willing to receive and use it. Every good gift comes down from Heaven. It is the essence of such goodness to heal wounds and repair breaches. It is never passive, because God is never passive. If Mr. Wilks is a good man, as I take him to be, then God is in his will in proportion as his will is good. In such case, God, who is goodness, works through him to accomplish his ends. So, you see, a good man is armed with the power of God himself to combat the enemies of goodness; not the man—he is impotent to combat evil; but the divine omnipotence incident to the goodness he welcomes into his soul, that does it. God does all the fighting. The fact that Mr. Wilks was thus misled, stimulates his will, which is his life, (for he who wills much lives much) to extinguish slavery—for God always inflows where there is a will to receive him. And thus the devil unwittingly brings slavery under the weight of the divine omnipotence. The devil can do nothing that is not useful—God permits nothing in his universe that is not useful, and the happiness of the good (so called) is in the act of performing uses. The present happiness of Mr. Wilks, therefore, consists in fighting slavery; and he is, as you see, propelled to fight by the devil himself. 'In vain do the heathen rage!'"

"Then what you call a burden to Mr. Wilks, is only a motive to influence his action?"

"That is it. It is a burden from the fact that he was instrumental to the mischief. So you see, the very burden is itself instrumental to the only happiness of an angelic spirit, to wit, doing good to others."

"I want to know one thing," said Lottie. "What is the reason Mr. Wilks was not right in his form of worship? He did as the Lord did and commanded."

"So the Lord commanded we should eat his flesh and drink his blood."

"What did the Lord mean, then, by washing his disciples' feet, and commanding them to wash each other's feet?"

"Ah, my dear little one you are just as wise as Peter was. When the Lord would wash his feet, he said to Peter, 'What I do thou knowest not now, but shall know hereafter.'"

"But Peter told the Lord he should not wash his feet."

"Just because he was ignorant of the meaning of the thing, as you and most people are."

"Well, what did it mean?"

"Precisely what the same thing meant in the Jewish Church and from Adam down. Jehovah reinstituted it for the Jewish Church, and they did not understand it any better, nor so well, as you and Peter—for they really supposed there was merit in the ceremony. The fact is, it is the expression of a great truth in the symbolic language of the most ancient people—a language which is preserved in both the Old and New Testaments, and from Adam to John the Evangelist. The corporeal man walks with his feet. They are the instruments of his will. Therefore, the term 'feet' among the Ancients, symbolized his spiritual walk or life. So water corresponds to truth—and if a man's walk or life is in obedience to truth, his feet are said to be washed by the Son of Man, who is the Divine Truth itself. In such case, his will being the motive power of the feet, directs them in charity. Therefore the Lord said, 'He that is *washed* needeth not *save* to *wash his feet*—but is clean every whit.' And therefore he replied to Peter, 'If I wash thee not, thou hast no part with me.' If a man's will is right, he will walk or live right—he will keep his feet clean. If men attend to their feet, they may be sure their heads are right. Not the opinions or doctrines, but the walk or lives of men, makes them partners with Christ. There is much head religion now, but precious little feet religion. Men are careful of their brains, and let their feet go to the devil."

"Why could not the Lord have told Peter and the others what the thing meant in plain terms? Why not say it right out, and not use signs which he knew they did not understand?"

"The disciples themselves were not prepared to receive the great truth this hieroglyph contained. It was therefore a cloud to their minds. They had not received the influx of the Holy Spirit which was to illuminate them and show them all things. The Lord, therefore, preserved and protected 'the word' in the antediluvian language. This is the reason he so often says, 'Clouds and darkness are round about him.' He is 'the truth,' and for wise reasons he 'makes the clouds his garment'—that is, he covers the truth of the word in letters which are a cloud to the minds of men. In this sense, innumerable passages, such as these, are intelligible—'The glory of the Lord appeared in a cloud,'—'The Lord descended in a cloud,'—'The Lord appeared to Moses in a cloud,'—'His strength is in the clouds,'—'He bindeth up the waters (which are the truths of the word) 'in clouds,'—'He makes the clouds his chariot,'—'The Son of Man will come in the clouds,'—'A cloud received him out of their sight,' &c., &c. Very few people now believe that Christ comes or goes in literal clouds; but great multitudes begin to see that when they quarrel about the letter of the word (the garment of Christ) the Lord himself disappears in the clouds. The progress of knowledge has opened the understandings and wills of many to see 'The Truth,' THE SON OF MAN, illuminating the letter of the word, which to them is his second coming 'with power and great glory.'"

"You say he makes the clouds his garment—had the Lord allusion to that fact or symbol when he said, 'They parted my garments among them, and for my vesture did they cast lots?'"

"Precisely. The garment is the letter of the word. This, 'the soldiers,' the sects, divide among them; but 'the vesture' is the true internal sense and meaning. They gamble for that, or in Scripture language, cast lots for it, and thus disperse the truths of the Church; but they cannot reach it—therefore it remains unprofaned and seamless."

"That is very beautiful!—but how are we to see Christ coming in the clouds?"

"It is a perception of the internal and spiritual truth which the letter of the word encloses or swathes. Perception is a divine coining or influx into the understanding or intellectual faculty—illuminating the letter of the Scriptures, awakening genius to discoveries in science, prompting inventions to benefit industry, and stimulating humane combinations, for the relief of the poor, the drunken and the enslaved, and the like. These are the tender branches of the budding fig-tree, indicating divinc illumination. The fig-tree, in Bible language, represents the natural good of truth, as the Olive does the celestial and spiritual good thereof. Because the fig-tree bore no fruit—no natural good—the Lord cursed it. So when 'her branch is tender and putteth forth leaves,' he has taught us that these temporal blessings will manifest his coming in the clouds or letter of his word. Christ comes to the minds of men, and is seen by mental eyes. The clouds are in the way now, but they are lighting up."

CHAPTER XVI

The last two chapters give a character of daily life at Mr. Preston's, for the two or three years Jarm lived there. It was a regular succession of industry, amusement and instruction. Before he came there, he delighted to spend his evenings abroad with young colored people in the amusements and dissipations of slave life; but now his inducements were at home, and he wanted no companions but those he found there. Manasseth Logue had so long neglected his claim to him, that his demand was becoming stale, and the Prestons hoped he had abandoned it. Jarm made up his mind to be a fixture in this good family for life. Alice had just taken on herself the duty of teaching him letters, and it seemed to be mutually understood that he had grown into the family, and was not to be separated from it.

On a fine spring's morning, some two and a half or three years from the time Jarm came there, very near the conclusion of one of those table-talks, such as is given in the last chapters, three large and rough men rode to Mr. Preston's, dismounted and fastened their horses, and, after knocking at the door, were invited in. Their aspect and motions were of the bully stamp, veneered with the artificial civilities of southern manners. There was a monitory shuddering felt all through this innocent and happy family. Jarm, especially, felt their presence as a touch of evil. Their looks indicated violent men, associated for a violent end; and though no weapons were visible, it was obvious they were prepared for war.

"It is Mr. Preston, I suppose," said one who seemed to be spokesman of the trio.

"My name is Preston."

"You have possession of a boy called Jarm, who was mortgaged to you by Manasseth Logue, to secure half or the payment of $550, with interest, some two and a half or three years since."

"Yes, sir."

"I have come to pay the mortgage for Mr. Logue, and take the boy back to him. There is $550 in gold and silver, the amount of the principal. The services of the boy, by the terms of the agreement, you were to have in lieu of interest; the money has been counted by these two gentlemen, and it is the true sum."

"Pardon me, sir," said Mr. Preston, "I am not acquainted with you, and though what you say may be strictly true, in a matter of this importance, I ought to have legal evidence that you are the agent or attorney of Mr. Logue, before I commit property of such value to a stranger."

"Very right, sir; there is my authority to represent Mr. Logue in this case," said the man, at the same time putting in to the hands of Mr. Preston a paper, which he opened, and read as follows:

> To whom it may concern. Know ye, I have appointed, and by these presents do appoint the bearer, James Nesbit, my agent and attorney, for me and in my name to pay and cancel a certain personal mortgage, dated —— which Mr. St Clair Preston holds upon my boy Jarm to secure the payment of a loan of $550. And I hereby authorize my said attorney to demand and receive the said boy of said Preston, and do every thing in law that I can or could do in the premises. Dated, &c.,
>
> Manasseth Logue.
>
> *State of Tennessee, &c—*
> Personally appeared before me, this —— day of —— Manasseth Logue, to me personally known, and acknowledged that he executed and delivered the above power of attorney, for the uses and purposes therein expressed.
>
> James Pillow, Judge, &c.

Before this conversation began, Jarm left the room and entered the kitchen, and Charley and the girls soon followed. The disappearance of Jarm awakened the suspicions of the visitors, and at the wink of the leader, his two companions stepped into the court yard and took positions to see any one who left the house. They did not know Jarm personally, but had no doubt of the man.

The impassioned dialogue of these disturbed and terror-stricken young friends, in the kitchen must be left to the conceptions of the reader. Jarm, however, was silent and tearful. His teeth were firmly set, and his countenance told equally of sadness, determination and resistance. His only reply to their numerous expressions of concern, was,

"Don't be disturbed; it is impossible to escape now. These bad men are armed with pistols. They are probably provided with irons; it is prudent to seem to be submissive. You must not be implicated in my wrongs; alone, I can bear them; half of them would crush me if the other half were on you. But mark me! I will not be a slave. My grief is that I must leave you." Here his lips quivered and his voice fell, but his prudence checked the surging sorrow, and with clenched fists, and swelling bosom, and determined emphasis, which shook his whole frame, he repeated in a low voice, "if I live, I will be free; I will not be a slave!"

When Mr. Preston had finished reading the power of attorney, he returned it to Mr. Nesbit and said, "it seems sufficient. If you take Jarm you will leave it with me of course."

"Certainly."

"Mr. Logue let his claim lay so long we began to suspect he had abandoned it."

"Great mistake. He values Jarm $1,000 at least, and is far from parting with him for half the sum."

"I can hardly think he will demand all that. My family are much attached to him, and for that reason I would pay any reasonable sum to retain him."

"Impossible!" said the man doggedly. "To tell the truth, Mr. Logue is displeased with the mode Jarm has been living here, and will not sell him to you on any terms."

"I am sorry Mr. Logue's feelings are unfavorable. It is true, Jarm has been useful to us and is an excellent fellow. I have treated him accordingly, and my family are loth to part with him; nor will they if they may retain him on reasonable terms."

"Altogether impossible! you may depend on't; at all events, if it is possible, you will have to treat with Logue. I have no authority of that sort; my duty is to take the boy and return him. That was him I suppose, who went into the other room just now."

"Yes, sir."

"Then there is your money and my authority to take him, and I demand Jarm."

"Of course I submit to the law and wait an early opportunity to confer with Mr. Logue in the matter; my legal rights are at an end, and I have nothing more to say."

The man bared his pistols, and was about opening the door into the room where Jarm and the family were.

"Stop," said Mr. Preston, "you will terrify my daughters. Please be seated. I will deliver Jarm to you, and guarantee you shall have no difficulty. Let me go and see him."

The man bowed politely.

"Certainly sir. All right sir."

Mr. Nesbit resumed his seat and spirted his tobacco juice into the fire, while Mr. Preston repaired into the other room, where all the family were collected. He entered in time to catch the last words of Jarm's above speech.

"I presume you know what these people are here for," said Mr. Preston to Jarm.

"O, yes. I am to be taken back to my old master. It is a dreadful disappointment; but I made up my mind to submit to it at once, and look to future possibilities for deliverance."

"Your conclusion is wise; we all love you Jarm, (here sighs and sobs were heard all around the board)—hush!" said Mr. Preston, "we must not let these men know how deeply they have afflicted us; nor show them any signs of it, if possible." Turning to Jarm, he said, "You need no other proof than you see around you now, and have always witnessed since you have been with us, that we love you; nevertheless, I have it in my mind to deliver you, if possible, from your bad case. You have gained our hearts by your qualities and conduct, and I shall be prompt to befriend you." Mr. Preston gave Jarm his hand as a pledge of fidelity, and added—

"Now we must be brief; good-bye, Jarm; my wife and children had best part with you here. I am sorry to say you need to do it at once, and prepare to leave with these men."

Having said this, Mr. Preston returned to Nesbit, and the family embraced their friend and bade him with tearful eyes and failing voices. The family never left the room until Jarm was packed and started away. They could not show themselves to the ruffians who had robbed them of their friend and companion. Jarm parted with them and appeared before the agent with his baggage, and said he was ready.

At this moment Mr. Preston said to Nesbit:

"You are prepared to put irons on Jarm, I suppose?"

"O, yes. The inference was the boy had been spoiled by you and your family, and might attempt to escape; therefore we brought the tools to secure him; indeed we always carry the tools with us."

"I want to ask one favor of you. I know there is no necessity of using those irons. Jarm has been a faithful boy since he lived with us. Mr. Logue will certainly find him improved, not injured. My family would be very sorry to see him go away in irons, and therefore I pledge you my honor as a man, that I will pay double damages for all losses that may occur from allowing him to return without shackles. He may walk or ride, with you or without you, and I am bound he shall return to his old master with all reasonable expedition. Mr. Logue may suffer no more harm in allowing him to return alone, than he did in sending him here alone. This I guarantee, upon the honor of a gentleman, and the strength of my estate."

"I am happy to oblige you," said Nesbit. "There is a mistake about this business. You are a gentleman, sir; I am a rough man, but know a hard case as soon as I get my eyes on it. I knew you were none of that sort the moment I saw you, and the short time I have been here gives me a high opinion of you. Old Manasseth has made a blunder this time. Jarm shall have a free passage home, and I shall represent his case and your case, so as to restore you and Jarm to his confidence."

"Thank you. Please accept this," handing Mr. Nesbit a half eagle, "as a signal of good will, and a happy termination of our affairs."[1]

Mr. Preston understood such fellows, and therefore knew that a trifling bribe would be twenty times its value in restoring Jarm to the confidence of his master, by means of the representations of Nesbit.

"Jarm, you may leave your duds with us and go ahead," said Nesbit, as he opened the door into the court yard, "we have an errand a little off the road, but we will overtake you or be home before you."

Jarm roused all the strength of his heart as he raised his hat to Mr. Preston and said "good bye," but in spite of him the big tear welled up under his eyelids, and his counterfeit voice failed of its intended emphasis; but when he turned to close the gate behind him into the street, and saw in the window the faces he was to see no more, all full of emotions he was attempting to suppress, his head fell by the weight of sorrow, and he turned and wept like a child as he walked away, turning again once only, while in sight, to drink through his eyes a last draft of agony from the loving hearts who were looking after him, from the only spot on earth which was now precious to him.

"Boys," said Nesbit to the two men in the yard, "let Jarm pass. It is all right; I have arranged with Mr. Preston that he shall be delivered safely. We

1. [Editor's note:] The half eagle is a US coin that was produced for circulation from 1795 to 1916 and in 1929. Composed almost entirely of gold, it has a face value of five dollars, but it quickly became worth more than its face value because of the rising price of gold.

have an errand at George's, you know," giving the wink. "Good bye, Mr. Preston."

"Good morning," said Mr. Preston, as he closed the door and retreated to his family.

"How is this? Here is quite a change of affairs," said one.

"This yellow boy is a part of the explanation," said Nesbit, as he tossed the gold Mr. Preston gave him. "It is an ample check for a draft of George's best whiskey, and good evidence that Preston is not the scamp old Manasseth takes him to be. It ain't the first time the old scoot has been fooled. Preston is as good a man as ever buckled; and as for Jarm, he is as true a fellow, you may depend on it. I would trust him for wit or honesty any time, before I would his master. The fact is, Manasseth made a blessed bargain for himself, and Jarm too, when he mortgaged him to Preston. He has made a first rate nigger of him, and Manasseth would have spoiled him, had he kept him."

"Then you ain't afraid to let the boy go back alone?"

"Pshaw, no. Old Preston's word is better than the Bank, and the fact that he has given it, is the best indorsement a nigger can have in these diggins. Every body knows him, and he must be a bad nigger indeed who is faithless to him after living with him two or three years."

"Why so?"

"Because he is reasonable, kind, just, merciful and everything else a man should be. I have heard the same said of him for years. Old Manasseth is the first I ever heard speak ill of him, and I have no doubt he was poisoned by some rogue. I need no more than the brief time I had with him to know he is not overestimated by the public. To tell the truth, his face, yes, and voice, had so much goodness and charity in them, that I was unhorsed—completely awed and floored. I tell you what, boys, if I was to live with that man two years, I believe I should be a good man myself. I feel that I am a good deal better for this interview."

"Pshaw!" said one "I saw much more to like in the girls than I did in the old man. I but squinted at him; but by Jippers! I couldn't keep my eyes off them while they staid in the room."

"O, you rogue; you didn't see enough to get a slight impression of the merits of that family. I tell you a white man or a black man can't live in it without growing good. It seems as if we had been disturbing a little heaven."

"I guess a drop of George's whiskey will cure all the disturbance it has made upon our souls."

"D—n the whiskey! To go from Preston's to George's is like passing out of Paradise into a hog sty."

"Well; here we are! Shall we go in among the swine, or stay here and dream of angels?"

Nesbit turned the gold in his hand and replied:

"Ah! you yellow rascal! You are the root of all evil! Here goes!" leading his fellow companions into the drinkery.

CHAPTER XVII

"This is too much—I cannot stand it. I could have lived there forever—I expected to have spent my days there. I desire nothing better than life with those good people. I can think of nothing worse than to be driven back to my old master and his family. I will not bear it—I will not be a slave. Henceforth I live to escape or perish! Had I supposed I was coming to this, I would have plotted with my friends and fled. I know they would have so advised if they anticipated this—and now, COME DEATH OR FREEDOM!"

The fore part of the above speech passed in Jarm's mind unuttered, as he was plodding his way to his old home from Mr. Preston's; but the last sentence leaped out of his mouth, and he spoke it audibly and with emphasis—not dreaming any one heard him. Alice often told him 'thoughts are heard in Heaven,' and there he was willing to be heard. But so filled was he with sad and indignant emotions, that he was unconscious of things about him, until awakened by a hand on his shoulder that made him start.

"Hallo, friend!—a little too loud. There are things a colored man may think, but not speak above his breath, until his eyes and ears assure him he is alone. What is up now?"

"You scare me!" ejaculated Jarm, as he grasped the hand of Mr. Wilk's Jerry, whose story we told along back.

"What's the matter, my good fellow? Where are you going? You look sad—what's up?"

"Did you hear me say anything?"

"Aye—aye, I heard you say a great deal in few words. 'Henceforth, death or freedom' is not a long story, but it is a great deal for a slave to say, as loudly and unguardedly as you said it just now. I only dare repeat it in an under tone—not because I am more a coward than other folks, but because I may be overheard by a poorer friend than you are."

"Jerry," said Jarm, looking him sadly and firmly in the face, "I know I may trust you. Did you ever think seriously of fleeing to a free State?"

"Think of it!—I have been thinking of it for ten years. I think of it every day—I am thinking of it to-day. If it was not for my poor wife and child, Tennessee would not hold me a month."

"Then you have a wife and child? I determined long ago never to marry until I was free. Slavery shall never own wife or child of mine. I pity you."

"I deserve it—they are the chains that hold me here. The links about my heart are stronger than the irons about my limbs. Were it not for the former, I would say as you did, 'Henceforth, death or freedom.' But where are you going?—explain yourself."

"I am going back to my old master—and what I want is to get into a free State and be free. I am determined—I am desperate!"

"I thought you were to live with Mr. Preston always?"

"I thought so, too."

"You were happy there?"

"O, too happy! I could have lived there forever. They are good people. The disappointment is greater than I can bear, and I won't bear it. I won't live with my old master. The worst he and his helpers can do is to kill my body, and that will free my soul. I learned many valuable lessons with those good people, and that is one of them. I tell you, Jerry, I will make a strike for freedom, if I die for it. I had rather die than be a slave."

"Well—but your mother, brothers and sisters—will you leave them?"

"Yes. As your wife and child are the only chains that bind you, so my mother, brothers and sisters are the only chains that bind me. It is bad to be bound to slavery by irons, but it is worse to be bound to it by heart-strings. Those strings will be stronger and sounder when I am clear of the incarnate devil that torments me and my family. I can do my mother, brothers and sisters no good while I am his slave—they can do me none. Life is a constant looking for evil to come. Besides being personally abused and outraged, we are liable to be sold apart forever, any moment. To be of any service to my mother or myself, I must be free; and I will be free, or die—so help me God!"

"Jarm, you are right. Were it not for my obligations to Col. Wilks, and prospect of buying myself, I would join you in a moment."

"Why not do it now? What obligation is on you to buy yourself? Necessity may make it a duty and an obligation—but he is a villain who created that necessity. God gave you freedom, and Col. Wilks has no right to make conditions to the grant. You are just the fellow I need to co-operate with me; have prudence, courage, and strength—together we can make our way to a free State, by endurance, stratagem, and bravery—I feel certain of it. In freedom, we may contrive for the deliverance of our kindred—as slaves, we see nothing but helplessness and despair. We must be free. Think of this until we meet again, if you are not prepared to act now."

"That I'll do. Indeed, I cannot help thinking of it, for the proposition sets my soul on fire; but when I approach the subject, another thing stares me in the face."

"What is that?"

"Col. Wilks saved my life when those bloody tigers were murdering me."

"What of that? He ought to have done more than that—he should have given you freedom, after all the money you have worked out for him with your hard hands. Your claim on him is infinitely greater than that he should not stand by and see you murdered. Mind you, Wilks was the man that thrust you in among those tigers."

"You are right, Jarm. I see it, but he don't—and the white people all around won't see it. It is so, I know; but after all, a sense of honor presses hard on me. I do owe life to him, that is a fact."

"You owe him nothing, Jerry. You dishonor God who gave you life, and to whom alone you are indebted for it, by talking as you do. Col. Wilks owes you freedom, without which life is a burden—and yet he demands of you money, a most unreasonable sum of money, before he allows you to have and enjoy it. Pretty story, that he and his father may rob you all your life long, and then bring them wild beasts upon you, and make a merit of saving you out of their paws."

"Jarm, we must part here—I'll think the matter over. Do you know John, of the Farney estate?"

"I know him well."

"He's the man to engage in the affair."

"Exactly."

"We'll see him. Good bye,"—and thus they parted.

Jarm was five miles from the Tombigbee. As a matter of prudence, he must seem to be glad to return—though the thought was hateful, and stirred all the desperate activities of his soul. He was soon there, and went through the ceremony of servile bows and counterfeit smiles to his master and mistress, and other false expressions of gladness. His mother, brothers, sisters and friends greeted him with tears of joy. Nesbit and his party had proceeded him, and given Manasseth a high opinion of his improvement and abilities, and he was readily installed the confidential servant and head man of the plantation.

Nor did he dishonor the station. His stay with the Prestons was to him a school of agricultural education, and he was eminently fitted to the trust. Under him the farm was put in better order than it had ever been—the fences were repaired or built anew—the grounds were prepared in season for the seed, and the budding grain and grasses and fruits promised an abundant harvest. Jarm affected the same care for the interests of the plantation that he would for his own, and this obtained from his master the greatest confidence, kindness and indulgence that a surly, selfish, drunken man can feel or allow to a cherished and valued chattel.

Of course all this industry and care on the part of Jarm, was adroitly counterfeited as a means to an end. Under cover of it, he was plotting to run away, and the hope of success only made it endurable. He now felt how unfortunate it was the Prestons had not anticipated his case, and informed him of the way to a free State—a piece of knowledge he valued above all things.

In the neighborhood of Manasseth's dwelt a family of poor whites, who, originally of Tennessee, had lately returned from Illinois, where they had emigrated, because they preferred Tennessee, or because they had not the means to get a possession and meet the difficulties of their enterprise.

This family resided some three years in Illinois, and the eldest child, now a boy about ten years old, often came in contact with Jarm. The family were very poor, and though white, had no means to claim superiority to an influential and trusty slave.

"How you have grown, John!" and Jarm to the lad. "Where have you been this long time?"

"I have been up to Illinois—we have all been there this two or three years."

"Where is that?"

"I shan't tell you."

"Pshaw! you don't know yourself—there ain't any such place as Illinois." This was the first time Jarm had heard of Illinois, and he meant to sift the geography and character of it from the lad.

"I say there is such a place!—don't you think I know?"

"What kind of a place is it, then? Let us see if you can tell anything about it."

"All the negroes are free in Illinois—they don't have any slaves there."

"Did you see any free negroes in Illinois?"

"Yes, a good many."

"What were they doing?"

"Why, they lived with their families, like other folks."

"Which way from here is Illinois?"

"Up that way," said the boy, pointing to the north-west.

"How many days does it take to go there?"

"We were a good many days coming home—but a man could go there on horse-back in less than a week."

"Do you have to cross rivers?"

"O yes, a good many—the Ohio River lays between Illinois and Kentucky. You have to go over that in a boat. It is a great river, and vessels are sailing up and down it all the while, except in the winter—then it is frozen over, and sometimes the boys skate on it, and horses and sleighs pass over on the ice."

Many other questions Jarm put to the boy, and elicited all he could of life in Illinois. He did not doubt the boy's truthfulness. The story charmed him, and he made up his mind to prepare to go there, where he might go and come as he pleased, and earn a house and home and farm with his own strength and mind.

About a mile from Manasseth's plantation was an old building, made of logs and slabs and boards rudely put together, for a school house, and meeting house for the methodists to hold meetings in. The floors consisted of hewed timbers, and the roof was covered with boards—swallows and wrens built their nests and chattered and warbled to their young in the roof and beams—while the bats huddled in the corners or hung in swarms from the rafters in the day time. This site was selected for the rough temple on account of its retired and wild position. The sect who fixed it up have a penchant for the forest, where "nature worships God in solitude, alone." The site of this building was flanked on the West and North by a formidable ridge of rocks, covered with vegetable mould which had been growing for ages, until it sustained stunted vines and bushes. Little streams of pure water enriched the sunbeams as they danced down its sides and sank into the gloomy woods, and formed a little brook at its base, in which small trout played to the very edge of the rocks.

Some quarter of a mile from this solitary temple, a huge flat rock projected from the mountain and entirely covered the little brook. It entered the mountain like a gigantic shaft, and descended towards the earth in an angle of about forty-five degrees, until its outer circumference dwindled to an edge a few feet from the surface of the brook, and spread over its entire breadth. This rock supported a thick fleece of aged moss, tightly woven with roots of green shrubbery which hung like a heavy blanket from its outer edge, and covered the water two rods or more, the breadth of the shaft. Under this cold roof lay a broad dark cavern, a fit retreat for wild beasts and savage men.

Some eighteen months after Jarm left Mr. Preston's, in a bright moonlight evening, after the sun had disappeared about half an hour behind the mountain, a solitary man merged from the dark woods and stood before this sylvan sanctuary. The shades of the mountain and forest intercepted the moonlight and concealed his identity and color. His deep, broad chest and frame, erect head, elastic, careful and firm step, evinced a great amount of strength, and his motions indicated that his eyes and ears were on the watch for some expected person or thing. He was about six feet high, a trifle below the height of Jarm, and somewhat broader. His anatomical proportions were compactly bound together with abundant muscle, showing, even in moonlight, evidence of great personal strength.

The man had been looking about a short time, when he heard the sticks crack under the cautious but heavy tread of another, whose large body appeared in sight, and stood a moment like a black picture on a dark back ground. He looked about him, and then gave a shrill whistle, which was instantly replied to by the first comer, as a signal of recognition and safety.

"Well, John, you are here before me," said Jerry, as he heartily locked hands with the first comer.

"Yes, I have been here some minutes. Where is Jarm?"

The reader will recognize in John the person spoken of by Jerry when Jarm was returning from Mr. Preston's.

"Jarm will surely come. The meeting was arranged by him, and he never fails."

"Of course, nothing will prevent him. If his master does not, he will be here in five minutes."

"Hark!"

"There is something coming!"

"Keep still!"

"There he is—it is a man—it is Jarm!"

Whistle answered whistle again, and the parties were immediately together.

"Here we are," said Jarm, "now for business."

"Talk low."

"Shall we go into the house?"

"No—better be heard here than there. If the white niggers find us there, they will be sure there is something in the wind. Follow me."

Jarm led them down the brook a quarter of a mile or so, and entered the cavern before described.

"Here we shall be neither seen or heard," said Jarm, as he struck up a light. "I lead you here because we shall need a place of deposit as well as conference, by and by, where we can be neither seen or heard by anyone not in the cave itself, and which is probably unknown in the neighborhood."

"This is a beautiful place for our business," exclaimed both of his companions.

"If we determine to quit this country for Illinois, or other place where masters can't wrong us," said Jarm, "and my mind is made up and has been a long time—we shall need a place not only to talk about it, but to deposit things necessary for our journey as we may get them. And now, boys, what say you to the main question—SHALL WE GO?"

"I shall go if I go alone," said John. "Come what will, I am resolved to get out of this country—life is worth nothing here. I had rather lose it in an attempt to escape, than to be eternally dying—that is my mind in the matter."

"I am with you," said Jerry. "The only trouble with me is my wife and children, and the means to be off, as I have often told you. But I am fixed—my wife and children are free—and if I get my freedom, they may come to me. I can do little or nothing for them here."

"One point is settled, then," said Jarm. "We are agreed to escape—that point is easy to arrive at—others are not so easy. It remains to know what provisions will be needed for the journey, and how we shall get them, and when and how to get off."

"We must have each of us a good horse, saddle and bridle, large saddle-bags of provisions and clothing, and an amount of money," said John.

"Yes, and we will need free passes, if we can find any body to counterfeit them."

In all these respects they allowed they were nearly or quite destitute, and that it would require time to make the preparations.

Jarm and John said, as to horses, saddles and bridles they were at ease. Each of their masters owned a crack young saddle horse of great value, which they much petted, and which were in their special care, and they often rode them in company on short excursions. They were of course acquainted with the abilities and habits of the noble animals. But their clothing, provisions and money, required time, care and industry to procure.

"May be it will be a year before we finish these preparations. In the mean time if our masters sell their horses, they will get others, there are a plenty of good horses among the man robbers all around, and we must take the best we can lay our hands on."

"It will be hard," said Jerry, shaking his head—"indeed it is impossible for me to take Col. Wilks' horse—it seems to me I shall forfeit my life if I do it. I owe something to the Colonel for saving me from those murderers. I cannot feel justified in rewarding it by running away with his property. You will take your own when you take your master's horses, or anything else they have—their lives, even. Not so with me—I must get a horse elsewhere. The memory (of what, under the circumstances, would be deep ingratitude) would torture me, and make my life a burden, did I turn my hands against the Colonel and his property. I could not bear it—I won't do it."

"All right—there is much reason in what you say. Did you take the Colonel's horse, or anything else of his, (yourself excepted) it would be used as an argument against our honour and justice. We should avoid doing that which will make them regret having done us favors. It will look better if you leave the Colonel's horse from a sense of gratitude, and take the horse of that villain Myrrick, who lives near him, and abuses his slaves so. There will be a meaning in the act which slaveholders will understand. The transaction will speak for our virtues. Though Col. Wilks is indebted to you beyond the value of all his horses, you are right, and wise in principle and policy, in your conclusions."

To the above sentiment all conceded.

"Well, then, we understand each other," said Jarm; "and for aught I see, the business of the evening is finished, and we may go home and plan to execute it."

"By the way," said John, "you know Ross, the poor, good old man, who lives on the corner of the woods by Col. Pillow?"

"Of course I know him—everybody knows him. While one hand was busy pouring a large estate down his throat, the other was equally busy giving it to the poor."

"He is the black man's counsellor and friend."

"Yes, and the white man's, too. Poverty will degrade any other man in Tennessee but Ross—his qualities keep him out of the reach of disgrace. Drunkard as he was, and poverty-smitten as he is, the whites love him for his nobleness, the blacks for his goodness."

"Won't he counterfeit a pass for us?" said Jarm.

"Of course he will—I have no doubt of it. But we must pay him for it."

"Pay him!—yes, liberally. He has wife and children who need bread and meat; and it will cost us nothing—that is, it will cost John and me nothing to get them for him. Our masters have robbed us of the fruits of our labor, and filled their barns and smoke-houses therewith. We have nothing to do but to take it and pay our debts with it. We can afford to supply his family with bread and bacon for six months, if he will make each of us a pass."

"Now this thing must be attended to. John, you know how to manage the card with Ross—he lives on your land, or near it—will you do it?"

"Indeed I will; and trust me I will do it right, and neither of you will be committed until the time comes."

"Now, then, let us go home—it is getting late. We shall meet again on the Sabbath, and in the mean time, if either has anything new, it is easy to find the others and give it to them."

Thus ended the first conference of these young men in regard to their escape. They walked together a little distance to the highway, and there parted in the direction of their homes. When they arrived there and lay down on their beds, the reflection that they were committed to each other, and to a measure, which, if pursued, would give them freedom, or send them in chains to the far South, or to the grave, kept them from immediate sleep. As each reflected on the peril of the case, he felt the embryo stir of a noble manliness, which, for a long time, resisted the advance of "nature's sweet restorer."

CHAPTER XVIII

The subject that now occupied Jarm's mind was to get money to run away with. One plan was to purchase a barrel of whiskey, and retail it at profitable prices. One afternoon, soon after his compact with his two friends, Manasseth and his wife went to visit their preacher, whose term had expired, and who was to leave for another place on the circuit the next day. Jarm embraced that opportunity to use his master's oxen and cart to bring from the distillery a barrel of whiskey, and place it on the premises out of his master's sight, where he might retail it and make money.

But the misfortune was, he was unable to complete the thing before his master's return. When Manasseth came home about eleven o'clock at night, he saw his team and cart were missing; and scarcely had he made the discovery, ere he saw Jarm coming at a distance with them. Supposing he was unseen by Jarm, he skulked in a corner of the fence, to watch his actions and get his secret. But Jarm was familiar with every object about, and with a keen eye on the look-out, saw at a distance the black spot in the fence, and scented his condition at once.

Here was a grave disappointment. He knew he should have a flare-up with his master, but by no means anticipated so serious a flare-up as the one he had. He supposed his master would rob him of his whiskey and get drunk on it—that he had made a bad speculation, and should be badly scolded, and that would end the matter.

Jarm drove his team past his master, while he was hid as aforesaid, in a natural and usual manner—passed the place where they were to be turned out, directly to the negro-house, and there rolled out his whiskey and deposited it under the floor, and returned to put out his oxen.

"Where have you been with my oxen?" said Manasseth, getting out from the fence.

"I have been down to the distillery to get a barrel of whiskey."

"How dare you steal my team to do your work?"

"Had you been here I supposed you would let me have the oxen; I did not suppose I should displease you. Had I so supposed, I would not have taken them."

"I'll learn you to steal my team and go off in that way! Turn them into the lot—I will see you in the morning."

And so Jarm did, and went to bed himself—but not to sleep, for he feared the loss of his property, and a conflict with his master more or less serious. Tired nature eventually overcome his senses, and he fell into refreshing slumber—from which he was soon awakened by the light and stir of the morning. He arose and made his master's fire, and went into the field to work without waiting for breakfast.

While in the act of making the fire, his master got up and left the house, and went straight to the woods and brought a bundle of whips, and laid them by the tree which was his usual whipping post. In the meantime, he sent Jarm's little sister to bring him some ropes. While Ann, all unconscious of the use for which the ropes were intended, brought and deposited them under the tree, Manasseth went to Jarm, who was working with great earnestness, and called him. Jarm affected not to hear. He called still louder, and Jarm, as if suddenly sensible of his master's presence, exclaimed:—

"Did you call me, master?"

"Yes, I called you. Why didn't you answer me? I'll wake you up!—follow me into the yard."

Manasseth passed on to the place of execution, and Jarm followed. When Jarm come into the yard, his mad master stood there, with the cords in his hands, and the bundle of sticks at his feet. The only clothing Jarm had on was his shirt and pantaloons.

On his way to this place, Jarm reflected upon the possibility that his master would attempt to tie and flog him, and resolved, come what would, he would not submit to it. He was willing he should take him on the leg and whip as long as he pleased—giving him a chance to dodge the blows. But he firmly resolved not to be tied and whipped by a mad man, or any other man. A few days before this he had a terrible experience on this point.

A neighboring planter's slave, provoked by jealousy, made a terrible assault upon him; and Jarm was compelled, in his own defence, to give him serious blows that disabled the assailant. Thereupon, the owner of the slave complained to a Justice of the Peace, and Jarm was convicted by the testimony of the jealous and perjured one, and sentenced to receive thirty-five lashes on his naked back, and Manasseth was adjudged to pay a sum in damages. The ridges on his back were still tender, and the agony in that case determined him never again to suffer mortal man to tie him up and flog him.

"Take off your shirt, you black rascal! I'll learn you to steal my oxen in the night and get whiskey! Off with your shirt!"

Jarm folded his arms and looked his master full in the face, with a steady and firm gaze.

"Don't stand there staring at me, you black dog! Off with your shirt, or I'll whip it off—hide and all!"

Jarm still stared and scowled at his master, but made no move to take off his shirt.

"You black scoundrel!—don't you mean to take off your shirt?"

"No!" growled Jarm, with a voice more like a provoked lion than a man.

Manasseth was now irritated beyond measure, and approaching Jarm with a rope, his face and eyes flashing fire, cried out:—

"Cross your hands, you rascal."

Jarm stood firmly and silently as before, his large muscles crawling on his great folded arms, and his eyes fixed boldly and defiantly on his master, who, by this time, trembled with uncontrollable frenzy.

"Cross your hands, or I'll take your life, you d—d black dog!" roared Manasseth, raising a large gad,[1] and aiming a blow at Jarm's head with all his strength.

Jarm avoided the blow by a motion of his head and body, and Manasseth, unable any longer to control his passion, flew at his bold and indignant slave to collar him, muttering in his rage:—

"Won't you cross your hands when I command you, you insolent rascal?"

Jarm growled out again, louder than before, a defiant "No!" At the same time he seized the mad man by the throat with one hand, and his breech with the other.

"Let me go!—let me go!" cried the terrified Manasseth, thunderstruck that his slave dare put hands on him.

"I'll let you go, and I'll go myself!" growled Jarm, both hands still clenched into him as aforesaid, and placing his right knee to his breech to aid his hands, he raised him from the ground and pitched him half a rod onto his head, turned on his heel, and ran for the woods.[2]

It is unnecessary to say that this transaction greatly disappointed and embarrassed both parties. Jarm was in no condition to attempt an escape,

1. [Editor's note:] According to John Brand's *Observations on the Popular Antiquities of Great Britain: Chiefly Illustrating the Origin of Our Vulgar and Provincial Customs, Ceremonies, and Superstitions* (London: George Bell and Sons, York Street, Covent Garden, 1877), a gad whip is an ox whip approximately ten feet in length. "Gad" is an Old English (Lincolnshire) measurement of ten feet, lending its name to the whip (1:131).

2. [Editor's note:] A rod is an Old English measure of distance equal to 16.5 feet, so Loguen is claiming to have thrown Manasseth approximately 8–9 feet.

and Manasseth in no condition to dispense with his abilities and labors. This extraordinary and daring onset on him, opened his eyes to the positive, manly, and uncompromising character of his slave. The onset had not personally injured him, but it brought him to his senses. Jarm fled out of his sight, but his gigantic form, determined look, and courageous bearing, remained daguerreotyped on Manasseth's memory, and awakened his respect. He felt that, though in Jarm's hands he was as a child, he had only put him out of his way—rather rudely, to be sure—under the highest provocation. To pursue and punish him, he saw would be to drive his chafed spirit to a desperate extremity, and that he should thereby lose him. He concluded, therefore, not to pursue him. Left alone, he believed Jarm would wander in the fields until his passions cooled, and then return to his labors, where he was greatly needed.

Thus was Manasseth disciplined to submission by the decision and bravery of his slave. Should all other slaves, or any considerable portion of them, manifest the same dignity and spirit, their masters would succumb to their manhood and give them freedom, or treat them justly—which, in effect, is to free them. Slavery can endure no longer than its victims are submissive and servile.

All ignorant was Jarm of the change in the mind and feelings of his master. On one point, at least, he had made him a sensible man; but Jarm did not know it. He fled to the woods, not doubting Manasseth was stimulated to the highest point of passion, and that he would rally the slave-catchers to hunt and shoot him; or, what was worse, return him to be scourged and tortured, and sold to Georgia. Of course he was in no condition to escape—he resolved, therefore, to go directly to the cave, the only attainable place of security, and consider what he could do, and what he had better attempt. Though he did not expect his project to escape would be so soon and seriously embarrassed, he did not regret that he had done what he did do. He hoped he had taught his master that to attempt to tie and flog him, was neither safe or wise, if he would retain him in his service. He had counted on the profits he should derive from the sale of his whiskey to increase his little capital to run away with—and he now concluded that the capital and profits together were sacrificed.

Though some masters were ashamed to get drunk on their slaves' whiskey, he knew his master was afflicted by no such delicacy. Right well he judged on that point. That very day Manasseth filled his jug with Jarm's whiskey and got drunk with it. Indeed the liquor was quite a pacificator, and through its taste and stimulus plead for Jarm. During all the time he continued away, it lay upon his master's mind like a charm, and held him in a dozy and contented negligence of Jarm and his affairs.

As has been before said, Jarm was in no condition to run away. He was without money or clothing beside the shirt and pantaloons he had on. The country, as he supposed, was notified of his elopement, and on a look out to take him. After examining the interior of the cave, as well as he could without light, and piling a quantity of leaves near its mouth for a resting place, he threw himself upon it, and began to study what to do. He felt that he was without a master, but his freedom was uncomfortably circumscribed and inconvenient. It would be hard to live it twenty-four hours, as he was nearly destitute of clothing and entirely destitute of food or the means to get any.

His destitution determined him to find at once some reliable friend to assist him in his emergency. It was now the forepart of a warm day in the spring, but he dare not expose himself in the sunlight, and must wait for darkness to cover him before he sought that friend. He knew hunger would overpower him at noon, and torment him until evening—and he could think of no antidote to its demands but roots and barks.

Never did Jarm rejoice more to see the sun go down than on that afternoon. So soon as the shades fairly covered the woods and fields, he took his course for John Farney's. John's master's name was John Farney, and he named his slave John. Because he was believed to be the son of his master, the colored people called him John Farney. Jarm started for John's because he was more accessible than any other friend of his, and because he knew him to be true as steel, and a good counsellor in his case. He might have gone home and awakened his sister and mother and obtained the articles he needed, but he knew it would be imprudent, and that John would do all he needed.

John supplied him with a tin cup, a blanket, a coat, tinder, flint and steel, (there were no Loco Foco matches in Tennessee then,) and what was more important, a plenty of cold bacon and bread, and promised to see his mother and sister and get his clothes.[3] He also promised to meet him at the cave with Jerry so soon as it was convenient. He further told him there was no noise or stir about his rencounter and escape,—and, indeed, it was altogether unknown at Farney's plantation.

Farney lived about four miles from Manasseth, and he and his slaves were likely to be soon informed of the rencounter. Their ignorance of it, made

3. [Editor's note:] Loco Foco matches were friction matches. The term originates from a self-lighting cigar, with a match composition at the end, invented in 1834 by John Marck of New York. He named it a "locofoco cigar," after the word *locomotive*, which by the uneducated was assumed to mean self-moving.

Jarm reflect that his master might have taken a different turn from what he expected. He went back to his solitary home, relieved and comforted. After lighting a pine knot with his flint and tinder, and eating a hearty supper of bread and bacon, and washing it down with water, he rolled up in his blanket on his bed of leaves, and instantly fell asleep, and so continued until late in the morning. The last two nights he slept little and his anxiety and excitement were very oppressive, he lapsed into slumber most profound, and awoke not until the music of birds, and the gurgling of the stream opened his ears, and the silver light on the surface of the brook opened his eyes to the fact, that the day was advanced, and that his bed-room, dark as Erebus in some places, would never be lighter.[4] He was ready dressed, but threw off his garments and plunged into the pure cold water at the foot of his cave, and then stept into the open air to feel the glorious sunlight, ere he sat down again to his solitary meal. His breakfast was the same as his supper, and soon disposed of.

4. [Editor's note:] In Greek mythology, Erebus is the personification of darkness and shadow; his name is used interchangeably with Tartarus and Hades since Erebus is often thought of as part of the underworld. Erebus can also refer to the underworld itself; it can refer to the darkness under the earth, imagined as the abode either of sinners after death or of all the dead.

CHAPTER XIX

Jarm now began to realize his destitution. Having finished his first breakfast at the cave, after a night of excellent sleep, and a morning of refreshing ablution, he remembered he was a prisoner. It was a dreary day to him. The beautiful sun shed its warmth and light, but not for him—his kindred and friends, driven to their tasks, might not come to him, nor could he go to them. He might not be seen out of his hiding place. The clouds that slavery gathered in his soul were colder and darker than the day-night that filled his dungeon, and he was borne down by a sense of unutterable injustice. He felt that it was bad to be poor, but insufferable to be so poor. Had he, like the Ocean-tossed Selkirk, been stranded on an Island among birds and beasts which were unacquainted with man, his soul might be content with external objects.[1] Or had he, like the beloved desciple, been thrown into some Patmos, where body and soul were free, he might have been sensitive to the voice and touch of angels.[2] But, alas! slavery fiercer than the winds, and more cruel than the persecutors of the Prophets, had driven him into the earth to shelter in perpetual darkness. Could he have walked out during the day without exposure to unimaginable wrongs—could he by any amount of carefulness have found his way to the Prestons, or even to friends near at hand—was he not obliged to be quiet in his cave, or skulk like a wild beast among the bushes, to avoid human eyes and savage bloodhounds—could he have dimly seen a way out of his discomfort and perils—if, to break the circle of present embarrassments, would not leave him in an impenetrable outer circle of woes on the plantation—if slavery had

1. [Editor's note:] Alexander Selkirk (1676–1721) was a Scottish sailor who spent four years as a castaway when he was voluntarily marooned on an uninhabited island in 1704. His travels are the probable inspiration for Daniel Defoe's novel *The Life and Strange Surprising Adventures of Robinson Crusoe* (1719).

2. [Editor's note:] Patmos is a small Greek island in the Aegean Sea. In the book of Revelation, it states that the book's author, John, was on Patmos when he experienced and recorded a vision from Jesus.

not, seemingly, driven him to the last extremity, and piled its insurmountable billows around him, he had not been cast down as he was. It was, indeed, a dreary day to Jarm; and when the sun went down, his soul reached the bottom of its troubled waters. He could stand it no longer. The fountain of feeling and tears burst open, and he fell upon the earth and prayed—

"O God, how long must I suffer? Pity, pity me, O my Father, and deliver me from these wrongs. Is there not mercy in Heaven for a poor slave? Help! help! O God, for I am helpless! Leave me not thus wretched!"

At this point, perfectly absorbed by his affliction, he was startled by a strong hand on his shoulder. At the same time a kind and familiar voice said to him:—

"Hallo! pretty boy! Here, you are, praying the Lord for help, and he has sent me, a poor creature to do the trick."

Jarm immediately sprang up and grasped the hands of Ross and John. The clouds departed, and the sunlight cheered his soul again.

"How glad I am to see you!" said he.

"Well, we come to make you glad. But what was you blubbering for when we came in?"

"Mr. Ross, I have some pluck, and can bear grief as well as most men, but I can't endure such a case as this. I think I can look my enemy in the face, and die fighting for my rights; but to die in this way—to perish on the rack of my own mind, is impossible. Oh, I have had a wretched day, and could stand it no longer. Therefore you found me as you did, crying for help. I had no companion or comforter on earth—why might I not seek one in Heaven?"

"You did right, and no doubt you found that companion and comforter, and he sent me, a forlorn old scoundrel to help you."

"Don't call yourself hard names—you are not a 'scoundrel.' If God uses scoundrels in works of goodness and mercy, it is in spite of them, and not because they delight in goodness and mercy, as you do. If you have the heart to do good, you have the heart of a Christian; and the good that is in you will overcome your evil, and rid yourself of it in the end. So I learned of the Prestons."

"But don't you know the Scripture says 'no drunkard shall enter the kingdom of Heaven?'—how, then, am I a Christian?"

"What does that mean?—is it an unpardonable sin to get drunk?"

"It is unpardonable so long as the man drinks. When he ceases to drink, and is a sober man, he is pardoned—he pardons himself. That is the way all pardons are granted. The truth about it is, that text applies not to alcohol drinkers—for, bad as they be, they may reform—in other words, be pardoned, for reformation is pardon. But the Scriptures tell us there are those who 'are drunken, but not with wine,'—who 'stagger, but not with strong drink.' They are those who are wiser than the word—who are drunk with self-intelligence—who are not sick, and therefore need no physician—who are righteous, and need no Saviour. The sin is in the spirit, the life, the affections. They are spiritual drunkards, drugged with self-intelligence, righteousness and wisdom. They reel to and fro, and stagger like a drunken man—their sin is unpardonable. There, can't I preach?"

"I wish all preachers would preach and practice as you do," said John. "But we must talk about earthly things. What is to be done with this poor Gentile? (pointing to Jarm)—and how are he and I and Jerry to get out of the hands of these christians, and find freedom?—that is the point."

"The best thing Jarm ever did in his life was to pitch his pious old drunken master heels over head." Turning to Jarm, he said, "I have been on the lookout to-day, and find the old hypocrite begins to think you are a boy of sense and spirit, and fit to have the charge of his business. He values you higher than ever, and will set no dogs on your track to chase you out of the country, mind that—at least so I think. But I will examine the case further, and in the meantime, prick up—don't be cast down. In three days I will guarantee you will be on better terms with him than you ever was before."

"For the sake of getting ready to run away, I want to get back to him. My means are in his hands, and they were hard earned. All I live for now, is to get freedom, and if I can't get that, I don't care to live at all."

"That is just my case," said John.

"Well, well, boys, keep quiet—it will come round. In a short time, you, Jarm, will stand better with the old man, and have a better chance to get the means you speak of, than ever before."

"About those passes?"

"O, I'll write each of you a pass when you are ready to start. John and I have talked that matter over."

"Well, I must make some money. I can make $50 by my patch this year—but not if I am shut up here."

"How large is your patch?"

"About an acre."

"How do you find time to work it?"

"O, I work nights only, of course—but the patch has the credit of raising a great deal of cotton, which I get by my wits. My master's son, John, is friendly to me, and I do things for him, and he steals his father's cotton and pays me liberally. I dicker with the slaves and they steal their master's cotton, and I put it all on my pile. So my crops depend quite as much on my skill at trade as upon my labor. By the way—have you given Mr. Ross any bacon yet?"

"O, yes—I handed him a ham yesterday."

"Give him another, on my account."

"That I'll do."

"We shall need to use you a great deal, Mr. Ross, and will pay as well as we can. We have no scruples to take property which our masters call theirs, because it ain't theirs—it has been earned by us and our kindred, and not by him or his. We would do no injustice to them, and so far as we can we are determined they shall do no injustice to us. The reason we escape from them, is, because they rob and wrong us all the while. We have well considered these matters, and are satisfied we are right."

"Of course you are right. No man ever lived that did not reason as you do—men are men because they so reason. And they are the more men as they get out of slavery. To take your own is just, as everyone knows by interior perception. Such perception is God, in every man, whispering—'get your rights and keep them.' By such interior perception God spoke to Adam, Noah, Moses, &c.—and this is what the ancients meant when they said, 'God spoke unto Adam'—'The Lord spoke unto Moses,' &c., &c. He never spoke to any man but by an internal perception, and his words are heard in the soul, not in the ears. A man's spirit never mistakes God's voice, saying, 'Get free—get your own.' And this voice every slave as distinctly hears, by his spiritual organs, as he hears the thunder by his natural ones. Go on, then, and be free. Take with you your earnings—horse, clothing, money—everything you need. You have a 'Thus saith the Lord' for it;—it is the command of God."

"That is the stuff—that is religion. It is full of charity and blessedness. If your preachers and class-leaders preached in that way, their awakenings would be of a different sort—they would howl to a different tune."

"Yes, indeed. If Christ should come in a new Jerusalem and preach that way, your master would kill him. Men no more know him when he comes in the spirit at his second advent, than they did when he came in the body the first time. They then thought he would come as a king—now they think he will come riding on a cloud or a white horse. The truth is, they don't understand the Bible. If they did, they would see him here now, separating the sheep from the goats, and setting the world in order."

"When shall I see you again?"

"In a day or so," said Ross.

"I hope you are right in regard to my master. I will submit to my fate a little longer for the sake of freedom—but I will not submit to be tied and flogged, nor will I go to him like a tamed and sneaking slave—I will be killed rather. I will go to him like a man, and he shall know he has gained nothing by attempting to tie and flog me."

"Right as a book!—you are an exception in slavery. Your master feels his dependence on you too much not to respect your manliness. He can't get along without you, and he knows you know it. From prudence and interest, he will not, as some masters would, drive you to despair. If I don't err, experience has taught him what you will and what you will not bear. Your manhood will raise you in his esteem and confidence. He values you at this moment higher than he did three days ago—at least that is my opinion—but I'll understand the case better in a day or two. Of course, you will be discreet, and approach him respectfully and frankly, as if you confided in his generosity and good sense—but I'll see."

"So I made up my mind to do—but I have no respect for his generosity or good sense."

"Neither have I," said Ross. "I rely upon neither the one or the other. I calculate on his discrimination in respect to his interest, only. I think he has sense enough to see that a quarrel with you won't pay. Manasseth Logue was never dull to scent a shilling, drunk or sober."

"You are right there."

"I have been telling you how to play the game with your master—for it is all trickery between master and slave. He that cheats most is the best fellow—if, being a slave, he is not found out in his cheating. So when you come to escape, if you do escape, and I have no doubt you will, you must be bold, and not fear to stop at the best house while in the slave states—you must act as freemen act. It is not enough to say you are free—you must act free. You are to get out of the country, of course, with all reasonable expedition—but, mark me; you are to go with heads up, and in the most public roads. If you go dodging and shying through the country, you will be suspected, seized, imprisoned and advertised—but if you ride boldly through, like freemen, you will get through unmolested."

"Do you say we must stop at the big houses?"

"Yes."

"Why?"

"Because it is the last thing a slave would do—and because again large houses are the most willing and able to entertain you."

In this way the parties talked until the evening was consumed, and then parted, mutually pleased—Ross, because he thought he had done something for the good of the poor fellows,—and Jarm and John, because they were encouraged and instructed by him. Jarm immediately rolled into his bed of leaves, and in the act of revising the conversation just passed, fell and woke not until the birds peeped on the boughs, and the gray light on the water, and the shade in the mouth of his dungeon disappeared. Then he awoke to repeat the ceremonies of the previous morning.

When evening came again, pursuant to arrangement with John, he started for the Farney plantation, and arrived there about nine o'clock. Perceiving there was yet a light in the great house as it is called, though it was about the size of an ordinary log house, he waited in the skirt of the forest for it to disappear. He had not to wait long before the house was all dark, and no sound of human life was heard but one soft, female voice, carroling a slave's song at the door of her cabin.

Jarm stepped lightly from his covert, and approached warily the spot where she sat, and by a token not new between them, made himself known. The voice of the girl sunk lower and lower, as she neared him, until the sound ceased to be heard, and she was in the arms of her friend. Quickly she flew back to the shanty and picked up a bundle of clothing, and hastened to the side of Jarm and delivered it to him, and then leaned on his strong arm and strayed into the forest. She was a beautiful slave, and Jarm was her favorite—but his heart was spoiled at the Prestons for love affairs. He was pleased with her company, person, and character, but his intent went no farther. He had long resolved never to be a husband or father, until he and his children could be free. He therefore discharged his obligations to the girl, by acknowledgements and caresses which were common to kind, young hearts of their class, and a disregard of which would seem cold and ungrateful.

"You have been over to our people?" said Jarm.

"Yes—I went this evening."

"Did you see mother and the rest?"

"Yes."

"Are they well?"

"Yes. Mr. Preston was there yesterday to buy you. He pressed Manasseth very hard, but the old wretch was unwilling to part with you at any price, and refused to name any sum that he would take for you."

"How did you find that out?"

"Maria and your mother both told me."

"Did Mr. Preston enquire for me?"

"Yes—he was very anxious to see you."

"How glad I should be to see him! He is a glorious, good man. Slavery would be nothing if masters and mistresses were like him and his wife and daughters. I never expect to enjoy myself as I did with those good people. O that I could go and see them!"

Supplied with clothing, Jarm shut himself in the cave and woods during the day, again, and visited his colored friends on the neighboring plantations, or entertained them in his rocky home, during the nights. His life was easy and social, but unnatural, constrained, and fruitless of preparation for a better country. His spirit tired of it, and he determined to put on a bold face and go to his master.

We pass over several interviews with Ross, John, and Jerry, in which their joint concerns, and his individual case, were talked of, and come to the interview between Jarm and his master. He had spent the previous evening with his friends at the cave, and was emboldened to take the step which would test the question of reconciliation. Early in the morning he fitted his dress for work, and took a circuitous route for home. He took a circuitous route, that his approach should not hint the direction of his concealment. He arrived just as the hands left for the fields, and found his master in the yard. For the first time in his life he approached him with his hat on his head. He touched it with his thumb and finger, bowed, and said, respectfully, as one equal does when he meets another,

"Good morning, sir."

"What do you want?"

"If you have anything for me to do, I will go to work."

"Have you been to breakfast?"

"Yes, sir."

"Go into the lot to making fence."

This brief colloquy was all that passed. But the tone and manner of it, signified to Jarm's mind, that the reconciliation was complete—Manasseth, who knew so little how to conceal passion, had not the least show of it. Jarm was satisfied his master was glad to see him, and that he entertained no intent to flog or injure him. If Jarm was tired of wild life, Manasseth was tired of filling his place on the farm.

From that day forward there was peace between Jarm and his master—not because they were really reconciled, but because it was the only means to secret ends. Jarm was peaceable as a war measure, and his master was peaceable as a measure of economy and policy. Like all slaves and slaveholders, (as a general truth,) they fell into a forced, hypocritical and false position, in which Jarm had the advantage, for he read his master's mind and motives like a book, while he was to his master a sealed book.

Jarm was very attentive to the interest of the plantation, and his master's eyes were effectually blinded thereby. The latter trusted the management of his farm to him, and allowed him many privileges. What remained of his whiskey, Jarm sold, which, with his little patch plantation, made sufficient capital to pay his way to the free north.

But notwithstanding Jarm's importance to his master, and the fidelity and industry of his mother and sisters, he was destined to experience another of those terrible blows upon his heart, which are ten thousand times more painful than death. His sister Maria was a young and beautiful slave mother, who lived in the smiles and caresses of her husband and three lovely children, one of whom was a babe at her breast. Her loving heart was bound to the hearts of her mother, brothers and sisters, by cords woven of heaven, and which could not be broken without impaling the very life of the whole family circle.

In the latter part of the summer, Jarm found himself in the midst of the following circle: a bluff and strong built man, having the dress, manners, voice and expression of a ruffian, with a pistol in his bosom and a whip in his right hand, attended by two three like ruffians, with Manasseth standing by, and two of them attempting to tie the hands of the beautiful Maria with a rope,—she resisting screaming and praying,

"Let me have my children—do let me have my children!"

"What you make such a d—d fuss for? Shut up, or I'll make you bellow for something—you have got to go—what is the use?"

"Give me my children and I will go anywhere—only let me have my children—I can't go without my children!"

The coarse and hard labors of Maria had given her great strength of muscle, and in the desperation of her affections it was no easy thing to secure her hands. The hard man who was attempting it, irritated by her screams and struggles, struck her on the mouth with the back of his hand.

"Shut your mouth, you d— d——."

The blood flowed freely from the mouth of the girl, and ran down her chin and neck, and she cried the louder—

"Give me my little children!—I can't leave my children!"

Internal agony gave desperate strength to her natural energies, and she resisted the united strength of all the men—screaming all the while, "Give me my little children!—O, take my little children with me and I will go—I can't go and leave my children!"

But the strength of the cruel men finally overcome the wretched slave mother, and she was forced into a wagon with them—her hands were tied, and she was held to her place, and driven screaming away. So soon as she found she must go, and there was no relenting, she prayed only for her babe.

"O, do give me my babe!—my little babe—I can't live without my babe. What will the poor little baby do?—do give me my babe and I will go with you—do let me have one child—I can't go without my babe!"

Crack went the whip, and just as expressive of sympathy was it as the curses and oaths of the wretches who made it crack—and the clattering of horses' feet, and rolling of the wagon, and oaths of the drivers, and moans and screams of the miserable Maria, mingled together, until they died on the ears of Manasseth and his wicked household. It was the last time poor Maria ever saw her children, mother, brothers or sisters, or any one of them. She was driven off alone, and left them to a like fate.

The lion-hearted Jarm was obliged to look on, riveted in his tracks by a sense of impotence and desire of vengeance. Nothing but a conviction that he would soon escape from the power that was wrenching his heart in pieces, held him from dashing his blood against the blood of the incarnate devils who were eyeing their gains amid the unutterable agonies of all his kindred.

CHAPTER XX

The terrible experience of the last chapter increased the impatience of Jarm. It was a stirring admonition, "that thou doest, do quickly." He hastened a meeting of his friends, to make final arrangements, and they determined to be ready with horses, clothing, provisions, money, arms, and passes, to start under cover of the first night of the holidays. The thought of remaining where he could be tortured by such unutterable outrage, was intolerable.

Manasseth Logue had four or five good horses. The one which Jarm appropriated was a young, high spirited, well-broke, beautiful animal. For fleetness, endurance, strength and beauty, it may be doubted whether there was a superior in the State. Having full charge of the horses and their feed, he petted and fitted this one for his purpose. Though perfectly orderly, he was often in the best meadows, oat and cornfields. Manasseth grieved that this good horse was being thus disorderly, little dreaming that his trusty Jarm pulled down the fences with his own hands, that he might have ingress to the best feed, and be fitted, at his master's expense, to carry his best slave out of the country.

The fall work was finally completed, and the religious season came round again, when it was convenient for these Christian slaveholders to have a time of taking care of their souls at the anniversary camp-meeting. There the three friends met again, for the last time, and their friend Ross met with them,—while their pious masters were mouthing their prayers and shouting their "Amens," they retired to hold a slaves' caucus in the mountain cave, and plot their escape.

"We must be ready to start the first holiday night," said Jarm.

"Agreed," said John; "I shall be ready."

"I'll try to be," said Jerry.

"It won't do to pass the holidays—we must go to Illinois before winter—and now about those passes?"

"There is one for each of you. I have dated them on the first of the holidays," said Ross.

Each of the parties then paid into his hand $10, in cash, and promised, before their departure, to deliver him flour, bacon, and other necessaries for his family,—a promise which they faithfully fulfilled. Of course, these articles were all secretly taken from their masters. Theft is the basis principle of slavery, and the little world in which the slave's mind and body moves, compels the conclusion that it is right to take from his robber every thing he can safely lay hands on. Nature and heaven know no law for the slaveholder. He is as much an outlaw in the slave's eye, as the slave is in his eye, and, therefore, justly exposed to every act of secret or open war, that the slave fancies may aid his freedom or convenience.

"Now, boys, remember what I tell you—nobody has a right to see your passes but a magistrate, and you are to deliver them to nobody but a magistrate," said Ross.

"But what if they stop us, in case we refuse to deliver them?"

"Knock them down—fight like lions. But you are not to seek a fight. You are to enquire if they are magistrates, and if they say "nay," tell them you are ready to show your passes to a magistrate,—but are not willing to deliver them to anybody you may chance to meet. Tell them you will go with them to a magistrate, and deliver your passes. Be civil—state your rights, kindly and calmly, but maintain them boldly and to the last extremity."

"We'll blow their brains out."

"Not until the last moment must your enemy know you have pistols. Your pistols must be your friends only in extreme cases. When you are driven to the point where you are to be seized or your adversary be shot, shoot him without compunction. Until you arrive at that point, keep your pistols covered up. If he won't give you food, rob him: if he won't give you freedom, shoot him."

"Lord speed the day!—freedom begins with the holidays!"

"Amen!"

"And now let us go and see what that bawling in the camp means."

Evening had already set in, the meeting was commenced, and the voices of the preachers and the shouts of the hearers echoed through the woods.

"I wonder if there is any religion in that noise?"

"Pshaw, no," said Ross. "Religion is willing and doing good to others—this is only bawling. The delights of religion result from doing good—the delights of this affair is in the excitement of self. Religion is merciful and rational—but this excitement is produced by the Evil One, to shut the eyes of their understandings to the unreasonable and merciless character of their own hearts. Look yonder—there is old Manasseth on his knees, now. Hear him cry aloud. Louder than that, old man!—Baal's deaf. That's it—beat the ground with your fists—take out your knife and cut your flesh and make the blood run, as your predecessor did at Carmel. What an old wretch he is!"

"What makes you say he is crying to Baal?—he is crying to God. What is Baal?"

"He is praying to god, to be sure—but it is a little shriveled-souled god, of just his own soul's size and quality. The ancients called that god BAAL—its true name is—self. All persons who worship from self love are worshipers of Baal.[1] He thinks, or pretends to think, he is praying to Jehovah—but in fact he is belching out the desires of his selfish heart—he is pleading to Baal for the benefit of his own infernal lusts. I'll bet you a guinea he has got a pistol in his bosom—and there it is—I see it sticking out, now—and if he saw you getting your freedom, he would jump up and shoot you."

"Of course he would shoot us, or otherwise murder us, if we attempted to get our freedom. Were it not so, they would not hold us long—you may bet your life of that. Pretty religion, that! I don't like Baal, if that is their god—he may do for slaveholders—I am determined to flee from their god and his worshipers."

"You will have to get out of the slave states, then. To use Bible language—those states "are the high places of Baal." Your master, Jarm, is well named, for his namesake of old built up the high places of Baal, and your master does the same.[2] Like Manasseth of old, he has shed innocent blood. Hear him—what a reckoning he will have with his crimes some day."

"I wish I understood the Bible as well as you do," said John.

1. [Editor's note:] Ross is referencing 1 Kings 18:18–40. Some Israelites had begun worshipping the god Baal. Wanting to prove that the Jewish God was the only true God, the prophet Elijah challenged the followers of Baal to choose which God was the true God. Both prepared a sacrifice. Followers of Baal prayed to their god to send fire to burn up the sacrifice, but nothing happened. When Elijah prayed to God, "Then the fire of the LORD fell, and consumed the burnt sacrifice, and the wood, and the stones, and the dust, and licked up the water that *was* in the trench. And when all the people saw *it*, they fell on their faces: and they said, The LORD, he *is* the God; the LORD, he *is* the God."

2. [Editor's note:] King Manasseh's reign is described in 2 Chronicles 33. He was the only son and successor of Hezekiah on the throne of Judah, ascending to the throne at age twelve and reigning for fifty-five years (698–643 BC). His reign is described as a relapse of the idolatry his father had banished, working to eliminate the worship of Jehovah from the land: "He built again the high places which Hezekiah his father had broken down, and he reared up altars for Baalim, and made groves, and worshipped all the host of heaven, and served them. . . . So Manasseh made Judah and the inhabitants of Jerusalem to err, and to do worse than the heathen, whom the Lord had destroyed before the children of Israel."

"So do I,—and I mean to understand it, when I get my freedom," said Jarm.

"You understand it now better than your masters," said Ross.

"How is that?—I can neither read or write."

"You can't read or write the external letter of the word,—but you do read and speak the internal letter and intent of the Bible—and your master knows no more of the latter than his horse, if we are to judge from his life. You understand this, don't you—'all things whatsoever you would that men do to you, do ye even so to them—for this is the law and the prophets?'"

"Why, I understand that I am to do to others as I would have them do to me—but that other thing, 'this is the law and the prophets,' I don't understand."

"It means that that rule of action is the sum of all the teachings of all the Bible,—'the law and the prophets' are the total of the Old Testament, which teaches only that sentiment—it is the pith and substance of the Bible, of all true religion—it is God's rule of life for himself and all his angels—in holding men to the same law, he does as he would be done by—for it is the rule of goodness and truth."[3]

"O, that everybody would teach and live such religion as that—we need not be here plotting to get away from these devil-deacons into Illinois, if they did. If I ever get to a free country, I mean to get learning and preach that religion, as the means of putting down the religion of the slaveholders. What a wicked thing it is, that our mothers, brothers, and sisters cannot be delivered until this religion is put down."

"They make a great fuss about religion, as if it required much learning and study to get at it. The truth about it is, it requires skill and study to give it a false face and cover it up. The children understand it better than the minister—it is to live right—it is to do justly—to do good to others, from a love of doing good, not because you are afraid of God or afraid of hell, but because it is your delight and life to do it. Afraid of God! Afraid of hell you may be, because hell is a perverted affection—it is self. If you suffer, your suffering is self-inflicted. Men never feared God until they fell—then Adam said, 'I was afraid.' Fear thyself, but don't fear God—rush into his blessed bosom rather, that is ever open to receive you. Now, boys, don't forget this injunction. I trust it is one of the last I shall give you—this may be the last time I shall see

3. [Loguen's note:] If we are to regard the letter of the Old Testament, and some of the New, much unintelligible, false and cruel. But if we seek its meaning from the science of analogy,—the science of the ancients,—we are overwhelmed with its divinity and mercifulness.

you—I would impress it upon your memories, have no fear of God—fear only yourselves and the devils, in the shape of men, who would enslave or corrupt you, and make you your own enemies. Yourselves and brother men are to be feared—God, never. He will be your friend whether you will or not—he never can be anything else—he loves his enemies—he loves even those cruel men that are praying there for mercy for themselves when they have none for you."

"God love his enemies! God not to be feared! Ain't that a strange thing to say?"

"It ain't common talk, I'll admit,—but it is true, notwithstanding,—and it is the true intent of the Bible, too. The Bible says, 'The fear of the Lord is the beginning of wisdom,' and that he is 'angry with the wicked every day'—but it must be remembered that the Jews, for whom it was written, had lost all spirituality—they were the swine of the Scriptures—they were inverted men, and saw things in a false and inverted order. To them, therefore, the Lord, instead of being loving and forgiving, was angry and implacable. They could only be influenced by fear,—and God, in mercy, ruled them through their fears and delusions. To them, truth was inverted and false—to them God was, of course, love inverted, and therefore angry, jealous and revengeful. The Book was written according to such false appearance, or it had been useless to the Jews. The fear that taught lessons of duty and wisdom, and the anger which appeared in the face of God, were seen through the inverted and perverse loves of their own souls. They had changed. God was the same never-changing, ever-loving being."

"Well, I love to hear you talk," said Jarm; "but those bawling hypocrites disgust me. I can't hear them any longer. By the way, I think I shall learn very little divinity until I get where I can think and act freely. As to Manasseth Logue, and all yonder crew, may God deliver me from them and their religion! Good bye."

"That's it, my lad! The angel of the Apocolypse is now saying to every slave, 'Whosoever *will*, let him come and take of the water of life *freely*;' and 'let him that heareth say, come;' and 'let him that is athirst come.' Flee, then, and slake your thirst freely!—the angel declares and God commands it; and no man may forbid it with impunity."

Jarm strayed into the woods, and came across his pet horse. He raised and curved his beautiful neck, and saluted Jarm with his usual whinner, and Jarm answered him by patting him and talking nonsense. He soon turned and examined a strange horse near by, whose points were not so good as his own. But the stray horse had a new, rich and beautiful saddle on his back—whereas, the saddle on his favorite was inferior and worn. It was not only new, but it was beautifully quilted, and its guilded stirrups reflected light like polished gold. Not doubting that the saddle was the property of some of the christian slaveholders who were carrying on in the camp, or carousing in the groggeries, he raised the question whether he had best appropriate it for freedom—and finally decided to take it by way of reprisal for slave piracy, and part satisfaction for its wrongs. As before said, in the eye of the slaveholder, the slave forfeits everything to his master;—so in the eye of the slave, the slaveholder forfeits everything to his slave.

He immediately took off the saddles and put his master's saddle on the stranger's horse, and then stripped the bridles off the horses' heads—leaving the throat latches buckled—and turned them loose—having previously fractured the girth of his master's saddle, so that he was sure it would be brushed from the back of the horse, and seem to be done by the horse himself.

Jarm left the bridles as he found them, fastened to small trees, and tossing the new saddle upon his back, he took a circuitous tramp to the old meeting house, and deposited it for his use.

The horses returned naked to their homes; and their owners, finding the bridles as aforesaid, inferred that they had stripped the bridles off their heads, and lost their saddles in the woods. Search was made for them the next day, but Manasseth's was the only one that ever came to light.

After Jarm deposited the saddle, he returned to the camp and met his friends again.

"Not gone yet?" said Ross.

"Not yet."

Jarm now explained to them what he had been doing.

"Let us go one side," said Ross. "These noisy Jews may overhear us, and it would be as bad for me as you, should they do so."

"What do you think of my saddle affair, Mr. Ross?" said Jarm. "You see, of course, what I think of it, by the act; and now I want to know whether you approve it as a just and right transaction."

"Exactly—exactly. 'An eye for an eye, and a tooth for a tooth.'"

"What do you mean by that?"

"Why, that is the law of retaliation—the law of mercy and Heaven. 'He that taketh the sword, (against the right, of course) shall perish by the sword.' If a man does good to his neighbor, he does good to himself—he does evil to him, he does evil to himself. When Christ told his desciples not to judge men, he added, 'for with what judgment ye judge, ye shall be judged'—'tit for tat.' In common language, that is the law of Heaven and Hell. If these christian rascals steal your freedom and bread, they forfeit to you their own freedom and bread. When God was about to rescue the Israelites from their masters, he told them to borrow their gold and silver and jewels, and take them along. Heaven knows no other law but this 'tit for tat' law."

"But we are told not to retaliate upon our enemies."

"Neither do we retaliate by this rule. The enemy does the mischief to himself. God's government is so that the wicked punish themselves. By shedding man's blood, which is divine truth, the bad man sheds his own blood—that is, he extinguishes truth in his own soul—and truth is spiritual blood or life. He kills himself—God don't do it. We are making our spirits all the while, and consigning them to Heaven or Hell—that is, we are constructing our eternal homes to suit ourselves."

"Old Manasseth would never allow such a thing as that."

"Not he. If a preacher should get on the stump there and declare this doctrine, the whole brood would draw their dirks on him. They could not bear it, because it is God's truth against slavery; it smites them where they live. It will be long before they approve the heavenly axiom, 'An eye for an eye and a tooth for a tooth,'—or in other words, 'as a man judgeth so shall he be judged,' or 'as he forgives trespasses so shall his trespasses be forgiven,' &c., &c. I tell you, as true as you live, every man, under God, is his own final judge, and sentences his own soul to Heaven or Hell. God, whose seat is in all our faculties, but endorses the decree. Those fellows are fixing their souls in Hell now. There are a plenty such meetings as that in Pandemonium."

"Well, well—my saddle has effected an important use already. It has been a capital text for a capital sermon. I believe in that preaching. In taking the saddle, I have been just to myself not only, but to the robber who claims it."

"We are agreed in that."

"There is one item of preparation that puzzles me to make. John Farney, have you got your pistols and ammunition yet?"

"No."

"Neither have I. We must have them immediately—Christmas is at hand. I see how it is—we shall have to employ you, Mr. Ross, to get those articles. It won't do for us to be looking round for pistols—you know it would make an earthquake in the country."

"Well, I can do it. I am going to Nashville next week, and if you give me the needful, I will purchase the lads for you."

"It is a bargain."

"Now, boys, I want to give you a special charge. You must be careful—I am involved in this affair as deep as you. You will put me in a fine fix if you let it be known I am helping runaway slaves to fire arms. I know you both, and can trust your honour. Still, I charge you to the utmost secrecy and care. A discovery in this matter would send you to Georgia, and me to the limb of a tree. Does your mother, brother, sister or sweetheart know anything about this?"

"No. It is one of the evils of slavery that a fugitive may not trust mother or sister or lover—nor may he confide in a brother, until he knows the strength of his love, and feels it as his own. No mortal among my relatives dreams of my intents, and as for a sweetheart, I have none. I did love a girl once, but her place and station are beyond my reach; and that is one reason that determines me to turn my back on slavery, until I can face it and fight to the death."

"You forget our Rachel," said John Farney. "If she is not yours, you are hers—and I am thinking she would make a pretty muss if she knew we were going to run away."

"Poor, innocent, good girl! It is not my fault she is partial to me. When we are gone, she will mourn sadly, and may take it in her head to be off too. Be assured, my dear friend, (addressing Ross) your name will never be mentioned in this affair. If my brother knows it, he never will know you had a hand in it, in any form whatever. This case is all our own."

"I did not suppose you would intentionally betray me, any more than you would yourselves. If this thing is to fail, it will be by carelessness, not treachery. Therefore I urge the utmost possible secrecy and care, every moment, and in every place. Life and death, liberty and slavery, the good to be done and enjoyed if you succeed, and to be lost if you don't succeed, depend on your cunning and courage and prudence. Shut up in this prison, you can't conceive the possible importance of this enterprize. You see it only so far as you are concerned, and only intend to be free, as other folks. The importance of your freedom to others is not thought of or imagined. To rid yourself of slavery is, an animal and a religious duty. That instinct reposes among the faculties of the soul before duty is there. It is an electric rod, which points to Heaven, all that attracts the divine spark which sets your souls on fire. You imagine you are self-prompted. It is a mistake. Divine love kindles the fire in your bones, which you cannot resist. Now, then, I am no prophet or son of a prophet, but I will predict that before you become of my age—before you are thirty years older—the whole land will cry out against slavery, and not only cry, but rise and expel it from the country. The Star in the East lights the horizon now, and ere your sun goes down—when it is in its meridian, if you live as long as I have—that Star will be in sight, rising and shining 'from the East even to the West,'—chasing the dreadful darkness away, and turning the clouds that make it into glorious light. Your corporeal and intellectual abilities, irrepressible impulses, and past experience, will make you an important element in the cold

North; and thousands of others, who, like you, will escape from this slave-cursed country, will carry in their bosoms, as you do, unquenchable fires; and the frosty North will melt upon their bosoms, whether they intend it or not. O, yes—would that I could live to see it! More progress is to be made in liberty, in religion, in polities, in science, in industry, in humanity, the coming thirty, than in the last hundred years. Slaves will be important agents of that progress. I scarce dare speak it. Such will be the intensity of intellectual light, that it will break through the crust of nature to the spiritual sun—the source of all light and all heat; for the light and heat of this world are only the natural and material coverings of the truth and goodness of the great God, which are constantly flowing from him through our sun into nature, to keep it alive."

"My dear friend, our freedom is a world of importance to us, and it is all we think of just now. It shall have all our industry and ability to attain it, for its own sake—beyond that we know nothing. If we can do anything to bring about the good things you speak of—though we hardly understand what you mean by them—we will do it for the sake of others. One thing we can do, if it comes to that, we can fight—yes, and we will fight, you may bet your life of that, when there is half a chance to break the yoke off the necks of our countrymen by breaking the necks of these impious men."

CHAPTER XXI

The evening before Christmas, though cold, was as clear and beautiful as Tennessee sky could make it. Jarm and John had their holiday passes, and no article was wanting to complete their equipment. They had stabled and fed their horses in the best manner, filled their saddle bags with clothing on one side, and bacon and chickens and bread on the other, and were ready for flight. So soon as the sun went down, Jarm went over to Farney's, and found him in the road, a little distance from his master's house.

"I have been waiting for you," said John.

"All ready?" said Jarm.

"Ready to a dot."

"We shall start at two o'clock, and take Jerry in our course—he will be waiting."

"Then good bye to old Tennessee? Won't we fire a salute when we get on free ground?"

"Three days will take us out of Tennessee—but how long we shall be getting into Illinois, I can't tell."

This conversation, and more like it, occurred as they proceeded slowly towards the negro house. At this point of the conversation, a voice, half scream and half groan, and loud enough to be heard at a distance, came out from the fence, very near them, and struck them with terror. Turning to the sound they saw Rachel in a delirium of excitement, produced by overhearing their conversation.

"Oh! dear!—you are going to run away!" cried the girl, whose affectionate sympathies were painfully excited by the possibility of a separation from one she loved.

"Hold your tongue!—hush! What do you make that noise for?" said John, in an undertone. "You are crazy!"

"O, I heard you talk—I know what you are at—you can't cheat me! What shall I do?" said the frantic girl.

"Shut up!—do you mean to cut us off from the holidays, and get us into the calaboose? Do you think we would go away and leave you?" said Jarm.

Jarm now took the girl by the arm, and led her to the kitchen, and soothed and quieted her, and drew her away from any suspicion of his escape; and, finally, wearied with her day's labor and the excitement of the evening, she fell asleep on his shoulder. The poor girl was tired, and slept soundly. Most anxious to be relieved of his charge, he quietly laid her on a bed near by, as he would a sleeping infant, and softly left the house. John, who was ready without, immediately put him on a nice horse, and he returned home, soon as possible, and let the horse loose in the streets; and he remained there, cropping the grass and bushes.

Without delay, Jarm saddled and bridled his own horse, and prepared for flight.

Now come a painful trial. To face hardship, and plunge, without experience, into an enterprize full of peril, did but stir the energy of his soul; but to take a last look at his mother, sisters and brothers was too much for him—but he could not leave without it. He had a lion's heart, when looking at the perils and terrors around him, but he melted down looking at those dear ones. The tear trembled upon his eyelids in spite of him, as he shook his half-brother Henry out of his sleep and called him aside.

"What do you want?" said Henry.

"Henry," said Jarm, "I know I can trust you. I am going to run away. This is the last time I shall see you, for I shall start in a few minutes—I could not go without telling you, that after I am gone you might tell mother about it. Were I to tell her directly, so much does she love me, I fear she would expose me. You must take kind care of her, I cannot be a slave any longer."

We will not detail the particulars of the conversation between these brothers. It was carried on with moist eyes and trembling breath. Jarm explained to Henry his preparation, and hoped on a future day to provide for them all. He knew he need not pledge his brother to secrecy, for he was the counterpart of his own soul. Nevertheless, they talked, of the necessity of secrecy. Henry approved the enterprize, and only regretted he was not a party to it. But a regard to their mother, required that one stay behind to soothe her in the dark days that would come to her.

The brothers entered the negro-house together. The silence was broken only by the loud respirations of the weary sleepers. Henry stood by the door, while Jarm approached his mother's bed-side, to make a last offering of love—and O! how deep and sacred was it! As he took a last look, his inmost soul said in a voice silent to sense, but audible to spirit and to God, "O, my mother! our bodies must part—our spirits, never. Where I go you will go with me. I can never be separated from my mother—never, never! Your master (he is mine no longer) may keep our bodies apart, but our souls he cannot part. O that you could go with me! I mean to embrace you again, mother. Forgive me, mother—I can't stay longer!" He wiped his eyes, and imprinted a last kiss upon her forehead. She stirred, and Jarm hid his light and retired.

Some conception may be formed of the sacred and touching sensations of the heart, but who will attempt to describe them? In the coming world, where spirit communicates with spirit, emotions are seen as in Eden, by the understanding which is the mind's eye. Not so in this outer world into which we have sunk by the fall. The good angels see them and turn them to use, but we are spiritually blind and helpless.

The brothers now embraced and bid each other a long farewell. Their affectionate communings were soon broken by the sound of horses' feet and John Farney, with overcoat close buttoned to the chin, rode up.

"My horse is lame—very lame, Jarm."

"That is bad—very bad."

"I'll let him loose and take that one," pointing to the horse Jarm rode over, which was still feeding by the road-side.

"That is a capital horse," said Jarm.

"I know it. I chose between the two, and regret I had not taken and fitted that one instead of this—but he is in fine order."

To set the lame horse loose, and put saddle, bridle and bags upon the other, was but the work of a moment; and he returned to Jarm and Henry about as soon as Jarm had his horse out and his load upon his back.

"Good bye, brother. Remember, mother must be ignorant of this at least one week, and longer, if she shows no uneasiness. Good bye."

"Good bye."

The last words of the two brothers were spoken faintly; and with a warm pressure of hands, they parted.

The cord was now severed which connected him to the home of his kindred, and it was some moments ere his experience of the keen night air restored him to a social state.

The travellers took the turf by the side of the path, and rode a while in silence, each occupied by thoughts peculiar to himself. It was, as we have said, a cold, gorgeous night. The moon and stars shone like burnished gold in an ocean of silver. The young men were alike dressed in a close buttoned overcoat, and their heads and hands were capped and gloved, so that they defied the frost in any shape, and at any point the winds might drive upon them. Its sharp edge stimulated their well fed and spirited animals, whose antics soon claimed their attention. Nor was the air less bracing and exciting to themselves. In spite of the scenes they were leaving, and the danger before and around them, they, too, began to inhale intoxication from the atmosphere, and feel it in the influx of freedom which the first step of their flight let in upon their senses. New life swelled their muscles; and ere they had gone two miles, they were side by side, curbing the impetuosity of their beasts, and presenting as gleeful, social, and formidable a platoon of might and courage as the star of Chivalry ever shone on. They called to mind that they had passes for the holidays, and if 'worst come to worst,' they felt they had strength and means to rout or ruin any three or four men the country could produce within their knowledge.

They were now nearing the estate of Col. Wilks, and hoped to meet Jerry provided like themselves, when they thought it would go hard with twice or thrice their number of ordinary men who might attempt to cross their track to freedom. How sad, then, to find him at the appointed place, unprepared for the enterprize. Situated as he was, he could not as readily as they possess the means of escape. They had but to lay their hands on anything of their master's which they needed; not so with Jerry. Though Col. Wilks had excellent horses, and provision in abundance, the fact that he rescued him from his murderers forbade his taking them.

We will not stop to detail the particulars of this interview. It is sufficient to say that Jerry could not be ready. They all felt this as a misfortune, but agreed that John and Jarm had best go on; and they pressed the hand of their unfortunate friend, and bade him a long farewell.

Though at least one third of their intended force was lost by this misfortune, their hopes and courage were not diminished. Jerry was a brave and strong man, a shrewd counsellor and terrible fighter, a close friend and boon companion, and therefore a serious loss. Yet they felt they were cunning and strong enough to go through without him. It is said disease preys on the senses, and that the patient therefore meets his fate with little pain or reluctance. So the slave, whose manhood is not crushed, loses attachment to life, and meets without reluctance the crisis that gives him liberty or death.

The interview with their friend was short, and the fugitives mounted their horses, now growing mettlesome with oats and oxygen, and turned to the North Star, which sparkled like a diamond on their path.

About six o'clock the same morning a stout colored woman, wearing a colored handkerchief in the shape of a loose turban on her head, was attracted by the appearance of two gigantic colored men on horseback, in the principal street of Nashville—their horses and themselves much freckled by the frost. Though she never turned her head or changed her step, which convinced the strangers that she supposed her interest as well as theirs required that she be neither seen nor heard but by themselves.

"There is a row up in the city," said she, "which, if you are strangers, you had best be mindful of."

Full well they understood (the travellers were no other than the young fugitives,) that the trouble related to their unhappy countrymen, and that they must be careful. It was arranged on the start, that if rivers were to be forded, John should take the lead; but if fighting was in prospect, Jarm should take the lead. Jarm therefore moved along, on a traveller's trot, up Main street, in the face of the people, and John followed the length of his horse behind him. The whole metropolis was in motion, but the travellers moved directly on about their business, like wise freemen, turning neither to the right or left,—carefully avoiding any matters not their own.

They soon found themselves moving through masses of citizens in a high state of excitement; but their appearance testified that they were strangers and early travellers, and their boldness saved them from any suspicion that they were fugitives. They were unnoticed but by the passing glance of an occasional horse amateur, who stopped to eye the beauty and motions of their noble animals.

They passed through the masculine population of the city, which had mainly rushed to the scene of action. Glad indeed were they when their horses' feet struck the bridge over the Cumberland River on the border of the city. But they were greatly alarmed to see there a toll-gate shut across their path. If they might avoid notice elsewhere, they knew they must attract direct attention at this important pass. As they advanced upon the bridge, a little boy presented himself at the gate to wait upon them. This new and unexpected peril, though it quickened their wits, did not embarrass their equanimity. It needed but a motion, which Jarm knew well how to make, to set his high spirited horse bounding as in a fright.

"Open the gate—quick!" said he, tossing a shilling to the obedient boy, as he rushed through, and told John to do the same.

They afterwards learned that they were in great danger at this point. The keeper of this gate being a lame man, he was employed by its stockholders for the double purpose of employing a moneyless cripple, and to detect fugitive slaves. It was a part of his bargain with his employers that he should criticise every colored person who came there, and be careful not to pass a runaway. It so happened, this morning, that his curiosity was attracted by the tumult, and he hobbled after the multitude to arrest or murder a handful of abused black men. Had he been at home, it is not probable the travellers could have passed without a severe cross examination—may be not without violence; for, under the circumstances, they would have forced a passage if necessary, and trusted to the strength of their horses and their own genius to avoid consequences. Happily the point was passed without trouble, and their minds relieved of great anxiety as they entered the open country beyond. They congratulated themselves on their good luck and began to think of breakfast for themselves and horses, and would have stopped at a farm house to eat, but for the following occurrence.

Between them and the house above mentioned, they met a little colored boy, who, from his size, they judged to be between four and six years old. The little lad was shivering, mourning, and crying piteously.

"What is the matter, boy?"

"They have been selling mother."

"When did they sell her?"

"This morning."

"Did the man who lives in that house sell her?"

"Yes."

"O, well—don't cry," and so saying, Jarm threw him a piece of a chicken's wing, and John gave him a piece of bread, which the poor fellow commenced eating with the utmost greed, apparently forgetting his wrongs and sorrows in his temporary good fortune.

"Who that ever had a mother could break and mangle a mother's and child's heart like that?"

"Curse the wretches! Don't let us stop at that house to feed—I should be tempted to shoot them!"

"No, no—I fear we would both fail to bear our selves as our case demands with such people. We will go on."

They passed by, and now and at noon, fed their horses at the corn stacks which they found in secluded places by the road, and refreshed themselves from their own provisions.

As yet they had little experience of freedom; they had never spoken with a white man in their new capacity, and feared a lack of assurance to save them from fatal embarrassment when put to the test.

When the evening began to drop its shadows around them, and their features were indistinguishable, they found themselves in front of a Baronial mansion, which stood in a large court-yard abundantly and tastefully ornamented with trees and shrubbery, and surrounded by a stone wall and iron gates. The scene, in its twilight drapery, to their unpracticed eyes, was full of inconceivable attraction and imposing grandeur.

"Dare we stop here?"

"We have got to stop somewhere, or feel and act like slaves—lay out, and be taken up for runaways, if we are stumbled on by white men."

"Will they keep us, think you?"

"To be sure they will."

"Courage, then!—here goes!" said Jarm. "Hurrah, there!"

The voice of a colored boy responded at the barn—to which was a gravel walk in a direct line from the large gate at the road. The boy came at once to the gate, and his master, who heard the call from the house, also came.

"What is wanting?" said the landlord.

"We want keeping for ourselves and horses to-night, sir. We are travellers."

"Open the gate, William."

The gate being opened, the travellers rode their horses into the yard, and it was immediately closed and barred behind them.

"Lead the horses to the barn, and take good care of them," said the host; and turning to the travellers, he said, politely, "Follow me, gentlemen."

To use an expression quite common now, the travellers were "taken down" by the politeness of their host; and when he took them by a circular path up a high flight of stone steps which led to the front door, and was about to usher them into a parlor blazing with light and fashion, they shrank instinctively back and exclaimed internally, "Conscience, we can't go that!" and instantly Jarm said to the man, "We are free colored men, and only want keeping for ourselves and horses over night."

"Very well," said the man—and turning to the door on the opposite side of the hall, he said, kindly,

"Walk in here."

The room was dark when they entered, but the landlord ordered a light, and wood and coals of fire were brought, and the host himself set to kindling them into a flame. Jarm was greatly embarrassed by the condescension of his landlord, and John retreated to the outer door to hide his confusion. Perplexed as Jarm was, he did not believe it was proper to be passive and see a white gentleman like his landlord build him a fire—he insisted, therefore, with all humility and civility, to do it himself. He was glad to bide the confusion his color did not conceal, by bending low and blowing the coals and kindlers into a blaze.

So soon as the fire blazed up, Jarm told his host they would be glad to retire early—if he had a "pallet" for each—which, in Tennessee, means a blanket,—they would be provided for the night.

The landlord gave the requisite orders, and left them to themselves. John, of course, returned from his temporary retreat. The room was soon warmed up, the pallets brought in, a hasty supper of bread and bacon consumed, the lights put out to signify they had retired, and themselves rolled up in their blankets on the carpet soon as possible—to watch, but not to sleep.

At this stage of their affairs, they were glad to avoid all intercourse with white men which they could avoid. The possibility that their landlord might return, kind and gentle as he seemed to be, and catechize them about their affairs, frightened them,—therefore they lay down at once and watched till morning.

When the clock struck four they were up, and called up William, saw to feeding their horses, saddled and bridled them when they ate their oats, and told William to find the amount of their bills, that they might pay and be on their journey.

They soon heard William in conversation with his master, asking him for the amount of charges.

"What! are they going so soon?"

"Yes, master—their horses are already prepared, and they wait only to pay their bills."

"Why, I did not think they were going so soon. I intended to have a talk with them in the morning."

"They say they are very anxious to be off, because they have many miles to ride to-day, to be at a certain place in time."

"Well, tell them to give you a shilling a-piece, and let them go."

"Bless God!" inwardly said the runaways. The shillings were paid, and they were let through the gate into the highway without delay.

CHAPTER XXII

As may be supposed, the young men were delighted to be alone again on the public highway. To them, their overnight experience was something like an escape from a den of lions. The weather continued freezing cold, but they minded it not, so intensely interested were they in their success. Their horses were well fed and cared for, and scarcely less lively than when they started.

Their own provisions furnished them again, and their horses were supplied as on the preceding day. When evening came, they found themselves in the presence of one of the most popular taverns on the road. It was quite dark, and they delivered their horses to the stable boy, like other travellers, and directed their steps to the house, which was glowing with light, and alive with the sound of many voices.

As they entered the hall, they met the landlord, and enquired if they could be entertained. He said "yes," and opened the door into the bar-room. They saw the room literally filled with white men, in all stages of intoxication. The fumes of tobacco and brandy, with the loud oaths of demented men, flowed in an overpowering torrent upon their senses.

"Don't take us in there!" said Jarm. "We are free colored men, and want to be by ourselves, and have supper, and go to bed, and be on our journey in the morning, early."

The landlord then led them to a private parlor, and left them. In a short time a servant came and said their suppers were ready.

Neither Jarm or John were ignorant of well provided tables; but to see one set for themselves, alone, was a new thing. Their table was furnished with broiled chicken, ham and eggs, coffee, sweet-meats, and etceteras. When they took their seats, servants stood behind them to obey their commands. They felt awkwardly but pleasantly, and exchanging significant glances, hastily sated their keen appetites with the best supper they ever enjoyed. After the cold food and cold ride of the last forty-eight hours, a warm feast like that was a great luxury.

They fell asleep soon after they felt their beds, and notwithstanding the bellowing of the crazy and drunken men, who, until after midnight, and even to approaching morning, made the house tremble with their demonstrations, they slept soundly, only, and occasionally, and partially, waking, to testify to the tempestuous excesses of the debauch.

At an early hour they awoke the hostler, fed their horses, paid their bills, and prepared to journey again. We give the following incident, illustrative of Jarm's luck and southern ways.

Jarm brought to the tavern a new cotton umbrella, and left it with the landlord. This umbrella some of the frolikers had taken, and left a new and beautiful silk one in its place. When the servant brought Jam's things, in the morning, he brought along this umbrella. "That is not my umbrella; mine is a new cotton one," said Jarm. The boy returned to his master and stated the case to him.

"Tell the d—d fool to take the umbrella and be off—who the d—l cares?—the silk umbrella belongs to the nigger"—growled the landlord from his bed, where it is not probable he had lain long. Of course Jarm made no more words, accepted the profitable exchange, unceremoniously thrust upon him, thinking it an ill wind that blows nobody any good.

The third day did not materially vary the experience of the fugitives. But when night overtook them, they stopped at a private mansion, which, they were told, belonged to a bachelor gentleman. They delivered their horses to the servants, to be cared for, as usual, and were led to the front door, and entered the room, where the proprietor sat reading.

"We are free colored men," said Jarm, "and want—"

"I'll colored men ye—you black rascals!" said the bachelor, as he reached for his cane, "if you don't get out of this room!"

The young men fled, of course, and avoided the blows the idiocracy or drunkenness of their host seemed willing to inflict. He did not follow them, but seemed satisfied that he was clear of their presence. The servants understood his peculiarities, and led them to the kitchen, and showed all the kindness they dare. But they were allowed neither supper or bed. Here again they had a night of fasting, added to anxious watching for morning, to be released from painful embarrassment. Two things only were they indebted to their crusty landlord for. Their horses were housed and fed,—thanks to the slaves for that,—and they, also, were covered from the cold winter.

Notwithstanding they were so shabbily used, the overseer showed them his sour and ugly face in the morning, and demanded a dollar for the use of beds which they never had. In the lion's mouth, as they were, they knew it was wise to be submissive. Jarm, therefore, handed the overseer a dollar bill, which had been condemned as counterfeit, and which he could no where else pass.

This piece of counterfeit paper, which had been imposed on Jarm, appeased the extortion of the crusty scoundrel, and they took their horses and departed.

They now entered the fourth day of their journey, without awaking the enemy, or eliciting attention to their real character. They were in excellent spirits, and congratulated each other upon their good fortune. From past experience, they believed to-day would be as yesterday and the day before, and that they should pass through without molestation. Their road lay through a thinly settled and uncultivated country, and it was rare they met a traveller. Under the circumstances, they dismissed fear, and amused themselves by recurring to the escapes, perils, and incidents of the journey. Those perils and incidents made them the more sportive, as they were exciting. Over their experience with the old bachelor, whose vengeance and hospitality were so spontaneous and peculiar, they made themselves merry and laughed heartily.

Full of health and glee, they progressed some four or five miles from their morning's starting point, when their attention was arrested by the appearance of three men on foot, who entered their path by a road in the wood at right angles with their own, about fifty rods from them. Instead of crossing and continuing along in the same road, the footmen turned and came towards them. Their merriment was abruptly hushed, and Jarm started ahead, while John fell behind, according to their arrangement. With their eyes steadily measuring the men as they advanced, they silently moved along on a moderate travelling gait.

So soon as the fugitives got sight of these men, they knew they were not gentlemen. On foot, and in a half shabby dress, they resembled a set of men known only in the south, who are most dreaded by black men, and despised by white men, to wit—negro-catchers. As they came nearer, it was evident they were able-bodied, and if their spunk was equal to their strength, it was certain, as opposed to Jarm and John, only, they were no despiseable force. Whether they had pistols or knives, the travellers knew not. Their only weapon in sight, was a heavy walking club, which one of them used, and which probably had been picked up in the path. They knew their own pistols were in order, for they fired and re-loaded them but a short time before. They made sure that they could be seized any moment, but determined to use them only in the last extremity, bravely trusting their personal strength to overcome the three, and relying on their weapons "to settle the hash," if necessary to victory.

When the parties came together, the footmen seized the horses by the bridles, and the following dialogue ensued:

"What is your name?" said one of them, addressing Jarm.

"Henry Robinson."

"What is your name?" addressing John.

"John Robinson."

"None of your d—d lies—whose niggers are you?"

"We are freemen."

"Where are you going?"

"We are brothers, going to see our mother in Kentucky."

"Have you got travelling passes?"

"Yes."

"Show them—let us see them."

"They are in our saddle-bags—we'll get off and show them."

When they had dismounted and tied their horses, they asked the ruffians if they, or either of them, were magistrates.

"None of your business—what do you want to know that for?"

"Because, if you are magistrates, or if any one of you is a magistrate, we are bound to show you our passes;—but if not, then you have no right to demand them. We are willing to go with you to a magistrate and deliver him our passes, if you doubt us—but we are not willing to deliver them to any one who is not a magistrate."

"Don't blarney with us, you black rascals—get out your passes, if you have got any, or come along to jail. We'll learn you manners—we don't believe you have any passes."

Conversation like the above was carried on with Jarm by one of the three, and a like conversation with John by another one—the ruffians demanding the passes, and the fugitives refusing to deliver them to any one but a magistrate.

Finding the young men obstinate, one of the ruffians took Jarm by the collar, while the other was busy with John.

"Come, along with me, you dog!" pulling him with his might.

"You have no right to take me, when I have a pass," said Jarm, hanging back, and nulifying the force of the draft on him.

"Come along, you d—d rascal, or I'll take your life," Jarm still hanging back, and remonstrating as before—waiting for the fight to begin in earnest by the assailants.

While thus engaged, the third man, covered by Jarm's assailant, struck him on the head with his club, which, for the moment, Jarm thought had ended the fight on his part, before it begun. His head flashed fire, like an exploding magazine, which was followed by darkness and faintness, that made him mindless and helpless. He reeled and was near falling, and the blood flowed freely from the severe wound made by the club. Jarm thought it was all over with him, as did the man who had him by the collar. He therefore let go of Jarm, to help the man against John Farney. John had already passed the bounds of self defence, and was dealing his enemy blows that made him reel and cry for help.

Jarm's brain now began to light up, and passion and vengeance came with its light. His strength came forth speedily, and he sprang like an angry tiger at the throat of the villain who struck him. The whole weight of his body was projected against the wretch, and he tumbled backwards over a log—and Jarm's knees, propelled by the weight of his body, plunged into his bowels and breast.

"You will lay still awhile, I guess," said Jarm, as he sprang from the lifeless man to rescue Farney from the assassins, who were pressing him hard.

When Farney's combatents saw Jarm coming, and that their companion was noiseless and motionless, they turned and fled, leaving that companion to the mercy of the conquerors. The victors pursued them a few rods, in separate directions, into the woods; but having no motive but vengeance in the pursuit, they returned, and found the prostrated man, motionless, with the club by his side. They felt that charity did not require them to see whether he was dead or alive, and without delay took their horses and fled with all reasonable speed, believing that the wounded and discomfited men would rouse the whole country in their pursuit.

A few moments wrought a great change in the condition, plans and feelings of the fugitives. As they rode, they made up their minds that coolness and impudence would no longer serve them—that they must abandon their original policy, and be fugitives in earnest. Leaving the main road, therefore, they took collateral and obscure ones, and travelled with great speed. As yet, their beasts made no complaint, and seemed able as at the beginning. Now, they put them to what, in their judgment, was the limit of their ability. At noon, and night, they fed them and themselves, in the fields, at the hay and corn stacks, and lodged there at night. They no more ventured on the general thoroughfare, or at private or public houses. Their policy now was, to be private and expeditious as possible to get out of the slave states.

The day after the above rencounter, they enquired of two slaves they met, the direct route to the Ohio River. After informing them of such route, the slaves said, two colored men on horseback, had given three notorious negro-catchers a dreadful fight, the day before, and that one of the latter had been killed, or nearly killed—that couriers had been sent along the road by the negro-catchers—that the slaves were greatly rejoiced at this, because these slave-catchers annoyed them, and were intensely hated by them. They said further, that though the slave-catchers were greatly excited, the people at large cared little about it; for they believed the brave travellers were free negroes—that none but free negroes would do as they did—that the white men were bad men, and deserved a flogging—and yet it was by no means safe for the fugitives to be caught, for the slave catchers would persecute them to death.

The slaves were satisfied from the appearance of Jarm and John, that they were the heroes who did the deed they were talking about, and said this to put them on guard.

On the morning of the second day after the rencounter, they found themselves in Kentucky, and forty-eight hour's ride, only, from the Ohio River, opposite Indiana, which, they learned, was a free State. Their anxiety was greatly stimulated to reach that point. They had spent the night under a haystack, which, with corn taken from a crib near by, served for feed for the horses and shelter for themselves. And now they started on a gait which they calculated would bring them to the river within time. It was a cold and dreary morning, but they were warmly clad, and vigorous as well by nature and habit, as by the interest at stake.

But their way was by no means a smooth one. It lay though a country of man-thieves, and wretches formed into banditti, to obtain a livelihood by way-laying, capturing, imprisoning, and depriving of their protection, such as they, and often selling them into slavery. Their danger increased from people of this sort, as they approached the free States.

About nine o'clock in the morning of this day, they discovered in the road before them, five men on foot. There was no way of avoiding them, but turning and fleeing, which would not only put them off their course and delay them in their journey, but would admit their guilt, and stir the country in their pursuit.

"Let us meet them," said John.

"Certainly—to turn and run would make us fair game."

"They are of the bad class, I know by their dress and walk. If they were gentlemen, we might hope to pass them without trouble."

"Just so—but we must make short work. If they stop us, let us not dally—if we must fight, let us not hesitate to give the first blow, after sufficient cause—and let it be a blow that will show them not only that we are in earnest, but which will leave their number of able bodies, less, by one."

"That's it—if it comes to my lot to strike, he that takes the blow will feel it;—but mind, if they have pistols! In that case they will have the hands of us, and there will be bloody work. The first motion of a pistol must be a death signal. Until we see such motion, however, we will be content to settle the fight with fists and clubs."

"They are on us—let us look right ahead and say not a word."

The parties soon came together, and the footmen came around the travelers, and began to catechise them, and demand their passes. As in the other case, they got off the horses under pretence to show their passes, but really to prepare for a fight. The colloquy differed little from the one they had with the combatants two days before.

The original arrangement in regard to fighting was now dispensed with. It so happened that one of the white men, who was more rude than the rest, put his hand on John Farney. Without waiting for further provocation, John gave him a blow in the eye, and sent him backwards almost to the ground. As if he had been kicked by a horse, the flesh above the eye was cut and fell over it, and presented a bloody and shocking appearance. No sooner did this most unexpected thing occur, than awakened by surprise, the assailants made a feint as if they would attack the young men, but their brawny arms and terrible determination, and astonishment at their courage, overpowered their pluck, and they fled with their might, John yelling behind them—

"Run, you white-livered cowards!"

There was no time to be wasted now. The interview and the combat were brief, but they served, so long as they lasted, to rest their horses. They mounted at once, and leaving the hat of the unlucky scamp whose eye was bruised on the field of battle, they fled the country.

They had not progressed far, ere they met an intelligent colored man. He was well acquainted with the roads to the River, and told them of an obscure one which was equally distant with the main road, and would be likely to deceive their pursuers; and should they be overtaken on this obscure route, they could easily cover themselves by the immense wood it traversed.

They had no time to consider chances, and therefore plunged into this blind road with great speed—and had occasion to thank their stars that they did so. They learned afterwards that the same slave who put them on this course, also put their pursuers on a false scent in the direction of the river at a point lower down.

Though their way lay through occasional corn fields, where they found abundant provision for their horses, they saw scarce a house or man the whole day. One more night they spent in the open fields among the stacks of corn and oats; and without meeting anything worthy of record, they arrived on the banks of the Ohio, late in the afternoon—a thing they had looked forward to with such concern as fugitive slaves only know anything about.

They went directly to the River, and there found a boat bound to the shore by the ice. Behind them lay the wilderness of stunted oaks and brush through which they found their path to the River. On the outer edge of the wood, and on the margin of the bank, stood a contemptible log shanty, which, in size and aspect, resembled a cross between a hog-house and an inferior human dwelling, with nothing about it to induce the suspicion that it had an inhabitant.

The first question, of course, was, how they should get to the opposite bank. The river was quiet in the embrace of Winter, and no sound was heard but the hoofs of the horses on the ice-bound pebbles, and the voices of the travellers talking of the safety of passing on the ice.

While they were discussing that subject, a door opened on the side of this miserable cabin, from which a man emerged and moved towards them. Of course their attention was earnestly fixed upon this new and unexpected object. Their first purpose was to assure themselves that the man was alone; that done, they were at ease. Though apparently a strong man, who did not seem to lack courage, they believed that either of them could manage him alone, and of course he would be a trifle opposed to them both.

"What you about there!" he exclaimed, in a coarse, rough voice, as he approached them.

"We want to get over the river."

"You can't do it."

"We must go over to-day."

"Well, you won't get over to-day. It is my ferry, and the boat is frozen in—and the ice is not strong enough to bear up a man, without the horses."

"What shall we give you to get us over with our horses?" said Jarm.

"Didn't I tell you it couldn't be done? Be off, you black d—ls! I know you—you are running away from your masters—and I would not help you over any how. But the thing is impossible—you can neither use boat or ice. It is uncertain whether you can in a week—so be off!"

"We will give you two dollars to get us over."

"Didn't I tell you it couldn't be done?"

"Well, name the sum we shall give you to take us over."

"It ain't my business to run niggers."

"But we are free niggers—name the sum we shall give."

"Free niggers, eh?—that may be. Well, if you are free niggers, then I will land you safe on the other side, if you will give into my hands five dollars a-piece before I start."

"We won't trust you so long as you can say 'scat.' If you will take us over, you will have your pay when your work is done, and not before."

"Well, since I have made the offer, if you will agree, upon honor, to pay me ten dollars when I get you over, then I will take you safe across."

"You old scoundrel! If *you* can take us over, then we can take ourselves over. We won't give you a single cent," said Jarm, leaping into the boat, and leading his horse along on the side to the end of it.

His eye now caught horses' tracks leading off on the ice.

"Come along, John," said he. "Here are tracks of horses' feet—we will follow them. We don't want any help from that lying old scoundrel."

"Get out of that boat, you black, d—l, or I'll break your head!"

"Your head ain't worth breaking," said John Farney. "But if you don't shut your lying mouth, I'll smash it," at the same time shoving his heavy fist near the cheek of the ferry-man.

"Come along," said Jarm. "Let the lying brute alone—he ain't worth quarreling with. If he don't leave peaceably, just put a bullet through his head—that will quiet him!"

The travellers now went along on the ice, leading their horses in Indian file, Jarm a little ahead. They left the Kentuckian foaming and swearing like a bedlamite, and kept their eyes intently upon the ice to see if it bent beneath them. Passing the center of the River, they felt safe, and for the first time raised their eyes to the opposite shore. When they started, that shore was scarcely perceptible through the milky atmosphere, but now a small village was visible a little distance from it, and three or four men were standing there, looking at them. The number of men soon increased to five or six. The fact was, that a light horse or two only had been led over, and it was still considered perilous for a heavy man and horse to venture.

As the travellers approached the shore, their color began to be seen.

"They are niggers," said one of the villagers.

"They are brave fellows, any how."

"I'll bet they are slaves running away. Let us take them up and get a pile."

"Agreed! D—n the niggers! We don't want them on this side!"

When they arrived at the bank, they were six or seven rods from these men. Now they had their feet upon free soil, it become a question what to do. A word or two only was said about it, when Jarm drew out his well loaded double barrelled pistol, and said, 'Let us fire!' John also took out his pistol, and they both pointed in the air, and each discharged both barrels. The report awoke an echo on both shores, and was heard at a great distance.

"Pshaw!" said one of the citizens, "they can't be slaves."

"They are free niggers," said another, "who have been to Kentucky to spend the Holidays with their friends, and have returned in a frolic."

"Slaves never acted in that way," said another.

"They are drunk," said another, "or they had not dared come over on the ice."

A brief colloquy of that sort dispersed these wiseacres into the village, with the exception of a colored man—who was shocked by the proposal to arrest and return them to slavery. He remained when the rest were gone, and went immediately to the young men.

"What are you firing your pistols for?" said he.

"We have been travelling many days to get to a free State, and we are free now. We fired our pistols to express our joy that we were safe from our pursuers, who we think we left not far behind."

"My dear fellows, you are little safer here than in Kentucky, if it is known you are slaves. Your pursuers will follow and take you here, and there are bad men enough to help them do it. Did you see those men standing with me out there?"

"Yes."

"They thought you were slaves, and agreed to take you back to your masters. But when you fired, they concluded you were free colored men, coming home in a frolic, after the holidays in Kentucky. Travelling on horse back, and shooting pistols in that way, made them so confident you were freemen, that they did not think it worth while to ask you any questions."

"I thought this was a free state?"

"It is called a free State—but the laws allow slaveholders to hunt their slaves here, and hold them, to take them back."

"Where, then, can we be safe? We cannot go back to slavery—we had rather die."

"Yes, and somebody will die before we go back," said John Farney, driving a ball into his pistol.

"There is no place in the States where you can be safe. To be safe, you must get into Canada. I am sorry to say that the only power that gives freedom in North America, is in England."

"How can we get to Canada?"

"Follow the North Star—do you know the North Star?"

"Yes."

"Have you any money?"

"Yes."

"There are those in the free States who will do what they can for you. Your danger is in falling upon enemies. It will not be safe to stop here a moment. Take that road, and go to Corridon, a small village about twenty miles from here, and enquire for a man by the name of——. He is an abolitionist, and will keep you and tell you what next to do."

The stranger said many other advisory things to the fugitives, in a brief discourse, which it is not necessary to relate.

The reader need not be informed that they received this information with great sadness and disappointment. Their joy was suddenly chilled, and their happy sky all black again. They were now more puzzled than ever to know how to act. The State where they were, forbid its citizens to hold slaves for themselves, but allowed and required them to hold slaves for others. Pecuniary speculations in slaves were limited to hunting, siezing, and replunging them into slavery. In this miserable way, there were too many ready to live on the miseries of colored men. They saw that ere they could attain freedom, they must track their way from point to point, and from abolitionist to abolitionist, by aid of the Star, through the dreary wilderness to Canada.

The joy, which a few moments before swelled like the sea, now ebbed like its tide—yet they were not discouraged. New dangers started up—but they had been educated to look danger in the face. Their lives had been a concatenation of disappointments and perils—therefore their spirits were hardy and brave. It is a blunder to suppose that American slaves are cowardly and spiritless. Ignorant and degraded they may be; and in some, the spirit of manhood is entirely crushed out—but the same causes strengthen and perfect the manly qualities of others—and it may be doubted whether, as a body, a braver people live. They lack wisdom and knowledge through no fault of theirs—but they are decidedly, if not pre-eminently brave.

CHAPTER XXIII

Instead of being in the promised land, the young men found they were further from it than they ever thought of, and an immense wilderness between, whose anti-slavery thoroughfares had never been opened—that wilderness, too, instead of an uninhabited waste, was full of enemies, dangers, and trials, such as at that day had rarely been encountered, and never recorded. And now, after having slept, for successive nights, like the beasts of the fields, in a dark, cold night, on the borders of a village in a so-called free State, they were met with the kind advice to walk softly away, so as not to awake the people, who would delight to seize and enslave them.

Nevertheless, they now felt they had been again saved by an unseen hand, and that their conditions, though harsh and severe, were a protection and a blessing. Had they arrived at the village a little earlier, they had inevitably fallen into the hands of slave catchers. Had they not fired their pistols as they did, they had not deceived and dispersed the bad men who stood ready to seize them. The blessed night now interposed like the pillar of cloud between them and their pursuers—and the counsel of their friend was as the voice of God speaking out of it, pointing their way, and directing them onward. Their acquaintance with the lives of Christians (so called) had led them to form a low estimate of popular Christianity—but they were not so obtuse as to infer that these deliverances were accidents. They served to revive in Jarm's memory the theology of the Prestons, and he was strongly impressed that God's angels were with him and would take him through. But had Mr. Preston been there, he would have told him that these experiences, and others like them, the land and world over, were the chanticlerian signals of the extinction of faith, and consequent tribulations which attend the birth of a new Jerusalem.

"What do you think of the case now?" said John, after they mounted and rode out of the hearing of their white friend.

"Bad—bad enough. But we are in great luck, after all."

"How is that?—twenty miles to a friend, hungry and sleepy, the horses tired—and in good luck?"

"It is evening—we had been off our guard entirely, and lost, had we been earlier; we were exactly in time to find the friend who just left us; our shooting saved us again and dispersed our enemies; the night covers our pursuers with darkness or sleep, to give us a chance to get out of their way. It is astonishing how lucky we have been. But we must not go twenty miles to-night. Our future safety depends much on our horses; and to go that distance, after all they have done to-day, is too much for them."

"We had best stop for the night at the first place that seems safe. We shall soon find if there is danger, and no small force will attempt to disturb us."

In this manner they talked until they came in front of a small Dutch groggery, with a tavern sign before it, about eight miles from the spot where they landed in Indiana. Here they stopped, as ordinary travellers. If there were any accommodations in the house, they were already occupied, and their lodging was a little empty log barn—their provisions for themselves were furnished from their saddlebags, and their bed was the bare plank beside their horses. They slept soundly on the hard timber, and took an early start for Corridon, twelve miles distant—where they arrived about eight o'clock in the morning.

They were not long finding the person to whom they were directed. He was a true hearted colored man, ready to advise and assist them to the best of his means. They spent the day with him. It was the Sabbath, and gladly would they have accepted it as a day of rest. But the certainty that the hounds were behind them, rabid for their blood, robbed them of the quiet necessary to repose. Their horses, however, whose strength had been so well tested, knew no danger, present or absent, and rested away their weariness.

The colored brother who entertained them, from absolute poverty, had grown to be a man of substance, notwithstanding the prejudice and injustice of pro-slavery men and laws. From him they received valuable information in regard to their condition in the free States, and advice to get out of them into Canada. But he knew little of the country. The most he could do was, to tell them they would find a valuable friend in a Mr. Overrals, of Indianapolis, about two hundred miles distant, as he supposed, in a north-westerly direction—but could say nothing of the intervening country and its inhabitants.

At midnight, the fugitives took the last lunch with their hospitable friend, and mounted their horses for Indianapolis. They were soon lost in an immense forest through which their path lay—and for three cold days and nights wandered about without food enough to sustain life, and without sight of human faces, other than the roving hunters, in whose camps they slept at night. Their path in the woods was circuitous and angular, and covered with snow—therefore they were mis-led from a north-west to a north-east course, and were travelling towards Kentucky. On the third day from Corridon, weary and hungry beyond endurance, they come into a country where white men lived, which was partially cultivated—but the inhabitants refused them food. Such was the extremity of their distress from hunger and cold, that their courage abated, and they began to talk of returning to Kentucky.

In this extremity, they came before a log house and asked for food. The landlord looked at them a moment with an expression of unutterable kindness, and said:—

"You are very hungry?"

"Yes."

"How long since you have eat anything?"

"We have eat very little for three days."

"Come in, my wife will get you a breakfast."

A boy then took their horses to the stable, and they followed the landlord into the house.

"Here, Elizabeth," said he, "are a couple of young men who are very hungry—they have had nothing to eat worth telling of for three days. I told them you would get them a breakfast."

The good woman turned her compassionate eyes upon the half famished strangers, and said:—

"Why, the poor creatures! They shall have breakfast shortly."

"How happens it," asked the landlord, "ye have been without eating so long—have ye no money?"

"Yes, sir, we have money, but were lost in the woods—and when we found our way out among the farmers, they turned us off, and refused to let us have anything to eat."

"I am sorry to say they are a set of broken down slaveholder's sons, who have squatted in these woods, and like their fathers and mothers, respect colored people as beasts of burden only. But ye are on a wrong course—you are going back to slavery again."

Kind as this man seemed to be, they dared not tell him their case. If nature and education made them strong and brave, experience made them cautious also—therefore they replied:—

"We are not slaves—we are free colored men."

"Where have you been?"

"We have been to the lower part of Kentucky to see our relatives, and are returning to Louisville."

John and Jarm had frequently heard of Louisville, and it was the only place they could speak of with confidence in this connection.

"Louisville is in Kentucky—you are going right back to slavery again. You are in a few miles of the river, which lays between you and your master—you should go back into the country. The nearer the river you be, the more liable you are to be taken and returned into Egypt. You should steer North and get into Ohio, or West, into Indianapolis, and then North, into Canada."

"We have a friend at Indianapolis that we started to visit—but since we got lost and suffered so much, we concluded to turn directly to Louisville."

Though they repeatedly denied that they were slaves, their host, disregarding their denials, continued to talk with them as if he knew their case exactly. He pointed his finger in the direction of Louisville, and said:—

"That is the way to Louisville. Keep clear of that course—it will take you right back to slavery. That is the way to Indianapolis, and that is the road that leads to it," said he, pointing to the north. "The further you are from Louisville and the river, the safer will you be."

During the conversation, the fugitives had their eyes upon the good woman who was cooking their meals, and the rich flavor thereof goaded their irresistible appetites. She, too, often turned to look at them, and plainly saw she was making them grateful and happy.

Such was the conversation between the parties for the few minutes the wife was preparing the bacon, coffee, &c.; and when she came, with a smile, and said their breakfast was ready, they thought no creature of Heaven could be more beautiful. It was charity, the dove which came down from God out of her heart and pictured its form in her face, that made her look so lovely. For the time, they seemed intromitted into the sphere of goodness, and saw and felt it in the uses this good woman was performing, which made her face shine like an angel's. In after life, when the fog of ignorance was swept from his mind, and his spirit had out grown whips and chains entirely, Mr. Loguen, on the stump and in the social circle, often returned to this case by lively memory, and spoke of it with a moist eye and swelling bosom. It is one of the Emanuels of his soul, to which it will cling forever.

It is needless to say that they enjoyed this meal greatly. The landlord and lady also enjoyed it with them. If it fed the bodies of the former, it fed the souls of the latter. Not to embarrass the young men, the host and lady withdrew by themselves, after charging them to be free and eat all they wished.

"Poor fellows!" said the woman to her husband.

"You love to feed the hungry, don't you, Elizabeth?"

"Yes, I do!" she said, with emphasis.

"Then you know what the delight of Heaven is, to wit, 'the doing good to others.' It is all the delight God has, and therefore it is a principle of Heaven that man never owns any good until he gives it away—then he treasures it up. Not only does God's happiness consist in doing good to the neighbor, but it makes the joy and growth of all his angels. It is the only genuine joy of earth and Heaven. Indeed, it must become our joy here, or it can never be there. The good we do others, we do to ourselves. So of the evils—I am afraid it will take the masters of those boys a great while to find that out."

"But they say they are free."

"Aye—but they are not free or they would not be in this plight. They are free if they get into Canada—otherwise they are slaves, and the worst of slaves. If they are caught, woe be to them!"

"How horrible the wickedness that compels a person to speak untruly, as the means of obeying truth and justice!"

"Truth and justice, in their internal and true significance, mean about the same thing. We are bound to be true to the internal principle, but are treacherous to it if we allow our external words and actions to give it to the destroyer—it would be casting pearls to swine. It is the intent of the heart that determines the moral qualities of words. Their moral meaning is their true meaning, and that is determined by the good or evil they purpose to do. Because slavery inverts principles, it inverts the use of words also. It is the greatest possible liar, and to give it facts to live on, is 'giving that which is holy to dogs!' It is 'to take the children's bread, cast it to the dogs,'—and ere this be done, Christ has charged, 'let the children first be filled,'—and there are the children, (pointing to John and Jarm.) The truth consists in preserving them. If our words betray them, we are liars, as well when we state facts truly, as when we state them untruly. Slave-holders forfeit their right to natural truth, as they do a right to their natural lives. You may as well say a slave may not knock his master down or kill him to get his freedom, as to say he may not tell him an untruth to get it. If the latter is a wicked lie, the former is a wicked murder. If a poor slave takes his master's horse to run away from him, he is not therefore a thief. Nor is he a liar when he tells an untruth to the same end. Slave-holders live a lie. They put themselves in a condition where God will not give them truth, and man may not. They must change their condition, as the prodigal did, before mercy and truth can come anywhere near them."

Having finished breakfast, they spent an hour or more with this good man and woman. After being warmed and fed, and clothed with clean shirts, and their horses were fed and rested, they prepared for a new start. These favors made a decided impression upon their spirits. The discovery of such hearts gave them courage to hope for more, and that their case was not desperate, even among white people. They had suffered intensely from cold and hunger, but they were revived again, and resolved to face any danger for liberty. Their only prayer was, that their enemy might meet them in any form but hunger.

"What shall we pay for our entertainment, sir?"

"You are off, then, are you? You are welcome to stay longer."

"We are anxious to be on our way, and are ready to pay for the trouble and expense we have been to you," addressing the landlord and his lady also.

"Your bills are paid, boys. To sympathize with the delight of my wife in doing for you, more than satisfies me for what you call trouble and expense. Our measure of payment, indeed, is pressed down and runs over already, and we should throw it all away, if we took one penny from your small means to pay your way to Canada. No, no—you are welcome, and may you fare no worse anywhere."

"We are most grateful for your unexpected kindness. You still speak of us as slaves. We value your generosity the more, because it was intended for that unhappy class of our countrymen. It is not necessary for us to repeat our denial in the matter. Our gratitude would be full had you entertained us as freemen, but we prize the act higher because you have done it to us as slaves—and now we have but one more favor to ask. Will you repeat the directions as to the course of our journey?"

"Can you read writing?"

"No."

"Take that road," pointing north, "and when you come to a four corners, take the left hand road, which will take you from Louisville and the River, north-westerly, towards Indianapolis. In the first village you come to on this left hand road, you will find two taverns—one of brick and the other of wood. Be sure ye stop at the brick one—and when ye have found the landlord, you may report yourselves to him with perfect freedom, for he is your friend. He will direct you after that, and provide for you while you are with him—and may God preserve ye," said the landlord, as both he and his wife pressed their hands kindly.

Touched by the kindness of these people, the young men started on their way, determined to obey instructions. The Providence that led them to these good people banished all regard for the flesh pots of Egypt, and they were stern in their determination to push for this new country called Canada. We call it new, because they never heard of it until they arrived in Indiana. Since Ohio, too, was named, the memory of it as the place where his mother was free, was revived. Besides them, Illinois, Indianapolis and Louisville were the only places they could name. These facts show how utterly unfit they were to be cross questioned, or even to respond to accidental enquiries in regard to themselves.

They left the house that entertained them so kindly, in great confidence of the good will of its inhabitants. But such had been their experience of the frauds and tricks of white men, that they had not gone far, ere they were pained by the possibility that even this good man (of the woman they could entertain no doubt) had laid a trap for them. So goaded were they by this possibility when they came to the four corners where they were to turn to the brick tavern, that they hesitated about taking the road to it.

The good angel prevailed over the bad one who suggested the falsehood, and they turned into the path they were directed to take, and arrived at Salem, Indiana, about half after nine in the evening of the same day.

They found the brick tavern to be a first class hotel for those days, in a new and thriving country village. The landlord's reception of them indicated the truth of all that had been told them, and they were kept like princes, compared to anything they had been used to. Nevertheless, the reflection that they were known or believed to be slaves, and that their road and stopping places were known also, was a thorn in their pillows, and they could not sleep. When the morning came, and they had forced payment on the landlord, against his protest to the contrary, and they were fairly under way again, with their hands unshackled and their bodies free, they were most grateful and happy. Now they began to be ashamed that they distrusted the sincerity of the hand that fed them so freely, and to feel that there was faith among white men after all.

The landlord at Salem directed them to a colony of colored people, distant an easy day's ride, on the way to Indianapolis, who, he said, would be glad to receive them. They arrived among them the same evening, and were most cordially welcomed.

This settlement was composed of fifteen or twenty farmers on as many small farms, which they owned in fee. Some of them had been slaves and obtained freedom by gift or purchase, and all were as happy as they could be, surrounded by those who despise and disfranchise them.

The three weeks the young men were detained here, was a succession of visits and ovations, in which they were the Apollos. The people, old and young, regarded them as stars dropped among them, attractive, alike for their social and personal qualities. John Farney was a light mulatto, of exquisite proportions, in which strength and grace equally predominated, and whose face was always brilliant with benevolence and wit. Withal, he was a graceful dancer, and gifted in all things to make him attractive among young colored people. Mr. Loguen always speaks of him with respect and admiration.

Our travellers lingered with these humble and hospitable men and women, until themselves and horses were fully recruited—and when they determined to leave, and replunge into the cold winter, and among the colder hearts between them and Canada, a rustic ball was got up to complete the circle of civilities, and celebrate their departure.

We stop, a moment, to give a brief passage, in this connection, upon African character.

The greatest philosopher of the last century says, love is the life of man, and that the African is the most loving of all the tribes of humanity. If this be true, the African has in him more of life than others of the human family. Take from a man love, and he can neither think, or move, or live. Affection is the life of the will, and moves the mind to think, and the body to act. One of the obvious results of this position is, that the African, having in him more of life than the European or the Asiatic, will survive and multiply under a greater pressure. Hence the cold blooded Indians of both continents are expiring under trials, which, to the African, would be scarce a burden. Another consequence of this surplus affection in the African is, that he sympathizes more than others with human suffering and enjoyment, and is therefore a more perfect receptacle for the influx of Divine affections, or, in other words, of Divine life. Hence, Africans are destined to grow in numbers and importance, in spite of superincumbent oppression, because their affections or life are more healthful and potent than others; and though crowded down now by wrongs to the lowest sensuality, in the order of Providence, as a race, they will first be regenerate, and become spiritual and celestial men. We venture these deductions from the idiocrasy of the African constitution.

Their intercourse with these kind people terminated the night of the ball, and they started on their journey again. During the night, the weather changed from cold and dry to warm and wet, and let them into new experience of northern life and travel. The moisture grew into a gentle rain that drizzled all day. The snow, of course, melted rapidly, and they were obliged to ford several rivers at considerable risk. On the second day, the rivers were amazingly swollen, and swept before them fences and bridges. When they came to a river called Sugar Creek, it discovered at the bottom, to them, a new and singular yellow appearance. It was quite deep and clear, and ran with great force; yet it seemed safe to ford it. To appearance, it was about the depth of the horses' breasts. Because of the color, they concluded it rolled on a bed of clay—not dreaming it could be other than solid earth.

Notwithstanding the depth and force of the torrent, they made up their minds to ride through it. According to this arrangement, John drove his horse into the water, and found it about half breast high in its deepest places. Jarm followed after. About the time Jarm was in the middle of the stream, and all was apparently safe, the foundation upon which John's horse walked broke beneath him and he sank so that the horses' head, and John's head and shoulders, only appeared above the stream. The next moment Jarm and his horse went down. The bottom of the river which they thought was clay, they now saw was ice, and its thick and awful fragments, broken by the weight of their horses, cast their frightful edges above the surface of the stream. It was a moment of terrible interest. The depth of the water below the ice they knew nothing of, except that it was beyond the reach of the horses. As they were sinking seemingly to a watery grave, they dropped the bridles on the horses necks and clutched their manes, and sank with them until their heads only appeared, and their strong and healthy animals swam them to the shore.[1]

"Luck again!" exclaimed John Farney.

"Luck indeed! But it is an awfully narrow escape, and leaves us in an uncomfortable plight!"

"Ha! ha! ha! We may as well laugh as cry," said John, at the same time pouring the water out of his saddle bags. "We shall know ice under water after this."

"It is awful luck getting into the water, but to get out of it as we have, is what we could not do in nine times out of ten. I believe the Lord is on our side, and by this He means we shall know it. We shall go through, I verily believe. Hurrah for freedom!"

"There is more good luck—do you see that log tavern up there?"

"Aye—that was put there for us. Let us hurry to it and dry our clothes, and line our stomachs with the best meats and drinks there are in it."

They were soon stripped of outer garments, and smoking before a huge fire, which extended half across the bar room. They did not need inform the

1. [Loguen's note:] We note another perilous adventure, which occurred the same day, before they came to Sugar creek, told by Mr. Loguen since the above was written.

They came to a river which overflowed its banks, and was half a mile wide. Jarm said it was madness to attempt to pass it, and insisted that they wait until the water subsided. But John Farney was resolved not to be delayed. An obstacle of that kind but stimulated his courage and love of adventure. He rolled a log into the stream, and laying his belly flat upon it, took his horse by the bridle, and swam to the opposite bank. Jarm waited anxiously on the hither shore, to see the possibility of the daring enterprise. Having succeeded in passing over, John hired a boat and returned to Jarm, who, assured by John's success, took his saddle and bags into the boat, and leading his horse by the side of it, was safely rowed across by his brave and resolute friend.

landlord of their case, for he witnessed it himself, and was struck with their courage or temerity. He was therefore ready to receive them, and allow the familiarity their good sense led them to adopt, as the means of concealing their real character.

On their first appearance at the tavern, they quaffed a deep drink of whiskey—not because they loved it, but to act like freemen—and at the same time called for dinner. While the dinner was making ready, they dried their clothes and killed time as best they could.

Seeing a newspaper on the table, and to cover the pretence that he was a freeman, Jarm took it and made as if he was reading it. Besides the capital (A) which he learned from Alice Preston, he was entirely ignorant of every letter of the alphabet. He was looking for that letter—but when he found it, to his deep mortification, it was wrong end upwards! By that, he knew he had the paper bottom upwards. He instantly threw it from him, and looked around to see if he had not proved the falsity of his pretense, by means adopted to credit it. Finding all was right, he took another taste of the whiskey, and turned to the fire—firmly resolved to let newspapers alone, until he reached a land where it was safe to handle them.

Having finished their purpose at the tavern, they started for Indianapolis, and arrived safely at Mr. Overrals of that city, in a day or two, without any occurrence worth relating.

Mr. Overrals, though colored, was an educated man, and had a large character and acquaintance among colored people; and was much respected by white ones, for his probity, industry and good sense. He received and befriended the fugitives, as was his custom with all others who came to him.

When they landed in Indiana and fired their pistols in joy of arriving on free soil, they acknowledged (as before related) to the friend providentially present, that they were escaped slaves; but to no other person did they admit it, until they found Mr. Overrals. To him they stated their case truly, and surrendered to his directions. For the future, he advised them not to conceal the fact that they were slaves, if it was necessary to speak of it at all, unless to those known to be enemies—for the reason that the people among whom they would travel, as a general thing, were more willing to befriend slaves than colored freemen. With such counsel, he sent them to a Quaker settlement, about forty miles from Indianapolis.

The Quakers received them with characteristic hospitality, and advised them to be careful and not bear to the east—that they had best go directly north, or north-west—for that emigrants from the slave States had settled into southern and eastern Indiana; that a large wilderness, occupied only by

Indians and roving hunters, separated them from settlers from the northern and eastern States—that those northern settlers were unlike the white men of the south and east—that they had been brought up in freedom, and knew nothing of slavery—that though they had an unaccountable prejudice against color, they would regard them with curious interest if they were slaves and would help them on to Canada. They also advised them that they were safer in this wilderness, among hunters and Indians, than with any other people short of those northern settlers, and advised them to go directly through the wilderness to them.

"Thee will stay with us until spring?" said a kind hearted Quaker to them.

"Thank you, sir—we are anxious to get to Canada."

"But it is very cold and stormy—thee has never known such cold and storms, and colored men can't bear cold as white men can. Thee had better stay with us until spring—thee will be welcome and safe."

"Thank you, sir—we make nothing of cold—we have found that we stand it better than white men. We can make no delay for such reasons. Ensure us from men, and we will risk storms and cold."

"Thee does not intend to say thee can endure cold better than white men?"

"We mean to say that is our experience. When we were little children, we wore thinner clothes than white children, and the white children shivered and suffered and complained more than we, though less exposed. So has it been since we have grown up. With less clothing and greater exposure, we suffer less than white persons of our age. We stand cold better than white folks."

"Everybody says white people stand cold best, and it must be so."

"We never heard it said in Tennessee—this is the first time we ever heard it pretended—depend on it, it is not true. We can travel where our masters, or their sons, or the slavecatchers, any of them, would perish. We will risk our case on that."

"Well—well—thee will act thine own pleasure—thou art free. I invited thee to stay through the winter because I knew thee was not used to the intense cold of the north, and because we supposed thee could not endure it as white people do."

"Thank you, sir—it is a mistake—our pursuers will have no advantage of us on this point—the truth is the other way. Colored people withstand cold better than white ones at the south, and we are willing to try it with them at the north."

The popular notion that colored people endure heat better, and cold not so well as white people, is a matter unsettled between them. In all his life, Mr. Loguen has been compelled to encounter the severities of both cold and heat, in company with white men, and as the result of his experience, he maintains that the white man has no advantage of the black man as to cold, and if the latter suffers less from heat, as is pretended, it is because his constitution is more genial. If it is true that the African has more of affection (which is heat and life) in him than the European, that fact may account for his ability to withstand both heat and cold better than the European.

CHAPTER XXIV

The Quakers supplied the young men with provisions and comforts, and they departed, through the wilderness, towards Canada. A frosty wind swept over the light snow, and cut their faces sharply. After half a day's travel, they passed beyond white men's log houses and clearings, into wild nature, where now and then, the Indians had mangled the forest and built their cabins. Occasionally, they met one or more Indians, to whom they bowed civilly, and received a half human response, which Indians, and those only who are familiar with them, understand.

The natives were a proud and stalwart tribe, dressed in their own costume, often ornamented with wampum and feathers, and generally armed with knives, or bows and arrows or rifles. Coming suddenly on them, as they did sometimes, the fugitives were startled by their ominous *umph* and imposing savageness. But after traveling among them and experiencing their harmlessness, they were quite disarmed of apprehension on their account.

The only annoyance from the Indians was their occasional lack of hospitality. For though generally they did not refuse them food and shelter, they sometimes did refuse them. Occasionally, too, they met white hunters in the woods, less reliable than the savages. These hunters told them to look out for wild boars, panthers, bears and wolves, especially the former monster beast, which they hunted with caution and peril. Not without cause, they feared to start up these terrible animals. They often saw their tracks, but if they came near the boars, they knew it not.

We said the Indians sometimes refused to entertain them—but not always did they accept a denial. One time, when night came on and they were thus refused, having provided for their horses, they lay down among their enemies in the wigwam, and slept on the watch, in contempt of them. As a general thing, they were received kindly, by night and day, and fed freely on the wild meats and indescribable dishes prepared for Indian palates.

In the middle of this great solitude, while treading their Indian path, at the close of an intensely cold day, as they hoped to a hospitable shelter, they began to feel the symptoms of one of those tremendous storms, which, at the north, make winter awful, sometimes, but which they knew nothing about. The wind grew louder and louder, and swelled into an appalling howl. The darkening atmosphere, filled with innumerable snow flakes, increasing the force of the hurricane, which scattered tops of trees around them, and occasionally tore them up by the roots and layed them with a horrible crash by their side.

To them, their case was strange, remediless and frightful. Their path was entirely obliterated by the tempest, and the pale snow light was about all they could see. In this dilemma, they gave the reins to their jaded horses, and trusted them to find a way to a house or barn among the Indians, while they whipped their arms and hands upon their bodies to repel the frost. But the eyes of the horses, scarcely less than the eyes of the young men, were blinded by the snow, and they were all alike helpless. They floundered among the trees, to the peril of the riders, and came at last to a field of bushes and small trees, that skirted the foot of a mountain or hill, at their left. This mountain, or hill, lay between them and the tempest, and broke its force—but in doing so, made it moan the louder and bellow its hollow thunder over their heads.

Here they dismounted, and allowed their horses to browse among the bushes, while they greedily devoured a portion of frozen provisions that they took from their saddle-bags, and then, by whipping their bodies as aforesaid, and other exercise, they kept off sleep and frost till morning. When morning came, most joyfully did they welcome it—not on their own account alone, but in regard to their poor horses, that needed rest and refreshment more than they. It was a terribly severe night, but not half so terrible as many they suffered anticipating outrages from their masters. They looked forward to daylight, and a refuge from the cold storm. But no day dawns for the slave, nor is it looked for. It is all night—night forever.

The earth was covered by a great depth of snow, which was unbroken by the track of man or beast. And still the storm raged, and the sky overhead resembled a crumbling snow-bank. The travellers were now lost, without a path to a human dwelling, or a star to show the point of the compass. But they could see—and from the growth of small timber inferred they were not far from Indian dwellings, and determined not to re-plunge into the woods, until they explored the brush-fields for an Indian's home.

They wallowed though the snow but a short distance ere they came upon cleared ground and a cabin; and they were kindly received and comfortably entertained in Indian fashion. It so happened that one of the natives talked bad English well enough to be understood by them, and acted the part of an interpreter. When the Indians found they had been lost in the woods, and in the storm all night, they (especially the women) expressed great surprise and sympathy. In justice to women, they, too, testified with a celebrated traveller, that in their extremity, they were sometimes repelled by white men and red men, but never by women, whether white or red. Woman, whatever her education or circumstances, represents the affectional element of humanity, and ultimates its uses in forms of kindness and love.

The horses were kindly sheltered and fed, as well as themselves, by these children of nature. But the wind continued to pile the huge drifts around their dwelling, and strip the great trees of their branches, or tear them up by the roots, and fell them with a noise louder than the tempest. They were therefore kindly detained twenty-four hours,—the time the storm continued,—and slept a double sleep, nourished by the bread and care of these sympathizing people.

In after life, when Mr. Loguen described the offices of religion in his lectures and speeches, he was often reminded of "the good of life," or "natural good," of these Indians, and contrasted it with the religion of the whites. The former are they, who, in the true meaning of the Scriptures, are "born blind," because without the Word of God, which is "the true light that lighteth every man that cometh into the world."

But that other class who have the Word, and yet spurn and oppress the needy, are they, who, in the ancient language thereof, "stumble at noonday." These, all the balsam of heaven cannot cure, because their blindness is internal, voluntary, and spiritual.[1] When the prevailing religion of Christendom

1. [Loguen's note:] To the antediluvians, natural things represented divine ideas, and men needed no letters or books to express them. Thus, "natural good," or the good a man does from natural reason, was represented by "clay." It is a condition receptive of spiritual good. The Scriptures treat it as the material of which Christians are made, thus—"as clay in the hands of the potter, so are ye in my hands." Again—"we are the clay and thou art the potter," &c. So Christ made clay, with his spittle to cure the blind man's eyes, signifying that the intellectually blind are restored to sight by truths, in the letter of the Word, symbolized by "spittle."

Much is said in the Bible of the poor, the maimed, the halt, and the blind. They are those who are principled in good, without truth. They are saved, because they joy in the light when it reaches them in this world or in the world to come. Of the offending foot, the Lord said, "cut it off; it is better for thee to *enter* 'halt' *into life*, than in having two feet," &c. It is "the poor, and the maimed, and the halt, and the blind," who dwell "in the highways and hedges," and "in the lanes and streets of the city," and not the rich and well fed gentlemen who build palaces and churches, and maintain priests, who come to the feast of Heaven. It was Lazarus at the gate, covered with sores, the evils of religious ignorance, desiring crumbs from Moses' table, who found a supply in Abraham's bosom. The rich man who had those things famished in hell. Better be an *Indian*

manifests the good of life, as did those heathens, then let that religion be given to the heathens, and not before. Better be "born blind," and live in ignorance, as they do, than "stumble at noonday as in the night," and "grope for the wall like the blind," as do the mind-enlightened Churches of Christendom. Give the heathen the word of God, and suffer its mysteries to be opened to their understanding by the touch of truth, as Christ did, rather than give it them through those whom he called "the blind leading the blind." In view of the selfishness, pride, and oppression, which pre-eminently prevail in all, so called, Christian countries, the Lord may well say—"Who so blind as my servant? or deaf as my messenger that I sent? Who is blind as he that is perfect?" Pardon the digression, reader—we return to our story.

The winds went down, and the sun rose clear again upon the snow-clad wilderness. But there were no paths, and the natives were slow to make them. The young men, therefore, were obliged to break their own track through the blind openings, pointed out to them, and it was a day or two before they found a firm road to travel on.

Eventually they arrived among the white settlers, on the northern borders of the wilderness. They found them, as they had been told, not like white men at the south. Their cultivations, agricultural and personal, were all different, as was evident in their talk and manners, houses and fields. Instead of insulting them as white men did at the south, by swaggering superiority, these men treated them as equals under the law, though not always with respect. As a general thing they were willing to entertain them—the public houses were always open to them, and they were never reminded that their rights were not equal to others—though often reminded that they could not occupy the same social level.

---

or *nigger* (modern Gentiles) in the good of life, as Jarm found these Indians, than the Christians who deprave and oppress Africans and Indians.

It was ordained by the Levitical law, that whosoever "had a blemish," that is, who was lame, blind, &c., "let him not approach to offer the bread of his God." These external blemishes symbolize intellectual and spiritual blemishes. External blindness, for instance, in ancient literature, signified lack of internal light or understanding of truth,—a blemish in the spirit, which made the man incompetent to touch, and therefore incompetent to the priestly office, though more receptive, perhaps, than the priests themselves, of heavenly things. Such blind one is in a condition to be compelled to the Lord's feast, while a pampered and selfish priest or deacon is positively shut from it.

This ancient representative literature, is the Divine Word in ultimates. A true interpretation of it, explains all that is mythical, and literally inconsistent, and sometimes meaningless and absurd, in the letter of the Bible. Prophetic language is heaven's language, and therefore Divine.

We shall not attempt to detail the particulars of their journey. Though tedious, trying, and full of hardships, and often very exciting, they are too numerous and monotonous to be recorded. Nor are we able to give the places through which they travelled. If ever known, they are forgotten. At Logansport, Jarm found his purse seriously diminished, and that he must in some way replenish it. To this end, he swapped his noble horse for boot money, offered him by a benevolent looking Quaker, who took advantage of Jarm's ignorance and necessities and his own false face, to cheat him.

Here, again, was illustrated the difference between a northern and a southern white man, not creditable to the former. This white Quaker cheated him badly, as to the ability and value of his horse, which a white man at the south would be ashamed to do, to a nigger, as they call a colored man. But Jarm needed the money, and he pocketed it,—and when he found he had been cheated, he pocketed the memory of that, too, and never failed to count it by way of discount upon the charitable pretensions of these really good people, of whom he had considerable acquaintance, in after life.

As a matter of prudence, they made no further enquiries, but trusted the North Star to lead them to Canada. But it was winter, and the sky often covered with clouds and storms—they were therefore often deprived of their stellar guide. By this means they were unfortunately led out of their course, and instead of arriving at Detroit, as they intended, they passed west of the lakes, and rode hundreds of miles from civilized settlements into a howling wilderness. Here they spent some of their nights in the woods, without fire or food, when it was intensely cold. The Indians sometimes entertained them kindly, and sometimes repelled them; but their language was as unmeaning as the growl of the bears and wolves they often scared up. Besides they occasionally passed over rivers and other places dangerous alike to the horses and their riders.

If the reader will remember that these hardships were endured with little food or shelter, he may form some conception of the hardihood and perseverance of these young men. And if he will further remember, that the same hardships were taken in exchange of the genial skies of their childhood, for the sake of freedom, he may form some estimate of the value they put upon it.

While plunging among the mountains of snow in this primeval wilderness, by the kindness of Heaven, they fell upon a hunter or trapper, who told them they were off their course hundreds of miles—that they had entered an illimitable wilderness, in the direction of the North Pole, and must change their course or perish. He put them upon a south-eastern direction, and after incredible hardships—which may be faintly conceived, but cannot be detailed—they arrived at Detroit. They entered the city in the night. We need not say that they and their horses were much jaded—as the weather had been for days, and still was, among the coldest of a northern winter; and as they encountered it with little food, and that the coarsest and most unpalatable, they were in a painful and suffering condition. They were nearly frozen, and they were nearly starved.

In addition to these miseries, they were little used to cities, and it especially embarrassed and alarmed them that this was the identical point their masters were likely to occupy to intercept their flight. Of this they were often told, and warned to be on the watch. Such, however, was, their determination for freedom, that cold and hunger, and death, even, were preferable to a return to slavery.

Under the circumstances, they concluded to separate, and fish in the obscure parts of the city for lodgings and entertainment. They thought if an advertisement was out for them, that it grouped them together, and that they would not be so likely to be recognized if separate as they would be together. Accordingly, one of them went in one part of the city, and the other in another—seeking the obscurest and miserablest place to bed and board—and such they found.

In the morning they met again, according to agreement, upon the spot where they separated the night before, and concluded to remain separate while in the city, and to cross separately into Canada the first moment they found the ice would bear them.

On the morning of the third day after their arrival at Detroit, Jarm led his old mare into Canada. When he put his foot on the soil, the angel of freedom touched his heart, and it leapt for joy. Cold, cheerless, and unpromising as everything looked without him, he felt the divine hand within him, and he instinctively exclaimed, 'O Lord God, I thank thee!—I am free!' But how different the scene before him from 'the picture which fancy touched bright' when he started from Tombigbee! Ignorant of men and climates, he fancied that where political freedom was, there nature and spirit smiled in harmony, and there was all but Heaven. He took it for granted that all would look upon all as brothers, which alone would make any climate heavenly.

John Farney came over soon afterwards, and they rejoiced together. John came without his horse and saddle, because the villains he staid with refused to let them go. Not for any claim they had against John did they retain them, but because they supposed John was a slave, and would not peril his freedom in a legal contest.

But this was not the only drawback upon their jubilation. They were nearly penniless; Jarm had fifty cents only, with the old mare, and John had less than that of cash—while his horse and Jarm's nice saddle were in the hands of the robbers over the river. The cold raging winter was new to them, and a serious obstacle in their new life. Besides, they knew not a soul in Canada; and at Windsor where they were, the people talked French only, and could not converse with them. Nature and humanity surrounded them like a globe of ice; but they rejoiced and thanked God with warm hearts. Spirit is independent of external nature. These evils moderated, but could not extinguish their joys.

They intended, upon landing in Canada, to have a holiday carousal. But they had been misled and harrassed until their money was gone, and their horses, too—for Jarm's was not worth the fifty cents he had in his pocket, while John's was with his robbers. They were disappointed, therefore, of their holiday. But they were deprived of the means of grosser comforts, that they might enjoy more refined and spiritual ones. So far as a jubilee was concerned, they were better without money than they would have been with their pockets full of rocks.

But the fact that John Farney was thus wronged, stimulated him to madness. He was resolute and brave, and swore he would save his property or perish. He left Jarm for Detroit, and it was the last time Jarm ever saw him. He heard he sold the horse, and Jarm's saddle with it, at compulsory prices; but how he was separated, and lost to Jarm, he never knew.

The loss of Farney specially distressed Jarm. He had been his companion in bondage from boyhood—they had travelled the wilderness together and he longed for him as a companion through the promised land and through life. He longs for him now, and ever will long for him as a dear brother. He has saught him and advertised him faithfully in the northern states and in Canada, and still seeks him as possibly among the living. If there is a being in the world that he loves, and that would rejoice his soul to fold in his arms, it is John Farney. He is sure John has not returned to slavery, for his brave and manly soul would not endure it. He thinks it most probable that he has been smitten down among strangers, and committed to a nameless sepulchre—that time has closed over him without a trace, but in Jarm's bosom, of his noble qualities.

Not being able to get employment at Windsor, and discouraged of further waiting for his companion, Jarm started on alone. Without money, he managed to get one meal a day for himself, and sufficient feed for his horse until he arrived at Chatham.

At Chatham his prospects were no better. Driven to his wits for dear life, he swapt the old mare for another and two or three shillings of boot money—put together a jumper—fastened the thills to the stirrup straps of his saddle, and thus rigged, mounted the vehicle and drove to London.

In the neighborhood of London he stayed with a farmer three or four days, to whom he sold the old horse for his board and a few shillings. Finding nothing to do at London, he availed himself of an opportunity to ride with a stranger to Ancaster, and in a like manner pushed his way through Dundas to Hamilton.

Of his situation at Hamilton at this time we let him tell his own story. In a letter to Frederick Douglass, dated Syracuse, N.Y., May 8th, 1856, he describes that situation, and contrasts Hamilton as it now is, with what it then was, thus:—

"On the western termination of Lake Ontario is the village of Hamilton. It is a large, enterprising place, amid scenery, placid, beautiful and sublime. It is in a delightful valley, which runs east and west. On the north is a beautiful lake, and on the south a perpendicular mountain towers up some two or three hundred feet, and hangs its brow over the village. Here are quite a number of our people, doing well so far as I could learn—able and willing not only to help the fugitive, but to join with able and willing white men around them to furnish him an asylum. How changed in twenty years! My dear friend, indulge me here a moment. Hamilton is a sacred and memorable spot to me; and I cannot slightly pass it. I could not stand upon its soil without a flood of sad and sweet and gushing memories. It seems to me, and ever will seem to me, a paternal home. I shall never visit it without the feelings which a child feels on returning after weary years to his father's house.

"Twenty-one years ago—the very winter I left my chains in Tennessee—I stood on this spot, penniless, ragged, lonely, homeless, helpless, hungry, and forlorn—a pitiable wanderer, without a friend, or shelter, or place to lay my head. I had broken from the sunny South, and fought a passage through storms and tempests, which made the forests crash and the mountains moan—difficulties, new, awful, and unexpected, but not so dreaded as my white enemies who were comfortably sheltered among them. There I stood, a boy twenty-one years of age, (as near as I know my age,) the tempest howling over my head, and my toes touching the snow beneath my worn-out shoes—with the assurance that I was at the end of my journey—knowing nobody, and nobody knowing me or noticing me, only as attracted by the then supposed mark of Cain on my sorrow-stricken face. I stood there the personification of helpless courage and finited hope. The feeling rushed upon me, 'Was it for this that I left sweet skies and a mother's love?' On visiting this place now, I contrast the present and past. No Underground Railroad took me to Hamilton. White men had not then learned to care for the far off slave, and there were no thriving colored farmers, mechanics and laborers to welcome me. I can never forget the moment. I was in the last extremity. I had freedom, but nature and man were against me. I could only look to God, and I prayed, 'Pity, O my Father—help, or I perish!' and though all was frost and tempest without, within came warmth, and trust, and love; and an earthly father took me to his home and angel wife, who became to me a mother. He thought a body lusty and stout as mine, could brave cold, and cut cord wood, and split rails—and he was right. I agreed to earn my bread, and did much more than that; and he rewarded my labors to the extent of justice. They paid me better than I asked, and taught me many lessons of religion and life. I had a home and place for my heart to repose, and had been happy, but for the thought that ever torments the fugitive, that my mother, sisters and brothers were in cruel bondage, and I could never embrace them again.

"My dear Douglass, you will not think it strange I speak of my case in contrast with the now state of things in Canada. Hamilton was a cold wilderness for the fugitive when I came there. It is now an Underground Railroad Depot, where he is embraced with warm sympathy. Here is where the black man is disencumbered of the support of master and mistress, and their imps, and gets used to self-ownership. Here he learns the first lessons in books, and grows into shape. Fortunately for me, I gained the favor of the best white people. My story attached them to me. They took me into the Sabbath School at Hamilton, and taught me letters the winter of my arrival; and I graduated a Bible reader at Ancaster, close by, the succeeding summer. All the country around is familiar to me, and you will not wonder I love to come here. I love it because it was my first resting place from slavery, and I love it the more because it has been, and will continue to be, a city of refuge for my poor countrymen."

In the spring after his first arrival in Hamilton, he hired himself to a farmer in the neighborhood, at $10 a month, to roll and burn logs in clearing land. From that time he never failed to find employment, at good prices, and to lay up money.

Having become a reader, after two years hard labor for good wages, and after acquiring the character of an able, faithful, and judicious farmer, in good repute as a man and citizen, he assumed the name he now bears. His paternal sir name was Logue—but he disliked that name, and added to it the letter n, to suit his taste. The name Jarm, which his master gave him, was an abbreviation of Jermain. His Methodist friends insisted he should adopt the name of Wesley for his middle name, which he did—and from this time forward was known only by the name of JERMAIN WESLEY LOGUEN.

In the spring of the third year after his arrival in Canada, he took a farm of 200 acres to work on shares. The operation was highly profitable, and at the end of the second year he had increased his little capital several hundred dollars; and being single, strong, persevering and spirited, was really independent. But unhappily he was persuaded to take a partner, and that ruined him. At the time he commenced with his co-partner, this farm was well stocked with his own animals and implements. But so soon as they harvested their large crops and prepared them for market, which cost much labor and money, they were all seized under attachments or executions against his partner, for debts previous to the partnership. And because Loguen was unacquainted with his rights, all his property, with the exception of his clothing, a little money, a span of horses, wagon and harness, worth about $300, was swept away by the creditors of his partner.

Disgusted and irritated by his fortune, he forthwith left that part of Canada, and invested the whole of his remaining capital in a house and lot in St. Catharines, and thus became a small proprietor under the crown of England.

But he did not stay at St. Catharines. He immediately crossed the lake into the States, and came to Rochester in the fall of 1837. Without property or acquaintance, his person and address commended him to the keeper of the Rochester House—then the most fashionable Hotel in that growing city. He was installed porter and confidential servant of the establishment.

Mr. Loguen was now about twenty-four years of age, of gigantic strength, temperate, moral, patient, and attentive to boarders and guests; and being economical in his receipts, he laid up from three to five and six dollars a day, and at the end of two years became possessed of a small estate. Among the boarders at the Rochester House at this time, was Gen. Champion, a bachelor resident of that city, of wide fame for wealth, purity, and benevolence. The qualities of Mr. Loguen attracted his special regard and when he distributed a Bible to each of the servants—as it was his custom to make them an annual present—he distinguished Loguen from the rest by giving him a large Polyglot family Bible, which he still retains in respect to the donor.

During Mr. Loguen's residence at Rochester, the peace and passions of the people and government of Canada were disturbed by some two or three hundred citizens of the State of New York, who, without authority, privately armed themselves and took possession of Navy Island, in Canada, and thus commenced what was popularly denominated the Patriot War.[2] The intent

2. [Editor's note:] Today, these events are known as the Upper Canada Rebellion and the Lower Canada Rebellion, which were uprisings against the British colonial government in 1837 and 1838. Collectively, they are also known as the Rebellions of 1837.

of this invasion was, to produce a revolution of the Province, separate it from England into an independent State, or annex it to the U.S.

On the night of the 30th of December, 1838, Sir Allen McNabb, who had the charge of the British forces to repel the invasion, sent a squadron of armed boats across the river, and seized and burned the steamboat Caroline, while fastened to the dock at Schlosser. In the melee, an American, one of the hands on the boat, was shot through the head and killed. The boat was burned because it was employed by the filibusters to carry men and arms and provisions from the American to the Canadian side.

The invasion of Canada on one side, and of the States on the other, and the slaughter of men on both sides, created intense excitement on the frontiers, and fears were entertained by some, that the passions provoked by these harebrained invaders, might mingle in the politics of the country, and bring on a general war.

The colored population of Canada at that time was small, compared to what it now is; nevertheless, it was sufficiently large to attract the attention of the Government. They were almost, to a man, fugitive slaves from the States. They could not, therefore, be passive, when the success of the invaders would break the only arm interposed for their security, and destroy the only asylum for African freedom in North America. The promptness with which several companies of blacks were organized and equipped, and the desperate valor they displayed in this brief conflict, are an earnest [example][3] of what may be expected from the swelling thousands of colored fugitives collecting there, in the event of a war between the two countries.

We write of facts, not of possibilities. Nevertheless, we may assert what is allowed on the other side of the lines, that these able-bodied and daring refugees are the most reliable fortress of national strength on the Canadian frontiers; and ere it is scaled by slave-holders or their abettors, a tale will be told that will make the ear that hears it tingle. And should pro-slavery folly and persistence raise the spirit of the North, or of any part of the country, to the point that admits the African element in a war for freedom, the blacks of Canada will be found overleaping national boundaries; and, gathering the sympathizing forces in the line of march, will imprint upon the soil of slavery as bloody a lesson as was ever written.

We have alluded to this flare-up on the frontiers, by way of introduction to the following fact.

3. Word missing in the original text.

During the same winter, Mr. Loguen went over to St. Catharines to dispose of his house and lot, of which we have before spoken. At this time, though the forces were still under arms, the back bone of the invasion was fairly broken, by the interference of the Government of the United States.[4] Nevertheless, while there he was urgently solicited by the Government of Canada to accept the captaincy of a company of black troops in the Provincial Army. We mention this fact, to show the estimate he had attained for fidelity, bravery, judgment, and manly conduct. But because the war had very nearly closed, and his brethren and friends were therefore out of danger—and because he was profitably employed at his home in Rochester, he respectfully declined the compliment, and having sold his lot, returned to his engagements.

4. [Loguen's note:] Inasmuch as the fillibusters made this assault on Canada without authority of any nation, State, or political power whatever, they were properly regarded by the Provincials as Pirates, and the captives were shot, or hung, or sent to Botany Bay. And inasmuch, also, as they were American citizens, who thus organized, equipped, and embarked from the United States, against a people at peace with them, they were subject to the penalties provided by Congress against such offenders. President Van Buren issued his proclamation for their rigid prosecution, and notified those who were or might be captured, that they would be left, without protection or sympathy, to the mercy of the Government they assailed.

The fillibusters were thus promptly taught that incursions for the conquest of northern Territory were less adapted to the national taste, than like forays for the conquest of Texas, Mexico, Cuba, and the Isthmus. The instant and decided check given to this northern move, effectually curbed unlawful enterprizes in that direction; and the only vent for national passions in this regard, has been found to lay at the South. The only prospect of increasing the slave power in the Senate and in Congress is that way, and there its attractions are irresistable.

CHAPTER XXV

At the Rochester House Mr. Loguen first heard the roar and felt the breath of the storm for the liberty of his countrymen. At the South, slavery shut him from a knowledge of public events; and hitherto, at the North, his circumstances limited him to the narrow circle of his own interests. Unschooled in the philosophy of history and the growth of humanity, he looked for nothing beyond that circle. He had been inaccessible to the spirits who were evolving the problem of liberty, and was insensible to the growing struggles against despotism every where. Eight hundred thousand slaves threw down their chains in the West Indies, and he heard it not. The early mobs, lynchings, and murders, the violations of the post office, and the rude attempts to stifle the tongue and the press, to prevent agitation, all went by and he did not know it. Happily, the powers of Church and State were impotent to keep down the volcanic fires which were struggling to the surface. Efforts to suppress them made them break out the more, and blaze brighter and hotter, until bastard priests and selfish politicians were driven to open alliance with the right on one side, and with the wrong on the other. Mr. Loguen could not be indifferent to the boisterous discussions about slavery in the bar room, and the more quiet and considerate ones in the parlors, where his business called him.

"Now what is the state of the Fig Tree?" said a gentlemen in a private parlor to another gentleman, whose conversation and appearance attracted attention and respect during the few days he had been there.

"There is a perceptible change since we last met. The branches are growing tender and the leaves multiplying. Have you seen Marcy's Message?"

"Yes. He recommends a law to put an end to these abolition gatherings, as disturbers of the public peace."

"In vain do the heathen rage, and the people imagine a vain thing. He may as well attempt to chain the winds and the lightnings. The devil's entrenchments are breaking up—his institutions crumbling—and the grand man is progressing to a new and better state."

"But what has that to do with the Fig Tree?"

"Why, there is such a thing as natural good. In God's Book, read by the Ancients—who could see spiritually and naturally alike—it was represented by the Fig Tree. When men loved rational truth, and sought it by the light of nature, they said its branches grew tender and the leaves put forth. The branches are the affections budding into leaves or rational truth. This natural good stimulates the rational and intellectual man to benefit his physical condition, as the means under God of opening the way to his lost spiritual condition. That is the substance and intent of the prophesy. The heart receives spiritual good through the understanding. If the understanding—which is the eye of the mind or soul—does not see and present the goodness and beauty of truth to the will, then the will can never embrace it. To this end, this is an age of natural light. Genius is put to the extent of its powers to produce natural good, to acquire wealth, distinction, and station. The mind, instead of the hand, is doing the world's work—hence Rail Roads, Telegraphs, Agricultural and Mechanical inventions, and the thousand and one artistic powers to supercede labor, which are conforming the affairs of this world to a new mental state; and hence, too, the corresponding combinations for the relief of the poor, the drunken and enslaved. These are the fig leaves, my friend. The understanding of the age has fallen in love with natural truth, that in its efforts to attain it, it may strike the current of moral and spiritual good and unite with them. How long will slavery, or other false thing of the passing age, be secure at such a time?"

"But, my dear sir, the Church, politicians, the intellect of the country, are largely on the side of slavery."

"Of course—where the carcass is, the Eagles are gathered. The Lord has prophesied that when the Fig Tree begins to warm and grow and show its leaves, the old Church will be a carcass, a corpse, and the Eagles, that is, the perverse rational and intellectual powers will feed upon its carrion. The Eagles are the Pope, the Priests, and sects, and politicians of every sort. The Christian Church to-day is in the state the Jewish Church was when it excommunicated its Lord. It is a dead carcass, dissolving as its essence is turned to uses. One says Christ is here, and another that he is there. Its sects have torn the Bible to pieces in regard to doctrines, while charity is crucified in their midst. We have no Bible, no Church, if it is not in the incipient love or heat which is thawing out the fig tree and making its branches bud again. I tell you God is in this heat—it is his life—it comes from his own great heart, the source of all life, and is therefore Omnipotent. My dear fellow, mark me—it is now September, 1839—see how this matter stands twenty years hence, if you and I live so long. Do you see that fellow there?"—pointing to Loguen.

"Well, what of him?"

"Why, he has heard so much about liberating the slaves that he is getting excited. He has been consulting me whether he had best go to Oneida Institute, and get Beriah Green to whet his sword, to battle in the war of Eagles. There are two kinds of Eagles,—one the understanding and love of truth, and the other its opposite."

"I admire your illustrations—but what did you tell Loguen? He is a dunce to think of leaving here. He is a great favorite, and is making his five dollars a day. What did you tell him?"

"I told him to stay here and attend to his business—that he would make a great sacrifice to little purpose—for that in my opinion emancipation depended on the progress of truth among the whites. But I believe he is determined to be his own counsellor. I expect he will go—there he comes."

Loguen had been passing in and out of the room during this conversation, and heard a considerable part of it.

"They say you talk of leaving for the Oneida Institute?"

"I have been thinking of it, and have about made up my mind to go."

"You are very useful here, and in good business—laying up money. Won't you make a mistake?"

"I can't be easy when there is a possibility of doing something for the freedom of my poor mother, brothers, sisters and friends. I lack education, and it seems as if it was my duty to acquire it, and use it for my kindred and friends."

"I am not going to argue the case with you. If you have made up your mind to go, the case is settled—but I am decidedly of the opinion you will regret it. I don't blame you for feeling deeply for your kindred—but I don't believe their interest will be advanced by surrendering your place here."

"I am not likely to want—I have not labored in vain for the last five or six years."

"I know you have laid up money—and what I want is, that you go on laying it up. How many thousand dollars have you in the bank?"

"O, my dear sir, I have got but little money. I have been a single man, you know—no wife or relation to provide for. I don't drink, or gamble, or dissipate in any way, as some of our people do. I have been very industrious and economical, and it would be strange if I had not saved a little money. What I want is, to make my money useful. I would make it a part of myself to that end only. If it takes a little of it to improve my learning, it will not be thrown away, I hope, and I shall have some left. Besides, I don't intend to break in on my little capital much. I shall spend the vacations in efforts to improve the colored people in Utica, Syracuse, and Rochester, and wherever else I may improve them—for it seems to me they have a part to act in this case, and need preparation to act well. In doing this, I trust Providence I shall not be a loser. Besides, I may spend some of the winters in service here. I don't think I shall reduce my capital much."

"Well, you will do as you please, of course—but I can't help thinking you err."

At the end of about two years from the time he entered the Rochester House, Mr. Loguen settled up with it—put his money in the bank—packed his clothes, and went to Whitesboro, and entered Oneida Institute, under the celebrated Beriah Green, the President of the Institute.[1] During the winter vacations of his first two years at the Institute, he returned to his post in the Rochester House, and earned more than enough to pay his expenses at the College—thus demonstrating that, if the door of education be open, colored youth, as well as white ones, may overcome the obstacles to education which poverty interposes.

The third winter after he entered the College, he went to Utica to learn the condition of colored people there, and institute a school for their children, and assist them to a higher plane of civilization. At that day, Utica was in advance of the cities of the North in regard to freedom—and its anti-slavery attractions secured the residence of an intelligent and spirited colored population. It was already renowned as the place where the Abolition Society of the State of New York had its birth in a mob, stimulated by one of the Judges of the Supreme Court[2]—and where the doctrine of the absolute anti-slavery character of the Constitution, and its utter incompatibility with slavery, even in the slave States, (which is fast growing to be public opinion) was first broached.[3]

1. [Loguen's note:] Mr. Loguen was induced to take this course by the Rev. F. P. Rogers, of Newark, New Jersey—a colored man of distinction, who was then a member of the Institute. Mr. Rogers spent a portion of the time he belonged to the Institute in teaching at Rochester, and there made the acquaintance of Mr. Loguen, in whom he discovered qualities and talents which, in his opinion, were due to the public; and having obtained his consent, made application at the Institute, and procured his admission, before was prepared to pass the required examination.

2. [Loguen's note:] Judge Beardsley.

3. [Loguen's note:] Two fugitive slaves, from Virginia, were brought before Judge Hayden, of the Common Pleas, under the law of '93, at the instance of two man-hunters from that State. The prosecution was conducted by Joshua A. Spencer, Esq., of Utica, deceased, and the defence by Alvain Stewart, Esq., of the same place, also deceased. It occasioned great excitement, intensely enhanced by one of the most ingenious, able, and touching arguments for the slaves that ever set a great audience in indignation and tears. The Judge delivered them

At this time, colored children were excluded from the common schools, though their parents were taxed for the support of such schools. At the request of the principal families, Mr. Loguen commenced teaching. The first day but three scholars came to school—but the number soon increased to forty, and they learned rapidly. At the close of the term, the people were desirous of a public school exhibition, and a large room was provided therefor. The children procured pieces to speak, and compositions to read, and clothes to wear, and presented themselves in all the pride of juvenile humanity on the stage, to a large and mixed audience. It was the first exhibition of colored children, it is presumed, in central or western New York. It succeeded admirably. Speeches were made complimenting the children for their proficiency, propriety and accomplishments, and thanking Mr. Loguen for the good he had done.

Mr. Loguen now began to feel the delight of living for use—the only real delight God allows to man. Men desire to serve in heaven, and are therefore happy—they desire to rule in hell, and are therefore miserable. If we had nothing else to prove the sin of slavery, it would be enough that it denies to the slave the heavenly joy of doing good to the neighbor. Inasmuch as religion and heaven consist in thus doing, the system is precisely infernal that forbids it—for that is the soul of all joy in earth and heaven.

The clauses in our State and national constitutions which forbid the governments of the country to establish religion, or to prohibit 'the free exercise thereof,'[4] assert and vindicate the basis principle of the divine constitution. The prohibition is as explicit in its application to the slave as to the freeman.

---

to the claimants, and they were accordingly imprisoned in a walled room, the door locked and barred, with armed bullies to guard it. But the brave colored men of Utica, armed with clubs, broke into the prison, and after a battle which made sore heads among the captors and bullies, rescued the slaves, and detained the claimants and bullies in the same prison, until the former were out of reach. So sudden and bold was this deed, that the enemy was dumbfounded, and the black heroes were never known to them. At that early day, Alvain Stewart, Esq., was condemned for asserting the unconstitutionality of slavery by some who have since been his able backers. He declared it on the stump, in the paper, and before the Courts. And especially in a memorable case before the Supreme Bench of New Jersey. His argument in that case was published in full, and was universally regarded as a glorious specimen of originality and strength of genius, power of argument, knowledge of first principles, of law, of the constitution, of touching and powerful combination of thoughts and affections, which demonstrate the lawyer, the orator, the philosopher, the great and good and heaven-gifted man.

4. [Loguen's note:] The clause in the Constitution of the United States on this subject reads thus: "Congress shall make no law respecting an establishment of Religion, or prohibiting the free exercise thereof."

Indeed, it is *se ipse* the inhibition of slavery. It is a positive guaranty that every human being shall be free to exercise all the privileges and indulge all the joys of his own religion. The whole fabric of slavery disappears in the presence of such constitutional provisions. What is religion but to live the command, 'Love God and the neighbor?' The Lord himself has told us "on these two hang all the law and the prophets,"—that is, everything relating to truth and goodness and human duty depend on them. What, then, can be more destructive of man's religion, than to take from him the right to know God and his duties, and thrust him, without rights, among brutes and things? Religion is truth in act; therefore the Lord said, "Ye shall know the truth, and the truth shall make you free."

While at the College, Mr. Loguen also had charge of a class of Sunday scholars at Utica. There he met, for the first time, Caroline Storum, on a visit to her friends. An intimacy commenced between him and Caroline, which ripened into mutual attachment, and resulted in their marriage on the day of the election of General Harrison in 1840, at the house of her father and mother, William and Sarah Storum, at Busti, Chatauque county, N.Y.

Mr. and Mrs. Storum emigrated from New Hartford, in the State of New York, to Busti, in 1816, when Chatauque county was new. They travelled in an ox cart, with all their effects, and purchased and took possession of one hundred and forty acres of good land, cleared and subdued it to a high state of cultivation, and made it one of the best farms of the county. They were both slightly tinged with African blood; but nevertheless were estimated by their lives and character among the well-informed and estimable citizens. Caroline was privileged with the best education country opportunities afforded. The standing and respectability of the family always protected her against prejudice of color, which effects so many of her race.

This connection was a fortunate event in the life of Mr. Loguen. Mrs. Loguen was about twenty years of age when married—of pleasing person and address, amiable, and of that best of breeding which undervalues the shining and superficial, and highly esteems the intellectual and substantial, the useful

---

A similar clause is in each of the Constitutions of each of the States. The Constitution makers and adopters either did not know what religion was, or they intended to give colored men—and even slaves, if there could be slaves—perfect freedom in matters of religion. If they did not so intend, then, happily, they were misled to adopt a provision which, in a clearer day, will secure a perfect foundation for just legislation and judicial action in regard to human rights. Freedom in Religion is freedom throughout.

and the good—qualities which fitted her to instruct her household, and even her husband, in some things,[5]—and to receive, comfort and bless the hundreds of fugitives from slavery who found an asylum at her house,—which, therefore, acquired the eminently appropriate appellation of the UNDERGROUND RAIL ROAD DEPOT AT SYRACUSE.

At Whitesboro he first made a public profession of religion, and united with the colored people's Church at Utica. His religious state long before made such a connection desirable; but his disgust of the Churches at the South, and North also, on account of their pro-slavery attachments, were so great, that he rejected all church relations until he found the colored church at Utica.

In speaking of a public profession of religion and uniting with the Church, we adopt the language of the age in reference to visible and external forms only. We may not leave the topic without saying, that a profession of religion and union with the Church, in the opinion of Mr. Loguen, are quite different things. The professions which men make with their mouths, and the Church unions they make for their convenience, are mere external things—often mere shams, and entirely empty of everything religious. There is but one Church, and he that performs Heaven's uses by doing good to the neighbor, in the very act of performing such uses, publicly professes the only true faith, and enters the true Church. Like the ancient Jews, who took the symbol for the idea symbolized, too many modern Christians (or Jews, for such Christians are scriptural Jews,) adopt the form for the substance, and make it of infinite account. It will be a glorious consummation, when that delusion, like the Levitical symbols, is dissolved by the truths, which, in these latter days, are forming a new Heaven and a new Earth.

5. [Loguen's note:] Mr. Loguen often says he wishes he was as well educated as his wife.

CHAPTER XXVI

In the year of our Lord one thousand eight hundred and forty-one, Mr. Loguen began his residence in Syracuse, and with the exception of five years—three at Bath, Steuben county, and two at Ithaca, Tompkins county, N.Y.—has resided there ever since.

The condition of colored people, and the progress of popular sentiment in regard to slavery in Syracuse, deserve a brief notice. There, as in all the country, the Churches and political parties were adapted to slavery as it was, and were unwilling to be disturbed by it. Indeed, it was the judgment of those bodies that the prosperity of both Church and State demanded that the old state of things be undisturbed. It has been a steady and persistent struggle with that idea, in the minds of politicians, ministers, and people, that has placed Syracuse in a precisely opposite position to that she occupied then. If Utica occupied the highest ground on this subject at that day, Syracuse, unhappily for her fame, occupied the lowest. She has been lifted out of her natural mud, and raised somewhat from her moral, political and religious mud, by cotemporary agencies.

We are told that men "can receive nothing unless it be given them from heaven,"—that "every good and perfect gift cometh down from the Father of lights." If, then, Syracuse has advanced in liberty and religion, inasmuch as she has done it in opposition to the external organizations of the city and country, we infer it is by the influx of divine goodness through the feeble few who stood by the right, and who, by virtue of such goodness, were stronger than the strongest. It is thus that divine love and wisdom are ever received by self sacrificing ones, and poured upon the darkness of the world. They form the connecting link between earth and heaven—they are the home of God—the true Church, whose divine activities overcome the world and preserve it.

In 1835, the anti-slavery men of the county of Onondaga assembled at the old Baptist church in the city, to organize a County Anti-Slavery Society. Among them, as visitors, were Gerrit Smith, Alvin Stewart, Beriah Green, William Goodell, Charles Stuart of England, and other illustrious agitators, who gave birth and embodiment to a new public sentiment in central and western New York. This proposition aroused the prominent men in the political and religious organizations of the city, to take measures to prevent it. The then leaders of the anti-Abolitionists were T. T. Davis, Judge Pratt, John Wilkinson, V. W. Smith, and others, who rallied the unthinking citizens into the convention, to prevent its action by their irregularities. The business committee reported resolutions and a constitution for the Society, and the convention passed the resolutions before the disorganizers came into it. Judge Pratt led off in a lengthy speech against the entire movement, followed by T. T. Davis and John Wilkinson,—all speaking at considerable length—when Beriah Green got the floor, and occupied nearly two hours in an argument of tremendous power, showing the dangers and atrocities of Slavery.

When Mr. Green finished his speech, the question was called for—but all attempts to put the question were drowned by the loud cries and disorderly conduct of the opponents. They would consent to hear speeches, but absolutely forbid a vote on the constitution. Being too few to vote the constitution down, they resolved to prevent its adoption by disturbance, and in that they succeeded. The meeting was adjourned for an evening session; but instead of meeting in the evening, as the anti-Abolitionists expected, the Abolitionists secretly retired to Fayetteville, in the same county, and completed their organization.

Determined in their purpose to prevent the formation of a Society, the anti-Abolitionists returned again to the Church in the evening, and found it shut and alone. There they appointed a venerable and respectable citizen to the chair, (Mr. Redfield,) and also appointed a committee on resolutions, of which V. W. Smith was chairman. A set of resolutions were reported by Mr. Smith, and passed by them, denouncing the purposes of the Abolitionists, and declaring it inexpedient to form an anti-Slavery Society in the county of Onondaga. These resolutions were paraded in the public papers—which also denounced the Abolitionists, and gloried over their supposed defeat.

Thus far, the resistance of the anti-Abolitionists showed a political front only; and the ministers and Churches, however they sympathised with such resistance, were mainly content to scout the Abolitionists, their principles and aims, as schismatical antagonisms to the unity of the Church, and therefore deserving religious condemnation. But the growing hostility to slavery originated in religious motives only; and its political manifestations were but the ultimation of interior convictions, which several prominent, influential, and eminently good men in the Church believed were wrought by the Holy Ghost, to be carried into their lives—or that their religion was a gross delusion.

The largest number of the Abolitionists belonged to the Presbyterian Church, the most popular and commanding congregation in the city, then under the charge of the learned and venerable Dr. Adams. All the Churches—the Presbyterian Church especially—were alarmed by the progress of anti-slavery in the city and country. Several of the truest and most reliable members of the latter Church were infected by the contagion, and it trembled with the revolutionizing sensations of its own bosom. The State Abolition Society, at this time, were scattering their tracts, papers and books, like the leaves of autumn over the State, at an immense expenditure of money, industry and learning—and its talented lecturers were gathering the people into the school houses and churches in many places, in spite of mobs and ridicule, and every form of abuse—pointing them to the history of slavery, its atrocities and meanness—and urging them to arrest its progress, ere liberty and religion, law and constitution, were defaced by its bloody steps.

In the year 1837, public notice was given that Rev. John Truair would lecture, on Sunday afternoon, on the subject of slavery, at a school house in Lodi, now a portion of the city of Syracuse. Mr. Truair was a worthy minister, and a powerful and eloquent debater.[1] Several prominent members of Mr. Adams' Church were attracted to this meeting, to hear the lecture of Mr. Truair. The venerable Doctor Adams, who prudently avoided the mention of slavery in the pulpit, and who thought it not right either to attend an anti-slavery lecture, or give notice thereof on the Sabbath, was deeply grieved at this supposed delinquency of those members, and made it the topic of severe censure the subsequent Sabbath.

The offending anti-slavery men, in consequence of this resistance of their minister to the holiest desires of their hearts, began to be sensitive to a separating point between themselves and him, and those of his Church and congregation, who, with him, cleaved to slavery as it was. They contrasted the cold sermon with the warm lecture, and the staid Doctor with the brave, enthusiastic and eloquent Truair. They began to feel that religion was a principle to be lived, and not an organization to be sustained, and therefore felt their attachment weakening as to the latter, and strengthening as to the former. The growing breach between the Abolitionists and anti-Abolitionists grew more distinct, from the fact that their minister (Mr. Adams,) would consent to a protracted meeting of the Church, only on condition that their favorite revival minister, Mr. Avery—who was also an Abolitionist, should not be the

1. [Loguen's note:] Father of the Messrs. Truairs of the *Daily Journal* office in Syracuse.

preacher thereat, and that Mr. Adams should select a minister for the occasion. The Abolitionists of the Church were revivalists, and vainly supposed that a protracted religious meeting would inflate minister and people with vital religion, to wit, the love of God and the neighbor—all that was needed to give freedom to the slave.

A plan was now seriously considered by the Abolitionists to part from Mr. Adams and his Church and congregation, and form an anti-slavery Church and congregation upon the basis of the broadest benevolence. A subscription paper was accordingly drafted and circulated among the people by S. H. Mann, Esq.; and such sums were contributed, that they immediately organized a congregational Society, and built a meeting house, and hired Mr. Avery for their minister. This Society and house were the rallying point of reform for the city and county, and for the State also, until the county and State became largely saturated with their sympathies.

So soon as this Society was formed, anti-slavery in Syracuse assumed an independent position and organization. It was a living embodiment of freedom, and opened its bosom to the charities of Heaven, and felt its arms strong by the divine influx—and fearless of parties and politicians, of calculating ministers and a consummated Church, put its hand to every good work.

But the Presbyterian was not the only Church disturbed by the new emotion of righteousness. All the Churches were more or less shaken by it. The Episcopal Methodists became largely receptive of it, and many of its members shrank from the infected body, so soon as their eyes opened to its companionship with this horrible crime. Such were the number and character of the seceders, that they formed a Society by themselves, under the pastorate of the Rev. Luther Lee, built themselves a church; and became an important link in the cordon of Wesleyan Churches in this country. Mr. Lee was an Ajax in debate, a fervent Christian, and of course an ardent Abolitionist. He soon formed around him a permanent and efficient Methodist anti-slavery power, which attracted the good and brave Methodists to co-operate with the Congregationalists in breasting the war against freedom, by the popular religious and political parties of Syracuse.[2]

2. [Loguen's note:] It is a pity all Methodists had not taken ground with the Wesleyans. But the little Spartan band of Wesleyans, to their honor be it said, were all who were then willing to stand beside God and the slave. They left the great body to the scourges of divine Providence for their fault in this matter. The evils that Slavery has wrought in its vitals now burn intensely, and its cold granite body is cracking with pro-slavery heat. Honorable efforts are being made in it, and in other great religious bodies in this country, to reform them in this regard. But

The excitement in the city affected not the city alone. It pervaded the county, and precipitated a change of sentiment among those who sustained slavery as it was. Prudent politicians and Christians, and all thinking men, were obliged to look respectfully at this antislavery power—entrenched, as it was, in its eternal truths and growing combinations, and to submit its claims to their reason and understandings.

It is not surprising that such men as John Wilkinson, T. T. Davis, and V. W. Smith, Esquires, eventually changed their views and positions, and came into conjunction with the almost universal sentiment of the city and country, in opposition to slavery. The strangeness is, that Judge Pratt, (and we name him because we have heretofore named him in connection with Wilkinson, and Davis, and Smith,) or any other person of any pretension to sense and integrity, could be found in Syracuse to retain their original hostility to universal freedom. It is only explainable by the fact that God invariably executes his righteous intents by antagonizing human agencies, and that thus the devils are instrumental of divine uses.

One more fact in this connection, will close the chapter of causes which dethroned the pro-slavery sentiment of Syracuse, and enthroned the opposite sentiment.

In the month of September, 1839, J. Davenport, of Mississippi, accompanied with his wife and child, and another white lady, arrived, with much show of importance, in Syracuse, and took lodgings at the Syracuse House—then, and still, a Hotel celebrated for its palatial accommodations. We called this female companion "another white lady," because nothing in her complexion, dress, or deportment, and nothing in the treatment of her that was publicly seen, designated her as one of the abject race. She was about twenty-four years of age, white complexion, straight brown hair, black eyes and full and

---

we never expect to see the Methodist Church, or Baptist, or any other Church, reformed. No Church ever was reformed. The order of Providence and Heaven is, that they perform their uses and perish. Like men, they begin in infancy, pass into maturity, old age, and death. When God is done with them, he lays them aside as a worn out garment, there to remain, until the day of universal charity consumes them. Noah, nor Moses, nor Christ, nor his Apostles, were reformers. They announced the end and positive incureableness of a past age or dispensation, and the opening of a new one, which was but the resurrection of the old one in a dress suited to the uses of the future—while the forms or shells of the past remain, as the Jewish and first christian Churches remain to kindle the fires of the millenial conflagration. The garments of the Lord are the opinions of the age in regard to him—and when those opinions cease to be available for his uses—when they cease to be vitalized by charity, as at the time of Noah, and of Christ, and at the present time, "as a vesture will he change them, and they shall be changed."

beautiful proportions. Citizens and strangers, caught by her personal attractions, turned to look at her as they passed, and never suspected she could be a slave. When she appeared in the coach or on the sidewalk, with Mr. and Mrs. Davenport, she was as richly dressed as her mistress, and seemingly entitled to equal civility and respect.

They occupied the most expensive accommodations, dressed and rode in the most costly and imposing fashion, and made a great sensation upon uppertendom in Syracuse. It was soon learned by the servants, and communicated to outsiders, that this beautiful southern girl was a slave—the property of Mr. Davenport. The fact that a woman so white and attractive was held as property, awakened curiosity and indignation among some who had no objection to black slavery—though many wealthy and fashionable citizens looked upon the case as a beautiful thing, and spoke of it as a sample of the elegance and bliss of Southern life.

Two citizens, William M. Clark and John Owen, having learned that this young lady felt keenly the restraints of slavery, and that rich dresses, and expensive baubles in her ears, and on her fingers and bosom, were no compensation for liberty, signified to her through the colored servants of the hotel, that if she dared, they would put her into Canada, and she should be free. She consented, and a plan was concocted by Mr. Clark, Owen, and those servants, to put her out of the reach of her master. But the terrible consequence of a failure excited her fears, and she revoked the agreement. Upon being reassured by the white and black men alike, that they would not fail, and that they would do their part so well that defeat was impossible, she again entered into the arrangement.

Harrict's—that was the name of the white slave—courage now revived, and she committed herself to the enterprize. A reconsideration of the matter satisfied her that, for her, the terrible consequences of slavery could not be aggravated, and that there was no hope for her but in freedom. She was aware her master had been importuned to sell her for $2500, for the worst of purposes, and she knew he had no conscientious scruples to deter him from yielding to the base intents of the purchaser.

Mr. Davenport now fixed the day of his departure to Mississippi. A single day intervened—the evening of which was spent at a select party at Major Cook's, as a sort of closing *fete* of the Syracuse fashionables to their southern friends. Harriet was at the party to take charge of the babe, and at a certain hour of the evening—which had been settled as the hour for her escape—she passed through the assembly, very naturally, and placed the babe in its mother's lap, and told her she wished to step out. The mother took the child without suspicion, and the beautiful white slave disappeared from her sight forever.

Not daring to hire a horse and carriage in the city, Messrs. Clark and Owen went into the neighboring town of De Witt; and employed a Mr. Nottingham, a farmer in said town, to be at the corner of the Park at the head of Onondaga street, to receive the girl at the time agreed on; while another carriage, furnished by the colored men at the Syracuse House, was to be at Major Cook's to receive the fugitive, and take her to Mr. Nottingham.

Harriet was bare headed when she got into the carriage, and it was cold—but the servants anticipated her necessities, and one put a hat on her head, and another gave her his overcoat—both intended to disguise her, and at the same time keep her comfortable. They then rode to the Syracuse House, and received her clothing from the window, and immediately deposited her with Mr. Nottingham, at the Park—and before Mr. Davenport suspected her, she was flying rapidly to the house of Mr. Shepard, in Marcellus—where Mr. Nottingham deposited his charge, safely and comfortably, the same night.

An observing citizen of Syracuse, in the year of our Lord one thousand eight hundred and fifty-nine, who had not lived through its intervening history, could by no means imagine the explosion this affair produced in the city. The rage of the man Davenport, so soon as the escape was known, was beyond bounds—and political and sectarian snobs, officials, and citizens, joined these mad ones in a chorus of indignation. Every man and horse was put in requisition to find the beautiful Harriet, who had so slily and foolishly fled from happiness and duty. No afflicted King or Queen ever had more, or more genuine sympathizers among their subjects, than had Mr. and Mrs. Davenport on that occasion.

The tide of feeling took two directions—one to find the track of the girl, and hunt her down and re-plunge her into slavery; and the other to hunt out the villains who dared to put their abolition in practice in Syracuse, and subject them to the terrible penalties of slave laws. But it was vain. The white and black men managed this enterprise so prudently and bravely, that no trace of the one or the other could be scented by the blood hounds. It was especially provoking to the anti-Abolitionists, that the spoil was plucked out of the mouths of the spoilers, while they were in the act of demonstrating their contempt of the Abolitionists—and that, too, in the presence of the Southerners, whose opinion of their strength, and of the impotence of the Abolitionists, they supposed they were establishing.

No crime was ever committed in Syracuse that excited so much blustering and active indignation as this. Expresses were sent to Oswego and in other directions, to head and capture the fugitive. The outrage was published through the press, then decidedly on the side of slavery; and the enraged slave-holder issued a circular, describing the person of Harriet, her ornaments and dresses, and offering a reward of $200 to whoever would return her to him, and $100 to any one who would inform of her whereabouts, that she might be captured.

The friends of liberty quietly but firmly pursued their course, notwithstanding the threats of their numerous and powerful opponents—who appeared before magistrates, and searched their houses, and disturbed their wives and children, to find the beautiful slave.

Harriet had enjoyed her asylum but a short time, ere her saviors learned that Davenport & Co., by means of some treachery not yet explained, were informed of her whereabouts. Happily, this information was given late at night, and the anti-Abolitionists determined early next morning to take and return her to slavery. Her liberators, however, were informed of the treachery the same night, and sent an express and took her from Mr. Shepard, and carried her to Lebanon, Madison county, and concealed her with a friend.

The next morning, the agents of Davenport & Co. arrived at Mr. Shepard's and demanded Harriet—not doubting she was in the house. Mr. Shepard made very strange of the matter, and so conducted that the agents, after searching the house, left for Syracuse—cursing the traitors, as they charged, who had humbugged them. The result was as it should be—the informer lost all credit for truth and honor, by all parties,—and what was worse than that in his esteem, he lost the one hundred dollars bribe which Davenport offered to quiet his conscience if he would assist in re-enslaving Harriet.

In the progress of these events, the case became known to Hon. Gerrit Smith, of Peterboro—who, since 1834, had lost his respect for the colonization scheme, and found in the abolition movement a channel for his benevolence, genius, eloquence and wealth. Mr. Smith expressed a desire that Harriet be brought to him at Peterboro, and promised she should be protected. She was accordingly taken to Mr. Smith, and tenderly and carefully secreted and comforted by him and his not less devoted and generous wife. Harriet staid with Mr. Smith's family several weeks, ere he supplied her with clothing and money, and sent her to Canada. There she afterwards became married to an excellent citizen, nearly as white as herself. When Mr. Clark visited her a few years after her escape, he found her a happy wife and mother, with a husband much respected for his well rewarded industry and good character. To his question, whether she would not be restored to her mistress in as good a state as when she left her, she replied she would have both her arms torn from her body before she would be a slave.

The brave men who set free this beautiful slave, never boasted of their success—nor did they think it prudent, in the time of it, to gratify the aching curiosity even of their friends, by telling them how, or by whom, it was done. Nor were the facts known, until Time, the barometer which indicates the states of the soul and of public opinion, showed the infamy of the transaction clean rubbed out, and the names of William M. Clark and John Owen upon a clear and beautiful passage of history.[3]

Such struggles with the social, political and religious powers of Syracuse, wrought largely upon public sentiment. The Abolitionists were few in number, but mighty through the great truths which attract the elements of power, to wit, love and wisdom—which, united, perform the uses of humanity, and without which, the masses fall into all the forms of antagonizing self-hood.

3. [Loguen's note:] We have taken much pains to learn the names of the colored operators in this case without avail, which we much regret, because we wished to put them on the record. Without them, Harriet would have continued a slave—and because, soon after Davenport became a bankrupt, if living, she would doubtless now be the cast off victim of a Southern Harem.

CHAPTER XXVII

Such was the state of things at Syracuse in 1841, when Mr. Loguen came to reside there. He found the colored people comparatively uncared for. He felt that his mission was to them, and by the license of Alder Chester became their preacher—and gathered the children and youth into a school, and taught them to read and write and cipher.

The controversy between the Abolitionists and anti-Abolitionists was now fast bringing them into notice, and they were becoming objects of regard by good and humane men and women. No man received Mr. Loguen with more cordiality than the venerable Doct. Adams, who offered to take him into his own house and family, in aid of his efforts to improve the colored people. But Mr. Loguen asked nothing for himself. He drew his own money from the bank, and bought him a house and lot, and became, and has continued, a freeholder and tax paying citizen. Real estate rose in value in his hands, and by industry and care, his early investments made him not rich, but in good credit. We speak of his property to show that it is the growth of his hard earnings the first six years of his freedom, and not contributions to his anti-Slavery lectures.

At this time, the colored people had a small house for worship inclosed, but not finished. But their minds were on the lowest natural plane, and unprepared for the simple truths of religion, much less to appreciate the high claims and profound truths of the Bible. Deprived of social and mental culture, they formed a suburban girdle of moral and intellectual darkness about the city. He hired a lot of Mr. Hoyt, near the Park, and opened a school for the children, and taught them to read and write. At the end of the term, he had a public exhibition at the Congregational Church, which was honored by a large attendance of white and colored people. The church was ornamented with evergreens, and their compositions and speeches were highly complimented by their hearers.

He next hired a room of Mr. Dunbar, in Salina street, but because it was too small, he set about building a new house near the old Baptist church, in Church street. Having enclosed the building, the people were so enraged at the project, that he moved it with oxen near McKinstry's Candle Factory, and kept a school in it the following winter, and had an exhibition as before. The house was again removed, and now stands on the tannery premises formerly of Bates & Williams, now the property of W. H. Van Buren.

The third year of his residence at Syracuse, he went into the southern counties to raise funds to finish the church building. At this time the slavery agitation had stirred the minds and passions of the people into a tempest, and the subject was mingling fiercely with the politics of the day. He made his first anti-slavery speech, on this tour, to a large audience in Prattsburg, Steuben county, at the request of Revd's. Judson and Adson, active abolition ministers, who invited him to preach and lecture. Elder Rowley was accidentally present, and so delighted was he, that he introduced him to the people of Bath, and procured him a settlement over a small congregation of white and colored people, with whom he labored three years—preaching Sundays and teaching week days. Before being installed, he attended the Annual Conference of the African M. E. Church, and was licensed as an Elder.

In the Fall of '44, Mr. Loguen's second year at Bath, the antislavery tempest broke into a rage, and the friends of Mr. Clay, and Polk, and Birney, candidates for the Presidency, had their orators of every grade in the field, attituding them to the breeze. In the midst of the excitement, Mr. Loguen visited the counties of Tompkins and Cortland, to raise funds to finish the church at Bath. On this circuit he met with circumstances that opened to him a new field—placed him in companionship with men of refinement, education and manliness, and secured to him a conspicuous and honorable position before the country. Until then he had made a single speech on slavery, and his public life had been limited to preaching and teaching. But now the spark fell amid the combustible elements of his soul, and kindled the fires which controlled him ever afterwards.

On a glorious Sunday morning, the latter part of September of this year, after the people had assembled in the churches, two gentlemen were seated in an office in Cortland village, the Capitol of Cortland county, and in view of the Presidential election, were mourning over the adulteration and debasement of the Churches as mighty obstacles in the way of freedom and Heaven, and mingling their sympathies for the Liberty Party, to them the only visible index of humanity and religion. No sound was heard save the heavy foot-fall of a stranger upon the solitary side walks, and the notes of the birds in the artificial forest that covered them. The gentlemen were members of the Presbyterian Church, of which Rev. H. Dunham was pastor—but that Church had passed under the dominion of partizans—the cold breath of the South had bitten it, and its seared glories, like the glories of autumn, were passing away.

"I have no heart to go to meeting," said one of them.

"Neither have I," said the other. "But O, if the Churches of the country were God's Churches, instead of man's, how quickly would this slave question be settled!"

"And who wants to go to meeting to hear a preachment about truths and doctrines, when all that is needed, and all that God demands, is a living charity?"

"True enough. It is not doctrines, however true, nor love, however pure, nor both united, however closely, that makes the christian. But it is truth and love united *in act*, in *life*, that perfects christian salvation. Hoarded manna breeds worms and becomes a curse. It is daily bread for daily use we need. The sheep on Christ's right hand represented those who were in the good of love—but not on account of that good were they beckoned into the kingdom, but because they lived the goodness in charitable deeds to God and the neighbor. The goats on Christ's left hand, too, represent, in the same ancient language, those who were in the truths of faith without the deeds of charity, and they were left to the consumption of their own infernal fires—not because they did not embrace truth, and preach and pray it, but because they did not live it in good to the neighbor. Religion is life, because it is love. It is man's when it is done—not when it is known and acknowledged, and undone."

"Who is that fine looking colored man walking all alone on the side-walk?"

"Sure enough! He is a stranger—may be a fugitive slave. Let us go and see him."

"You seem to be a stranger," said one of the gentlemen, approaching him. "Can we be of service to you?"

"I thank you, gentlemen. My name is J. W. Loguen, and am a stranger here. I want to make an appeal to these rich churches for a small sum to finish our house at Bath. I have been to see all the ministers, and they were not willing to give me a hearing."

"Do you ever talk on slavery?"

"I can talk on slavery."

"Were you ever a slave?"

"Yes, sir—twenty years a slave in Tennessee."

"If we will get you a hearing in two of these churches, will you address them all on slavery at five o'clock?"

"Yes, sir."

The gentlemen seated Mr. Loguen in the Presbyterian church, and after the service, Mr. Dunham stated his case and introduced him to the congregation. He then made his appeal, and received a handsome contribution. In the afternoon he visited and addressed the Baptist Church with like success. Having made a fine impression, and the largest notice being given at all the meetings, the Baptist house was filled to overflowing at five o'clock, to hear him on slavery. The people were *qui vive* on this subject, and a fugitive slave speaker was a person of great interest.

Mr. Loguen did not enter the pulpit, but fell upon his knees before the altar and the people, and poured out the passion of his soul for the redemption of the slave. He thanked the Divine Mercy that led him from the house of bondage, and prayed the same mercy to open the way for all his people. He did not ask God to smite his enemies, if it was consistent with his goodness otherwise to deliver them; but if his poor countrymen could not be delivered without blood, then he prayed God strike quickly. "How long shall my poor brethren suffer? Smite, O God, if smite thou must, and let them out of the hands of their tormentors! Have pity on us. How long shall our little children be torn from their parents, and our innocent sisters and daughters and mothers be give to pollution? O! give me my mother! Thou knowest how she is robbed of her children, and flayed and tortured because she grieves for them. My little brother and sister on one occasion, and my beautiful sister Maria on another, torn from her, and driven, screaming, away, by cruel men, who lashed her body and covered it with her dear blood, because she struggled and prayed for her children!"

No prayer ever made in Cortland melted the people like that. It is impossible to describe it. Suffice it to say, there was not, probably, a dry eye in the great assembly when it ended. Look which way you might all were in tears.

When he rose from his knees and wiped the water from his brow, he stood a moment confused, as if he had forgotten his audience while he talked with God. He adjusted his face and form as if he had come suddenly into a new presence, and then commenced his speech in the timid language of a child. He apologized for his lack of education and habit of speaking on any subject. He had but once before spoken on slavery, and the only qualification he had, he said, was his practical acquaintance with it. He wanted to do justice to it, for it was the burden of his soul.

He then proceeded to detail the features of this terrible despotism as he had felt them and seen them stamped on others. The souls of his hearers were put upon the rack, and their passions burned like fire under his unpretending but harrowing eloquence. When he had them fairly in his hands, he charged them—"Vote this hated monster quietly to death, or its fangs will drive deep in the bosoms of your children. It is the law of divine retribution. You can not allow that monster to tear out our eyes and preserve your own intact. You may not allow it to stupify and demoralize our masters, without feeling a corresponding stupor and demoralization yourselves. I tell you the evil is past endurance—the Justice of God cannot endure it. Heaven's gathering vengeance waits your decision to-day—my poor oppressed countrymen are charged with it to the brim. Do you ask if I will fight? Ah! do you suppose a war upon God and humanity can be carried on, from one side alone? Yes, I'll fight, if fight I must. We were never made to have God's image ground out of our hearts without resistance. If our rights are withheld any longer, then come war—let blood flow without measure—until our rights are acknowledged or we perished from the earth. White men fight—all men fight for their freedom, and we are men and will fight for ours. Nothing can stop the current of blood but justice to our poor people!"

The above is a poor specimen of some of his thoughts on that occasion.

The liberty men of Cortland were so delighted with this specimen of Loguen, that they set him on the stump for Mr. Birney, in opposition to Clay and Polk. Appointments were made for him to speak at the principal places in the county, and he filled them with ability and success. In this circuit, his soul became so absorbed with his theme, as to divorce him, in a measure, from the pulpit, and to set him beside the slave in a life-long war for liberty; and he has continued a public speaker in his behalf ever since. The liberty voters of Cortland county this same year increased to between six and seven hundred, and credited Mr. Loguen for his agency in producing the result.

So soon as the campaign of '44 was over, John Thomas, then of Cortland, persuaded Mr. Loguen that it was his duty to enter the field as an anti-slavery lecturer, and gave him a letter to Hon. Gerrit Smith, commending him for that service. Mr. Smith entertained him over night, and wrote Mr. Thomas, saying, in substance, "What a man you sent me! I invited him to pray in my family, and he prayed so feelingly for his mother that he set us all in tears."[1]

About this time his term at Bath expired, and he accepted a temporary call from the colored people at Ithaca to be their minister—where he labored two years, and did important service. During this time, so numerous and importunate were his calls to lecture on Slavery that he determined to put himself in

1. [Editor's note:] See the editor's introduction for more information about the relationship between John Thomas and J. W. Loguen.

a position to answer them without interfering with other obligations. Accordingly, he dissolved his connection at Ithaca, and returned to his property and friends at Syracuse, and preached to the African Church there, when not called elsewhere to talk on slavery. From that time forward, his life has been a series of incessant activities, for the freedom of his family and race.

CHAPTER XXVIII

The citizens of Cortland were so pleased with Mr. Loguen, and so overcome by his love for his mother, that they determined to purchase her and give her to him, and employed John Thomas to negotiate with Manasseth Logue to that end. Mr. Thomas opened a correspondence with him, and concluded a bargain for Cherry at the price of $250. The sum was raised by subscription, and Nathaniel Goodwin, then of Cortland village, now of Albany, took a letter of Attorney from Mr. Thomas, and went to Tennessee to pay it and bring her on.

Mr. Goodwin arrived at Columbia in the evening, and finding that Manasseth lived about eleven miles off, and that he could ride there only on horse-back, slept till morning, and then went to the livery for a horse.

"You are a stranger, I believe, sir?" said the livery man.

"Yes, sir—I am from New York. This is the first time I have seen Tennessee."

"I knew you was a yankee at first sight. I guess you are after that old slave woman, but you won't get her."

"Pray, how came you to know my business?"

"Manasseth brought all Thomas' letters to me. The matter has made talk here. It is believed Jarm has a finger in the pie, and I advise you to be still as possible, for the abolitionists have made us very susceptible, and a spark will set us all on fire."

Goodwin mounted his horse, and trotted through a half cultivated country, until he came to a cluster of mean log houses. The center one was Manasseth's dwelling, and the surrounding ones were for his cattle and slaves. He rode up to the house and "hallooed" in the unceremonious style of the country. A decriped and bloated old man appeared, and claimed to be Manasseth Logue, and invited him in.

"My name is Nathaniel Goodwin, of Cortland Co., N.Y. I am here, as the agent of Mr. Thomas, to pay for a slave woman he bought of you, and to take her away."

Manasseth admitted the contract, but was inquisitive to know whether it was made for Jarm's benefit. Goodwin admitted that it was. He was advised by his brother and others, at Louisville, that in case enquiry was made about Jarm, to state the facts frankly. They judged, and judged truly, that the facts were strongly suspected at Columbia, and any attempt to conceal them would probably lead him into difficulty. Manasseth told Goodwin that he would be glad to take the money, and let Cherry go—but the rule of slave-holders was "that they shall not sell a slave to a slave"—and the people of Columbia were so certain the contract was for Jarm's benefit, that they would not let her go until Jarm had bought himself.

Goodwin then told him that Jarm would never buy himself.

"Then I shall go and take him; he is my property."

"You can no more take him and make him a slave, than you can the Governor of New York. He is a man of property—a preacher of the Gospel, and loved and respected the country over."

Manasseth and Goodwin altercated this point until after dinner; then the former enquired of Goodwin if he wished to see Cherry. Having an affirmative answer, he sent for her. In a short time an aged colored woman entered the room, dressed in a single coarse garment, which covered her from her neck to near her ankles—leaving her head and feet bare. She appeared to be about sixty years of age, stout and healthy, for a woman so old—though her slow and heavy foot-fall and bent neck, told of age and hardship. Manasseth left her alone with Mr. Goodwin.

"Is your name Cherry?"

"Yes, master."

"Did you ever have a son you called Jarm?"

"Yes."

Her countenance lost its vacancy, and she turned her eyes with obvious intent on Mr. Goodwin.

"Should you like to hear from Jarm?"

"Yes, master—but he died long ago."

"Should you like to be free and live with him?"

"O yes, master."

By this time her attention was fixed intensely on Mr. Goodwin.

"Jarm is not dead—I came from him a few days since. His friends sent me to buy you and take you to him. He wants to make you free and have you live with him."

The dew gathered plentifully on her eye lashes, and her frame was struggling with strong and deep emotions.

"O, I should like to see Jarm and live with him. He must come here and live with me—master will never let me go and live with him."

"O no—he can't come here—he will be a slave if he comes here. Besides, he is a preacher, and owns houses and property, and is very much known and loved by everybody all around the country. More than that, he has a wife and children, and he would not be willing to bring them here."

"How does Jarm's wife look?—how I should like to see her! Is Jarm's wife a slave?"

"O no—there are no slaves where Jarm lives."

In the midst of this conversation, Cherry's daughter Ann came into the Room. She was the property of a neighboring planter, and had been informed that a man had come from New York to purchase her mother and take her to her lost brother, and she was permitted to come and see the stranger, and hear from him and talk about him. It was this daughter that, in the opinion of Manasseth, fastened the heart of Cherry to Murray county. She was the only child not sold out of the country.

"Go, mother—by all means go with the man, and live with Jarm and be free—and one of these days I'll get away and come and live with you," said the animated and stout young woman, whose appearance testified her relationship to Jarm.

Here the sister and mother entered into minute enquiry of Jarm's looks, his age, the looks and ages of his wife and children. His property and condition, his intelligence, wisdom and influence, seemed not to interest them—but any personal peculiarity they sought to treasure in their memory, to hang their hearts on. His mother did say once, "It is just like Jarm to preach." The interview was a luxury to Goodwin—he felt the heart of Loguen stirring in his bosom, awakening emotions of tenderness and love. But he was obliged to close it. Accordingly, he dismissed them, assuring them that he would obtain Cherry if he could, and take her to her son. When he took them by the hand to dismiss them, they wept together—and supposing they might have no further interview with him, they piled their separate messages to Jarm upon his memory.

"You have concluded not to part with Cherry, then?" said Mr. Goodwin to Manasseth.

"I could not, if I would, until Jarm purchased himself."

"That Jarm will never do, I am persuaded—and our business, of course, is ended. I came here on an errand—I have finished it, and must return to Columbia to-night."

Manasseth urged Goodwin to spend the night, but he peremptorily declined; and about two o'clock in the afternoon, started on his return. But

Manasseth, unwilling to part with him, and still hoping he might yet get Jarm, or get his value, walked a mile or two by the side of Mr. Goodwin's horse and two or three over-grown sons with him—all the while urging Goodwin to persuade Jarm to buy his freedom. Finding they could get no consolation from Goodwin, they separated.

Mr. Goodwin returned his horse to the owner at Columbia, who congratulated himself upon the truth of his prophesy, and then took the stage to Nashville, where he arrived about sunset. After supper, the landlord invited his guests to go to meeting with him, and hear Bishop Soule 'give the abolitionists *fits*.' It seems the Annual Methodist Conference of Tennessee was to conclude a long session that night, with a sermon from the far famed Bishop—and the landlord inferred that he would smite the abolitionists, of course.[1] Mr. Goodwin being an abolitionist dyed in the wool—though he regarded the Bishop as a downright Atheist, yielded to the proposition—being curious to see and hear the man who was breaking the Church to pieces by his fanatical adhesion to the sum of villanies.

The congregation was large, and the sermon prosy, in the style of proslavery northern preaching—without a bit of the life which the devil-element of slavery would give it. The only characteristic feature of the case was, that the white people filled the basement, and the galleries were draped with black people; and when the venerable Bishop finished his talk to the whites, he lifted his eyes up to the black circle around his head, and said, very solemnly:—

"And now, my dear colored children, let me say one word to you. Be good children—be obedient to your masters and mistresses for the Lord's sake, and keep your minds and hearts intent on your Heavenly Master, who has ordered your condition in the world, and by-and-by you will die and go with us to the white man's Heaven."

1. [Editor's note:] Joshua Soule (1781–1867) was a bishop of the Methodist Episcopal Church (elected in 1824) and then of the Methodist Episcopal Church, South. He was an opponent of Calvinism, Unitarianism, and Universalism. In the 1844 division of the Methodist Episcopal Church over the issue of slavery, he sided with the South.

CHAPTER XXIX

When Mr. Goodwin returned and told Loguen he could not have his mother until he owned himself, he was deeply grieved and indignant. He felt wronged and insulted by the proposition. The result of this effort set him to the extreme of hatred against slavery. His whole time and talents and passions were given to war with it. Where there was excitement, there he was to inflame it—where there was none, there he was to set the fire blazing. He was in the spirit on the Lord's day and every day. Scarce a Sabbath has passed but he stood before a large congregation in some part of the country to electrify the people with his spirit.

Mr. Loguen was stationed at Syracuse in '46, and remained there to '48, when he was made presiding Elder for one year, and appointed to preach in the city of Troy. He went to Troy in the spring of 1850, and continued there until the fugitive slave act—which was passed the 7th and approved the 18th Sept., 1850—when he was advised by his friends, and urged by his wife, to leave his charge and return to Syracuse. He was more exposed than any fugitive in America to be seized under it—for the reason that he had published himself on the stump and in the pulpit and the papers, all over the North, as a defiant fugitive from slavery. Not to attempt to re-enslave him, was an admission that the Government dare not test the strength of the law in such a case; or that the claimant and officers dare not trust their persons in the attempt.

Mr. Loguen arrived at Syracuse the day before the Citizen's Convention to consider the fugitive act, to wit, the 3d day of October, 1850. That convention, so important in its consequences and results, deserves a brief notice. The act had been published in the Liberty Party Paper, and transferred to the Whig Journal. It had also been noticed in the Democratic Standard, the leading dailies in the city. The latter papers disapproved it indeed, but spoke of it with the prudence of mere partizans—while the Liberty Party Paper assailed it with fervent indignation, and attempted, by stirring appeals, to induce the people to forget their parties in positive resistance to it; and yet the people were as unruffled as a summer's sea.

In this state of things, Thomas G. White, of Geddes, an unambitious, plain man, came to the editor of the Liberty Party Paper, and said, with more than usual earnestness:

"I know the people of Syracuse won't stand this, when they come to understand it."

"But how will you make them understand it?"

"I will get up a large convention to discuss the subject—and I want you to sit down and write a call for such a meeting on the spot. I will circulate it among the Whigs and Democrats, and we will have such a meeting as has never before been in Syracuse."

Whereupon the liberty party editor wrote the following call and gave it to Mr. White:

"The citizens of Syracuse and its vicinity, without respect to party, are requested to meet in the City Hall, on Friday evening, the —th day of September inst., at early candlelighting, to make an expression of their sense of the act of the present Congress, generally known as the fugitive slave law, but entitled, 'A bill to amend an act entitled an act respecting fugitives from justice and persons escaping from their masters.'

"Dated September 26, 1850."

Mr. White took this circular into the street, and presented it to the first man of anti-slavery sympathies he met, who was not an abolitionist—but not until he had invited several to sign it, and was turned off, did he find one willing to head the list, and that man was George L. Maynard, Esq., now Sheriff of the county. Some said they had not read the act—others were unwilling to lead in a measure of that kind, and others wanted to consult political friends—for they would do nothing to discompose the order of parties. Having obtained Mr. Maynard's signature, he had less difficulty to get the sixteen or seventeen other names to the paper—many of whom were prominent free soilers and abolitionists. Having these few names, Mr. White printed the call in the Whig and Democratic dailies of the city; and afterwards caused the time to be altered to the 4th day of October. This expedient of Mr. White started the people from their slumbers, disengaged them from demagogues, and kindled the flames, which, afterwards, consumed party cords like cob-webs, and swept the country with a conflagration which was spiritual and sublime.

When Mr. White and his friends left the city to attend a State Convention at Oswego, the 2d day of October, it was doubtful whether the people would be sufficiently aroused to the subject. But when they returned, they rejoiced to find that C. A. Wheaton had acquainted himself with the startling provisions of this law, and had Mr. White's call printed in a large hand bill, and posted and circulated in all parts of the city, and that the public passions begun to blaze. In addition to this, as we said before, Mr. Loguen made his appearance in the city on the 3d, and passed around among the citizens the next day like a moving fire brand. Many of his friends joined his wife to urge him to retire to Canada for the present—but he deferred a conclusion on that subject, until the meeting.

The people of Syracuse and vicinity, on the evening of the 4th, filled the City Hall to overflowing, and Alfred H. Hovey, Esq., then Mayor, was led to the chair, and the following Vice Presidents chosen, to wit: Ron. E. W. Leavenworth, Hon. Horace Wheaton, John Woodruff, Oliver Teall, Robert Gere, Hon. Lyman Kingsley, Hiram Putnam, and Dr. Lyman Clary; and Vivus W. Smith and L. J. Gilbert were appointed Secretaries.

So soon as the meeting was organized, the impatient audience called long and loud for Samuel R. Ward, a distinguished black orator, who made a most stirring speech, which was greatly applauded.

Mr. Loguen was then called on, and took the stand. He looked over the great assembly, and said:

"He was a slave; he knew the dangers he was exposed to. He had made up his mind as to the course he was to take. On that score he needed no counsel, nor did the colored citizens generally. They had taken their stand—they would not be taken back to slavery. If to shoot down their assailants should forfeit their lives, such result was the least of the evil. They will have their liberties or die in their defence. What is life to me if I am to be a slave in Tennessee? My neighbors! I have lived with you many years, and you know me. My home is here, and my children were born here. I am bound to Syracuse by pecuniary interests, and social and family bonds. And do you think I can be taken away from you and from my wife and children, and be a slave in Tennessee? Has the President and his Secretary sent this enactment up here, to you, Mr. Chairman, to enforce on me in Syracuse?—and will you obey him? Did I think so meanly of you—did I suppose the people of Syracuse, strong as they are in numbers and love of liberty—or did I believe their love of liberty was so selfish, unmanly and unchristian—did I believe them so sunken and servile and degraded as to remain at their homes and labors, or, with none of that spirit which smites a tyrant down, to surround a United States Marshal to see me torn from my home and family, and hurled back to bondage—I say did I think so meanly of you, I could never come to live with you. Nor should I have stopped, on my return from Troy, twenty-four hours since, but to take my family and moveables to a neighborhood which would take fire, and arms, too, to resist the least attempt to execute this diobolical law among them. Some kind and good friends advise me to quit my country, and stay in Canada, until this tempest is passed. I doubt not the sincerity of such counsellors. But my conviction is strong, that their advice comes from a lack of knowledge of themselves and the case in hand. I believe that their own bosoms are charged to the brim with qualities that will smite to the earth the villains who may interfere to enslave any man in Syracuse. I apprehend the advice is suggested by the perturbation of the moment, and not by the tranquil spirit that rules above the storm, in the eternal home of truth and wisdom. Therefore have I hesitated to adopt this advice, at least until I have the opinion of this meeting. Those friends have not canvassed this subject. I have. They are called suddenly to look at it. I have looked at it steadily, calmly, resolutely, and at length defiantly, for a long time. I tell you the people of Syracuse and of the whole North must meet this tyranny and crush it by force, or be crushed by it. This hellish enactment has precipitated the conclusion that white men must live in dishonorable submission, and colored men be slaves, or they must give their physical as well as intellectual powers to the defence of human rights. The time has come to change the tones of submission into tones of defiance,—and to tell Mr. Fillmore and Mr. Webster, if they propose to execute this measure upon us, to send on their bloodhounds. Mr. President, long ago I was beset by over prudent and good men and women to purchase my freedom. Nay, I was frequently importuned to consent that they purchase it, and present it as an evidence of their partiality to my person and character. Generous and kind as those friends were, my heart recoiled from the proposal. I owe my freedom to the God who made me, and who stirred me to claim it against all other beings in God's universe. I will not, nor will I consent, that, any body else shall countenance the claims of a vulgar despot to my soul and body. Were I in chains, and did these kind people come to buy me out of prison, I would acknowledge the boon with inexpressible thankfulness. But I feel no chains, and am in no prison. I received my freedom from Heaven, and with it came the command to defend my title to it. I have long since resolved to do nothing and suffer nothing that can, in any way, imply that I am indebted to any power but the Almighty for my manhood and personality.

"Now, you are assembled here, the strength of this city is here to express their sense of this fugitive act, and to proclaim to the despots at Washington whether it shall be enforced here—whether you will permit the government to return me and other fugitives who have sought an asylum among you, to the Hell of slavery. The question is with you. If you will give us up, say so, and we will shake the dust from our feet and leave you. But we believe better things. We know you are taken by surprize. The immensity of this meeting testifies to the general consternation that has brought it together, necessarily, precipitately, to decide the most stirring question that can be presented, to wit, whether, the government having transgressed constitutional and natural limits, you will bravely resist its aggressions, and tell its soulless agents that no slave-holder shall make your city and county a hunting field for slaves.

"Whatever may be your decision, my ground is taken. I have declared it everywhere. It is known over the State and out of the State—over the line in the North, and over the line in the South. I don't respect this law—I don't fear it—I won't obey it! It outlaws me, and I outlaw it, and the men who attempt to enforce it on me. I place the governmental officials on the ground that they place me. I will not live a slave, and if force is employed to re-enslave me, I shall make preparations to meet the crisis as becomes a man. If you will stand by me—and I believe you will do it, for your freedom and honor are involved as well as mine—it requires no microscope to see that—I say if you will stand with us in resistance to this measure, you will be the saviours of your country. Your decision to-night in favor of resistance will give vent to the spirit of liberty, and it will break the bands of party, and shout for joy all over the North. Your example only is needed to be the type of popular action in Auburn, and Rochester, and Utica, and Buffalo, and all the West, and eventually in the Atlantic cities. Heaven knows that this act of noble daring will break out somewhere—may God grant that Syracuse be the honored spot, whence it shall send an earthquake voice through the land!"

The words of a strong and brave man in the hour of peril fall like coals of fire on human hearts. The people knew Mr. Loguen and loved him. They knew he was a slave, and, trembled for him. They listened with keen sympathy and breathless attention to his brief speech. They knew it was no occasion for Buncomb for any body, and least of all for him. His manliness and courage in a most trying crisis electrified them. He uncapped the volcano, and oppressed sympathy broke forth in a tempest of applause.

By this time every seat and aisle and nook and corner of the room was filled to the utmost, and the cry arose from all parts of the excited multitude:

"The chair! the chair!"

The great audience now forgot they were partizans, and remembered that they were men. They were drawn together by the enthusiasm of a great idea, and that idea was stirring, defiant, revolutionary and sublime. Except with a few, that idea was unuttered and unknown to each other.

The Mayor made a short but spirited and significant speech. He said, among other things:

"The colored man must be protected—he must be secure among us. Come what will of political organizations, and fall where I may, I am with you. I hope I may never be called to obey this law. But should the alternative come, I shall—well,—I hope I shall obey, *law*—(unbounded applause)—let us act deliberately. We are right—this is a righteous and holy cause." (He sat down amid loud and repeated cheers.)

The Business Committee now reported resolutions and address to the people. The resolutions read by Mr. Sedgwick denounced the fugitive slave law—for that it purposely exposed the persons of citizens to the last and worst of outrages, and at the same time deprived them of all legal and constitutional protection, the trial by jury, habeas corpus, the right of appeal, and the privilege of counsel—for that it was charged by a diabolical spirit, and marked by a cruel ingenuity, offensive alike to white and black men—assailing, as it did, the laws of nature and of God—they therefore declared it null and void, and called on the people everywhere "to oppose all attempts to enforce it." They denounced Daniel Webster as responsible for the act, and President Fillmore for approving it, and recommended a Vigilance Committee of thirteen, to see that "no person is deprived of his liberty without due process of law." The Address, read by Mr. Wheaton, embodied the same sentiments, and urged the people, in obedience to God, to "arise in their majesty" and set the act at defiance.

The resolutions and address effectually set free the tempest, and it burst forth from the great assembly in the loudest demonstrations. The sense and spirit of the meeting was no longer doubtful. Stirring addresses were made by Mr. Sedgwick, Mr. Raymond and Mr. May; and after the Chair announced the Vigilance Committee, the meeting adjourned to Friday evening, the 12th October, 1850.

The names of the Vigilance Committee thus announced were C. A. Wheaton, Lyman Clary, V. W. Smith, C. B. Sedgwick, H. Putnam, E. W. Leavenworth, Abner Bates, George Barnes, P. H. Agan, J. W. Loguen, John Wilkinson, R. R. Raymond and John Thomas.

With one exception, there was perfect harmony in this meeting. As it was drawing to a close, in the midst of its deep and burning enthusiasm, J. H. Brand, Esq., a young Democratic lawyer, took the stand, uncalled, and opposed the resolutions and address, and cautioned the meeting against hasty action. He believed the fugitive law to be constitutional and valid, and declared, if called upon, he would aid in its execution. The audience instinctively hissed their disapprobation, but immediately hushed by compassion and pity, and extreme regret that there was a youth in the city willing to set sail in life to the visable infamy of such a statute. The young man sat down amid the universal sorrow which an expressive silence declared for him.

During the week between this meeting and the next, popular feeling swelled and intensified, and the pimps of power—for there were a few such—had little opportunity to find their affinities amid the resistless whirl of popular passions. They were silent, or spoke cautiously in the face of the tempest. At an early hour on the 12th October, the City Hall was again filled, and a large surplus tide of men were set back to talk the matter over in the public rooms, or at their homes. It was the most astounding and stirring coming together that ever occurred in Syracuse.

The meeting was addressed by William H. Burleigh, Judge Nye, C. B. Sedgwick, Rev. Samuel J. May, Rev. R. R. Raymond, Mr. Titus, and J. W. Loguen. If it was large in numbers, it was larger in its spirit and power.

All that was combustable in free, enlightened, arid generous humanity, was already ignited, and the breath of the orators fanned the flame, until it wrapt the city in a general and inextinguishable conflagration, which cleansed the public mind of all fear of federal power, and revealed in the inmost heart of the county, its living principle—to wit, "No man shall be taken from Syracuse a slave, and no power shall force the fugitive slave law upon it."

We conclude the chapter by briefly saying, that the friends of the administration followed the above meetings by another of their stamp; and B. D. Noxon, a venerable counsellor, was their chairman, and Major Burnet, and others, were Vice Presidents. But this counter Convention proved a failure, and its officers deserted it. Hon. Daniel Webster also visited the city, and addressed the people, and told them that their proposed resistance of the law was treason.

"These men," said he in his speech, "had better look to their language and actions, for the law may be enforced. The fugitive slave law will be executed in all the large cities. *It will be executed in this city, at the time of holding the next Anti-Slavery Convention*, if a case arise."

CHAPTER XXX

The 1st of October, '51, is a memorable day in Syracuse. "The next anti-slavery Convention" after Mr. Webster's speech, was then and there held, and the city was thrown into consternation by an attempt to execute the slave law. About noon, C. A. Wheaton came into the Liberty Party State Convention, and announced that a man was arrested as a slave in the city, and that he was at the office of U.S. Commissioner Sabine. A vote was instantly taken to adjourn to Sabine's office, and assemble again when the slave was delivered.

The County Agricultural Fair had attracted to the city people of substance and respectability from abroad in great numbers—the Convention was numerously represented—the Judges of the Court were holding one of their terms, attended by lawyers and litigants—and the politicians far and near were in the crowd. The best opportunity, therefore, existed, to help the government suppress an attempt to rescue the slave, if the people would do it. It is said that the agent, Rev. James Lear, of Missouri, had been in town days before that time, and at the instance of the Marshal, waited this general gathering as favorable to their aims—that they expected sympathy and assistance from it; or they expected to perfect a victory over rebellion, which should be to the greatest extent comprehensive and impressive. An amazing error was leading them into a blaze of light in regard to the pride and courage, spirit and integrity of Syracuse. It needed this additional spark to the iron flask to explode the powder within, and scorch and scatter and blacken the government and its abettors.

The members of the Liberty Party Convention, probably to a man, walked quickly to the office of Commissioner Sabine. If such a convention usually exhibit a collection of marked faces, the exhibit may be supposed to be then eminently striking. Their procession was a signal of alarm to the throng through which they passed—stopping only as they met a friend to explain themselves, and plant a kindred feeling. The young and active led the way—middle aged followed with elevated brow and firm tread—age-stiffened limbs, brought up the rear—and the faces of all, relieved of every shadow that would obscure the brilliancy of their indignation, were attracted to the chained slave in the Commissioner's office.

In the meantime, William L. Crandall, an intelligent, impulsive and chivalric citizen, hastened to the Presbyterian church, and vigorously tolled the bell—and instantly every bell in the city (the Episcopalian excepted) sounded the tocsin of liberty. The amazing mass of citizens, men and women, friends and enemies also, in a very short time had their minds on the poor mulatto—who, until then, was undistinguished, but was destined henceforth to be the subject of the most sublime and beautiful passage in the history of freedom.

The Court room of Mr. Sabine, and the stairs leading to it, were rapidly wedged with the bodies of the conventionists, in whose faces the slave read unmistakeable trust, courage and rescue. The appearance of the triplicate band of Marshals and their armed posse, about the large, bold-browed and handcuffed slave, was not less unique than that of the determined spirits that surrounded and assured them, that their safety lay in the respect or fear of the masses for the law and its penalties. They were armed—but the mighty mass before them might cover and crush them in spite of revolvers. The abolitionists were taken by surprise, and with the prudence of wise men, took time to think.

So soon as Mr. Wheaton gave the above notice, he proceeded to the Court House, and retained counsel for the slave—while the Hon. Gerrit Smith and the Hon. Leonard Gibbs took seats by his side as his voluntary defenders.

"I am Gerrit Smith—your friend," whispered Mr. Smith. "I shall defend you at any expense, and leave no stone unturned to secure your freedom."

"You ain't Gerrit Smith, are you?"

"Yes—and I mean you shall have the best counsel, and to stand by you with my fortune."

The countenance of Jerry brightened. What fugitive slave, if he has been in the country a short time, has not heard of Gerrit Smith? or sitting by his side, is not inspired by the aura that surrounds him?

Jerry was a cooper by trade, and was actually on his seat at work when he was seized. He was alone, the other workmen having gone to their meals. His back being towards the kidnappers, they seized him from behind and threw him on the floor, and ironed him, before he had time to resist, under the cowardly pretence that they had a warrant against him for theft. And not until he was set before the Commissioner was he aware of the cause of his arrest. Then the agent, Lear, approached him, smiling, with a—

"How do you do, Jerry?"

The truth flashed on Jerry's mind with all its intensity and horror but he suffered not a muscle to change the expression of his face or body. He sat down like a chained tiger, amid armed ruffians more hateful than tigers, and to his eye more wicked than devils.

"Who is this Jerry?" said Mr. Loguen, as he passed from the Hall and marched rapidly to the Court Room.

"I know him. He is a short time from slavery, and has few acquaintances. He is stout and brave, and could not be taken without stratagem."

"I see there is concert in this villainy. They had their mind on taking somebody, and have picked him. Why didn't they take me? There are spies in the city speculating on our blood."

"Yes. There are two policemen who would think it a fine thing to hunt up our history and bring our masters on us for a price—and it is not unlikely there are one or two young lawyers who would unite in the game."

"But what are you going to do, surrounded, as we are, by snares and scoundrels?"

"I shall stay and defy them."

"Here we are, at the office—the first ones. Shall we go in? How do we know they will not grab us?"

"Let them grab. Now is the time to try the spunk of white men. I want to see whether they have courage only to make speeches and resolutions when there is no danger. Let us be here at nightfall, and if white men won't fight, let fugitives and black men smite down Marshals and Commissioner—any body who holds Jerry—and rescue him or perish."

They then went up the stairs together, and showed themselves boldly in the presence of the Court, the Marshal, and his armed retainers. The mass crowded up behind them and shoved them in their very faces. Such was their position when Messrs. Smith and Gibbs took seats by Jerry, and the following additional colloquy was had between him and Mr. Smith:

"I believe," said Jerry, "if I should throw myself upon this crowd, they would help me to escape,—they look like friends."

"They are friends," said Mr. Smith, "but not yet. I mean you shall escape—but not yet."

In the mean time, Mr. Gibbs claimed that the prisoner should not be bound when on trial, and raised other questions—all of which were overruled. The Commissioner said, however, that he had not power to order the shackles taken from Jerry, but wished him unshackled, and advised the Marshal to release him, which he refused to do. The great crowd were anxious to release Jerry, but there was no concert among them. Each had determined he should not be taken away, but had not determined how to prevent it. The Court adjourned for dinner, but the abolitionists remained by Jerry without dinner. In the meantime, Jerry put the same question to one of them he put to Mr. Smith, and he, inconsiderately, advised Jerry to throw himself on the crowd and escape.

Acting upon this hasty advice, Jerry, with eyes, flashing fire, and the strength and agility of a tiger, threw himself across the table, scattering papers and pistols, Marshal and constables, and lay upon the bosom of the multitude, who made room for him, but closed upon the kidnappers, and effectually separated them from him; and before the captors could follow him, he was flying through the crowd in the street. Then, a great multitude, friends and enemies alike took up the chase in the utmost confusion—the former to assist Jerry and embarrass his pursuers, and the latter to retake him.

Jerry ran as fast as he could with fetters on his hands; and doubtless it was owing to the fetters, which were both a mark and an embarrassment, that he was not covered by the crowd, and lost in the great surge of humanity around him, whose voice at a distance was as the roar of the ocean. About half a mile from the starting point, a carriage was brought to take him off; but Peter Way and Russell Lowel, city officers, got at him and prevented him from entering into it. Now the popular wave returned, and Way and Lowel, the assistant kidnappers, pressed a truckman into their service, and with other help, got Jerry into it, after a scuffle which left his body bare and bleeding, with nothing to cover it but pantaloons and a part of his shirt—and then one of them mounted the vehicle, and sitting on his body to keep it down, rode through the streets to the Commissioner's office.

Indignation had now risen to blood heat—though nothing was as yet done but to embarrass without striking the kidnappers. Even then, had a blow been struck, the pent up passions of the multitude would have broken restraint, and by force of sympathy come into the order of desperate battle.

"The devil's to pay!" said Harry Allen to the other Marshals who had been imported from Rochester and Auburn, &c., to help do this infernal deed. "It won't do to take him to Sabine's office. We'll take him to the Police office and shut him in the back room, and shackle his feet, too, and put a strong guard over him. Where is Charlie Woodruff, Green, Shuart, and the other boys?"

"Let me tell you the bullies won't be sufficient. We must have the militia. You may have the militia to help execute the laws."

"I'll call the militia—but I begin to fear we chose the wrong day for this business."

"It is a blunder. These fellows show more spunk than I looked for. It is a pretty business if the Government must fall back before them. We shall be disgraced, and the fugitive law be dead in Western New York. Here is Charlie Woodruff, the Greens, Morrow, Welch, Forman, Lowel and Way, &c. We can guard the prisoner in the back room—but if there is a general rising, our only safety is in the militia."

Poor Jerry, naked and bleeding, with fetters on both hands and feet, was hustled into the back room and put under the guard of the above persons; and Marshal Allen hurried after Sheriff Gardiner, and commanded him in the name of the United States to bring the militia to his aid. The Sheriff, mistaking his duty as an officer and citizen, instantly called upon Capt. Prendergast, and ordered him to the assistance of the Marshal. Capt. Prendergast was an Irish Militia Captain of the sham democratic stamp, who, with many of his countrymen, are fooled into the belief that to be free themselves they must make slaves of other poor people.

Things did not now look to the Marshal as at first. Then he was in high glee. He met Mr. Wheaton in the street, and with triumphant face, and a voice half jocose and all insulting, said:

"Now is your chance, Wheaton! I have got a slave here in Sabine's office. I give you notice that you may not say I stole the march of you."

Poor man! He thought all was safe then. Now, he is looking with dismay and terror to bring Capt. Prendergast and the militia, secretly and rapidly as possible, to the Police office for his own safety. How ignorant was he of the spirit of the youth of Syracuse! Wheaton instantly went to the Captain, and asked if he had been called to bring the citizen soldiers to the aid of the Marshal.

"Yes," he said, "I am commanded to bring out my company to keep the peace."

Mr. Wheaton warned him that keeping the peace was a different thing from hunting slaves—that the Sheriff was the officer of the State, and the State knew nobody as a slave. If the Sheriff put his hand on a man as a slave, he committed a breach of the peace of the worst kind, by the laws of the State. Slave-catchers must do their devil's work without the aid of the State.

This call for the militia caused a general murmur of indignation in the city, which reached the ears of Col. Origen Vandenburgh, and he hastened to Prendergast and asked:

"Is it true you have ordered the militia to interfere in this slave case?"

"Yes—Sheriff Gardiner calls upon me to bring them to keep the peace."

"Then I countermand the Order," said the Colonel. "If the States, with their Marshals and army, can't take a slave from so peaceable a city as this, they are in bad business. Anyhow, my soldiers shall not voluntarily help them, for no better reason than the cowardice of the officials trembling before the outrage they are committing. My soldiers shall never be kidnappers with my consent."

This act of Col. Vandenburgh was soon known through the city, and greatly applauded. But the slave-catchers were indignant at the interference of Wheaton and Vandenburgh, and the Marshals and serviles who had Jerry in charge, were disappointed and dismayed.

In this stage of the case, to form a nucleus of popular action, Thomas G. White invited a few brave spirits into the counting room of Abner Bates, to settle upon some plan of action for rescuing Jerry. They met, and adjourned to meet at Dr. Hiram Hoyt's office at early candlelight, and to bring with them as many good and true and brave spirits as they could vouch for.

Very early in the evening, the following persons appeared at Hoyt's office, viz.:—Doct. Hiram Hoyt, Doct. James Fuller, Doct. R. W. Pease, Gerrit Smith, Samuel J. May, John Thomas, Charles A. Wheaton, Samuel R. Ward, Jermain W. Loguen, Samuel Thomas (Cazenovia,) Linneus P. Noble, (Fayetteville,) Washington Stickney, (Canestota,) William L. Crandall, R. R. Raymond, Caleb Davis, Montgomery Merrick, Abner Bates, James Davis, J. M. Clapp, C. C. Foot, (Michigan,) James Baker, Jason S. Hoyt, Edward K. Hunt, George Carter, Peter Hollenbeck, James Parsons, Lemuel Field, William Gray.

It is not certain that the above list is perfect—nor is it easy to make it so. It is quite probable a few other persons were at this meeting who are not named. For though judges were appointed, and each individual presented to such, judges vouchers for their honor and reliability, and their names were written down, the writing was prudently destroyed, that it be not a possible evidence of so-called treason or conspiracy. It was thought politic to keep in the dark, to escape legal persecution. And now some of these brave men have left the country, and others, with the victim Jerry, have gone to their last account.

When each had proved his title to a place in this Congress of freedom, they gave an emphatic opinion that Jerry must be taken from his captors and set free, and that Syracuse should not be disgraced by his taking off, be the consequences what they might. Some said, that Mr. Sabine would deny the claim, because the evidence would fail to establish it. But if such were known to be the result, they could not be deterred from releasing him by force. The opinion of Gerrit Smith on that subject was enthusiastically applauded.

"It is not unlikely," said Mr. Smith, "that the Commissioner will release Jerry if the examination is suffered to proceed—but the moral effect of such acquittal will be as nothing, to a bold and forceable rescue. A forceable rescue will demonstrate the strength of public opinion against the possible legality of slavery, and this fugitive law in particular. It will honor Syracuse, and be a powerful example everywhere."

The possibility that the opportunity might pass to strike a blow which would be a lesson to the dough faces of the North and the blind men at the South, instead of deterring, precipitated determination, and nerved these men to strike quickly, and in a manner to give the blow the greatest possible effect in all directions. It was the only treatment the law deserved.

While this meeting was in session, the liberators had agents at the Court room, to watch the kidnappers. Ira H. Cobb and Rev. L. D. Mansfield kept their places in the Police office, to know that Jerry was safe, and to give information if an attempt was made to put him beyond the reach of the people, who were assembled in large numbers before the office, with a manifest anxiety to fall in with any attempt at rescue. As the darkness increased, the assemblage increased. It was estimated that not less than 2500 or 3000 persons had assembled, ready to obey the hand which, by an overt act, should tap the tempest within them.

To hold this large mass of citizens at the office, until the session disbanded and gathered into it, the rescuers at the Doctor's office deputed Samuel R. Ward and C. C. Foot of Michigan, distinguished anti-slavery orators, to take the platform before the Police office, and hold the multitude by their address and eloquence, until the liberators arrived. Gallantly and bravely did Messrs. Ward and Foot execute their commission.[1] By turns, their loud and clear voices rolled through the moist twilight until night set in. They were heard distinctly at the Empire and Syracuse houses, and the passers in the streets caught the sound, and reminded of the imprisoned slave, merged into the black mass at the police office. Those who dare not trust themselves near, lest they be impli-

1. [Loguen's note:] The following incident has been furnished the Editor:—When Mr. Foot had finished his speech, Rev. J. R. Johnson commenced speaking, from the window in the third loft. The Sheriff ran up stairs to him, and commanded—"Stop speaking, or I will arrest you!" "I have done," said Mr. Johnson, "but as you command me to stop, I shall begin again, to test the liberty of speech." Addressing the audience, he said, "The Sheriff commands me to stop—do you say I shall stop?" "No! Go on—go on!" said a hundred voices. Here Mr. V. W. Smith interfered, and kindly requested him to stop—for that he feared the crowd would break through the floor of the Journal office. Whereupon Mr. Johnson turned to the Sheriff and said—"Mind you, I stop at the request of Mr. Smith—not from a regard to your order." "What is your name?" resolutely demanded the Sheriff. "Joseph R. Johnson." The Sheriff booked it. "What is your residence?" "Syracuse, Gertrude street, No. 23." "You shall be remembered," said the Sheriff. "The next time we vote, you, too, will be remembered," cried out Doct. Potter. The Sheriff immediately returned to Mr. Johnson, and took him one side, and said in a soft voice, "I am a public officer and must keep the peace—*but betwixt you and me there is no difficulty!*"

cated—the leaders of parties, as well as openly committed partizans of slavery, and all cowards, gathered into groups at safe distances, to see if the people had courage to set Jerry free, as they had resolved in their conventions they would free any slave thus arrested. When the rescuers entered the crowd from Hoyt's office, about eight o'clock in the evening, the great square was filling with the women of Syracuse, who took stands out of the reach of danger, to see the battle which they prayed would set the bondman free, though it periled the blood of their sons, brothers and husbands.

The rescuers had been in the crowd some ten minutes, before any demonstration was made. During that time, they were seen, some with clubs, and others with axes under their overcoats, while others were arming themselves with rods of iron from a pile before Mr. Wheaton's Hard Ware store. All this time the orators, well knowing the great idea with which the body they addressed was pregnant, and waiting painfully its ultimation, showered their inflammatory eloquence on their brains.

Finally, one of the rescuers, anxious for an overt act, and pained intensely by the delay, cried out at the top of his voice from the crowd, "Bring him out! Bring him out!"

Soon after this call, a stone from the crowd dashed out a light of glass, and fell among the lawyers, Marshals, constables, serviles and Commissioner, to the peril of their bones. This was followed by another, and another, and the Commissioner hastily delivered Jerry to the Marshal, and adjourned the Court until morning, and escaped.

The missiles now came thicker and faster—the assailants walked boldly to the windows and broke them in with clubs and axes—sash and glass together were dashed upon the floor within and the platform without.

When these initial acts were done, no shouts of the actors attended them. The air but gently murmured the approbation of the assembled city, as distant thunder responds to lightning. It was not the case of men moved by rum or party madness to destroy property and rights and laws. It was the throes and agonies of good and great minds giving birth in nature to interior affections. Throes and agonies, pregnant more of bliss than pain while ultimating in the outer world the sentiment which makes Heaven within—"thou shalt love thy neighbor as thyself"—a sentiment on which all happiness and all order depends. It was obedience to divine dictates that made their acts sublime, and left them on natural minds, the living symbols of great truths to be felt and lived, but not expressed. Fallen humanity has no letters or words to express sentiments so spiritual and exalted, as the delivery of a slave crushed by the weight of a great and guilty nation. None to describe the power of that sentiment, when it gives its representative to nature, and like the incarnate Deity, brings its enemies down.

The assault on the window took the uninitiated by surprise, and for a moment the popular wave subsided to take a second thought; but the act, inspiring as an angel's tongue, electrified them with a common impulse, and drew them to a bolder position, whence, the love of freedom inflamed to madness, forced them into the midst of the war. Amalgamated by a common sympathy, not a man retired, or wished to.

Now the war went on in earnest, and the Police Justice and constables, smitten with consternation, circulated among the patriots, not daring to lay a hand on them. Harry Allen, the U.S. Marshal, pale with fear, borrowed an overcoat of another Marshal, and using it as a disguise, escaped through the crowd to the Syracuse House, and remained there. Rev. Mr. Lear, overcome by the same contagion, sneaked up stairs into the office of Doct. Hubbard, a highly respected citizen, who, in courtesy to Lear's democracy hid him in a hole and covered him out of sight, until the indignation passed by.

Before the Rescuers left Doct. Hoyt's office, they talked of the manner the Police office should be entered—and it was thought best not to enter it until every window and door and particle of wood-work were demolished—not until even the casings under the windows which came down to the platform on which the orators stood were destroyed, and the whole room was open to the assailants.

When Marshal Allen retired, he delivered Jerry to Marshals Fitch and Swift, and they held him in the back room, with their retainers Woodruff, Green, Marrow, Shuart, and others, locked the door, and guarded him with clubs and pistols—while Ira H. Cobb, L. D. Mansfield, and others, remained in the Police office.

The sash and lights being broken in, the assailants now attacked the casements with axes and bars of iron—but so firm were the fixtures, that progress lagged behind their patience, and several strong men went to a pile of hemlock plank near by, and took therefrom a board about ten feet long and four inches thick for a battering ram. As they approached, the crowd opened at the command of one of their number, William L. Salmon, of Granby, Oswego county, a brave and true man, who called aloud:—

"Open the way!—Old Oswego is coming!"

By the application of this powerful instrumentality the casements were soon stove in, and nothing remained to the rescuers but to enter and conquer the police, constables and rowdies, who were retained to guard the outer door of Jerry's prison. The foundations of the city now seemed to be shaken, and all the men and women assembled. Clinton Square, on both sides of the canal, was dotted with hats and bonnets. It was a general coming together to witness the most daring and stirring event that had occurred on the continent. The excitement among them was intense, without tumult, and seemed to surround the two or three thousand actors at the Police office as a celestial guard, and stimulant of their manly and heroic qualities.

The assailants now rushed through the apertures into the office, led by J. M. Clapp, Peter Hollenbeck, James Davis, and others. The entrance from without was nearly simultaneous to the extinction of the lights within. At this moment, Messrs. Cobb and Mansfield, without concert with each other or the assailants, turned off the gas and left the room in darkness, mollified by the distant street lamps and the light of heaven only. A momentary scuffle with the police concluded the victory, and peace settled upon the dark court room.

At this moment, driven to desperation and insane by fear, the besieged, more by instinct than predetermination, used their revolvers. The body of the besiegers who were drawn into the combat by irresistable sympathy, were startled by the report of a pistol, aimed in the dark at Mr. Clapp and those who entered the office with him. At the first report of the revolver, soon followed by a second, the original rescuers remained firm, while the great multitude without, as if surprised by a question of life or death, like two dark waves swayed in different directions—one part towards the bridge north of the steps, and the other to the south.

These parting waves of men quickly halted a few feet only from the platform, and listened and looked with intense emotion for a groan or a corpse from among the sons of freedom, resulting from this attempt at murder. The immense mass that filled Clinton square heaved with like emotions, and gazed with an anxiety which cannot be expressed, for some motion from which they could infer a fatal result. The suspense was awful, but it was temporary. At this moment, Thomas G. White came out from among the rescuers, upon the platform, and said with a loud voice:

"Come up!—come up, gentlemen! They have fired all their powder!"

The parted mass of men were now fired up to the blood point, and rushed to the rescue, determined to set Jerry free, come life or come death.

The partition between the rescuers and the victim was a strong one, and the door was locked. In pursuit of the plan thus far adopted, they determined not to enter the prison through the door, where they might be shot down—but to enter it over the partition between them and their enemies, after they had broken it from its fastenings and tumbled it upon their heads.

Now, again they siezed their huge plank and other weapons, and plied them against the partition, with a force that struck the besieged with consternation.

Marshal Fitch, now mad with desperation, again partially opened the door, and pointed his pistol at one of the rescuers, and received a blow on his arm from a rod of iron, wielded by his intended victim, which broke the bones, and the pistol and arm fell down together.

The partition thus assailed was firmly built; but the huge battering-ram, axes and iron bars soon loosened its fastenings. As it began to give way, the hearts of the Marshals and rowdies who were guarding Jerry also give way. They knew they must soon face the men whose blood they had provoked to the point of mortal combat—and also, by daring to defy the United States and rescue Jerry, showed they intended to meet the consequences. Under such circumstances, Marshal Fitch, distracted by pain and fear, leaped out of the north window of the room onto the side of the canal, with his broken arm, and escaped—and Woodruff, Swift & Co., soul-stricken and trembling with a sense of danger to their persons, hastily opened the door and thrust Jerry into the arms of his friends—and by so doing prudently consulted their own safety.[2]

Jerry was received at the door by Peter Hollenbeck and William Gray—both colored men, and the latter a fugitive slave.

The huge hemlock was now dropped, the sound of axes and iron bars ceased, and raising the thrilling bondman, the rescuers, for the first time, uttered a shout of joy and triumph. The joy of the bondman touched the hearts of the rescuers like a galvanic shock—the great heart of Syracuse assembled there felt it as a unit, and broke open with gladness, faintly expressing its quality and intensity.

2. [Loguen's note:] So soon as Fitch fired his pistol and closed the door, Peter Hollenbeck, a brave and powerful colored man, hurled a brick at the door in reply to the pistol. The missile went through the door, and grazed and slightly wounded the head of Jerry. Smitten with terror, his keepers, Woodruff, Foreman, and others, covered themselves with boxes, or crowded into the closet, to be out of harm's way—leaving Jerry helpless and exposed on the floor. Peeking his head from under a box, as a turtle sticks his head from under his shell, Woodruff cried out:—

"I say there!—haven't we a right to let the prisoner go to save our lives?"

"Yes!—yes!"

"Hallo. Jerry! Go out there among those folks!—you can quell this riot!—go right off!"

"How can I go with feet and hands shackled? Open the door and let them in, or take off my irons and let me do it, you coward! I am not afraid of them—they are my friends."

"Go out!—why the d—l don't you go?"

"How can I go, I say? Are you so cowardly crazy as not to know you have chained me so I can't go?"

Brought to his senses by the brave Jerry, Woodruff, quick as lightning, opened the door and shoved Jerry into it, and crept back to his shell again.

Possessed of the slave, their black brother redeemed, his heart's blood repeating its pulsations of gratitude and love upon their bosoms, they forgot their hatred of tyrants and detestation of wrong doers, in the sweet gushings of Heaven that trickled in their bosoms, and filled their mouths with praises and shouts of thankfulness—not like the expression of infernal delight from a rum-born riot—not like the heartless explosion of a party triumph, or the senseless demonstration of sectarian conquest or martial battle, indicative alike of starved and sunken spirits measuring the decay of churches and empires—unlike any of these—the shouts of the multitude for the rescue of Jerry were the music of Heaven in the soul, celebrating the birth of a new era in politics and religion—the jubilee of the incarnation of a celestial sentiment, which, like the mountain stone seen by the prophet, has grown and is to grow, until it fills the republic and gives liberty to the continent—until liberty and religion come up to the level of that act, and read their conquests and their brotherhood in the "sea of glass" before them.

When Jerry was received, his body was mostly naked—being covered only by tattered pantaloons and shirt, which hung on him in rags—and what was worse, sadly pained by a wounded rib, and otherwise bruised by the harsh treatment of his captors.

His powerful and heavy frame was perfectly helpless because of his shackles. The rescuers tried to raise him on their shoulders, but could not. They then put their hands under him and carried him in their arms. When he arrived upon the platform, the joyous thousands clapped their hands and shouted:

"There he comes!—there he comes! Hurrah!—hurrah!"

At this time Clinton Square bristled with human heads. The Empire and Syracuse houses, and all other buildings from which the spectacle could be seen,[3] were draped with anxious spectators of both sexes. Few families in the city were unrepresented among the thousands that saw Jerry descend the high platform—many being moved to tears at the scene, every item of which passed through their souls and set them shouting and weeping and moving towards Jerry, the point of attraction. Before him, behind him, and by his side, moved a mighty mass, which the Marshals, politicians and rowdies, in sympathy with the prosecution, might look at, but dare not touch.

3. [Loguen's note:] It was a clear, star-light evening. We need no other thing to show how utterly unreliable were the witnesses for the United States in the suits against Reed, Brigham, Salmon, Cobb, and others, who were indicted for rescuing Jerry, than their testimony that the night was cloudy and dark. It seems, though the rescue was open and above board, their enemies were so excited and darkened by fear, that they could scarcely identify an opponent or state a fact.

Instead of taking Jerry out of the city, the rescuers took him to the densest part of it, and set him down at the front door of the Syracuse House, in Salina Street, where the Judges of the Supreme Court and its officers, surrounded by fastidious politicians, were huddled together to look at him. Though it is impossible to name all the persons who took part in carrying Jerry in this imperial procession, special notice is due one of them.

When Jerry came down the steps, his head and one of his shoulders were delivered to Moses Summers, one of the editors of the *Daily Standard*, then the democratic organ of the city. Mr. Summers did not quit that position, but as after stated, until Jerry entered the carriage that took him off. As the procession was passing the Townsend Block, it was assaulted by B. L. Higgins, one of the democratic Aldermen of the city, at the point where Summers was engaged. Summers instantly quit his hold, and laid the officious Alderman in the gutter, and again took his position. Higgins got up out of the dirt, and followed by the side of the procession, and again stepped in front of it and commanded the liberators to lay Jerry down and obey the laws. Full of the spirit of the occasion, Summers gave his place to Peter Reed, a colored man, and turned upon the meddling Alderman and knocked him down. This quieted the officious Alderman, and Summers returned to his place again.

From the door of the Syracuse House Jerry was taken and deposited at the Rail Road Depot—but the mass was so dense that the carriages to take him off could not come to him—and still the tumult was so great that but few knew where Jerry was.

When in prison, it was an object to collect the people—now it was important to disperse them, that he might find a place, unknown to his enemies, where his chains could be broken, and he could refresh his bruised and broken body with food, medicine and slumber. Several rescuers now ran in opposite directions through the crowd, crying "Fire! fire! fire!" This was a successful *ruse de guerre*. The masses, wild with excitement, ran every way, crying "Fire! fire! fire!"—some, doubtless, scenting the stratagem, and others falling into it.

In a short time Jerry was left alone with James Davis, Jason S. Hoyt, Moses Summers, and a few other brave and stalwart men, who lifted him, groaning with pain into a carriage, and he was taken, by a circuitous route, to a colored man's house in the eastern part of the city. A proposition to call at Doct. Hoyt's office and have his wounds dressed, was overruled in regard to prudence. As the carriage rolled away, the Liberators sent up a "Hurrah!" at the top of their voices, which drew up the sympathizing voices of thousands in all directions, and the heavens vibrated with delight.

Without delay, Jason S. Hoyt brought his cutting bar—a powerful instrument—and cut Jerry's shackles apart, leaving each of his limbs free, but bruised and bleeding, and encumbered by the dissevered irons. Not daring to leave Jerry with the colored man, he was disguised in female attire, and led from house to house among the colored people, who were willing to receive him, but who, nevertheless, those who had him in charge, to wit, Jason S. Hoyt, James Davis, &c., feared to trust, because of a possible lack of prudence or discretion. Therefore they led him to the house of Caleb Davis, on Genessee street—a man whose heart was big with the love of liberty, and whose mind they knew to be charged with qualities fitting their purpose.[4] Mr. Davis opened his door at midnight to the rap of James Davis.

"We have a man here who wants shelter under your roof."

"Are you pursued?"

"No."

"Bring him in—it is too late to ask questions. It is needless to strike lights—take him up stairs and put him to bed. He wants rest, I have no doubt."

The bruised body of Jerry was soon composed to sleep, and his brave rescuers also.

Davis kept Jerry at his house four days—had tools made to break the irons from his ankles—and at the end of that time he was sufficiently healed to start for Canada.

On the evening of the 5th of October, 1851, Jason S. Hoyt procured a noble span of horses from the livery stable of the late Mayor Woodruff, and drove into his own yard in the rear of Caleb Davis' dwelling house, and there received Mr. Davis and Jerry. Davis and Hoyt mounted the seat, and laid Jerry on his back under them, and covered him with straw, and started for Canada. Mr. Davis went as a sort of body guard to see them fairly on the way. James Davis and Doct. Potter also preceded them to see the coast clear, and to receive Caleb at Oneida Bridge and return him to Syracuse, as they did do.

Hoyt was directed to an individual some twenty-five miles from Syracuse, whose name is forgotten. Scarcely had they parted with the Davises and Doct.

4. [Loguen's note:] Mr. Davis was then nearly sixty years of age, of powerful frame and robust health. He was in the army during the war with England in 1812, and one of the brave men who raised the bridge at Plattsburg. Coming to Clinton Square on the afternoon of the day of the rescue, and finding it full of people, and that a call had been made on the militia to suppress an attempt to rescue a slave, he returned and told his wife—who was a fervent abolitionist—"If the militia come out, I will come out, too—there will be enough to turn out. We will see if citizens soldiers will shoot us."

Potter, when they were vigorously pursued—and Jerry, most anxious to make his freedom secure, proposed to take to the fields.

"No, no!" said Mr. Hoyt, "I provided this instrument (showing a six barrel revolver,) for a crisis like this. It is carefully loaded and ready for use. You must now take this iron bar, provided for you, and if they outspeed and attempt to take us, you will strike to kill and I will shoot to kill. It shall be a life struggle!"

This proposition suited the daring spirit of the slave, and the compact for freedom or death was made with a zest. In the meantime, Mr. Hoyt put his horses to the greatest speed compatible with safety. For a while the enemy actually gained on them, but after a race of some seven or ten miles, Hoyt's horses proved of strongest bottom, and left the pursuers out of sight. Arriving, as Hoyt supposed, at the friends house who was to receive Jerry, he drove directly into the yard and into the barn, and closed the door, to be out of sight of their pursuers, if they had not turned back in despair—as it seems they had done. This freedom was taken with the farmer without consulting him. He soon got out of his bed and showed himself.

"Here is a man who wants a passage to Oswego," said Mr. Hoyt, pointing to Jerry.

"I understand it—we have heard all about it here," said the man, in a voice indicating both surprise and fear. "We don't approve of the thing—but since you have come to me, I won't betray you. It is my neighbor, there, you are after. I will go and call him—but mind you, I take no part in breaking the laws."

In ten minutes the excited farmer brought in his more cool and considerate neighbor, who, addressing himself at once to Hoyt and Jerry, said:

"If you have anything for me to do, I am ready to do it—I ask no questions."

"I want you," said Mr. Hoyt, "to take this man and deliver him at Oswego before morning, that he may take the boat for Canada."

In a brief time Jerry was on the road with his generous conductor, and in due time was safe in Oswego. In the morning he took an early boat to Canada, and arrived there the same day in good condition—where he lived, respected for his industry, morals and general character, until taken off by death.

Thus ends a brief of the Jerry Rescue—a model tragedy of sublime significance—which resurrected the spirit of freedom and respect for law—overrode the power of slavery in the Empire State—broke the charm of party—gave freedom to conscience and righteous politics—compelled the respect of political aspirants, and like the brazen serpent, today, demands that such aspirants look to it and live, or turn from it and die.

CHAPTER XXXI

The slave Jerry was now rescued—the government boldly nullified, and the telegraphic wires were sending the good deed through the continent. It remained to be seen that Syracuseans would meet the recoil of their heroic conduct with persistent resolution and wisdom. At this point, the pro-slavery partisans and officials hoped to clutch the ephemeral pluck of Syracuse and crush it. They waited the cooling of the fires, to see the people tremble through fear of legal penalties, and crouch into subjection at the sight of their doings.

The test of character was to come. To meet the crisis, and not suffer the revolutionary spirit to chill, the leading minds seized the prestige of the rescue to assemble an immense meeting of the people, to baptize anew in its fires, and commit them to an open endorsement of the rescue, and strengthen the feeble by pledging the public support to whoever might be prosecuted therefor.

Of course a small portion of the citizens could crowd into the City Hall at this meeting; but such as could not get in, met at the public houses and other public places, to consider the same subject. The meetings, within and without the Hall, glowed with like indignation at the attempt to make Syracuse a hunting ground for slaves—repeated their detestation of the fugitive slave law, and their admiration of the men who bravely set it at nought. The more cautious and timid citizens, becoming familiar with this transaction, were attracted by its goodness and beauty; and not a few of them, at the meeting and elsewhere, were free to unite in the endorsement of it, and pledge their sympathy and support to the actors therein, to the extent "of their lives and fortunes and sacred honor."

The friends of the rescue were now much multiplied and encouraged, while their enemies were reduced to a mere court party of discouraging and contemptible diminituveness. It only remained to be seen whether the government could enforce its bloody enactment in Syracuse. Orders were issued from Washington for a stern execution of the law, and the offending citizens prepared to meet the malice of the political powers through the Judiciary already degraded to their use.

Jermain W. Loguen, and the fugitive slaves to a man, were heart and hand in the rescue. But they stood in different circumstances from the rest of the rescuers. To the latter, the penalty was fine and imprisonment only; to them, it was more terrible than the penalties for murder and treason. The provisions of the act delivered them, without trial, to perjured claimants, to be taken to distant States, to be beasts of burden for life. Many citizens, who, with him, engaged in the rescue, and were liable to its penalties, were especially anxious for Mr. Loguen. To take him from Syracuse and return him to bondage, would be so notable a triumph for slavery, as to be published through the land to the discouragement of the friends of freedom. And though nine-tenths of the people would have periled their lives and property to avoid the calamity, they were anxious to escape such a complication of affairs.

To avoid the complication just named, many citizens of wisdom and influence, so soon as Jerry was out of reach, advised Mr. Loguen to retire until the skies cleared up. So concerned were they, that they called at his house, when he was surrounded by his wife and children, and urged him, with much earnestness, to do so. At first, he had no ears to listen to the proposition—because it was directly opposed to his resolution, considerately formed. On being told what was then, and still is, generally believed, that his master was near to claim him, and that he would most certainly be siezed under the law, he spurned the idea of fleeing from him or it—or secreting himself from either. To do either, was a concession that his dignity and manhood would not consent to. He declared his resolution to go and come as before, in the face of day, and meet the Marshal and his master with weapons, in the conflict, if need be.

But the wishes of Mr. Loguen, in this regard, were destined to be overruled. The entreaties, and even tears, of his wife, conspired with the entreaties of his friends in the city, and he submitted to what he regarded a sad mortification—not for his sake, but for theirs.[1] Having made up his mind to leave Syracuse temporarily, to avoid a trial supposed to be very near him, he packed up at once, and retired to Skaneateles, and found an asylum in the family of the late Lydia Fuller, which was ever open to the fleeing slave. Mrs. Fuller was the aged widow of the late venerable James Cannings Fuller, Esq., a Quaker gentleman of talent and fortune. After passing through the conflict of West India Emancipation, in his own country, he emigrated to the United States,

1. [Loguen's note:] It was then currently reported that James R. Lawrence, Esq., the Dist. Attorney of the United States, had given out that Mr. Loguen would be siezed and returned to his master, at all events, as one of the consequences of the Jerry Rescue.

and settled at Skaneateles, just in time to give his hand and tongue and purse to the cause of African freedom in his adopted country. He came to America for quiet and repose, after a laborious and expensive European conflict—but unexpectedly and providentially to meet the enemy in his entrenchments, and leave his body in the field of battle. He was a man of strong mind and unshrinking courage. The latter quality fitted him to face many mobs, and the former to soothe and instruct them—and both qualities, combined with the sleepless impulses of his heart in behalf of the slave, attracted the respect and admiration of abolitionists, and will command the blessings of all true men, now the star of freedom is rising.

Mrs. Fuller and family were glad to do good to their persecuted friend, and watched him and supplied him with all things his case needed—but they could not keep him. Good as they were to him, he felt that he was a voluntary prisoner, and his restless spirit could not brook restraints, imposed though they were by the truest friendship. If he must be a prisoner, he resolved it should be on larger limits, where he could be useful to others, if not to himself. Indeed, it was a religious principle with him, that the good he did others, was, in fact, good to himself.

After a residence of three or four days with these good people, he thanked them for their kindness, and said he must leave them and go to Canada without delay. To this the Fullers consented, on condition that they keep his horse, free of charge, until his return, and that he be taken to Canada at the expense of his friends.

Early in the morning, Sumner Fuller, son of Lydia Fuller, harnessed his own horse to the family carriage, and rode him into Rochester, to the house of Samuel D. Porter, a man eminent for his fidelity to the slave. Porter immediately procured a livery, and himself and Fuller and Loguen rode to the steamboat landing on the lakes, and there left him. He immediately took the boat for Lewiston, and passed over the bridge at sunrise on foot into Canada at Queenston.

He was now in Canada, where he first drew free breath—where he planted his foot many years before with unutterable enthusiasm. Slavery drove him there in both cases—but how different his circumstances and feelings now from what they were then! If words could not utter the joy he then felt, neither can they faintly picture the swellings of his bosom now.

The first time, in many days, he was alone. He had seen the last man turn sorrowing away and leave him to drag his heavy heart over the river. It was against his own judgment and the passions of his nature to do so. The panorama of his life arose in his soul like an accusing presence, as he passed along.

Its soul-stirring objects and scenes and motives surrounded him, and uttered an implacable *ne exeat* every step he took. But, right or wrong, the die was cast. His friends had committed him, and it only remained to suffer bravely and briefly as possible. He parted from the objects his heart loved, to enter the mental world within him, and see those objects in a form inexpressibly touching and overpowering. His history and its relations from infancy were present in the intellectual firmament, surrounded by his longings and aspirations, and hopes and prospects. Time and space passed away, and all he lived for in the past and present were grouped in his sight, and melted his heart. He felt the throbbings of his wife's and children's hearts against his own—the loves of his mother, brothers and sisters scattered and chained, the prayers of his outraged race—the generous labors of the abolitionists, and the brave blow just struck at Syracuse—the upheaving of mighty freedom throughout the land—the unutterable interests at stake, and his vile expatriation, oppressed him to tears. So absorbed was he with this mental scenery, that the great river rolled beneath his feet, and the mighty cataract thundered in the distance, and the birds sung over his head, and the landscape spread its gorgeous prospect before him, with-out awakening his senses to the outer world. His heart, his duties, his life's aims, his whole soul was on one side of the river and his body on the other. Intensely excited, he gave vent to his feelings and tears, and talked aloud:—

"Has it come to this? Is slavery yet so mighty that I must quit my country that my friends be not burdened by my person and rights? Must I be elbowed out of it because God gave me a dark skin and Manasseth Logue robbed my mother's cradle? Shall the battle of freedom be fought, and I not suffered to engage in it? And who shall engage in that battle if I may not? Tell me that slavery is a creature of law! Away with such blasphemy. It is the offspring of a soul that knows no law—no truth—no God, and given up to live a lie. If the Constitution and statutes endorse such a stupendous falsehood, which they do not, God demands that they be hated and trampled on. Even the damned are free to live their infernal lusts, to this extent only, that they trespass not upon the freedom of others. God only restrains men at the point where they assail the rights of their fellow men. Within that limit they live as they will, on earth and in Hell. It is the law of all laws—the law of Heaven—and of earth and Hell because it is the law of Heaven. At this pass, God has stationed all the energies of the human soul, and commands them 'to arms' to resist the least attempt to pass it. Those energies are God's body guard to defend the central principle of his spirit and kingdom, 'thou shalt love thy neighbor as thyself.' The axiom, 'resistance to tyrants is obedience to God,' has its origin here. All just war begins here, because all law begins and ends here—it is the Thermopylæ of the universe, and God stimulates every motive of the soul to defend it,—for his whole government is staked on it.[2] Aye, that is the moral of these old battle fields—that is the language of this huge pile to the brave Brock whose shade marks its daily crescent on the spot where I stand.[3] Spirits of Lundy's Lane![4] what were your wrongs, compared to mine? What your motives to fight, compared to those that are inflaming and bursting the vitals of my guilty country? What other motive can God employ to stir me to mortal resistance, beside those that are burning my heart and seething my brain this moment? My wife and children trembling for their outraged husband and father, surrounded by trembling white men almost as timid as they—my mother, brothers and sisters, and kindred and race embruted—the very color God gave us made a mark of dishonor by the tyrant whose blood my revolver thirsts for! The tide of progress rising, too, and breaking its waves at Syracuse and elsewhere, and bellowing above the storm, 'NOW OR NEVER!' Come bloody battle, I say—I care not how bloody, if these outrages continue!"

We do not give the exact words of Mr. Loguen, but its substance and spirit only. How long his soliloquy lasted, he did not know. As we have before said, he was lost in the flood of his emotions, and his voice rolled through fields and forests, and was heard by people at a distance, who, not knowing his case, questioned his sanity. So soon as they came in his presence, they mutually recognized each other. He knew them as fugitives he had helped to Canada, and they knew him as their benefactor and friend.

2. [Editor's note:] The battle of Thermopylae was fought between an alliance of Greek city-states, led by Sparta, and the Persian Empire of Xerxes I during the second Persian invasion of Greece in 480 BC. A Greek army of approximately seven thousand men fought a Persian army that was alleged by ancient accounts to have numbered in the millions (modern estimates suggest a number closer to two hundred thousand) to defend a narrow pass that controlled the only road between Thessaly and central Greece. Although vastly outnumbered and ultimately unable to block the pass of Thermopylae, the Greeks were able to hold off the Persian army for seven days. The battle of Thermopylae has been used by ancient and modern writers to illustrate the power of a patriotic army defending their native land and courage against impossible odds.

3. [Editor's note:] Sir Isaac Brock (1769–1812) was a major general in the War of 1812. He was responsible for defending Upper Canada against the United States. He became known for collaborating with Shawnee chieftain Tecumseh, called "the Hero of Upper Canada," after winning several battles against the United States. He was killed in the battle of Queenston Heights.

4. [Editor's note:] The battle of Lundy's Lane was during the War of 1812, which took place on July 25, 1814, in present-day Niagara Falls, Ontario, Canada. It was one of the bloodiest battles of the war and one of the deadliest battles ever fought on Canadian soil.

The State of things at Syracuse was already known in Canada, and a brief explanation of his case sufficed to discover his sanity to his companions and fellow sufferers. They immediately took him into St. Catharines, where, and in the vicinity, there were many other fugitives and colored men. These, with many white men, to whom his eminent labors and sacrifices for the slave were known, received him with respect and honor. They immediately employed him to preach to the colored people, and to teach the parents and children. His religious and literary labors were eminently blessed. A great awakening commenced among his hearers, which added to his Church many converts. This was a great satisfaction to him. Of course his religion was of that sort which embraced both the poor and the enslaved. Thus was he preparing a soil, by religious instrumentality, to receive the many sons of sorrow he afterwards sent there. Driven, as he was, from his family and country, his benevolent activities mollified his bereavement and made his expatriation more endureable.

When the spring arrived, his desire to return to Syracuse was irrepressible; and though informed by letters from his friends, that he and many others were indicted for a part taken in the rescue of Jerry, and that the Attorney of the United States held a warrant for his arrest—and though some of those friends exhorted him to stay in Canada, his love of freedom, family and country, and great desire to share in the trials of the abolitionists, determined him, in the spring of '52, to return to Syracuse and face his foes. He was ashamed longer to yield to counsel which shocked his manhood. The fact that he had so yielded, for a few months, aroused his energies, and discarding all opposing counsel, and all fear of consequences, he returned and threw himself defiantly in the midst of his enemies.

He was received by his family with an excess of tremulous satisfaction—but when he appeared in the streets, with a bold brow and a firm tread, all eyes were turned to him. But if many hearts trembled for him, such trembling found no sympathy in his own bosom.

"How could you—how dare you come back?" was the enquiry of many prudent ones; and his uniform reply was:—

"Because I was ashamed to act like a criminal or a slave any longer. If the Marshal has a warrant to serve on me, let him serve it—but if he attempts to take me as a slave, let him beware! I respect no process that disregards my manhood."

The warrant against Mr. Loguen, which had been so long waiting his return from Canada, must now be served. But such was his known character for strength, bravery and spirit, that the Marshal, though he desired only to go through the form of an arrest and take bail, which he knew there were hundreds in the city ready to give, was unwilling to meet him alone, even for a formal execution of his process. His bold return was evidence that such process, or any peril incident to his condition as a fugitive, had no terrors for him. The audacity of his movements impressed the consciousness of the U.S. Marshal in the form of a warning and a prophecy. His prudence, therefore, cautioned him to take such a course in the execution of the warrant, as should not arouse the lion in the veins of this just and brave man.

Hon. Charles B. Sedgwick, of Syracuse, was the friend of Loguen—a stern nullifier of the fugitive slave enactment, and a learned and valiant counsellor of the indicted rescuers. He was a member of the Vigilance Committee of the city with Mr. Loguen, and in him the latter had implicit confidence. The Marshal knew this, and therefore called on Mr. Sedgwick to go with him to Loguen's house, and explain to him the limits of the process, and advise him to submit to it, and allow Sedgwick and others to be bail for him. Mr. Sedgwick complied with this request, and they went to Loguen's house for the purpose, but found him absent in the city.

When Mr. Loguen was notified of the above visit, he readily avowed submission to any arrest that did not purpose to sieze him as a slave—but at the same time insisted he would not be bailed by sureties for any offence under the fugitive act. Charles A. Wheaton, and others, called on him, and offered to be his sureties—but he replied to them all, that they must not bail him, for that he would not give any name but his own for bail. If arrested, he would be committed, if sureties were demanded. He would do nothing that seemed to imply that this nefarious act had the least force.

Harry Allen, the Marshal, having learned that Mr. Loguen would submit to his arrest, and that his own person was safe if he attempted to serve the warrant in an officer-like manner, met Mr. Loguen, and politely informed him he had a warrant against him, founded on an indictment for rescuing Jerry.

Mr. Loguen said he was aware of the warrant, and told him to serve it. Allen then presented a blank bail bond for his appearance, and Loguen signed it. On inquiring who he would get for sureties, Loguen replied:—

"I will get nobody to be my sureties."

"Why, it is mere form. There are thousands in the city who will sign the bond with you. If you request it, Sedgwick and Wheaton, and almost every other good citizen will sign it. All I want is to serve my process and go about my business."

"I positively forbid Sedgwick or Wheaton, or any other person to be my bail. If my own bond is not sufficient, you must commit me. With me the giving surety is not form—it is substance."

The Marshal found he could not then be induced to give sureties; he therefore left him for the present, determined to see him again, when he hoped to be successful. Again and again he saw him, and found him persistent in the determination, and was obliged, himself, for appearance sake, to procure them against Loguen's consent. He presented the blank privately to Abner Bates and Hon. C. B. Sedgwick—they readily signed it, and he returned the process.

This was shrewd management of the Marshal. Had he arrested Loguen, and attempted to lead him through the city to prison, it would have been like throwing a fire brand into a powder house. It would have been a sight the people could not endure, and the city would be in flames about him. Already had he been indicted for arresting, or attempting to kidnap Jerry. His circumstances were critical, and he knew that to commit Jermain W. Loguen, in a case like that, would inflame Syracuse to madness, and enrage the county, and the flames would spread over central and western New York.

Not long after this, an event occurred to test the public concern for Mr. Loguen, and to show what the people would do in case he was seized as a slave. On his return from Canada, he engaged, as before, in passing through the country, collecting funds to aid slaves, and stirring the people to meet the fugitive law with physical resistance—even to the shooting, or otherwise killing the Marshal or claimant, if need be, to prevent the return of a slave.

But he needed his horse and carriage, which still remained at Skaneateles with his friend Lydia Fuller. He took the cars in the morning to go after them. It so happened that Marshal Allen and two or three police officers were on board the same cars, armed with heavy clubs or batons of office. Mr. Loguen was well acquainted with these men—but the last thing to enter his mind was to fear them.

"What in the world has started out the civil police of Syracuse with their clubs?" said Loguen, as he walked carelessly and pleasantly and took a seat near them in the cars. "Where are you going?"

"We are going to Auburn."

"Have the prisoners rose in rebellion, that our whole corps is called there with clubs to help put them down?" said he, with a waggish smile.

They laughed, and made a sportive reply, which gave no idea of their intent.

On board the same cars, and in conversational proximity, were two ladies from Ithaca, Tompkins county, to wit: Mrs. Brum and Mrs. Lewis, acquaintances and friends of Loguen. On his way to the Junction, the point of his departure from the cars to Skaneateles, he filled up the time in playful colloquy with the Marshal and his companions on one side, and polite conversation with the ladies on the other.

These ladies, all the way, were oppressed with the apprehension that the officers obtained a foreknowledge of Loguen's departure from the city, and followed to arrest him at a distance from his friends. They heard the talk between them and Loguen, and the manner of it intensified their suspicions and fears. Arrived at the Junction, the officers led the way out of the cars, and Loguen bid the ladies good by, and carelessly followed them with his usual stately and reckless carriage.

The feelings of the ladies were now wrought to an excess of alarm, for they inferred that this was the identical point where they intended to arrest him. And as but one of the constables returned, when the cars started for Auburn, leaving Mr. Loguen and the rest behind, they were overwhelmed with the conviction that their pretence of going to Auburn was a sham, to lead Loguen into a trap, and that they had actually sprung it upon him and seized him. On their arrival at Auburn, they published these facts, and the story was immediately circulated through the city that the U.S. Marshal, assisted by a corps of constables, had arrested Jermain W. Loguen at the Junction. The city was instantly thrown into a tempest—for Mr. Loguen was a favorite there as at Syracuse. Mechanics dropped their tools—merchants and customers, citizens and laborers left their business, and ran about the streets to learn the truth of this report, and to gather armed men for his rescue.

John R. Hopkins, a devoted friend of freedom and of Loguen, instantly resorted to the telegraph office, and sent a despatch to Charles A. Wheaton, of Syracuse, purporting "The news by the western train just arrived is that J. W. Loguen was arrested by the U.S. Marshal and a posse of constables at the Junction this morning." The church bells at Syracuse were immediately set tolling, and the citizens rushed into the streets to learn the cause.

"Loguen was arrested at the Junction, by Marshal Allen and his posse, and is being hurried secretly out of the country!" was the cry through the streets, from store to store, and from house to house—and the whole city was convulsed by excitement. For the moment, business ceased, and a concern for Loguen engrossed the passionate attention of the people. The cause and the effect was as an electric shock.

"How comes this?" said one.

"What are the facts?" said another.

"To the Congregational church!" said another.

"Yes, to the Congregational church, and look into this case—and if it is true, take measures to rescue him!"

"We'll save him, if it costs the life of the Marshal!"

"Yes, and our own in the bargain!"

"To the Congregational church! To the Congregational Church!" was the universal cry.

The streets were immediately filled with citizens, hastening to the Congregational church. The various expressions of their faces, all indicating the stern passions of their souls, was a subject for a painter. Some were armed with revolvers—others declared they would arm and pursue and shoot the kidnappers and save Loguen—others handled their rolls of bank notes, and offered money to defray the cost of the enterprise. Mr. Wheaton was already at the house, and as people arrived, explained to them the facts in the case; and that they act under no mistake, he was advised to telegraph back to Mr. Hopkins, and request him to return the particulars.

While these things were going on at Syracuse, Mr. Hopkins, by the advice of Hon. Wm. H. Seward and others, at Auburn, proceeded directly to the Junction, and followed up Mr. Loguen, to be assured in the premises, and in case he was arrested, to telegraph the fact in every direction through the country.

Hopkins learned at the Junction that Harry Allen, with the constables, armed as aforesaid, did leave the cars there as reported, and that Mr. Loguen rode off in the Skaneateles stage. He immediately proceeded to Skaneateles, where he arrived a little afternoon, and found Mr. Loguen seated at the dinner table with the family of his generous and great hearted friends, the Fullers. He took a seat by his side, and while sateing his appetite with good things, gave a history of the great fire at Auburn which the "little matter" had kindled, and from a grave affair it became a subject of amusing entertainment.

Mr. Loguen arrived in Syracuse that night, and was hailed by many of the citizens as he passed along, and informed of the commotion in his absence. Not having heard from Auburn or Skaneateles through the telegraph or from the men sent to the latter place, the alarm, though settled to a rational determination, had by no means subsided. He often heard his name pronounced from the side walk, as he rode along, and occasionally—

"That's Loguen!"

"That's him—I know his horse and carriage," &c.

Having given evidence of his return to some by his personal presence, he passed as privately and rapidly as possible, most intent to get home and quiet the intense anxiety of his wife and children.

Scarcely had he arrived at home, and gladdened his anxious family by his presence, soothing and laughing off their fears, when a delegation of citizens knocked at his door—who, after congratulating him on his return, and pleasantly noting the popular survivance of a glorious humbug, earnestly invited him to return into the city and address the people, who were rejoicing under the stimulus of a delightful reaction.

He thanked them for the honor of their visit and invitation—and more especially he thanked them and the citizens of Syracuse through them, for their generous concern and manful demonstration during his absence—but respectfully declined to return to address the people, on account of the lateness of the hour and the weariness of his body.

CONCLUSION

The indictment against Loguen was never tried. Those indicted with him were Enoch Reed, (colored), W. L. Salmon, J. B. Brigham, Ira H. Cobb, James Davis, Moses Summers, Montgomery Merrick, L. H. Salsbury, W. L. Crandall, Prince Jackson, (colored), William Thompson, (colored), Stephen Porter, and Harrison Allen, (colored). The three first named only were put on trial. Reed was found guilty—not of a crime under the Fugitive Act—but on a count for resisting process, prudently annexed to the main charge—and he died pending an appeal from the verdict. Salmon and Brigham were tried and acquitted. The Jury disagreed on the trial of Cobb, and his case was never again brought up. The prosecutions and trials were, of course, political prosecutions and trials; and immediately after Mr. Cobb's trial, the parties which intended them for their good, found them a burden and a curse. The act became infamous and the zeal for victims under it died with the party that enacted it. The indictments, like the statute, having failed their end, were left to perish by legal outlawry and public contempt.

Some of the defendants were poor men, and some of them colored men; but the readiness with which the wealthiest, wisest and best men, at Syracuse and Auburn, (where many of them were let to bail,) volunteered to be their sureties, is proof that poor men and colored men, rich men and wise men, may sympathize in a common interest. The rescuers and their bail balanced their persons and property against the Government, in a desperate struggle for supremacy. The only method that great minds and heroic hearts could adopt to put the infamous law on trial, was to throw themselves against it, and trust the energy of public virtue and publican opinion to lead them in triumph over it. Such has been the history of Freedom in all time; and such the history of the popular triumph over the Fugitive Slave Law in Syracuse. The Judges, Conklin, Nelson and Marvin,[1] were the tools of guilty power, and leaned,

1. [Loguen's note:] The Grand Jury of Onondaga County indicted Harry Allen for attempting to kidnap Jerry, upon the assumption that the Fugitive Slave Act under which Jerry

with inexpressible meanness and servility, against the heroic defendants; but an Omnipotent public opinion carried them through, and consigned those Judges, and the law and liberty-killing statute, to perpetual impotence and dishonor.

The gentlemen who volunteered to give bail in these cases, were Alfred Cobb, Wm. H. Seward, George Barnes, Hiram Putnam, S. J. May, Wm. E. Abbott, R. R. Raymond, Seth Height, Abner Bates, Charles B. Sedgwick, and C. A. Wheaton. Besides these, Horace White, Hamilton White, E. W. Leavenworth, and others, signed a written indemnity to any body and every body who would bail them, at Syracuse or elsewhere. Hon. Gerrit Smith, who was one of the rescuers, volunteered as their counsel, and associated with him C. B. Sedgwick, D. D. Hilis, Le Roy Morgan, J. G. Forbes, and Gen. Nye.

The contest between the people and the Government having terminated, Mr. Loguen walked into the U. G. Rail Road Depot with the pride and boldness of a conqueror, and welcomed to house and aided to Canada one thousand and five hundred fugitives. From that time to this, his time, talents and fortune have been exclusively and laboriously devoted to that business—he has pursued it with an energy, perseverance and success that has attracted the admiration of the country.

We have now finished the story of Jarmain W. Loguen. It would be supererogation to pursue it further. When his career is ended, another volume may give the supplement of his life and character. We purposely avoid contemporary occurrences, which more properly belong to that volume than to this. We name but one of them, and that because it is of a public character, only to pass it by in the order of events. We allude to the controversy between himself and Rev. H. Mattison, in regard to the claims of the U. G. Rail Road upon the congregation and preachers of the M. E. Church. That controversy consists of a series of letters and replies, published first in the newspapers, and afterwards in a pamphlet, and circulated through the country. We believe it has found a grave in the charities of two christian hearts, and a mutual desire to cleanse the world of human slavery. But the nominal Church and the political parties of this country have fainted in the conflict. In regard to sectarian and party supremacy, they openly consent that the heaven-defying villainy shall live.

And now, when the slave has no hope from Church or State,—when the measure of his tears is full—when his wrongs have involved the heavens

---

was arrested was unconstitutional and void; but Judge Marvin, of the Eighth District of New York, bent his servile spirit to the uses of slavery, sustained the act, and let the criminal go.

in blackness, we wait the fulfilment of Mr. Jefferson's prophesy—and with him, look to the Almighty Father to demolish slavery "by his exterminating thunder." The coldness with which the politics and religion of this country turn away from the slave, is sad but irresistible proof that slavery must go down in blood.

APPENDIX

Testimony of Rev. E. P. Rogers.

THE following article, from Rev. E. P. Rogers, was written for a Preface to this Book—but it came too late to be used for that purpose; and we give it a place in our Appendix.[1]

Early in the winter of '38, I became acquainted with the Rev. J. W. Loguen.

Being then engaged as a teacher of a public school, in the city of Rochester, N.Y., Mr. Loguen made application, and was cheerfully received as a pupil. Having been brought up in Tennessee slavery, which institution, wherever it is found, never fails to bequeath to its victims the miserable inheritance of ignorance, he was of course without education, save the little which he had gleaned from time to time, by his own persevering efforts.

But though the taskmaster had fettered his limbs, and deprived him of learning, yet it was evident that his soul was unshackled, and his lofty spirit unsubdued.

I am not aware that Mr. Loguen made any secret of the fact that he was a fugitive, and, then, as now, bid defiance to his claimant.

During the winter which Mr. Loguen was under my tuition, he improved rapidly in the primary branches of education; and at the same time manifested a strong desire to be serviceable in some way to his down-trodden race.

The writer, being about the same age of Mr. Loguen, and both being in pursuit of knowledge with a view to future usefulness, a close intimacy sprang up between us which time has not impaired.

1. [Editor's note:] Reverend Elymas Payson Rogers (1815–1861) was an African American minister and educator. He studied for the ministry at the Oneida Institute, obtaining his degree in 1841. Rogers became known for writing satiric political arguments in octosyllabic couplets, using precise, well-structured verse with many historical allusions. After working for many years on behalf of the African Civilization Society, Rogers sailed to Sierra Leone in 1860 but died shortly after arriving.

Observing that Mr. Loguen was a man of uncommon energy of mind, and of a truly benevolent spirit, I soon became anxious that he should enter upon a course of study, in some of the liberal institutions of the day.

In the following Spring, when about to return to the Oneida Institute in Whitesboro', N.Y., of which I was a member, (at that time presided over by Rev. Beriah Green, a well known scholar and philanthropist,) I urged Mr. Loguen to avail himself of the benefits of that Institution. His friends, likewise, of whom he had very many in Rochester, (among whom was Mrs. Sherman, now the wife of the writer,) counselled him to go forward and prepare for a higher calling.

Mr. Loguen, yielding to the solicitations of his friends, who clearly saw that he was a man of no ordinary abilities, entered the preparatory department of the Institute the same season, and commenced a course of study, which, had time and means permitted him to finish, would have placed him among the best scholars in that Institution.

The day upon which Mr. Loguen entered the Institute, was an auspicious one for him—because it brought him in contact with students of aspiring genius, most of whom were the open and avowed enemies of slavery, and the advocates of equal rights, and frequently listening to President Green upon those great subjects, whose words in those days touching the rights of man, "were as if one inquired at the oracle of God," it is not strange that Mr. Loguen, particularly as these truthful sentiments found a ready response in the deep chambers of his soul, should be so influenced thereby, as to dedicate himself to that particular branch of the anti-slavery work, in which he has since been so successfully engaged.

Such was Mr. Loguen's progress at the Institute, that at the end of the first term he was able to teach an excellent school in Utica.

And after spending some two seasons at the Institution, where, by diligence and christian deportment, he won the confidence and esteem of both students and professors, and during that time making himself useful as a Sabbath School teacher and exhorter among his brethren in Utica, he was happily united in marriage to Miss Caroline Storom, a lady in every way worthy of him, entered the ministry, and settled at Syracuse, N.Y., where he has since acted in the double capacity of religious teacher and Superintendent of the *Underground Railroad.*

Since Mr. Loguen has been engaged in the noble work alluded to, he has been well known to the public, and his biography will be eagerly sought by thousands who have heard his eloquent appeals, and listened to the outrages which heartless tyrants perpetrated upon him and his unfortunate relatives.

From the first, I beheld in Mr. Loguen a noble spirit and manly independence, as well as other qualities indicative of future greatness and usefulness. But little did I think a few years would find him occupying one of the proudest and most responsible positions, among those who care for the oppressed in this land.

But it is even so; Jermain W. Loguen is unquestionably one of the most distinguished men in the country, in the particular field in which he labors; and not only in this country, but also in old England, thousands of anti-slavery men and women are familiar with his name, and the history of his labors for the last few years.

On account of the interest felt in his life and labors, in England, Mr. Loguen's work will doubtless have a wide circulation in that country.

To say nothing of the hundreds of poor heart-broken fugitives, who have been sheltered and cared for by Mr. Loguen, and who have been sent on their way rejoicing by means collected by his own hand, he has done much in various other ways to aid the anti-slavery cause. He has lectured in towns and cities, and preached in many pulpits in western New York; and wherever he has been, he has done much to remove prejudice against the colored man, and to break down the prevailing opinion that the black man is naturally inferior to the white man.

And as none can feel for the fugitive from slavery as he can, who has been crushed by its power, and whose heart has been made to bleed by its cruelties, let us never fail to encourage those having the requisite qualifications, to aid others, escaping from the land of despotism to the land of the free.

Such conduct is not only according to the dictates of humanity, but a plain and solemn duty which God requires man to perform.

If the words of the Bible, "hide the outcasts and betray not him that wandereth," mean anything at all they mean that it is the duty of Christians and philanthropists to do all that Mr. Loguen and his patrons have done for the last few years, for those who were justly entitled to their sympathy.

And not only is the fugitive peculiarly fitted for the work of aiding those who have just come from the house of bondage, because of his experience in suffering, but none can describe so graphically the workings of Slavery, and present so clearly its different phases, and make so stirring and pathetic appeals as he.

Undoubtedly, Douglass, Bibb, Brown, Clark, and others, would have been distinguished men had they been raised on the soil of freedom; but neither of them would have been able to portray the wickedness and cruelty of Slavery with such amazing power, had they not been within its grasp and felt its heavy scourge.

Multitudes have listened to Mr. Loguen on the subject of Slavery, and thousands have been moved to tears by his affecting narrative.

His book, written in a clear and vigorous style, will contain a full and complete history of all events connected with Mr. Loguen's escape from bondage, and of what he has since been able to do for his brethren, both bond and free. And we have reason to believe that the present work will be most favorably received by all classes in community, whose hearts are not benumbed by the influence of slavery.

May heaven smile upon this new effort of Mr. Loguen's to aid the sacred cause of liberty, and may the noble sentiments contained in the work, kindle anew the hatred of philanthropists to the accursed system of American Slavery.

Newark, N.J., August 1, 1859. E. P. Rogers.

Loguen's Position

BY E. P. ROGERS

They say I have a daring look—
A bold and fearless mien:
For this I'm not accountable,
As shortly will be seen.

I am athletic, they declare,
And strong in every part,
With lurid vengeance in my eye,
And mischief in my heart.

But let each one be slow to judge,
Until my tale is told,
In which the reason will appear
Why I am tart and bold.

I am a panting fugitive—
I fled from Tennessee,
From chains, and whips, and bloodhounds, too,
In search of Liberty.

'Twas there I saw my sister flogged,
And heard her thrilling prayer,
Oh! spare me, master! master! Oh,
For God's sake, master, spare!

I and my mother felt the lash—
Our sufferings who can tell!
O Slavery! thou bloody fiend,
I hate thee worse than hell!

And now they wish to drag me back
To servitude again;
But never, no! so help me God!
Will I endure the chain.

I would not turn upon my heel
To flee my master's power;
But if he comes within my grasp,
He falls the self-same hour!

I know 'tis God-like to forgive—
Perhaps I may be wrong;

But, were your soul in my soul's stead,
You'd doubtless feel as strong.

Hasten, O God! the joyful day
When Slavery shall not be;
When millions now confined in chains,
Shall sound a jubilee.

[From the Wesleyan]
Interesting Correspondence

The following letter to the Rev. J. W. LOGUEN from his old Mistress, and his reply to her, will be read with interest by our readers. Mr. L. is a clergyman and gentleman of high standing in this community; and any attempt to capture him will involve consequences that we hardly dare picture to our imagination.

Letter From Mrs. Logue

Maury Co., State of Tennessee,
February 20th, 1860.

To Jarm:—I now take my pen to write you a few lines, to let you know how we all are. I am a cripple, but I am still able to get about. The rest of the family are all well. Cherry is as well as common. I write you these lines to let you know the situation we are in—partly in consequence of your running away and stealing Old Rock, our fine mare. Though we got the mare back, she was never worth much after you took her; and as I now stand in need of some funds, I have determined to sell you; and I have had an offer for you, but did not see fit to take it. If you will send me one thousand dollars and pay for the old mare, I will give up all claim I have to you. Write to me as soon as you get these lines, and let me know if you will accept my proposition. In consequence of your running away, we had to sell Abe and Ann and twelve acres of land; and I want you to send me the money that I may be able to redeem the land that you was the cause of our selling, and on receipt of the above named sum of money, I will send you your bill of sale. If you do not comply with my request, I will sell you to some one else, and you may rest assured that the time is not far distant when things will be changed with you. Write to me as soon as you get these lines. Direct your letter to Bigbyville, Maury County, Tennessee. You had better comply with my request.

I understand that you are a preacher. As the Southern people are so bad, you had better come and preach to your old acquaintances. I would like to know if you read your Bible? If so can you tell what will become of the thief if he does not repent? and, if the blind lead the blind, what will the consequence be? I deem it unnecessary to say much more at present. A word to the wise is sufficient. You know where the liar has his part. You know that we reared you as we reared our own children; that you was never abused, and that shortly before you ran away, when your master asked you if you would like to be sold, you said you would not leave him to go with any body.

Sarah Logue

Mr. Loguen's Reply

Syracuse, N.Y., March 28, 1860.

Mrs. Sarah Logue:—Yours of the 20th of February is duly received, and I thank you for it. It is a long time since I heard from my poor old mother, and I am glad to know she is yet alive, and as you say, "as well as common." What that means I don't know. I wish you had said more about her.

You are a woman; but had you a woman's heart you could never have insulted a brother by telling him you sold his only remaining brother and sister, because he put himself beyond your power to convert him into money.

You sold my brother and sister, ABE and ANN, and 12 acres of land, you say, because I run away. Now you have the unutterable meanness to ask me to return and be your miserable chattel, or in lieu thereof send you $1,000 to enable you to redeem the *land*, but not to redeem my poor brother and sister! If I were to send you money it would be to get my brother and sister, and not that you should get land. You say you are a *cripple*, and doubtless you say it to stir my pity, for you know I was susceptible in that direction. I do pity you from the bottom of my heart. Nevertheless I am indignant beyond the power of words to express, that you should be so sunken and cruel as to tear the hearts I love so much all in pieces; that you should be willing to impale and crucify us out of all compassion for your poor *foot* or *leg*. Wretched woman! Be it known to you that I value my freedom, to say nothing of my mother, brothers and sisters, more than your whole body; more, indeed, than my own life; more than all the lives of all the slaveholders and tyrants under Heaven.

You say you have offers to buy me, and that you shall sell me if I do not send you $1,000, and in the same breath and almost in the same sentence, you say, "you know we raised you as we did our own children." Woman, did you raise your *own children* for the market? Did you raise them for the whipping-post? Did you raise them to be drove off in a coffle in chains? Where are my poor bleeding brothers and sisters? Can you tell? Who was it that sent them off into sugar and cotton fields, to be kicked, and cuffed, and whipped, and to groan and die; and where no kin can hear their groans, or attend and sympathize at their dying bed, or follow in their funeral? Wretched woman! Do you say *you* did not do it? Then I reply, your husband did, and *you* approved the deed—and the very letter you sent me shows that your heart approves it all. Shame on you.

But, by the way, where is your husband? You don't speak of him. I infer, therefore, that he is dead; that he has gone to his great account, with all his sins against my poor family upon his head. Poor man! gone to meet the spirits of my poor, outraged and murdered people, in a world where Liberty and Justice are *MASTERS*.

But you say I am a thief, because I took the old mare along with me. Have you got to learn that I had a better right to the old mare, as you called her, than MANASSETH LOGUE had to me? Is it a greater sin for me to steal his horse, than it was for him to rob my mother's cradle and steal me? If he and you infer that I forfeit all my rights to you, shall not I infer that you forfeit all your rights to me? Have you got to learn that human rights are mutual and reciprocal, and if you take my liberty and life, you forfeit me your own liberty and life? Before God and High Heaven, is there a law for one man which is not law for every other man?

If you or any other speculator on my body and rights, wish to know how I regard my rights, they need but come here and lay their hands on me to enslave me. Did you think to terrify me by, presenting the alternative to give my money to you, or give my body to Slavery? Then let me say to you, that I meet the proposition with unutterable scorn and contempt. The proposition is an outrage and an insult. I will not budge one hair's breadth. I will not breathe a shorter breath, even to save me from your persecutions. I stand among a free people, who, I thank God, sympathize with my rights, and the rights of mankind; and if your emissaries and venders come here to re-inslave me, and escape the unshrinking vigor of my own right arm, I trust my strong and brave friends, in this City and State, will be my rescuers and avengers.

Yours, &c.,
J. W. Loguen.

Appendix

Index

APPENDIX: *Selected Letters*

In addition to exchanging letters with many abolitionists, ministers, temperance supporters, friends, and critics, Jermain W. Loguen was a frequent correspondent to a variety of newspapers. Included in this edition is a selection of letters that Loguen published in various abolitionist newspapers. The letters were chosen to illustrate Loguen's skills as an orator and writer, providing further insight into his views and experiences as an abolitionist. References in the letters to Loguen's early life in slavery show connections between the personal testimony of his antislavery lectures and his public letters to the personal narrative of *The Rev. J. W. Loguen.* These letters further support the argument for Loguen as author of his own life story by revealing a writer who not only conveyed his arguments elegantly but was also active in the oral and written political and social debates of his time.

To Frederick Douglass

Frederick Douglass launched the abolitionist newspaper the *North Star* in 1847. In the first edition, he explained his reasons for publishing a specifically African American–owned paper, emphasizing that he did not want to seem ungrateful to white abolitionists such as William Lloyd Garrison, who published an antislavery paper named the *Liberator.* Douglass explained that those individuals who suffer injustice must demand redress, so African American authors, editors, and orators must have their own paper to express their voices. The *North Star* would go through two name changes, to *Frederick Douglass' Paper* and then *Douglass' Monthly,* ultimately becoming the longest-running black abolitionist paper in the United States, although it always struggled financially. As indicated in the letter below, antislavery lecturers like Loguen not only subscribed to and communicated through the paper but often acted as agents, selling subscriptions during their speaking circuits.

Syracuse, Feb. 8, 1848

MR. FREDERICK DOUGLASS—Dear Sir:—
I have for some time been taking as many papers as my slender means would admit; but I have been favored by our friend and brother, Samuel J. May, with the perusal of your excellent sheet, and come what may,—poverty, the want

of a full meal, or a well-covered back, or even the discontinuance of other periodicals that I highly value,—I am determined to take the North Star. I regard it as the star of promise to the millions of our downtrodden brethren in this miscalled land of liberty, and can no longer hesitate to do what I may, at any personal sacrifice, to keep it high above the horizon. Never should it be allowed to act, until the darkness of slavery passes away from the land, and the sunlight of universal and impartial freedom absorbs its rays.

I am myself a fugitive from the land of whips and chains and might never have made my escape had there been no North Star. For nearly a month, I desired no other light than that which came by its rays. The light of day was darkness to me. I was obliged to skulk and hide myself from the sun. But when the North Star shone upon my path, my spirit revived, and I dared to press on towards a land of freedom. I left behind me an aged mother, sisters and brothers, who are still, I presume, wearing the yoke of bondage, dragging out years of living death. And what can I do to relieve them! Nothing directly. Indeed, the fact that I have escaped has probably increased the vigilance of their keepers. The thought of this, at times, embitters the joy of my deliverance. My only hope for them is in the "God of Battles, who is on the side of the oppressed," and in the further diffusion of the sentiment and the love of liberty. As a powerful instrument to the production of this effect upon the public mind and heart, I welcome your labors as an editor, and long to do all I can "to strengthen your hands and encourage your heart." I love your paper because "it forgets not Joseph," but pleads for his deliverance, speaking boldly, pointedly in his behalf—daring even to say to the mightiest slaveholder, "thou art the man." May God make you a skilful and mighty potter, to remould all the clay in our land.

I shall be happy to do what I may to procure other subscribers to the North Star, if it will not interfere with the arrangement of your agencies.

Enclosed I send you my subscription for one year; and add my repeated assurances of respect and affection.

Yours for the poor and crushed slave,
J. W. L.

North Star, February 18, 1848

To Henry Bibb[1]

Loguen's letter to Henry Bibb, a journalist and fellow antislavery activist, offers details about life on the abolitionist lecture circuit and indicates that Loguen has been

1. Henry Bibb (1815–54) was a slave-narrative author and journalist, founder of Canada's first black abolitionist newspaper, the *Voice of the Fugitive*. He is best known for publishing

helping white abolitionist Gerrit Smith carry out a land-grant scheme to protect African American enfranchisement. Loguen defends himself against what a reader can infer to be accusations of mishandled money or embezzlement, but Loguen does not identify the source of the complaint. Loguen was highly regarded among abolitionists and his community, so it is possible that the accusations he defends himself against were an attempt by proslavery activists to discredit his character. The land-grant scheme occurred in 1846, when Gerrit Smith gave roughly fifty acres of land in the Adirondacks to each of three thousand poor blacks from New York. The New York Legislature had reinstated a twenty-one-year-old law denying black men the right to vote unless they owned $250 in land or a home. In response, Smith announced a settlement plan that would endow three thousand grantees with plots of land, enabling them to attain the right to vote and become self-sufficient as farmers. Unfortunately, the well-intentioned project did not ultimately succeed because the majority of those individuals who received endowments were from the city and completely new to farming, lacking experience or skill to prosper in an agricultural setting.

Syracuse N.Y. Aug 13 1852

Dear Friend Bibb,
I am here on the ground, contending for my rights, and the rights of my enslaved brethren; by the help of the Lord I shall try to do my duty, and be true to the cause of universal freedom. And I think every man will allow that I have enough to do, warring with slavery and slaveholders without stopping often or long with those who misrepresent and traduce me. I have neither time nor taste for personal altercations especially with those who ought to be united with me in contending against a common enemy.

All I have any desire to say now, is, that if any one of all the recipients of the bounty of that great hearted man Gerrit Smith, will show that I ever charged himself or any other one, from one dollar to two dollars and fifty cents (as has been alleged) for procuring their deeds, &c., I will pay that man every cent back and for the use of his money from the time he will show that he paid it to me, up to the present hour. No, my friend, that statement, let it be made by whomsoever it may be, I declare to be a sheer falsehood. I have travelled many miles, hundreds in all, to get deeds for the grantees of Mr. Smith's lands and in other services for them, but I never made any money out of such transactions, as those whom I have served are ready to testify.

Narrative of the Life and Adventures of Henry Bibb, an American Slave (1849), which details the abuse he suffered under slavery and his escape to freedom. Bibb's narrative was well known during the antebellum era, and his story is credited with being the inspiration for George Harris in Harriet Beecher Stowe's *Uncle Tom's Cabin* (1852).

In this county alone I obtained deeds for more than 23 persons, while I was living in Ithica Tompkins Co—and I never charged them a cent for the service. In some other counties the grantees knowing the time and pains I had expended, did of their own accord and free will give me some 50 cts, some one dollar, some more as they chose, and others gave me not a cent.

I never charged any of them however, more or less. Those that gave me any thing, did it because they were pleased so to do—and those who did not give me any thing were welcome to my services.

This is all I know about the matter. If any body thinks he knows any thing discreditable to me in this respect, let him produce his witnesses, and prove what he alledges against me. I trust what I have now said will be enough to satisfy the honest and candid. It is hardly worth ones while to satisfy others.

I have been much encouraged on the whole, since my return. I have never had larger audiences than I have been favored with in several places. Sunday before last, it was estimated that more than 2000 people were assembled in a grove near Rockton, where I preached. I have many invitations to speak else where, some which I purpose to accept after my return.

Frederick Douglass and I expect to visit some parts of Canada, and hold meetings the latter part of this month.

I am much interested I assure you in your good paper. It is doing valuable service for the poor enslaved, and for those who are ready to flee, and have fled from this oppressive country. I hope that many will fall in with the proposition that I made to you in my last. I wish you to put me down from the 1st day of this month. I will bring it all up if I am spared. I send you now a part of what I owe you, the rest shall be coming in due time. Do not allow yourself to get discouraged, you are gaining continually on the confidence and kind regards of the people of this country. Truly Yours,

J. W. Loguen

Voice of the Fugitive, September 9, 1852

To Frederick Douglass

Loguen writes to report on his activities on the Maine lecture circuit, demonstrating the strong link between the antislavery and temperance movements, which is also a significant theme in *The Rev. J. W. Loguen*. Loguen also refers to the 1853 National Convention of the Colored People of the United States, which included 140 delegates from nine states and was held in Rochester, New York, for the purpose of "improving the character, developing the intelligence and maintaining the rights of Blacks."

Syracuse, August 5th, 1853

Frederick Douglass, Esq.: My Dear Friend:—I would not intrude myself upon the columns of your paper, if I did not feel deeply interested in the same great cause that it so ably advocates, and that it is doing so much to forward. I am anxious that you should have along list of learned and able correspondents, knowing that this would give more credit and character to your columns than the writings of a poor, obscure and unfettered fugitive, such as I am—and especially of one who is not only a fugitive, but a prisoner, under the hellish Fugitive Slave Law, for loving liberty, not only for myself, but also for a brother *Jerry*. For this, I (with others,) am to be tried in an American Court, on the fourth Tuesday of September next, at Canandaigus. In this I glory, I can well assure you. I once traveled nine hundred miles through the American wilderness, having many rivers to swim, many mountains to climb, and many four-footed blood hounds to fight, because I loved liberty better than I did slavery. The Lord was on my side and helped me through. And now, sir, I am to be tried in a Republican Court of Justice, for the same horrid crime—for loving liberty for a brother. Well, as I am no Baltimore platform man, I am glad of it. I go for agitating, and agitating again. I believe that slavery has yet to be done away with, whether by agitation or bloodshed. And I sometimes think that I care not which. But of course, I leave all this with the God of the oppressed, hoping that one way or the other may open quickly. My dear friend, I have an old grey headed mother, and sisters, and brothers, all in slavery at this time. And, as God is my Judge, I would much rather today hear of them swimming in blood, and nobly contending for their rights, even at the cost of their own lives, than have them remain passive slaves all the rest of their days. I would willingly yield up my life even on this consecrated soul of Syracuse, rather than be a slave again; and I feel ready to try titles at any time with the slaveholder, or his meaner lickspittles of the North. *Death is sweeter than slavery.*

When I took up my pen, I did so with the intention of saying something with regard to my late tour in the good Temperance State of Maine. I had a glorious time, I assure you, with the noble Maine Law men.—They are not only opposed to making man a slave to rum, but they are also opposed to making him a slave to his brother man—I mean, of course, the true Maine Law men; for that one cannot progress without helping on the others. So, I believe that all true Temperance men are also abolitionist, and that abolitionists are all Temperance men and women. The Maine law is working gloriously, under the guidance of such noble souls as the

Hon. NEAL DOW,[2] Rev. A. WILLEY,[3] GENERAL FESSENDEN,[4] and many others of like note, in Portland and elsewhere. Clean work is made by the Maine law, I assure you. I traveled more than two hundred miles in that State, and found there many true friends of the slave. I also found three gentlemen who are travelling in that State, all the time, as lecturing agents. One of them, named John Marshall, is trying to do something to help our friend and brother, Calvin Fairbanks, out of trouble. The names of the other two, are —— Gurley,[5] and Henry Gloucester. The latter is well known in parts of the far West. He is a brother of the Rev. James N. Gloucester,[6] of New York. They are all colored men, and are doing good work. It is so said in Maine. I should think it would be well, and might do good, if these gentlemen would report themselves through *Frederick Douglass Paper*, in order that the world might know what we are doing to help ourselves. For the world is watching that publication. It is, in truth, our world wide organ. I think they might do much in Maine to help the *Frederick Douglass Paper*. Do you rejoin, "Ah! And so might you, brother Loguen!" Well, I will. Please put me down for fifty new subscribers, this year, commencing the 1st day of August, 1853; and if I do not fulfill my engagement, I hope you will expose me to the world for gross neglect of duty.

I left Maine, where I found many willing to hear Anti-Slavery truth, long before I wished in order to attend the GREAT ROCHESTER CONVENTION; and I rejoice that I did so. I regard that Convention as an era in the history of the free colored people of this country and, as one not regarded as being free by the laws of this land, I feel deeply interested in the

2. Neal Dow (1804–97) was nicknamed the "Napoleon of Temperance" and the "Father of Prohibition." He was a founding member of the Maine Temperance Society in 1827 and was later elected mayor of Portland as a Temperance Whig in 1851. As mayor, Dow was credited with leading the passage of Prohibition in the state, referred to as the "Maine Law."

3. Rev. Austin Willey (1806–96) was a preacher, abolitionist, author, and editor of the antislavery paper *Advocate of Freedom*.

4. Samuel Fessenden (1784–1869) was a member of the Massachusetts Legislature (1814–16) and the Massachusetts Senate (1818–19). He was major general of the Massachusetts (later Maine) militia, supported temperance, and was an ardent abolitionist.

5. Ralph Randolph Gurley (1797–1872) was a minister and abolitionist who served as an agent and administrator for the American Colonization Society. Gurley lived in Washington, DC, where he served as chaplain of the House of Representatives for the Twenty-First, Twenty-Second, Thirtieth, and Thirty-First Congresses.

6. James Newton Gloucester (birth and death unknown) was an African American minister and abolitionist. He was the son of John Gloucester, founder of the first Black Presbyterian Church in Philadelphia. He also served as principal of the African School in Carsville and supported Lewis Tappan's American and Foreign Anti-Slavery Society.

doings of that body. The sight of the noble men whom I beheld there was reviving my soul. I had no idea that such men lived, as yet, in the United States. I had been accustomed to look at a few who were mostly to be seen upon the surface of the water. I tell you, my dear sir, that we slaves (as the law calls us,) thank Almighty God for raising up such noble free men as were in that Convention. Although it was thought not to be wise, by some of the delegates, to put any one of that assembly in a very conspicuous position, unless he had been born free, or in some way come in possession of his freedom by law, I know that you, friend Douglass, and many other noble minds, did not sympathize with any such idea, and would not do so for a moment. So I, as being identified with the slave portion of this land, would not hear of such a thing, but felt that I was regarded as a *man among men*, and I yet feel so. I know that you and many others are too pure to entertain such feelings and that you regard a man as a man, be he bond or free. So I am going to give all my powers to carry into effect the doings of that Convention, God helping me. Excuse my dear sir, the length of this letter, as I do not trouble you often; and believe me ever in the cause of oppressed humanity.

Sincerely yours,
J. W. Loguen

Frederick Douglass' Paper, August 12, 1853

Refugees in Canada

When his antislavery lecture circuit took him into Canada, Loguen would write reports to fellow abolitionists and to readers in New York of the progress of his visits as well as the status of fugitive slaves who were residing in Canada. These reports provided an opportunity to thank benefactors and encourage additional donations by updating them on the status of those people they had assisted. The descriptions also allowed Loguen to further the public argument against slavery by offering directly observed evidence of the industriousness of free blacks, countering proslavery arguments that maintained slavery as a method of improving what they pronounced to be a lazy or unskilled population. Also important to Loguen was addressing the racism that existed beyond slavery, even in the free states, so it was important to contrast the ways in which free blacks—less encumbered by the limitations of American-style racism—were able to prosper.

Syracuse, Dec. 20, 1853

Knowing many of your readers to be interested in our people in Canada, as well as in this country, I have thought proper to say a word about them.

I have just returned from a short visit there and I must say that I found those who have left this country on account of slavery and its wicked laws doing much better than I had expected from sundry reports from that "land of the free." If the fugitives can only get there they can take care of themselves excellently well, with few exceptions. So far as I could learn, they are accumulating property faster than the colored people residing in the State of New York. A few families suffer from want there, just as in this or any other community, on account of sickness or other misfortune. Poverty, under such circumstances, is no dishonor. Some are poor from bad economy,—which should not be surprising among the people brought up in slavery, for slave holders themselves are sadly lacking in economy, and of course do not teach it to their slaves.

Had my brethren in Canada only to contend with *poverty*, it would be of little moment, but they have to meet with *too much* of American prejudice, and that in its worse form. The great majority of them, however, are doing much by their upright course to lessen or do away with this prejudice. There is a class of persons in Canada as well as in the United States, who esteem a man according to his moral worth. Now as we cannot change our color, we must make up our minds to endure the caprice of such as best we can, in this country or any other.

I attended several religious meetings while there, and it affords me great pleasure to report to the Vigilance Committee and to other friends in this city and vicinity, that I saw many fugitives whom they had personaly aided during their passage on the Underground Railroad. They were, with scarcely an individual exception, doing well and sent many heartfelt thanks to their good friends in Syracuse, whose kindness they can never forget.—They remember the good deeds and the kind words of their dear friends. While listening to their relation of things said and done while with us, I was strongly reminded of what the Savior says, in Matthew, of kindness done to "one of the least of these, my brethren." Some I found who seemed to know little of Christ when among us, but are now living members of his Church—having sought him in their time of need and found him ever true to all his promises.

It is said that some of the best common mechanics in Canada are found among the fugitives. I saw some of them. One is a blacksmith from my native State by the name of Lindsay, who is reported to be wealthy. He ran away some years after I did, but has fairly excelled me in accumulating this world's goods. He has a fine looking and happy family. I might name others, once fugitives, now in prosperous circumstances.

I would say to the kind friends of this city, that I distributed the contents of that box of clothing to the best advantage I could among the destitute. Those just arriving are generally most needy. I think the liberal and well-timed donation forwarded by friends here and in Paltneyville and

Williston enabled me to relieve some cases of real suffering. Many and heartfelt thanks are sent you in return. In conclusion I will say, though they may suffer *some* in Canada for the first year, yet their sufferings will not compare *at all* with what they endure for the same time in slavery, and after the first year they will take care of themselves.

J. W. Loguen

Anti-Slavery Bugle, January 14, 1854

To Frederick Douglass

Although Loguen modestly claims poor writing skills, his letters belie his actual abilities. Describing himself as an "untutored slave" not only demonstrates how far his mastery of writing has come but also highlights another abuse of slavery—the denial of access to education—against those individuals it subjugates. In the letter below, Loguen demonstrates the interconnection of political and religious arguments over slavery as well as his passionate and deep involvement in the social, political, and legal maneuvers to abolish slavery and counter proslavery expansions.

Syracuse, March 7, 1854

My Dear Douglass:—It is a long time since you have heard from me. I have been too much engaged to write. Indeed, writing is not my *forte*, to use a Yankee phrase. I can talk some; and a good deal in the style of an untutored slave. Had I not been horribly wronged, as you and all our race, I think I should have been a very still, quiet man. Oppression has made me mad; it has waked up all my intellectual and physical energies. It has compelled me to talk not a little in my poor way—but not to write much. A cruel school-master has been my only education.

You have learned, ere this, that Syracuse is a great place. There is a new thing under the sun here. We have a class of Christian Democrats, who meet every Sabbath in the City Hall, and fill it full, and sing, and pray, and read the Bible, and preach, every man for himself. That is, they claim that one Christian is no more a priest than another, but that all should preach according to their gifts; and that *charity*, not *doctrine*, is the foundation of the true church. These meetings have caused great excitement.—Growing out of them is a Biblical debate between our good friends, Luther Lee[7]

7. Rev. Luther Lee (1800–1889) was an evangelist, editor, and abolitionist. He served the Underground Railroad as a recruiter of agents and a conductor of fugitives. On behalf of

on the one side and S. J. May on the other—the former maintaining the tri-personality of the Godhead, as affirmed by Orthodox Christians in this and other countries; and the latter denying it, and maintaining the unity of the Godhead. Floods of people, the elite of the city, pour into these meetings every night that is not forestalled by some other popular demonstration. Well, let them agitate. There is nothing like getting the people to thinking.

But this Nebraska business is the great smasher in Syracuse, as elsewhere.[8] It is smashing up platforms, and scattering partizans at a fine rate. Political scoundrels are adopting the question of the famous Daniel with much concern, "Where shall I stand?" Even James R. Lawrence smites the traitor Douglas, and spits upon his infamous bill. This atrocious villany of that enemy of God and man, (Douglas.) is doing a fine work for the slave, (but no thanks to him.) It is making new constitutions, new laws, and organizing physical forces to carry them out, expressly for the slave. The people are becoming ashamed to have any connection with the ungodly course that many of their Congressmen pursue, when in power, for the sake of party. They are beginning to say now, "Let those traitors do what they will for slavery, we will trample their statues under our feet." They are becoming ready to draw the sword and fling away the scabbard, and that is what must be done. The time is coming when blood is to flow in this cause; and let it come I say I am always prepared in my own person for that event. I resolved long ago to face the tyrants on their own soil, and die there, if need be, for my poor people. So long as God spares my life, it shall be spent to defy all slave laws. They wish me to buy myself; I say I won't. Nothing in the world is so good for the slave as this Nebraska bill. It is such an outrageous assault upon all laws, all compacts, and rights and honor, that a political slaveholder will be no more respected hereafter, than a political Satan. I want the North strongly committed against it; and then pass the bill, and we need not look far for the day when Northern freedom will begin to grapple his iron sinews about the enemy, and crush him to death wherever he can find him, be he North or South. I do most profoundly sympathize

---

the New York State Anti-Slavery Society, Lee lectured across the state, criticizing Christian churches for failure to publicly denounce slavery, earning him the nickname "Logical Luther." Lee offers an account of the debate between himself and Rev. Samuel J. May in his *Autobiography of the Rev. Luther Lee, D.D.* (New York: Phillips & Hunt, 1882), pt. 4.

8. Loguen is referring to the Kansas-Nebraska Act of 1854, which created the territories of Kansas and Nebraska, opening new lands and repealing the Missouri Compromise of 1820. Whether to allow slavery in the new territories was hotly debated during the bill's passage, and it was ultimately decided to allow settlers in those territories to vote on it. The act was designed by Democratic senator Stephen A. Douglas of Illinois.

with the sentiment of Lysander Spooner,[9] Esq., to the Boston *Commonwealth* the other day. Says he:

"I am not in favor of making nor keeping any compacts with slavery in regard to the boundaries. I am glad to see that slavery intends neither to make nor keep any such compacts with freedom. I don't believe the constitution authorizes any such compromises. I am glad that all excuses for the discussion of such compacts are likely soon to be swept away. I hope the Nebraska bill will pass; and I hope then to see freedom and slavery meet face to face, with no question between them, except which shall conquer, and which shall die."

That is the stuff. There is no virtue, no honor whatever in any compact made with slavery. The parties to any such compact are equally disgraced; their guilt and infamy are equally deep and damning. That is the sentiment of our fathers of the Revolution, (yes, *our* fathers;) and if that principle is not written in our history, let it be recorded now—the sooner the better. It would be a capital time now to test the compromise of 1850 in Syracuse, by an attempt to arrest and return to bondage a fugitive slave. I would like to see such an attempt made.

Let me give you, my dear friend, a fact here which is significant of the state of feeling at Syracuse. The democrats made their city nominations last Friday—Thomas Alvard, Esq., an old Hunker, in the Chair. The Convention unanimously nominated A. Harvey, Esq., for Mayor, and sent a committee to notify him of it, and request him to come to the Convention. He came and made his speech, expressing his regret that they had made such a choice, but did not decline. Said he, (and this is the significant thing,) raising his hand, with great emotion and characteristic emphasis:

"If I am to be the Democratic candidate for Mayor, I wish the Democratic party, and all the electors to understand my position on this slavery question. I am now and forever opposed to the encroachments of slavery upon one inch beyond its present accursed limits. If they vote for me, they must do it with that most explicit understanding."

His speech electrified the house. So, my dear sir, you see that we are a moving people. I tell you, we are fast getting up to the *Jerry level.* It is becoming the popular sentiment; and there is no safety until it is the practical law of the land—scoundrel statutes to the contrary notwithstanding.

9. Lysander Spooner (1808–87) was an entrepreneur, political philosopher, radical abolitionist, and somewhat controversial character owing to his radical theories. Spooner published his most famous work, *The Unconstitutionality of Slavery*, in 1845, which was well received among many abolitionists, including Gerrit Smith and Frederick Douglass, and argued that the Constitution did not support slavery.

That point reached, and the cry will be "Freedom or Revolution." Then let them add territory to territory as they please; it shall be for freedom and not for slavery.

I am in great demand about these times. The Nebraska bill is waking the people up in all parts of the country. I have of late been holding very large meetings in the Cos. of Herkimer, Wayne, Cayuga, and Onondaga. I have never been so much driven about by the popular demand for lectures on slavery. I can scarcely meet half the demands upon me, which come from all parts of the compass; and such audiences as swell up on these occasions are inspiring. I sometimes wish we had fifty Douglasses, Morells,[10] and Watkins's[11] in this State, and as many Days,[12] Browns, and Gaines, in Ohio; and Wagoners,[13] Jones,[14]

10. Loguen may be referring to Benjamin Morrell (1795–c. 1839), a sea captain and explorer who also lectured against slavery. William Lloyd Garrison refers to a Captain Morrell in his book *The Abolitionist; or, Record of the New England Anti-Slavery Society* (Boston: Garrison & Knapp, 1833) and describes him as a "voyager on the coast of Africa" who advocates the abolition of slavery, arguing that "nothing but a total, unqualified prohibition of this soul-debasing traffic by every power in both hemispheres . . . can afford any rational hope of its final abolition" (102).

11. Loguen is likely referring to Frances Ellen Watkins Harper (1825–1911), an African American writer, lecturer, abolitionist, and women's rights activist. According to Frances Smith Foster in *A Brighter Coming Day: A Frances Ellen Watkins Harper Reader* (New York: Feminist Press at CUNY, 1990), she was an important part of the abolitionist lecture circuit, and African American papers frequently published reports about her activities and speaking engagements. Two years after Loguen published this letter, Harper made a circuit through New England in 1856 and spent time at the Loguen home. In an 1856 letter to William Still, Loguen mentions that Harper has just departed their home, writing, "Miss Watkins is doing great good for our part of the State. We think much indeed of her." *Still's Underground Rail Road Records: With a Life of the Author* (Philadelphia: William Still, 1886), 158.

12. Loguen is likely referring to William Howard Day (1825–1900), an African American editor, minister, educator, lecturer, and abolitionist. Like Loguen, he was a supporter of John Brown and the failed Harpers Ferry raid in 1859. He led campaigns for black suffrage in Ohio and advocated for the repeal of so-called Black Laws that prevented free blacks from settling in the state without extensive documentation and patronage.

13. Loguen may be referring to Henry O. Wagoner (1816–1901), an African American entrepreneur and Underground Railroad agent who also wrote for the *North Star* and *Western Citizen* abolitionist papers. He also corresponded with and supported John Brown.

14. Jones is a common last name, and there are a number of Joneses who figure in abolitionist and Underground Railroad history. Loguen may be referring to John Jones (1816–79) or John Albert Jones (1806–?), both agents of the Underground Railroad in Illinois. John Jones was a tailor and real estate agent who managed a way station in Chicago and aided abolitionists in the fight to repeal Illinois Black Laws. John Albert Jones was an attorney in Tazewell

Parkers,[15] in Illinois—and God with them all—and then what a mighty work would be done for the outraged slave. May the Lord send them forth, is my prayer. I shall answer those demands on me in the cause as well as I can, and you may occasionally hear from me. We shall have an eventful year to look upon, next August, when our State Council assembles in our city of salt.[16] I am calculating for an interesting time. I read the letters from Washington with much interest, from Miss Julia Griffiths.[17] We are now beginning to see what a lasting impression our good and noble friend, the Hon. Gerrit Smith, will leave upon this nation. Millions of my poor people have their faces turned to him, with their eyes filled with tears of blood, looking for deliverance. He is our Congressman.—The under-ground rail-road is doing a great business this winter; we pass about one a day. Excuse my length. I am

Yours, for Liberty,
J. W. Loguen

Frederick Douglass' Paper, April 4, 1854

To Frederick Douglass

Loguen sends another report on the progress of his lecture circuit and indicates that the Underground Railroad is regularly assisting the passage of fugitive slaves northward. Loguen resided in and was very active in New York, but in this letter he refers to similar abolitionist activities occurring in neighboring Pennsylvania.

County who facilitated the transfer of fugitives, hiding them beneath a trapdoor in the bedroom of his home.

15. Loguen is likely referring to Byrd Parker (birth and death unknown), who escaped slavery in North Carolina and settled in Chicago, where he promoted the Underground Railroad, sold subscriptions for *Frederick Douglass' Paper*, and conducted missions for the African Methodist Episcopal Church.

16. Syracuse was often referred to as "the Salt City" or "city of salt" because salt production was its dominant commercial activity until the 1860s. For more information, see Roberta B. Miller, *City and Hinterland? A Case Study of Urban Growth and Regional Development* (Westport, CT: Greenwood Press, 1979).

17. Julia Griffiths (1811–95) was a British abolitionist who worked with Frederick Douglass and was one of the founding members of the Rochester Ladies Anti-Slavery Society. After Douglass visited England, Julia and her sister Eliza followed him on his return to the United States, where Julia remained nearly eight years, assisting him with the writing and editing of the *North Star*.

Madison Co., Dec. 4, 1854

My Dear Friend Douglass:—I am now snowed in within six miles of our good and *glorious friend*, GERRIT SMITH'S house, and I can feel the influence so sensibly of this MODEL man among white men, that I have thought that I could not improve the time better than to write a few lines to my model man among colored men; and that man is FREDERICK DOUGLASS. I know of nothing that will be more agreeable to me, than to report to you a little of my whereabouts. I am in Clarkville, very comfortably situated, (after a hard day's work on the Sabbath,) in the kind family of N. S. Cady, Esq. of Clarkville. I had meetings at Canastota and this place; they were well attended for such a day, for it snowed hard all day. The meeting in this place in the evening, was a sterling one, and I talked to the people as well as I knew how. It seemed to have a good effect upon them, and I think good was done. I had a good time myself with Brother Stuckey's people. I was to go North to-day to attend other meetings; but the snow—O the snow, it compells me to disappoint, and will for some days. There are some things we cannot overrule, you know, in this world. I am trying, in connection with talking on slavery, to do something for our brethren that are so nobly struggling from bondage to freedom; and a noble struggle it is, to try to be free. We are passing them every week, more or less.

I congratulate you on your late *triumphant tour* at the West, and your safe return to your own State again, where hundreds of us rejoice to know that you are one among us for we consider it an honor to live in the State where your influence is felt, as it is in the State of New York. Would to God we had a FREDERICK DOUGLASS in every State of this wicked and hellish Union of political and church devils. O that every man among us would truly be himself, and not ape after those that would use us meanly, for their own convenience. (O, let us be men and not apes!) We cannot all be Douglasses; but we could do a mighty work in this land for outraged humanity. I rejoice at the stand that some of our friends have taken in the State of Pa., in inviting FREDERICK DOUGLASS to their State, where much has been done by some to destroy his influence.—We are happy to see such honorable names among the many—as Dr. J. J. Gould Bias,[18] Prof. C. L. Reason,[19]

18. Dr. James Joshua Gould Bias (?–1860) was an African American minister and conductor on the Underground Railroad in Philadelphia along with his wife, Eliza.

19. Professor Charles Lewis Reason (1818–93) was an African American mathematician, educator, political activist, and abolitionist. In 1837 Reason worked with Henry Highland Garnet and others on an effort to gain suffrage for African American men. He was later one of the coauthors of the Call for the New York Negro Convention of 1840. In 1847 Reason and

and Wm. Whipper[20] and others. If the LORD will enable you to raise such a flame for liberty, in other parts of the State, as you did in Sugar Grove, Pa, last summer, I shall rejoice greatly; for that was a time that will never be forgotten by many of the friends in Sugar Grove, Pa. I have seen a great many men that called themselves the ministers of the most high God; (and many of them, no doubt, were;) but I never, in all my remembrance, saw the man that looked more heavenly to me than did FREDERICK DOUGLASS, the beautiful Sabbath day that he stood in that Grove to address the hundreds that had come from afar to listen to his unbounded eloquence. But enough from us, for the half cannot be told by our pen.

Truly your friend,
J. W. L.

Frederick Douglass' Paper, December 15, 1854

To Frederick Douglass

Loguen clearly advocated for women's rights in addition to praising and welcoming the efforts of female antislavery activists. While many abolitionist New York Democrats held to patriarchal views that maintained that women's place was in the home, focused on domestic concerns, antislavery activists in upstate New York generally promoted women's rights as well as slavery reforms and saw the issues as interconnected. Loguen worked with and praised the efforts and accomplishments of women's rights activists and female abolitionists, including Harriet Tubman, Frances Ellen Watkins Harper, Elizabeth Cady Stanton, and Susan B. Anthony. In the following letter, Loguen praises the work of a Delaware Ladies' Anti-Slavery Society. He also deplores those individuals who work for the abolitionist cause for personal gain rather than moral good, and his defiant resolutions to fight slavery with any necessary force echo many of the statements—such as "Resistance to tyrants is obedience to God"—that appear four years later in *The Rev. J. W. Loguen.*

Mr. Frederick Douglass: Dear Sir:—I am at present laboring in our common cause, among the rough hills of Delaware. I find many warm hearts that respond to the truth, and am touched with the story of the

Charles B. Ray founded the Society for the Promotion of Education among Colored Children, and in 1852 he became the first principal of Philadelphia's Institute for Colored Youth.

20. William J. Whipper (1804–76) was an African American businessman and abolitionist who wrote for the *Colored American* in addition to cofounding the American Moral Reform Society and publishing its newspaper, the *National Reformer.* Whipper and his wife, Helen Lee Whipper, established an Underground Railroad depot in Columbia, Pennsylvania.

slave's wrongs. The portion of the county in which I have been laboring, is noted for its prompt attendance at these meetings. Men and women often travel miles to listen to a lecture on slavery. A strong desire is felt by man to see and hear a fugitive slave, and thus my meetings are largely attended.

I have held two meetings in the village of Franklin—the locality of the "Delaware Institute." The last was the largest I have attended for a long time; and I felt encouraged in my mark. We have many true friends in Franklin. There is a "Ladies' Anti-Slavery Society" here, which is in a flourishing condition, and accomplishing much good—Would to God that woman's voice might everywhere be raised against the damning wrongs which crush our race. How eloquent might it be in hastening the hour of our deliverance. Mrs. Stillson, President of the above Society, and her husband, are true hearted friends of our cause. I saw on their table on striking proof of their devotion to the slave, viz: *Frederick Douglass' Paper*. Wherever this paper is read, I find men and women whose hearts are true to the slave who labor for the colored man's good as well as the white man's. In this they differ widely from many I have found of late, who are very willing to work in the name of the slave, *if the thing pays*, and the pay goes directly to *their pockets*. The colored man is "all right;" he is a "good *nigger*" so long as he will worship at their shrine, and pour money into their coffers; but let him only presume to think and act for himself, like an independent and accountable being, and above all, to put his own penny into his own pocket, and he is no longer a "good *nigger*!" Away with such arrant hypocrisy, that would save a man from the clutches of the slave-driver only to fasten upon him the shackles of another despotism! I am sick of all such friends of the slave. The less we have of them the better. From such we may well pray to be delivered. Years ago, while a toiling slave in Tennessee, I resolved, that with the help of God, and the energies he had given me, I would cast off the chain, and be a slave no longer. "Liberty or Death!" never came from a more earnest breast than when I uttered it there before my God!—My residence in the North has not diminished, but has rather strengthened the firm resolve I then took. I will be no man's slave, be he called friend or foe be he in a church or out. God helping me, I will be a MAN—I will wear no chain!

I have also passed through a portion of Otsego Co., since I left home, and had some fine meetings and, what is better, found a few sterling friends. Alas! I found many, too, who are temporizing—"policy men"—men only about half "dyed in the wool"—While thinking this over, the worse of that great, and noble, and pure man, GERRIT SMITH, (how many hearts beat joyfully at the mention of that name,) came to my mind. He says in his letter to Wendell Phillips: "I admit that it requires only a small number of right-minded persons to sustain the American anti-slavery cause, and carry it forward to victory, and that even this small number cannot be supplied."[21] Alas! that in so holy a cause, these words should be true. O consistency! thou art a jewel; would that thy lights were not so rare.

But, notwithstanding these discouragements, our hearts are often made glad, by finding honest persons, who are laboring for universal freedom. In these two counties, I find what is rare, devoted ministers to the Gospel, who preach against man-stealing as well as against sheep stealing, and against the atrocious cruelties of woman-whipping and cradle robbing in America as well as in any other part of the world. Among these noble ministers, I found Elder J. N. Adams, and Elder George Post, both Baptists, with many of other churches. Would to God that *all* the ministers were as true as these. Slavery would soon be numbered among the things that were and are not. They are *do* ministers as well as *say* ministers; and our Savior says, "Inasmuch as ye have *done* it" not inasmuch as ye have *said* it.

I have spoken two or three times every Sunday, and with a few exceptions, every evening through the week, for the last three weeks; and I feel to go on in God's great name, doing battle for our bruised and down trodden brethren. As I have before said to you, dear friend, I say again—we want more true soldiers in the field, who are not afraid to die, if need be, in our great cause—men and women, too, who feel the cause at heart sufficiently to stand alone, with God's help, and fight on and ever, and not quit the field or be frightened by persecutions, prejudice disagreement with so-called friends, Fugitive Slave Bills, slave hounds, kidnappers, or any other instruments of the devil; but who will stand with sword in hand, contending for God and liberty! Let them not wait for some church or society to send them forth and push them onwards. Let the love of justice and truth, the cries of bleeding humanity persuade them forth, and God will sustain them. Every man and woman must be within himself an embodiment of all a church or society can be for good. For myself, I am willing to cooperate with others, so long as I can do so and maintain my manhood. Beyond that I will not go.

I am now getting up Fugitive Aid Societies wherever I may, to stand by every fugitive who will take a stand in the free States and maintain it at all hazards. *The time has come for us to stop running!* Such as can not nerve

21. Wendell Addison Phillips (1811–84) was an attorney, libertarian orator, and contributor to the *New York Tribune*. After his wife, Ann Terry Greene Phillips, a member of the Female Anti-Slavery Society, converted him to abolitionism, Phillips gave up practicing law and joined the Massachusetts Anti-Slavery Society. He collaborated with agents of the Underground Railroad at his home in Boston and became well known for issuing radical speeches that agitated against slavery.

themselves up to this, and feel like going to another land, we must help; but we want everyone to feel that it is his duty to stand; and we want those who come in with us to feel like standing by them. We have some true hearts enlisted already, and we hope to have many more. Let such remember that God will bless the right and the true.

I would like to say to the Slaveholders and all others, just here, that the Underground Railroad was never doing a better business than at present. We have had as many as sixteen passengers in one week in this city. I speak officially, as the agent and keeper of an Underground Railroad Depot. Let them come; we have some true hearts ready to receive them, and God will raise up more.

I send you a copy of our Constitution and By-Laws. Please give them an insertion in your good paper. "Speak the Truth—God defend the Right."

Truly yours,

J. W. Loguen

PREAMBLE.

The undersigned, believing that Liberty is not only one of the God given rights of man, but one which he should rightfully enjoy in whatever place seems to him, fit, and believing, too, that the cause of human freedom would be better subserved by fugitives from Southern Slavery, taking a decided stand to sustain and protect themselves in the nominally free States of the union, rather than by their fleeing elsewhere, do form them selves into an Association to be governed by the following.

CONSTITUTION.

Article I. This Association shall be known by the name of the Fugitive Aid League.

Art. II. Although this Association will not object to assisting fugitives in making their escape to another land yet it proposes, and shall continue to propose to itself, as the more appropriate object of its action, the aiding of those unfortunates, by every means that may be necessary to elevate themselves to the proper level of respectability and manhood, in this land which has been both the witness and agent of their degradation.

Art. III. The officers of this Association shall be a President, Vice President, Secretary and Treasurer. These, together with five others, shall constitute an Executive Board; this Board shall have power to devise By Laws for its own regulation and government.

Art. IV. The duties of those officers shall be such as are ordinarily understood to appertain to their respective offices.

Art. V. In order to create such a fund as may be required for effecting the object of this Association, a travelling agent shall be appointed by the Executive Board, who shall solicit aid in behalf of the League for all who are well disposed towards it, and shall report his proceedings to the Executive Board, as the Annual Meeting, and at any other time at which he may be called on so to do by that body.

Art. VI. All persons who approve of the principles and objects of this Association may become members of it, by paying an initiatory fee of one dollar, and the additional sum of one dollar annually.

Art. VII. The head quarters of this Association shall be, for the present at Syracuse, at which place regular meetings shall be led on the fourth Wednesday of the months of January, April, July, and October, in each year. The meeting in January shall be the Annual Meeting of the Executive Board, and shall have power to call special meetings of the Association when it is deemed necessary.

Art. VIII. This Constitution may be altered or amended at any regular meeting of the Association, by a vote of a majority of the members present, provided that the proposed alteration or amendment shall have been formally submitted in writing at the regular meeting immediately previous, at which time the Annual Report of the Secretary Treasurer and Executive Board shall be presented, and elections held to appoint officers for the succeeding year.

Frederick Douglass' Paper, April 6, 1855

To Frederick Douglass

African American men had the legal right to vote in many Northern states, but accessing that right often proved very difficult. In New York a person was required to own property valued at least $250 to vote, excluding poor whites and most African Americans. Although activists filed grievance petitions, legislators largely ignored them. In the following letter, Loguen describes participating in an 1855 effort to organize at the local level and circulate such a petition to address African American men's suffrage. According to Phyllis F. Field, activists worked to circulate such petitions while also educating eligible African Americans on their rights, voter registration, and the power of their ballots.[22] The African American press played a significant role in promoting these efforts.

Syracuse, April 9, 1855

Friend Douglass:—I noticed an article in your paper, several weeks since, calling the attention of your readers to the manly efforts which our

22. Phyllis F. Field, *The Politics of Race in New York: The Struggle for Black Suffrage in the Civil War Era* (Ithaca, NY: Cornell Univ. Press, 2009), 94.

brethren are making in Pennsylvania, in behalf of their God given and man-stolen rights, as citizens of that State. You also gave a very good and timely hint to our friends in this State; and I agree with you that we should be up and at work here, for the acknowledgement of the rights which God gave us as citizens of the Empire State. I took the watch-word for you and commend the work. I got up petitions to our Legislature, and sent them broad cast over the State, to such friends as I thought would circulate them for signatures and forward them to such members of the Legislature as they thought best. I should say that I sent none east of Albany, or Troy. I thought our brethren in New York and Brooklyn, would attend to the matter in that part of the State. I circulated one in Onondaga County; and was happily disappointed in seeing so many of the old party leaders willing to put their names to it. Men, who, a few years ago, rallied to deny the colored man, the elective franchise, were seemingly willing to do all they could to restore us as a people, to our long lost rights, by attaching their names to a petition which asked the Legislature, to so amend the first section of the second Article of our State Constitution, by striking out all after, and including the words, "But no man of color," &c., that said Constitution shall, in truth, secure to all what is promised in its preamble the blessings of freedom. It was signed by many of our first citizens and sent to Hon. D. P. Phelps. I see that a little noise has been made on the subject in the Legislature. May we not hope that this manifest change in the feelings with which our cause is regarded by our former opponents is indicative of something bright and glorious for the colored man. Does it not show a revolution in the public sentient, which is destined to lead to a full recognition of our inalienable rights?

I hope that my brethren, to whom I have sent petitions, have done their duty; but if they have not, I hope they will resolve with me to commence early, and be well prepared for the next sitting of the Legislature. Let us send into that body a flood of petitions from every county in the State, let them know and feel that the sentiment of the people is being enlisted in behalf of equal suffrage.

"Eternal vigilance is the price of Liberty." I think the times are very profitous for us to labor. Amid the confusion of parties, and the death-struggles of old political dynasties, we cannot fail to accomplish much with proper exertion. Therefore, let us work together, and God will help us.

Yours for the work,
J. W. Loguen

Frederick Douglass' Paper, April 20, 1855

To Frederick Douglass

Loguen's letter about John Brown—as well as the enclosed letter from Brown—underscores his stance that violence and war are necessities justified by God to end slavery and secure the rights of enslaved African Americans. Loguen was an early adopter of this position, which was in contrast to abolitionists Frederick Douglass and William Lloyd Garrison, who belonged to the New England Non-Resistant Society and believed in the power of moral suasian to end slavery, distancing themselves from violent rhetoric that might turn off a white audience. However, after the Fugitive Slave Act of 1850, the Kansas-Nebraska Act of 1850, and John Brown's raid at Harpers Ferry, Douglass's views began to shift toward a justification of violence as self-defense against slave catchers and then to forcible liberation.

The following letter from Mr. LOGUEN, which we find in Frederick Douglass' Paper, will be interesting to his friends in this vicinity.

> Dear Friend:—What an age we live in! The year 1859 will be ever memorable in the annals of all future time! The 2d day of December, 1859, will hereafter be looked upon as a sacred day to the holy cause of human freedom; made so by the noble sacrifice of John Brown and his brave compeers.—When we contemplate the work designed to be accomplished at Harper's Ferry by these heroic men, words are powerless, and language fails to express one's thoughts! We thank God that ever such a man as John Brown lived. And though Virginia may think she has put him to death, yet he lives—lives in the hearts of every liberty loving individual in our country. Yes, in the hearts of the poor, crushed, bleeding slave, for whom he sacrificed life. Life was as dear to him as to us. Yet when compared to the cause of freedom which laid so near his heart, it seemed to him of small value. He did all one could possibly do—lay down his life. And he himself said 'he could not better serve the cause he so much loved than to die for it.'
>
> The death of John Brown has struck the heart depths of our own people, and will be the means of uniting them more closely in feeling and sympathy. For to know that there are those among their white brethren who are willing to risk even life itself in their behalf can but inspire them to noble deeds of daring in the defense of their own lives and liberties.
>
> In all my travels among our people, I find but one feeling in reference to this matter, namely: a universal endorsement of John Brown's operations at Harper's Ferry, to the fullest extent. This, to my mind, is encouragement. The enemy has hitherto succeeded in keeping us divided. I thank God for the unanimity of feeling which now prevails among us as a people.

And my prayer is that it may continue so to prevail until the last chain of oppression shall be stricken off from all our enslaved brethren.

To justify the brave deeds of the hero of Harper's Ferry, requires more real nerve of soul, than is exhibited generally by those in our day who talk a great deal about freedom. We have been at a loss some times to know who were our true friends. But the blow struck for liberty at Harper's Ferry is bringing the genuine lovers of impartial freedom to the surface. This, itself, is cause for devout thankfulness to God. Our people have now the opportunity of learning who are their real friends, and of uniting with them in efforts of emancipation. Even our poor fugitive brethren and sisters, as they come on their flight to Canada, seem fully to appreciate and understand the intention of Brown at Harper's Ferry. All parties are getting to see this affair in its true light. Slaveholders fully understand it, and well they may, for they read in it the hand-writing of God, describing the certain overthrow of their accursed system. But it cost the life of brave John Brown and his noble compatriots to bring about this result. And I hope, dear friends, that we as an outraged people, may use this well begun work, so as to achieve the glorious designs proposed by it, namely: the liberation of the slave, and his religious elevation in the scale of being. John Brown was a firm believer in the true Gospel of Jesus. The religious improvement of our oppressed people was one of the cherished objects of his life. In a letter to me dated Boston, Mass., May 17th, 1859, he said:

Rev. J. W. Loguen:—My dear Sir:—I will just whisper in your private ear, that I have no doubt you will soon have a call from God to minister at a different location. I trust you will obey that call; unless we can secure a strong religious influence among the early settlers, we may as well abandon the idea at once of having a good town. "Who is there among you of all his people; his God be with him and let him go up to Jerusalem." I passed by you the other day sick—and better now and getting on well. Let God be praised. Your friend in truth.

John Brown'

I give this letter to the public, that the Nero Wise, and his bogus democratic friends may know and understand that John Brown's religion did not commence after he was taken at Harper's Ferry; and that long before that event occurred, other measures, looking to the moral and religious elevation of our downtrodden people, were in contemplation by the good man.

At Harper's Ferry, the white man and the colored alike mingled their blood in the holy cause of Freedom. They struck a deadly blow at the black heart of American Slavery—a blow from which it cannot recover. I hope all true men and women will follow it up until slavery is blotted out of existence.—The blood of the martyrs of Harper's Ferry shall be avenged. In God's great name I trust this event may be the beginning of the speedy end of Slavery in this land.

The signs of the times are ominous of a glorious future. Let the colored people of the free States be wide awake to the development of God's providence in relation to slavery. They have a very important part to act in the work of emancipation. Let them learn bravely to do and dare for the cause of Freedom by the heroic example of John Brown. 'They that would be free, must first strike the blow.' 'The price of liberty is eternal vigilance.' Yours for God and Liberty,

J. W. Loguen
Agent of the U.G.R.R.

Syracuse Daily Journal, February 18, 1860

INDEX

JENNIFER A. WILLIAMSON is director of gender mainstreaming and women's empowerment at ACDI/VOCA, a global development organization, and a former instructor of English and women's studies at the University of North Carolina at Chapel Hill. She has previously taught at the University of Maryland–College Park. She is the author of *Twentieth-Century Sentimentalism: Narrative Appropriation in American Literature* (2014) and the head editor of *The Sentimental Mode: Essays in Literature, Film and Television* (2014). Her research and publications focus on gender, women's writing, domesticity, the sentimental tradition, class, and slave narratives and constructions of race.